The Life of Yellowstone Kelly

The Life of
YELLOWSTONE KELLY

JERRY KEENAN

University of New Mexico Press
Albuquerque

YEAR   PRINTING
10 09 08 07 06   1 2 3 4 5

Library of Congress Cataloging-in-Publication Data

Keenan, Jerry.
  The life of Yellowstone Kelly / Jerry Keenan.
     p. cm.
  Includes bibliographical references and index.
  ISBN-13: 978-0-8263-4035-1 (cloth : alk. paper)
  ISBN-10: 0-8263-4035-0 (cloth : alk. paper)
 1. Kelly, Luther S. (Luther Sage), 1849–1928. 2. Pioneers—West (U.S.)—
Biography. 3. Scouts and scouting—West (U.S.)—Biography. 4. Frontier
and pioneer life—West (U.S.) 5. Indians of North America—West
(U.S.)—History. 6. West (U.S.)—Biography. 7. Yellowstone River Valley—
Biography. I. Title.
 F594.K25K44 2006
 978.6'302092—dc22
 [B]
                              2006017248

Book design and composition by Damien Shay
Body type is Utopia 10/14
Display is Birch and Mesquite

For
Carol
who has lived
with Luther Kelly
almost as long
as I have

and for
Brother Rod
who kept the faith

In memoriam
Dignum et justum est

Past dim, untrodden trails,
the paths of yore whence all
wild Creatures sped their way
into the fastnesses beyond
the Old Frontier, and like
a dream of long ago.

Luther S. Kelly

January one,
nineteen hundred twenty-eight

Contents

List of Illustrations

Acknowledgments

During the unusually long gestation period of this book, I have enjoyed the help and encouragement of many, some of whom have already followed the subject of this book into that bourne from which no one returns. It gives me pleasure here to acknowledge those still living as well as those who have stepped off this poor ledge, as Luther Kelly once described the process.

For help received during the preparation of this book, I would like to thank the following institutions: the Amon Carter Museum, Fort Worth, Texas; Anchorage (Alaska) Historical Society; Brigham Young University Library, Provo, Utah; Center for American History, University of Texas, Austin; Colonial Williamsburg Society; Western History Department, Denver Public Library; Geneva (New York) Historical Society; Germantown (Pennsylvania) Historical Society; Library of Congress; Montana Historical Society; National Archives and Records Services; Smithsonian Institution; Norlin Library, University of Colorado, Boulder; the U.S. Army Military History Institute, Carlisle Barracks, Pennsylvania; and the United States Geological Survey, Denver, Colorado, and Anchorage, Alaska.

Individuals who have been especially helpful include Allison Cowgill, of Fort Collins, Colorado, who tracked down some difficult reference material on Kelly's Alaskan and Nevada experiences. Wendy Diamond and Michael Mulcahy of Paradise, California, shared the hospitality of their home during our visit to their community. Susan Doyle and her husband, Dr. Roger Blair, of Pendleton, Oregon, supplied helpful medical background information on Luther Kelly. Carol Edwards and Joe McGregor, USGS, Denver Federal Center, were most helpful in locating Alaska photos relevant to both the Glenn and Harriman Expeditions, while Jill Schneider of the USGS, Anchorage office, supplied copies of the Walter Mendenhall journals of the Glenn Expedition.

Ernest J. Emrich, Reference Specialist, Manuscripts Division, Library of Congress, located copies of correspondence between Luther Kelly and William Howard Taft. David Kessler, Photo Archivist, Bancroft Library, went out of his way to search for photos relevant to both of the Alaska expeditions of which Kelly was a part. Holly Klinzman, Parachute (Colorado) Public Library, provided material pertaining to Kelly's Colorado years. Richard Lea of Fort Collins, Colorado, shared his knowledge of Medal of Honor recipients from the frontier army. John D. McDermott, Rapid City, South Dakota, provided anecdotal material on Kelly from his files and made helpful suggestions about sources in the National Archives.

At Norlin Library, University of Colorado, Boulder, the staff of the Inter-Library Loan Department obtained books and microfilm so essential to the needs of any researcher. Likewise, the Government Documents section in Norlin, particularly Debbie Hollis, Peggy Jobe, Linda Rogers, Suzan Winters, and LeAnne Walther, were always ready to provide assistance in locating federal documents.

Helen Plumer, Amon Carter Museum, Fort Worth, Texas, and Holly Reed, National Archives and Records Services, Washington, D.C., provided photos, as did Laury Gould, Montana Historical Society Archives. Thanks to Tom Child for preparing the final drafts of the maps, and to Ginny Hoffman for her editorial expertise.

Others who merit thanks include Nick Aretakis, William Reese and Co., New Haven, Connecticut; Casey Barthelmess, Miles City, Montana; Lauren Bufferd, Special Collections, Chicago Public Library; Wallace Dailey, Theodore Roosevelt Collection, Harvard College Library; Bruce Dinges, Arizona Historical Society; John Doerner and Kitty Deernose, Little Bighorn Battlefield National Monument, Montana; L. Boyd Finch, Tucson, Arizona; the late John A. Gable, Theodore Roosevelt Association; Lisa Gezelter, National Archives and Records Services, San Diego, California; the late Michael Harrison, Fair Oaks, California; Bruce Liddic, Syracuse, New York; Lois McDonald, Paradise, California; George Miles, Beinecke Library, Yale University; Thomas Minckler, Billings, Montana; Brian McAllister Linn, Texas A&M University; Stephen C. O'Malley, formerly of the Geneva (New York)

Historical Society; the late John Popovich, Billings, Montana; Marion Rosenbaum, Germantown (Pennsylvania) Historical Society; Douglas C. Scott, Midwest Archaeological Center, National Park Service, Lincoln, Nebraska; Richard Sommers, U.S. Army Military History Institute, Carlisle Barracks, Pennsylvania; Kim Walters, Southwest Museum, Los Angeles; and Constance E. Williams, Civil War Library and Museum, Philadelphia.

Several individuals deserve a special note of thanks for their more than generous help and support. George Bille of Paradise, California, whose father knew Luther Kelly well during Kelly's years in Paradise, graciously loaned photos from his collection and provided helpful insights into the Paradise area itself.

Brian Dippie, The University of Victoria (B.C.), and Paul Hedren, National Park Service, O'Neill, Nebraska, read the original manuscript and offered many helpful suggestions.

Dr. James S. Brust of San Pedro, California, supplied an assortment of anecdotal material, including photos, and graciously visited Huntington Library, San Marino, California, on behalf of this project. His encouragement and support throughout cannot be overstated.

Jerome A. Greene, National Park Service, Denver, Colorado, one of the preeminent frontier military historians, was ever ready to offer guidance and encouragement and to suggest additional sources.

The Kelly family, descendants of William D. Kelly I, including the late Luther W. Kelly Sr., Luther W. Kelly Jr., William D. Kelly II, William D. Kelly IV, Alice and Buford Orndorff, and William McAllister, were most gracious in making available information in their possession.

Louis E. Sdunek, a descendant of Alice May Kelly's niece, Mrs. Louis Sdunek, although unable to provide any hard data about Luther Kelly, was nevertheless most interested in the project and was pleased to tell me what he did remember about his own family's knowledge of Kelly.

Patrick Schroeder, Daleville, Virginia, mined the National Archives in Washington for relevant material pertaining to Luther Kelly's years at San Carlos, Arizona.

Luther Wilson, director of the University of New Mexico Press, and his staff provided patience, support, and encouragement throughout the publication process.

Finally, and by no means least, I shall never be able to adequately thank my wife, Carol, for her cogent observations and comments during our many discussions about Luther Kelly's life. Her unflagging support has meant more than she can possibly imagine.

For all those I may have inadvertently overlooked in compiling this list of acknowledgments, I humbly beg pardon. And of course, it goes without saying that I alone bear full responsibility for any errors of commission or omission to be found in these pages.

Introduction

I suppose many biographers could describe that special moment when they first became enamored of their subject. In my own case, I walked into a bookstore (the name of which I have long since forgotten) in Napa, California, one afternoon in the autumn of 1957. While browsing the shelves, my eye chanced to fall upon a novel, *Yellowstone Kelly*, by Clay Fisher (a.k.a. Will Henry). Intrigued by the title, I took the book down and began to read. Quickly warming to the subject and the author's style, I wound up buying the book and that was it, though of course I did not realize exactly what had happened here. At the time, I was twenty-five and believed myself well read on the history of the American West, and yet the name Yellowstone Kelly did not ring a bell. How had I managed to miss a fellow with such a fetching name?

Notwithstanding, I proceeded to devour the novel and soon discovered that Kelly's memoirs had been published by Yale University Press in 1926 and that Kelly himself had died in Paradise, California, two years later. The hook had been set. In the years since, I have found that novels (movies, too) often inspire me to dig further and learn more about a historic individual or event.

At any rate, from here I moved on. As I began to learn more about Kelly's life, I grew increasingly astonished to find that very little had been written about the man, despite the fact that his had been a truly remarkable life. Oh yes, there had been a movie and two other novels, but if anything they led both viewer and reader far afield from the real

Kelly story, which included service as an army scout, Alaskan explorer, soldier in the Philippines, and Arizona Indian agent.

In 1958, Warner Bros. released *Yellowstone Kelly*. The film, based on the Fisher novel, starred Clint Walker—about as unlikely a looking Luther Kelly as one could hope to find. The strength of the Fisher novel lay not in its particular fidelity to history—or to Kelly's life, for that matter—but in the author's ability to write an engaging novel that captured the flavor of the Montana frontier, while introducing readers to an unusual figure from those distant days. The Warner Bros. film failed to capture the novel's flavor and managed to stray even further from the truth. Two Peter Bowen novels, which appeared some thirty years later, while cleverly written, are notable only for their outrageous twists on Kelly's life.

I decided, probably with more arrogance and naiveté than I realized at the time, to undertake the telling of Luther Kelly's life. Research began about 1960, though in those early days it was more a matter of collecting information about Kelly as I chanced to find it, rather than serious historical research as such. Unfortunately, the demands of parenting and earning a livelihood meant slow and erratic progress, but there were always small discoveries that managed to keep the flame kindled.

Early in my research, I learned that in addition to his published memoirs, Kelly had a second, unpublished manuscript that dealt with his experiences in Alaska and the Philippines. That manuscript had been bequeathed to a nephew, with whom I was subsequently able to establish contact. As it turned out, the nephew remembered the manuscript but had no idea as to its present whereabouts. I decided that it had probably been tossed out during the course of some spring housecleaning, but I always held out hope that one day it would surface.

Although Luther Kelly's nephew had been unable to provide me with the missing manuscript, he did put me in touch with an older brother who had actually lived with Kelly and his wife at San Carlos, Arizona. Unfortunately, after an interesting exchange of letters, this older nephew relocated and I lost contact.

In the spring of 2003, I learned that the long-sought Alaska-Philippines manuscript had turned up and been acquired by Yale University's Beinecke Library. I was ecstatic. How fortuitous it was that this manuscript should be discovered in time to be used in my own work. What a stroke of extraordinary good fortune.

When I retired in 1990, I was finally able to devote all my time, more or less, to telling the Kelly story. In that year I was fortunate to have an overview article on Kelly's life published in *Montana: The Magazine of Western History* and was exceedingly gratified when the article received the Western Heritage Award for "Best Magazine Article" presented annually by the National Cowboy Hall of Fame. In addition to the award, the article provided an unexpected bonus: contact with the descendants of the older nephew previously mentioned, whom I now learned had since passed away.

Then in 1996, my research revealed that the manuscript Kelly had originally submitted to Yale University Press had actually included his Alaska-Philippines experiences. Yale, however, based largely on the recommendation of M. M. Quaife, whom the press had contracted to edit the manuscript and write an introduction, chose to publish only that portion of the narrative dealing with Kelly's Western frontier experiences. I could not imagine why a life so rich and extraordinary should be told only in part. Early on, I decided my effort would be the whole nine yards or nothing.

Luther Kelly's life can scarcely be thought of as ordinary. He was an unusual man, an individual with a unique blend of skills. Those who knew him were always quick to testify to his courage, dependability, and moral exactness. He was also a man of consummate modesty and a delightful, almost mischievous sense of humor. And he combines these qualities with a wonderful gift for literary expression.

But Kelly's strengths had to be observed firsthand to be fully appreciated. It would have been tough to make them resonate on anything like a résumé. Accordingly, in his middle years, past the time of the wilderness wanderer, he was forced to rely on the support of those who had known him personally. Theodore Roosevelt, Nelson Miles, George Bird Grinnell, and Jesse Matlock Lee went to bat for him on more than one occasion. Yet he never leaned on any of them, never pushed or prodded.

It would be easy to criticize Kelly for the way he used influence to seek political appointments, but he was no more out of line in doing so then than he would be today. And he always operated within the system. What is important here is to recognize that while Luther Kelly used influence, he did not *abuse* it and, unlike many others, never sought a government position for which he was *not* qualified.

Because of his compelling sense of modesty, much of Luther Kelly must remain forever unknown, and I suspect that suits him just fine. Having said this, however, it also needs to be pointed out that he also longed for the recognition he believed was his just reward, much as we all do. However, he would never press the issue, as his friend Theodore

Roosevelt had done for his own Medal of Honor at San Juan Hill. Kelly believed he deserved a medal for his conduct at the Battle of La Lud in the Philippines, but he never sought to make a case for himself. The recognition, in his mind, should have come as a matter of natural course, without him having to seek it.

Writing a biography of Luther Sage Kelly has been an enjoyable, fulfilling, and at times maddening undertaking. When one writes a biography of a well-known historical figure such as Abraham Lincoln or Theodore Roosevelt, one is blessed with an embarrassment of riches in terms of original source materials. Such was far from the case with Kelly.

Source materials covering the first twenty-seven years of Kelly's life—essentially from childhood until he joined the Fifth Infantry as a civilian scout—range from scarce to nonexistent. Accordingly, I was forced to rely heavily on his published memoirs and correspondence in order to reconstruct that portion of his life.

During various periods of his life, Kelly was acquainted with a number of prominent people—including Theodore Roosevelt, Nelson Miles, William Howard Taft, and E. H. Harriman—as well as a great many military figures with whom he had served during the Indian campaigns on the Northern Plains and later during the Philippine Insurrection, as it was then called. Numerous references to his presence may be found in the standard histories of the Indian wars, the official records of the Philippine-American War, and various personal recollections. And if there was not an abundance of these recollections, what was there was striking. When someone did write something about Kelly, such as his conduct at La Lud and Surigao in the Philippines, it was almost always in complimentary terms. Still, I yearned—lusted might be a better word—for additional details that would have served to more fully illuminate Kelly's life. He was, for example, a member of Theodore Roosevelt's second-term "tennis cabinet," and T.R. says he knew Kelly in the old days, but says nothing about how that relationship came about. Unlike contemporaries such as William F. Cody, Luther Kelly preferred to walk in the shadows, leaving only thin traces of his passing; thin, all right, but enough to tell us he was there. He was an elusive figure who moved through history as stealthily as he did while scouting for Nelson Miles. The trail was there—sometimes with gaps, often faint, but withal visible enough to follow, or so I judged.

Kelly's published memoirs conclude in 1885, but for him much adventure and excitement was still to come. Indeed, the period between 1885 and his retirement in Paradise, California, in 1915, embrace, in my opinion, the most interesting period of his life. Fortunately, his unpublished memoirs, official records, and a fair body of surviving personal correspondence provided a wider range of source materials to draw on in reconstructing this period of his life. In any case, I believe this narrative offers a reasonably accurate portrait of Luther Sage Kelly.

What follows then, is the story of an unusual man, as best I have been able to tell it. Yellowstone Kelly was surely the equal of those other, better known frontier luminaries: Daniel Boone, Buffalo Bill Cody, Kit Carson, and Davy Crockett. But he was also an exemplary soldier and explorer, an able administrator, and a gifted writer.

Cody, Carson, and Crockett have become icons of American culture, and if the public at large possesses only scanty information about these individuals, their names are still highly recognizable. Certainly all were frontiersmen *par excellence*, but none went on to accomplish what Kelly did following his own time in the West. What Kelly did was to reach out beyond the frontier of his young manhood to seek adventure and fulfillment on the then far-flung frontiers of Alaska and the Philippines. In a sense, the others never really left the frontier that gave birth to their respective identities, and yet each is far better known than Luther Kelly, whose name remains known almost exclusively to historians and students of the Indian wars on the North Plains.

Although Yellowstone Kelly was the subject of one movie and three novels, the others have been featured in both mediums numerous times, and Boone and Crockett in particular have had wide television exposure. Indeed, for a time it seemed as though every boy in America wore a coonskin cap and imagined himself to be Davy Crockett. That kind of repetition serves to create an enduring public image. By comparison, the name Luther Kelly has yet to find a niche in the public consciousness. Thus, he remains a figure in the shadows, today as in his own time.

If this recounting serves to bring the name Luther Sage Kelly out of the shadows to its merited place of recognition, I shall have received full satisfaction.

Prologue

The procession left the Commercial Club at 2:30 that afternoon, moving slowly on foot to the soulful dirge and steady thump of muffled drums from the Rotary Club's boy's band. West along Third Avenue the retinue proceeded, turning south at Broadway to First Avenue North, then east to Twenty-second Street, where autos were boarded for the final leg of the journey to the crest of the "rim."

It was an impressive group, headed by color bearers, then city officials, Boy Scouts, the band, and a firing squad. These were followed by a solitary horse with boots reversed in the stirrups and a saber hanging from the saddle. Finally came the casket itself, resting atop a flower-bedecked wagon drawn by four horses, followed by pall bearers and an honor guard of veterans old and recent.

Most evident were the younger veterans of World War I, but here and there could be seen a few old soldiers in blue, aging members of the G.A.R., from the Spanish and Indian Wars. Proud and straight they marched, these veterans from an era long since passed but not forgotten in the minds of those remaining few who had known and tasted the times of which they had been a part.

This day, the twenty-sixth of June, 1929, was warm and pleasant, typical of the season here in the magnificent valley of the Yellowstone River. It was a day he would have appreciated, he who now lay peacefully within the confines of his flag-draped casket.

Reaching the "rim," the casket was removed from the wagon and placed next to the prepared repository that would soon claim it for eternity. This final resting place, overlooking the great sweep of valley below, was a grand spot indeed—made a man's heart ache with the beauty of it all, not to mention the memories.

From here, a man could gaze out across as fine a view as God ever created. From here, he could look downstream, eyes squinted against the glare of bright sunlight coruscating off the rushing waters of the Yellowstone and recall the time he had come upriver on the old *Far West* with Grant Marsh and Sandy Forsyth back in '73.

Just to the east rose Pompeys Pillar, that towering chunk of sandstone that had served as a register of historic passage from Lewis and Clark to the present, and offering a view nearly as splendid as that currently spread out before a man's musing gaze.

Two days' ride to the south—allowing, of course, that a man had a good horse under him—stretched those tawny slopes where George Custer and his men found their immortality.

To the north lay the Judith Basin, the Big and Little Belt Mountains, and a score of other places that hearkened back to a time when life was sweet and strong; when a man was seldom out of sight of the vast buffalo herds that swarmed over the land, and the aroma of ribs roasting over an open fire produced a contentment of the spirit now vanished along with the herds themselves. Ah yes, if a man had to settle on a final spot, he would be hard pressed to improve on this.

Presently, Mr. Ben Harwood addressed the group, briefly recounting the life of this man to whom they had come to pay their last respects. When he had finished, David Hilger, secretary of the Montana Historical Society and official representative of the state of Montana, paid tribute to the deceased.

Then the firing squad assembled and at the command,
fired a volley toward the azure sky, the report trailing
off into the high lonesome distance of this waning,
early summer afternoon. Finally, American Legion
buglers stepped forward and in a moment, the plaintive
melody of taps rose above the gathered assembly like
the far, thin cry of the wolf whose own presence in this
country was now but a memory, like the remains of
the man honored by the haunting refrain that bade
him farewell.

And so now, finally, it was finished. After nearly four score years and a life that most little boys imagine somehow will be theirs and most old men reach back for wistfully, Luther Sage Kelly had come home at last to his beloved Yellowstone Valley.

Chapter One

GENEVA TO THE MISSOURI,
1849–1868

**Along Seneca Lake and the deep woods
that bordered it I passed many a happy day
of my boyhood.[1]**

Accumulating to Indian legend, the Great Spirit once placed his hands in the earth's soft molten rock, and from the imprint of his outstretched fingers was sculpted the beautiful Finger Lakes region of central New York. By all odds this is an undeniably lovely land, from its warm, deep, verdant summers to the cold, white stillness of its winters. It is as well a land rich in history. The combination of the great natural beauty and history of the area seems an especially appropriate setting for Luther Kelly's early years. "I first saw the light among the wonderful Finger Lakes of central New York," he recalled many years later, "in the historic region made famous by Red Jacket and other noted chiefs of the Iroquois Confederacy."[2]

The Finger Lakes themselves are eleven in number, of which Lake Seneca is the deepest at 630 feet. Seneca's next-door neighbor, Cayuga, is the longest of the group, reaching 40 miles from north to south.[3]

Prehistoric peoples are thought to have inhabited the area as early as 8,000 B.C. More recently, the Finger Lakes region was the home of the famed Iroquois Confederacy, composed of the Senecas, Cayugas, Oneidas, Onondagas, Mohawks, and Tuscaroras. Of these, the largest and most powerful were the Senecas, the "Keepers of the Western Door" in the Iroquois scheme of things, who dwelled in and around the lake that draws its name from them.[4]

Throughout the intercolonial wars between France and England, the Iroquois had by and large been loyal to the British Crown, and remained so during the American Revolution, when their ranks were reinforced by a substantial number of colonists opposed to separation from England. As a consequence, the area was an important staging ground for Indian-Loyalist raids on New York and Pennsylvania settlements. In response, Gen. John Sullivan's "Sherman-like" march through the region in the summer and fall of 1779, destroying crops and villages, effectively ended the Loyalist-Indian threat to the colonial frontier.[5]

Sullivan's campaign not only brought a much-needed measure of security to the frontier; it also marked the end of Iroquois presence in the area and in so doing cleared the way for new settlers, who began pouring into the region following the end of the Revolution. The young nation pulsed with land fever, and schemers were rampant.[6]

The country around Lake Seneca proved particularly inviting to incoming settlers because of its agricultural possibilities and strategic location. The area lay astride the natural east-west corridors across New York. Moreover, the lake itself offered a natural water route to the south and east. Here was a ready-made means for commerce and people to flow into and out of the region, and on a year-round basis since the lake seldom froze, despite the severity of the region's winters.[7]

By 1800 a settlement of sorts had begun to take shape at the foot of Lake Seneca, which had once been the site of a principal Seneca village known as Kanadesaga, a name that would eventually be supplanted by that of Geneva.[8]

Among the early arrivals in Geneva was one Ebenezer Kelly. Born in Amesbury, Massachusetts, in 1768, Kelly married Elizabeth Cheney in 1789. With the end of the Revolutionary War and freedom from the restrictions of English rule, many settlers began pushing west and the Kellys were no exception. Shortly after their marriage, the couple moved, first to Haverhill, Massachusetts, then to Bristol, New Hampshire, where a son, Luther, was born in 1803. At least one other child, a daughter, was also born to this union, though her identity seems not to have survived.[9]

The Kelly line from which Ebenezer was descended had its North American origin in John Kelly (1615–1644) of Newbury, England, who arrived in the Massachusetts community of the same name in 1635. Little is known of John Kelly's background and lineage, except that he emigrated from the parish of Kelly in Devonshire, England.[10]

Ancestors of both Ebenezer and Elizabeth had been involved, one way or another, in the fighting and violence that touched New England during this colonial period, whether in warfare with the French or with the Indians. Ebenezer's father, Jonathan, had fought in the French and Indian War. Jonathan's wife, Sarah Foot, was the great-granddaughter of Capt. Samuel Foot who had been tortured to death by Indians in 1690. Elizabeth Cheney was the daughter of Lt. Daniel Cheney and was the third great-granddaughter of Hannah Dustin, whose story of capture and subsequent escape from Indian captors (after braining her sleeping guards with a tomahawk), was one of the best known Indian captivity narratives in colonial history.[11]

Sometime between 1810 and 1820, continuing their westward migration, the Kellys arrived in the nascent community of Geneva. Here, Ebenezer provided a living for his family by building spinning wheels and manufacturing cloth. About 1820 the family moved once more, this time to a farm near Marion in Wayne County, northwest of Geneva, where Ebenezer died in 1829.[12]

In 1822, Ebenezer and Elizabeth's son, Luther, perhaps concluding that the farm was not for him, returned to Geneva, where he went about establishing a life better suited to his skills and inclinations. Shortly after returning to Geneva, Luther applied for and was accepted as a member in the Ark Lodge of the Masons. The following year (1823) he was raised to the rank of Master Mason and would later serve twelve years as Grand Lodge Officer.[13]

It is not known what young Luther did to earn a living during these first years in Geneva. He may have had a small inheritance, or perhaps he simply took on whatever work he could find while trying to establish himself. However he came by it, he seems to have been a man of some means and, judging by his later record, ambitious and energetic as well.

The year 1825 witnessed two important events in Luther's life. In April, he purchased a lot on Williams Street and constructed a large brick house thereon. That same year he also entered into marriage with Charry M. Hall.[14]

In 1834, in partnership with his brother-in-law, Sanford Hall, Luther purchased the store of one James McClure at Number 10 Seneca for the foreclosure price of $1,800. The business, known as the Golden Eagle, seems to have been a combination drug and grocery store. The business evidently grew and prospered, allowing Kelly to indulge in the acquisition of additional real estate. His presence in Geneva was noticeable beyond the pale of his business, too. He continued his active role in the Ark Lodge and the Methodist Church, where he was numbered among the leaders and was undoubtedly in the forefront of those who led the drive to construct a beautiful new Greek Revival church on the corner of Main and Seneca. The impressive structure was dedicated in 1840 and occupied the site where Geneva's Civic Center now stands.[15]

If Luther Kelly's business had prospered and his civic involvement had grown in the two decades following his return to Geneva in 1822, the autumn of 1841 marked a time of sadness in his life when Charry passed away on September 23 after a long and painful illness. Although the marriage had lasted sixteen years, there were no children.[16]

Kelly did not long remain a widower, however. Seven months later, on April 26, 1842, he married twenty-six-year-old Jeannette Eliza Sage of Chittenango, the daughter of Col. Hezekiah Sage. As with Luther's forebears, Jeannette's line, through her father, was deeply rooted in colonial New England.[17]

Luther's second marriage proved as fruitful as his first had been barren, with Jeannette giving birth to eight children during the next fifteen years. Infant and child mortality rates were high in those years and it was a rare family who did not know the pain of losing one or more children. The Kellys were no exception. Luther and Jeannette's first four children would die before reaching adulthood. The eldest, Sarah Elizabeth, born in 1843, died a decade later at age ten. Mary, born in 1844, would reach sixteen before succumbing. The next two children were boys. Luther Mortimer arrived in 1846 and Clinton in 1847; both would die in 1849.

But if 1849 was a year of dual loss for Luther and Jeannette, it also marked the arrival of a third son, Luther Sage, born July 27. Another son, William Dunham Kelly, arrived three years later, in 1852. In 1855 the last daughter, Anna Jeannette, was born, and finally Albert Frederick in 1857.[17]

These were busy years for Luther in the community as well as at home. In addition to operating his business and pursuing his work in the church and in the Ark Lodge, he was also more than a little active in civic affairs, serving as village president from 1848–1849. In 1852, he was appointed Office of Collector by the Canal Board, a position

Luther Kelly (1803–1857),
father of Yellowstone Kelly.
W. D. Kelly Family Collection,
Author photo.

Jeannette Eliza (Sage) Kelly
(1816–1890), mother of
Yellowstone Kelly.
W. D. Kelly Family Collection,
Author photo.

regarded as lucrative, at least by the editor of the local paper. Lake Seneca was then a vital north-south artery that connected Geneva to the Erie Canal and gave the city access to the eastern part of the state.[18]

Luther Kelly was apparently not a man inclined to shy away from controversy. He was involved in a fight to make what was then known as Genesee Park into a public park and was also noted as one of "The Eight Champions" who saw the Ark Lodge through a difficult period when feelings ran high against Masons and indeed threatened the total collapse of Freemasonry in the state of New York.[19]

In 1826, Capt. William Morgan of Batavia, New York, authored a book purporting to reveal the hitherto carefully guarded secrets of Freemasonry. Dissemination of the work by David Miller, publisher of the Batavia *Republican Advocate*, sent a shock wave through the Masonic community. A request by a committee of Masons to cease publication was rejected by both author and publisher. Shortly thereafter, a fire broke out in Miller's printing office, though whether the blaze was accidental or intentional is unclear.[20]

Morgan, meanwhile, had been incarcerated in the Canandaigua jail on a debtor's charge. On 11 September 1826, persons unknown, after paying Morgan's debt, forcibly removed him from the jail and apparently took him to old Fort Niagara where he was last seen on the nineteenth. Morgan was widely suspected of having been murdered by angry Masons.[21]

Although there was no evidence implicating the Masonic Order in Morgan's disappearance, the incident touched off a powerful wave of anti-Masonic protest that swept across the state and nation with a fervor that lasted for a decade. More than 90 percent of the lodges in New York State were compelled to relinquish their charters. In Geneva, Ark Lodge's substantial land ownership, together with the steady guiding hand of Lodge Master Luther Kelly, enabled the lodge to survive these perilous times.[22]

The most controversial episode in which Luther Kelly was personally involved was when he was named postmaster in Geneva. In 1854, Kelly is alleged to have employed political chicanery to secure that appointment. The charge was leveled by S. H. Parker, editor of the *Geneva Gazette*, who had been appointed postmaster barely a year before, during the outgoing Fillmore administration, only to find himself suddenly replaced when Franklin Pierce took office. "Yesterday the news came," Parker wrote in the first of two columns to appear in the *Gazette*, "sudden and startling as a thunderclap that Luther Kelly has been appointed Post Master at Geneva, in place of S. H. Parker, removed." Whether indeed Luther Kelly was guilty of any scheming will never be known. Moreover, coming as it did from his predecessor, the implication appears a bit suspect.[23]

Shortly after receiving his appointment as postmaster, however, Luther was stricken with apoplexy, and his illness apparently caused Mr. Parker to hold off on further comments. The stroke was not serious enough to incapacitate Luther permanently, however, because he appears to have been back on the job soon thereafter. And Parker, wasting no time in resuming his diatribe, reported that

> "we were relieved from official connexion [*sic*] with the
> National Administration. We breathe freer and feel lighter
> of heart than ever. As our successor has so far recovered
> from his paralytic stroke as to enter upon official duties,
> the causes which impelled us to withhold for the time being
> a few facts in regard to our removal and his appointment
> no longer exist; and we shall therefore pay our respects
> to him next week. We'll make 'the galled juice wince,'"
> he added with a twist.[24]

It is not likely that any of the Kelly children—which numbered three now following Sarah's death in 1853—with the possible exception of ten-year-old Mary, had any real inkling as to the serious nature of their father's illness. Young Luther Sage was but five and his brother William only two; they would enjoy only three more years with their father. In the interim, however, they would be joined by two additional siblings: Anna Jeannette on Christmas Eve 1855 and Albert Frederick on October 29, 1857.[25]

As it often does in such cases, the first stroke proved a herald of what was to come. On February 14, 1857, Luther was felled by a second stroke at age fifty-four, his death occurring virtually on the eve of the conception of his last child, Albert. Luther Kelly was buried with full Masonic honors and laid to rest in the Washington Street cemetery, where Jeannette would join him thirty-three years later.[26]

The Geneva that Luther Kelly left behind had evolved into a cultural center of upstate New York. Although there was access to the Erie Canal, the routing of that famous waterway through Rochester and Syracuse had largely spelled an end to the community's original dream of becoming a major commercial center, but it had become important in other ways and thus had grown and thrived despite falling by the wayside as a prosperous canal port.

Geneva had grown as an agricultural center and was home to a number of varied business enterprises, including several successful nurseries and a farm implement manufacturer. The community's real strength, however, seemed to be concentrated in its religious and educational institutions. Indeed, one historian has observed that by 1836, there were thirteen schools of one kind or another to serve a population of three thousand.[27]

Presumably, Luther's estate left the family in reasonably comfortable circumstances, judging from the success of his drug store and salary as postmaster, together with his property holdings. In any event, it would appear that Jeannette had no financial constraints in providing an education for her children.

There are no extant records showing where the Kelly children attended school, although there was certainly ample opportunity for them to do so. In point of fact, between 1830 and 1870 eleven private schools were founded in the community to complement a public school system that had been introduced in 1815. In 1839, Schools Number One and Nineteen were combined to form Union School, and it seems reasonable to think of young Luther and his older sister being part of that student body, although Mary may well have attended one of the several local schools for young ladies, such as the DeLancey School for Girls, which opened its doors in 1856. William, Anna, and baby Albert were of course too young for school at the time of their father's death, though William would soon be of age.

Young Luther's boyhood seems to have been typical for his time and place. Like many youths he was attracted to the great outdoors: woodcraft, Indian lore, and wildlife fascinated him, perhaps even a bit more so than most. "Along Seneca Lake and the deep woods that bordered it I passed many a happy day of my boyhood, encroaching, no doubt, upon many hours that should have been devoted to school." If this be considered a classroom of a different sort, he evidently learned his lessons well. We may assume, too, that he acquired some proficiency with firearms during this period because when he entered the army just a few years later, he had already developed the skills necessary to be a successful hunter.[28]

Kelly's penchant for the adventure and solitude that so characterized his rich and varied later life, found its earliest expression in these sylvan haunts along the shores of Lake Seneca. Here perhaps he imagined himself as Natty Bumppo moving silently and stealthily through the woods, ever watchful for the evil Magua and his Huron war party. Or perhaps the shore of the lake served as the beach of a deserted island on which, he, as Robinson Crusoe, found himself stranded and alone. These and a thousand other imaginings of boyhood were here dreamed, and in this crucible of great natural beauty was first planted the seeds of a truly remarkable life.

The world that Jeannette Kelly's now fatherless family found itself in was on the threshold of a tumultuous time. Talk of secession, abolition, and war was growing stronger. By 1854, the *Geneva Courier* was printing antislavery slogans in every issue. Interestingly enough, however, Geneva was not totally devoid of sympathy for the South, as several families from Virginia were numbered among the area's earliest settlers. Generally, though, abolitionist sentiments ran high in the community. In the 1856 election, a strongly Republican Geneva supported John C. Fremont over James Buchanan by a two-to-one margin and provided equally staunch support for Lincoln in 1860.[29]

In 1860, sadness again touched the Kelly family with the death of sixteen-year-old Mary on June 14, thus making the fourth of Jeannette's eight children to die before reaching adulthood. Young Luther Sage, who had become the man of the family following his father's death, now became the eldest sibling as well, at age 11.[30]

With the firing on Fort Sumter in April 1861, a wave of patriotic spirit swept across the nation. Geneva was no less immune to the fever that gripped the rest of the country. The community's Republicans viewed the trial by sword as the only way to deal with the question of slavery once and for all.[31]

Many years later, Luther Sage Kelly could still recall the heady excitement of those first days of the war. "There was marching by night of 'Little Giants' and 'Lincoln Clubs' in resolute and solemn array, and I yet recall how the oil dripped down from dusky, smoky torches onto black wide-awakes and capes. . . . Nearly everybody wore a rosette of red, white, and blue, and some of these were very gorgeous indeed."[32]

Now nearing his twelfth birthday, Luther Kelly also remembered looking on with envy not long afterward, when the 126th New York Volunteers, who had been training in the area, marched down Main Street, led by some of his schoolmates, now ready to march off to war as drummer boys. "I deplored the fact," recalled Kelly, "that my youth and my position as eldest in the family rendered it imperative that I remain with my mother, sister, and brothers."[33]

It is not clear exactly when young Luther entered Geneva Wesleyan Seminary in Lima, about thirty-five miles to the west, but it was probably late 1864 or early 1865, during his fifteenth year, which was about the right age for a young man of that era to continue with the next phase of his education. Unfortunately, none of the school's records have survived so we have no way of knowing how Luther fared academically, either prior to his matriculation at Geneva Wesleyan or after; whether he was attentive to his lessons, or was preoccupied with the adventure of a war that was passing him by. However, judging from his later writings, it seems reasonable to suggest that he was probably at least a fair student, particularly when it came to poetry, literature, and history, topics that would interest him throughout life, a trait he shared with sister Anna, herself a writer and Browning scholar.[34]

By 1865, the war was winding down and Kelly, who would turn sixteen in July, could resist the lure no longer, even though he was not yet of age. One can picture this earnest young man pleading for his mother's permission to join the army. In all likelihood, the request was refused at first, then reluctantly granted in the face of persistent pleas.[35]

After approval by a local board, Kelly was sent off to Rochester, New York, where he first attempted to enlist in the Fourth New York Cavalry, only to be turned down because of age. One can imagine Kelly telling the recruiting officer that he was not quite sixteen, but that he did have his mother's permission, which evidently was not enough to convince the recruiter. Refusing to be dissuaded, however, Kelly tried again and this time was successful. He does not admit to it directly, but implies that having been foiled by honesty the first time, it would not defeat him in round two.[36]

And so Luther Kelly now found himself in the army; it would prove to be the first of two military experiences in his life. Not realizing the distinction between volunteers and regulars, he had unwittingly signed up for the latter and accordingly was now a member of Company G, Tenth U.S. Infantry. In due course he would serve in the volunteers as well, but that was more than three decades in the future and at the moment, his thoughts were on the rapidly concluding Civil War and the role his company might still play in that conflict.[37]

From Rochester, Kelly joined other new recruits for transfer to Governor's Island, New York, where they were housed in historic Castle William, a forty-foot-high stone edifice built during the War of 1812. Here the recruits remained for several days before boarding a transport bound for City Point, Virginia. Three decades later, Kelly would return to Governor's Island as an employee of the War Department.[38]

Because it served as Gen. Ulysses Grant's field headquarters, City Point, Virginia, had, by 1865, become the *de facto* center of Union military operations.[39] Accordingly, this small and otherwise rather obscure landing on the James River was a scene of great hubbub and

Pvt. Luther S. Kelly, Co. G,
Tenth U.S. Infantry,
about 1865.
Luther S. Kelly Memoirs.

activity. Here, Kelly and his companions found much confusion, with soldiers bustling about on every sort of duty. Eventually, the new recruits were issued equipment and assigned to various companies as replacements.[40]

On 9 April 1865, Gen. Robert E. Lee surrendered the Army of Northern Virginia to General Grant at Appomattox Courthouse, effectively bringing an end to four years of fighting. Shortly afterward, Kelly's battalion of the Tenth Infantry marched to Richmond, then on to Washington where it encamped south of the Potomac River and remained there until after the forthcoming Grand Review. The military family is often small. Kelly would meet his present battalion commander and adjutant many years later in the Philippines when each was a brigadier general and Kelly a captain of volunteers.[41]

At some point, while the battalion was marching through Virginia, Kelly developed swollen veins in his left testicle, a condition that produced considerable discomfort. The army surgeon provided him with a support that Kelly wore in all but the hottest weather, when wearing the device proved "unbearable." He would be afflicted with this problem for the remainder of his life.[42]

The Sixth Corps, Army of the Potomac, which had been unable to participate in the Grand Review, was to be honored with a parade of its own. On 6 June, Kelly was selected to be part of a fifty-man guard detail to be posted around the reviewing officer of the Sixth Corps. It was his first official duty of any real consequence and an exciting moment for a young man who was still some seven weeks shy of his sixteenth birthday. The parade itself took place on 8 June. Kelly recalled the event with clarity. "Long before daybreak we were on the road marching through the misty, fog-covered stretches to the Potomac. On either side, as we passed, could be heard the morning call of bugle, fife and drum, and stentorian voice giving commands to morning cavalry."[43]

After crossing Long Bridge, the detail paused to rest along Pennsylvania Avenue. Hungry, Kelly purchased a small pie from a black woman, but found that it looked much better than it tasted and so, with hunger unappeased and poorer by a "shinplaster," he had learned firsthand the timeless principle of *caveat emptor*.[44]

As the review got underway, music signaled the approach of a column of mounted police, followed by the Sixth Corps, called by some the most famous in the entire Union Army. Once commanded by Gen. John Sedgwick, affectionately known as "Uncle John" and who had been killed at Spotsylvania, the Corps was now led by Gen. Horatio G. Wright. Kelly was mightily impressed with the bronzed and bearded veterans that paraded past him, none of whom he recognized except for one figure whom he thought might possibly have been the flamboyant George Armstrong Custer.[45]

"[S]o they passed," wrote Kelly, "horse, foot, and artillery, followed by camp followers and 'bummers' in strange and quaint attire gathered in foraging forays on the flanks of armies."[46] It was a thrilling pageant for a young man to be part of, even if not as an actual participant. It is not difficult to imagine Luther Kelly visualizing himself as one of these returning veterans, swinging down Pennsylvania Avenue with a long, proud step, being greeted as returning heroes. A heady experience, but it was also a long day for the guards. Kelly recalled that as the commanding officer of each new unit passed, they had to stand at present arms "until our fingers and arms ached with tension...and our arms became numb with saluting."[47]

Following the review, Kelly's battalion went into bivouac on Kalorama Heights north of the city. After a time, the unit was moved into the city proper and quartered in some old barracks. Here, between lousy conditions and the stifling summer heat of the nation's capital, Kelly and his comrades spent a largely uncomfortable summer.[48]

Relief came in the fall, when the battalion boarded a train for transfer to St. Paul, Minnesota. On 10 November, Kelly's Company G, together with Company A were assigned to Fort Ripley on the Upper
Mississippi River. Created in 1848 to monitor the terms of the 1837
Treaty with the Winnebago Indians, and to generally maintain peace in
central Minnesota, Fort Ripley (called Fort Gaines until 1850) was located on the east bank of the Mississippi, about seven miles below that
river's junction with the Crow Wing River.[49]

With winter fast approaching, there was little to do at Fort Ripley.
Very likely Kelly felt right at home here, as the winters in north central
Minnesota were undoubtedly much like what he had experienced in
Geneva. When spring finally arrived, Kelly recalled that he liked to take
his rifle and "ramble through the silent forests and along the pebbly
banks of the Mississippi and its tributary streams."[50]

On 14 May, Company G was ordered to Dakota Territory, first to
Fort Abercrombie on the Red River, thence to Fort Wadsworth. The
country gradually took on the look and character of the prairie as the
column headed southwest. Settlements were fewer and more remote,
but they did pass a number of small lakes, one of which usually managed to provide a nice bivouac area each night. Here, Kelly, being an
expert swimmer, managed to amaze his comrades with his "long
under-water dashes."[51]

Although game was frequently observed during their march, Kelly
noted that the men assigned as hunters seldom returned with anything. Accordingly, with the kind of quiet confidence in his own ability that was to characterize his adult life, Kelly approached the
commanding officer and asked for permission to see what he could
bring in. When asked if he had experience, the young man said no, but
pointed out that since the experienced hands did not seem to be faring
very well, he would like to try his luck. Permission was granted and
Kelly promptly proceeded to go out and bring in a deer, which earned
him the appreciation of his comrades. It was the first big game animal
he had ever killed and his timing could not have been better.[52]

Fort Wadsworth, later to be renamed Fort Sisseton, lay some seven-
ty-six miles southwest of Fort Abercrombie, in northeastern Dakota
Territory. Built in 1864 as an outgrowth of the 1862 Minnesota Sioux
uprising, Fort Wadsworth was one of several military outposts created
to provide protection for overland traffic along the Cheyenne River
Road from Minnesota to western Montana. Four of these posts—
Abercrombie, Ransom, Totten, and Wadsworth—covered the route
from Minnesota to the Missouri River, along which were located two

Fort Wadsworth, Dakota. Luther Kelly was stationed here with Co. G, Tenth Inf.
in the spring of 1866. The post was later renamed Fort Sisseton. This view shows
the fort in August 1988. *Author photo.*

additional forts, Buford and Stevenson. The later addition of Forts Ellis
and Shaw extended the line of protection as far west as Montana's Sun
River. In due course, Kelly would become well acquainted with both
Forts Buford and Stevenson.[53]

Company G arrived at Fort Abercrombie on 1 June and paused only
briefly before pushing on to Fort Wadsworth, which was reached on
the seventh. The post, recently vacated by a battalion of the Second
Minnesota Cavalry, a battery of light artillery, and a company of
"Galvanized Yankees," was to be Luther Kelly's home for the next year.
Located in the Kettle Lakes region of the *Coteau des Prairie* (highland
of the prairies), it was an area of considerable spiritual importance to
local Indian tribes. It was also a region rich in game, and given his
recent success, Kelly was more than likely given ample opportunity to
bring in meat for the garrison.[54]

In the fall, Kelly, now a corporal, was directed to take three mule-
drawn wagons to Sauk Centre, Minnesota, a journey of 120 miles, and
pick up a load of potatoes and vegetables. Though he was but seventeen, Kelly had evidently demonstrated a strong sense of responsibility to his commanding officer to be entrusted with such an assignment.

For personal transportation and armament, Kelly was furnished a horse and carbine. A mixed-blood guide and interpreter would accompany him. Kelly's instructions specifically forbade any other individual from attaching himself to the party. The first day out of Fort Wadsworth, however, Kelly was joined by a sergeant from another company who was also on his way to Sauk Centre for supplies. In the best interest of practicality, the two decided on a generous interpretation of Kelly's instructions and the sergeant became an unofficial member of the party.

It proved a mutually beneficial arrangement. The sergeant was evidently glad not to have to make the journey alone and Kelly, though never one to shy away from solitude, was probably happy to have an older, noncommissioned officer along. Should anything happen, it would be nice to have the sergeant available for counsel.[55]

As they got closer to Sauk Centre, the guide pointed out places where the Sioux uprising had struck with a heavy hand just four years earlier. While Union and Confederate armies were flailing away at each other in Maryland, Virginia, Kentucky, and elsewhere in the summer and fall of 1862, southern Minnesota had been terrorized by rampaging Sioux warriors. Hundreds of settlers had died, and not a few Indians as well. When finally the killing had stopped and order was restored late that fall, many of the Sioux had fled toward the setting sun to join their Lakota brethren in the western reaches of Dakota Territory. Many of those apprehended, however, were tried and found guilty of murder. More than three hundred were sentenced to hang, but President Lincoln commuted the sentences of all but thirty-nine. Another was later saved from execution on the grounds of specious testimony. Accordingly, on 26 December 1862, thirty-eight Sioux were hung from a scaffold in the streets of Mankato, Minnesota, in what has been called the largest public execution in U.S. history. Doubtless, the stories of the Minnesota uprising that Kelly heard on this journey and elsewhere made an impression on him, though certainly not enough to dissuade him from later moving into Sioux country by himself.[56]

At Sauk Centre, then "a straggling village of one street," and the future home of writer Sinclair Lewis, they loaded the wagons "with potatoes, onions, and turnips" from one of the nearby farms, where they remained for several days, enjoying the farmer's hospitality. The sergeant also knew a family of German settlers who invited the men to share a meal with them. That night Kelly enjoyed the pleasure of a "genuine feather bed, the kind in which you lose yourself." The next day they began what proved to be an uneventful return trip to Fort

Wadsworth, where the vegetables were turned over to the post quarter-master. Kelly was pleased. His first independent assignment had gone smoothly and it had been a most pleasant interlude to boot.[57]

Like most all western military posts, life at Fort Wadsworth was anything but exciting and eventful. Kelly says little about his time here, except to say that "[t]he aspect it [Fort Wadsworth] presented was cheerless enough, with not a tree nor a foot of cultivated ground."[58]

Living conditions at these posts were usually abysmal and the daily routine dull and laborious. Often the garrison spent more time on work details than on soldiering. There was little that was glamorous about soldiering on the western frontier, certainly not the pay. Privates earned the munificent sum of thirteen dollars a month. As a corporal, Kelly would have drawn an additional two dollars.[59]

As with the daily routine, the menu was spare and monotonous. Typically, the daily ration consisted of salt pork, bacon, beans, rice, dried apples, and coffee or tea. Beef was occasionally available from contractors. Sometimes the men hunted and fished, or planted gardens to supplement the less-than-appealing army bill of fare. Although there were instances when gardens planted at these military posts were highly successful projects, Kelly's journey to Sauk Centre to procure vegetables suggests that, for one reason or another, such was not the case at Fort Wadsworth.[60]

In spring of 1867, Companies G and H were ordered to build a new post at the forks of the Cheyenne (Sheyenne) River in south-eastern Dakota Territory, near the present town of Lisbon, North Dakota. The site of the new post, to be known as Fort Ransom, had been personally selected by Gen. Alfred Terry, commanding the Department of Dakota. In addition to safeguarding overland traffic, Fort Ransom would also be able to provide protection for the Northern Pacific Railroad.[61]

In mid-June, the battalion, consisting of five officers, eighty-one enlisted men, and five Indian scouts, marched out of Fort Wadsworth, arriving at the future site of Fort Ransom on the seventeenth. Winter was evidently late in bowing out that year, because Kelly recalled that there was still some ice to be found along their route of march, and dead buffalo were to be seen everywhere. It was Kelly's first view of the great shaggy beasts.[62]

During that summer and fall, construction of the new post proceeded. Little timber was available from the surrounding countryside except for what could be procured along the river bottoms. The limited supply of local timber may have been supplemented by lumber freighted in from St. Cloud, via Fort Abercrombie, as Kelly recalled that floors in the log quarters were composed of boards.[63]

During the winter of 1867–1868, Maj. Joseph Whistler, command-ing at Fort Totten, came down to inspect the new post. Although it is highly unlikely that Kelly had any contact with Whistler on this occasion, their paths would cross again while both were serving under Col. Nelson A. Miles, Kelly as chief scout for the District of the Yellowstone, Whistler as lieutenant colonel of the Fifth Infantry.[64]

With the arrival of April, Kelly's three-year enlistment expired. He was three months shy of his nineteenth birthday. The past three years had provided an opportunity to grow that he would not otherwise have had. The military experience is unique in that respect, quite unlike any other in life. The army had filled a need, but he was now ready to move on. As he put it, "I was too much enamored with the free full life of prairie and mountain to suffer the restriction and dis-cipline of another period of service in the army, especially in time of peace." Thirty years later he would view things a bit differently, but right now the lure of distant vistas was too compelling an attraction to remain in uniform.

Chapter Two

FORT BUFORD TO FORT PECK:
Adventures Along the Upper Missouri,
1868–1870

When my business at St. Paul was completed I embarked upon a project I had long cherished. This was to proceed to the Canadian settlement of Fort Garry and from there journey westward, wherever the spirit of adventure might lead me, until I had reached the wild country at the headwaters of the Missouri River.[1]

The region drained by the Upper Missouri and Yellowstone Rivers had fired the imagination of more than a few since Lewis and Clark first returned with reports of their extraordinary odyssey. The sixty-odd years since their journey across the western half of the continent had witnessed the rise and fall of the mountain men and the fur trade; steamboats on the Missouri River; and the discovery of gold in Montana. Here was a country where opportunity and success awaited those with enough savvy and determination to track it down. A wholesome helping of good fortune wouldn't hurt, either. But for others, such as young Luther Kelly, it was simply a land that beckoned with high adventure.

That Kelly was imbued with a spirit of adventure, there seems little doubt. He was also a romantic, as any reader of his memoirs will quickly discover. With the exception of sister Anna, who shared his literary bent, neither trait seems to have been present in any other members of his immediate family; certainly not his father nor his brothers, all of whom found their niche in the world of commerce. Perhaps it was an earlier ancestor who contributed these particular characteristics to Luther's gene pool.[2]

Kelly had known about Lewis and Clark before his unit was assigned to the frontier. And surely he had heard tales of the Upper Missouri country from other soldiers, transient frontiersmen, and emigrants on their way to and from the Montana gold fields. Given his interest in history and his romantic bent, coupled with a love of the wilderness, these stories undoubtedly exerted an irresistible pull on him.[3]

Luther Kelly was not the first young man who yearned to strike out into *terra incognita* on his own, but not all who dreamed such dreams sought to make them a reality. One had to be possessed of a certain spirit supported by an ample supply of gumption to venture forth in harm's way, which is exactly where he was bound. The tools he carried with him were great physical skills and a quiet confidence in his own ability to succeed.

It might be suggested that Kelly's decision to head west alone could be laid at the feet of youthful naiveté and ignorance; after all, it is said that those who know little fear little. Perhaps there was some of that at work here, and yet throughout his life he was to demonstrate time and again a restlessness of spirit; a predilection to answer the call of a new adventure seemingly without regard for danger.

This is not to suggest that Luther Kelly was a man devoid of physical fear. He would have been the first to scoff at such a notion. Kelly knew fear as much as anyone, but it never held sway over him, never kept him from whatever it was he wanted to do. On occasion he was given to a bit of reckless behavior, but mostly he was governed by a strong measure of common sense that blended well with his confidence and determination.

Kelly seems to have been able to always maintain his poise, often in some pretty tight situations. His duel with the Sioux while carrying mail between Forts Buford and Stevenson in 1869; his conduct at the Battle of Wolf Mountains in 1877; and his defense of the U.S. provincial office and civilian community at Surigao in the Philippines in 1903; all attest to this particular quality in his makeup.[4]

Before venturing west to see the Upper Missouri River country, there were a couple of intermediate stops to be made. First, in order to cash his pay vouchers, it was necessary to travel to St. Paul. That taken care of, he would head north and visit Fort Garry, a place about which he had heard a great deal and long wanted to see.[5]

Kelly had undoubtedly heard stories of Fort Garry and the Red River traders throughout his three years in Minnesota and Dakota. Forts Ripley, Wadsworth, and Abercrombie all lay within the traders' sphere of movement. Accordingly, there is a better than fair chance that he saw one or more of these caravans (or "brigades," as they were known), and it is not surprising that his naturally curious and adventurous eye would have been drawn to these colorful merchants of the prairie.

It was early April when Kelly left Fort Ransom. Spring was in the air and the countryside was flooded with melting snow. On this first leg of his journey, Kelly accompanied the mail carrier and his dog sled as far as Fort Abercrombie. His personal belongings rode on the sled, while the new young civilian strode along behind. "I managed to keep up with him during the first thirty or forty miles," Kelly recalled, "though not without making some strong drafts on my store of reserve energy." At Fort Abercrombie he was able to board a stagecoach. The remainder of his journey to St. Paul at least would be less demanding.[6]

Lying nearly five hundred miles northwest of St. Paul, Fort Garry (present Winnipeg, Manitoba) served as the Canadian terminus of a flourishing trade with the Minnesota settlements. This prosperous economic enterprise was conducted by a colorful group of mixed-bloods called *métis* or *Slotas*. These people were descendants of French trappers and traders who had intermarried with Indian women. Their numerous offspring adopted the Indian way of life almost entirely and eventually came to comprise virtually a tribal entity unto themselves. The métis were also known as the "Red River traders" or "Red River people," because their sphere of trading consisted of a network of trails that ran from the Minnesota settlements through the valleys of the Red and Minnesota Rivers to Fort Garry and on into the western Canadian provinces. Their trading activities frequently brought them into contact with the Lakotas.[7]

The most distinctive aspect of these Red River traders was their unique two-wheeled cart, the design of which had evolved over time into an extraordinarily efficient vehicle, particularly well adapted to the terrain over which it passed. These carts, about six feet square, were constructed entirely of wood, without a single nail or bolt. They were mounted on five-foot-high wooden wheels, three to five inches in width and covered with green buffalo hide. When the hide shrunk, the wheel then possessed a nearly cast-iron hardness. The carts could be pulled by either a single oxen or horse. Capable of carrying up to a thousand pounds, they were also models of versatility. With the wheels removed and attached to the underside of the cart, they could easily be floated across a deep waterway, even while fully loaded. One draw-back, however, was the horrible squeal created by the wooden wheels rubbing against the wooden axles. It was said this Hadean screech could be heard for three miles.[8]

After he had cashed his pay vouchers and taken care of other busi-ness—he doesn't say what, but it may have been some administrative details connected with his separation from the army—Kelly bought a horse and headed north to Fort Garry. It was now May. Spring lay strong on the land as he rode north up the Red River Valley, "through a land of gentle slopes." The journey was pleasant enough for the young man to recall with clarity, baking bread over an open fire and savoring his com-munion with nature.

For the most part it was a solitary journey, except for one night spent with a Frenchman unable to converse in English. Kelly, on the other hand, knew no French, so it was essentially a silent camp. On another occasion, upon reaching a small river, he encountered a canoe filled with Chippewa (Ojibway) Indians. The moment touched a responsive chord in his romantic soul. He would remember it for the rest of his life. Indeed, when describing it more than half a century later, the incident reads like a scene out of Cooper and perhaps at the time he even imagined himself a latter-day Hawkeye: "The gaily decorated canoe, the handsome young men that manned it," he wrote, "their garments garnished with bead, feather, and porcupine quill work, the slow easy movement of the paddles, all in a set-ting of green forest that bordered the sluggish stream, formed a picture that has fixed itself in my memory." The Indians were friendly and took him across the river in their canoe while his horse trailed along behind at the end of a rope. Upon parting, the Indians presented him with three roasted muskrats, which made a fine meal, as he recalled.[9]

There is no indication of how long Kelly spent in Fort Garry, but while there he met a party of Montana miners who had come there to spend the winter, the cost of living apparently being less in Fort Garry than in the gold camps. Kelly found these miners to be a friendly bunch and they in turn seemed to take a shine to him. Perhaps his youth moved them to take him under their wing. They gave him pointers about the country through which he would be traveling and showed him how to tie a diamond hitch, the *par excellence* method for securing cargo to the back of a mule or horse. Mastering the intricacies of throwing the diamond hitch, however, was not a skill easily acquired and despite the miners' instruction, Kelly failed to get the hang of it. Not until some years later, through the patient instruction of one of the army's mule packers, did he finally manage to master the art of the diamond hitch.[10]

The miners attempted to persuade Kelly not to continue his journey alone. It was much too dangerous, they said, especially for a tenderfoot so young and inexperienced. The area was frequented by Sioux war parties that would quickly pounce on a lone traveler. But Kelly was not to be dissuaded and so, bidding farewell to his Montana friends, set out for the Upper Missouri.[11]

Heading west from Fort Garry, Kelly crossed the Assiniboine River, and eventually fell in with another brigade of Red River traders bound for the buffalo grounds, there to hunt and make pemmican (dried and preserved buffalo meat), one of their stocks in trade.[12]

Kelly found these mixed-bloods a pleasant lot and enjoyed their company. He was also attracted to their handsome coats, one of which he promptly bought. Called, not surprisingly, a Red River coat, these garments were made of high-quality blue broadcloth with brass buttons and a hood. He lost no time donning his new coat, which, in tandem with a red "Assumption" waist sash he had also adopted, made him feel like a "free lance of the prairie."[13]

The exact route taken by Kelly and his trader companions is not clear. We do know they headed west from Fort Garry. At some point beyond the Assiniboine River, they turned south and crossed the boundary line, entering Dakota Territory (present day North Dakota). Somewhere along the Mouse River, about halfway between Forts Totten and Stevenson, the traders encountered a party of Hunkpapa Sioux, one of whom was a rising warrior named Sitting Bull. Among the traders was a Santee Sioux and his wife who pointed out that Kelly was an American. As the Hunkpapas gathered about him in a threatening manner, Kelly maintained his poise, but it was a tension-filled moment, one that he did not forget. Eventually, the Sioux departed and all of the trading party, or at least Kelly, breathed easier.

Kelly later recalled that Sitting Bull appeared to be about thirty years of age and

> had a round, pleasant face, and wore a headscarf of dirty
> white cloth, while most of his followers affected black
> headgear. I suspected that the stiff leather cases tied to

some of the saddles contained war bonnets, as I saw feathers
sticking out of the pouches.... They were armed with rifles
and trade shotguns in addition to the usual bow and quiver
of arrows. They reported killing a white man a short time
before near the mouth of the Yellowstone.[14]

Kelly does not say how he recognized Sitting Bull, but he was probably informed by one of the traders, who had a good working relationship with the Sioux. Sitting Bull especially recognized the economic
value of these traders and tolerated their presence in his country more
than any other non-Indian group, and this shield may very well have
saved Kelly's life. However, despite reassurances from the traders, his
safety probably seemed much less obvious than the circumstances suggested. In fact, he was "nearly scared to death" and that night slept
with his rifle close by. During the course of the night, a light rain fell,
prompting one of the Red River people to check on the covering of his
cart, and in so doing nearly stepped on Kelly's head. Instantly, the
young man was on his feet, rifle leveled at the inadvertent intruder,
who feared for his life. Seeing who it was, Kelly relaxed and explained
that he thought it to be the Sioux war party returning.[15]

The Red River traders' stock in trade was pemmican, made from
buffalo. After a hunt, all hands went to work butchering the animals
and bringing the meat back to camp, where it was cut into slabs the
thickness of a man's finger and hung out to dry. After the drying
process, the meat was lightly toasted over coals, then cut up and placed
in rawhide sacks and covered with hot tallow or marrow fat. One pound
of this concentrated food is equal to about ten pounds of fresh meat
and will keep in good condition for one to two years. "The Red River
people sold tons of it to trade posts," recalled Kelly.[16]

Not long after the encounter with Sitting Bull's group, Kelly parted
company with his Red River companions and headed southwest toward
the Missouri River. In his ears rang the warning of one old trader who
had befriended him: "Look out for the Sioux, boy."[17]

By his own account, Kelly continued his journey in an unhurried
manner. Undoubtedly his keen eye was ever on the watch for Indians,
but at the same time he also remained observant of, and sensitive to,
the character of the region through which he was passing. Approaching
the Missouri River divide, he could see beyond that mighty watercourse
to a "forbidding-looking country, under the shadow of low-lying clouds
far on the western horizon."[18] Later, in recreating the moment for
his memoirs, Kelly's romantic bent came to the fore. "It was, indeed,"

he recalled, "a land of broils and feuds, where dwelt many tribes of men of different tongues, whose pastime was war until the white man came, who warred against none, but fought all because opposed."[19]

His initial contact with the "wide Missouri" was apparently something of a disappointment. The great river rolled along through a narrow valley, between treeless bluffs. "Perhaps not in hundreds of miles," he later wrote, "could the river have presented to the stranger a more unattractive aspect than at the bend where I touched it." Here, horse and rider refreshed themselves with a drink of the "mighty Minnishushu," after which Kelly imagined where the men of the Lewis and Clark expedition must have stood while patiently hauling their great keelboat upriver.[20]

Resuming his journey, Kelly soon encountered two Indians whose tribal identity was unknown to him. He quickly concluded they were not Sioux, however, because of their hairstyle. He was learning. Probably through a combination of signing and the spoken word, Kelly was able to communicate with the pair, who informed him that a large white community was but an hour's ride downriver. Since the community proved to be Fort Berthold, where the Arikaras, Mandans, and Gros Ventres banded together for mutual protection against the Sioux, it is likely that the two Indians Kelly met were from one of these tribes.[21]

Originally established as a trading post by the Northeastern Fur Company in the 1840s and later acquired by the American Fur Company, the post was named for Bartholomew Berthold, one of the founders. Fort Berthold had also served as a military post during the 1860s, but had been abandoned by the army when Fort Stevenson was built, fifteen miles downriver, in 1867.[22]

Kelly proved something of a curiosity when he rode into Fort Berthold. We can picture the young man passing through the high wooden gates, into the courtyard of a post that was square in design, its walls consisting of the log buildings that opened onto the center court. Garbed in his handsome blue Red River coat, Kelly probably turned more than a few heads. He recalled that the agent graciously arranged for him to have food and quarters during his stay.[23]

Kelly would call Fort Berthold home until late fall, finding much there of interest. By his own admission, he was a curious young man and took note, for instance, of the nearby Indian burial ground, where rested the decaying corpses of many who had succumbed to smallpox. He explored the surrounding countryside, educating himself about the Indians and the flora and fauna, as well as the land itself. Curiosity about his surroundings would prove a lifelong trait.

The time spent here stood him in good stead later on. Fort Berthold proved an excellent classroom and Kelly an apt pupil. Here he was able to observe Indian trading practices and agricultural techniques in the fields of Indian corn and squash along the rich alluvial bottomlands of the Missouri River. He studied the design and construction of the conical dwellings used by the Indians who lived close to the fort, noting that these earth- and grass-covered exteriors helped to maintain a comfortable year-round interior temperature. He also learned about lodge etiquette, seating arrangement, and the traditional smoking ritual. He tasted Indian cuisine and experienced the salubrious effects of the sweat bath.

> There is nothing like the vapor bath in an Indian sweat house in its good effects; you recline on a robe on the ground while the water oozes from every pore. An Indian may have traveled fifty or a hundred miles in the saddle or afoot, or danced all day and night; he will then immediately hie himself to a sweat bath and feel invigorated for new effort.[24]

He also witnessed the various festival celebrations, including the annual Sun Dance, spiritual apex of the Plains Indian year. Surely it must have been a riveting experience for a young man of nineteen to watch this excruciatingly painful ritual wherein an individual hangs suspended from thongs secured to his flesh until either the flesh or the thongs finally gave way. Certainly nothing in Geneva had prepared him for such an event.[25]

And when not observing or experiencing Indian life and customs, there was plenty of country to be looked over, though of course one had always to keep a wary eye out for ranging Sioux war parties. The area was evidently a hunter's paradise. "The land swarmed with game," Kelly remembered, "so that one could ride north for hundreds of miles and never be out of sight of buffaloes and their attendant friends, the agile, keen-eyed antelopes, who gave the alarm on approach of danger."[26]

During his sojourn at Berthold, Kelly purchased a .44 caliber Henry repeating carbine and a supply of cartridges for fifty dollars from one of the post traders. Like most frontiersmen, Kelly became very attached to his weapon; it became virtually an extension of himself. On one occasion, when the Henry was out of commission, he substituted an old Springfield, which he had encased from muzzle to butt in the skin of a large bull snake and personalized it with the sobriquet of "Old Sweetness." But the Henry was Kelly's favorite weapon and served him faithfully for several years, until eventually replaced with a Winchester. Though not noted for its stopping power, Kelly nevertheless used the Henry to bring down plenty of game, including buffalo.[27]

Berthold also provided Kelly with an opportunity to become acquainted with several individuals who would either cross his path later on or achieve some degree of frontier notoriety. "Red Mike" Welsh, a colorful character, would later team up with Kelly to hunt wolves. Another trader at the post was Fred Gerard,[28] a man of considerable experience with Indians. Eight years later, Gerard would be a participant in the Battle of the Little Bighorn. Fortunately for him, he was with Reno rather than Custer, and so survived that debacle.[29]

Despite his solitary habits, Luther Kelly was not a misanthrope—far from it. He had no difficulty making warm and lasting friendships, both red and white. While at Berthold, for example, he developed a fast friendship with a chief known as Sun-of-the-Star. "I was always welcome in his lodge," Kelly recalled. Nearly ten years later, he encountered Sun-of-the-Star, who immediately recognized his young American friend, and the two enjoyed a pleasant reunion.[30]

By the time November rolled around, Kelly had begun to grow restless. The upper reaches of the Missouri continued to beckon and he decided it was time to move on. Evidently he sold his horse and headed upriver on foot, keeping his route of travel close to the riverbanks. In this way, he increased the likelihood of avoiding a Sioux war party, which would also have been more apt to spot him had he been mounted.

He traveled light, carrying nothing more than a pair of blankets, some extra ammunition, and a knife, in addition, of course, to his new Henry repeater. He makes no mention of it, though one imagines Kelly was also wearing his Red River coat, which would have felt good, since it was cold enough for ice to have formed along the river.[31]

At dawn on the second day out of Fort Berthold, he came upon a small village of log huts, which proved to be a winter encampment of Mandans who were up and about and who quickly made him welcome despite the early hour. During breakfast he was encouraged to spend the day and night with his hosts and decided to do so. That night, after an unsuccessful day of hunting, the pipe was smoked and pleasant conversation followed, the exchange being facilitated by one of the young women who spoke good English and was able to translate. Later, when Kelly retired, he was offered a bed partner, but declined, saying he always slept alone.[32]

The following day he continued on to the next village, where he again enjoyed Mandan hospitality. From here, he resumed his upriver journey, accompanied by the son of his host. Despite the fact that neither could speak the other's language, Kelly remembered that their time together was enjoyable. At a place called the "Painted Woods," a stretch of timber along the Missouri River between the mouth of the Little Missouri and the Yellowstone, Kelly's companion turned back to his own village and Kelly continued on to Fort Buford alone.[33]

The autumn twilight was deepening as Kelly reached Fort Buford, located in a bend of the Missouri near that river's junction with the Yellowstone. It was a lonesome land of raw, wild beauty, and rich in history as well. Away to the north swept rolling prairie, where buffalo still roamed in considerable numbers, while to the south stretched the badlands of the Little Missouri River and the future haunts of Theodore Roosevelt. Upriver a few miles was to be found the ruins of old Fort Union, in its day the prime fur trading post of the region, but whose location was deemed unsuitable for a military post and thus resulted in the creation of Fort Buford.[34]

Built during the summer of 1867 on a site personally selected by the department commander, Brig. Gen. Alfred Terry, and named for the late Maj. John Buford of the Inspector General's Department, the post was currently garrisoned by five companies of the Thirty-first Infantry. Situated as it was in the heart of Hunkpapa Lakota country, Fort Buford, like Fort Phil Kearny down in Wyoming, suffered continual harassment at the hands of the Sioux, who looked upon the presence of the soldier fort in their territory with high dudgeon. Indeed, earlier that year Buford had been the subject of a wild—and as it turned out, false—rumor, reporting that the garrison had been massacred.

Indian problems were not the only thing that plagued Fort Buford in the first months of its existence. Whiskey was another. During the course of an evening that involved considerable drinking, both the post commander, Capt. William G. Rankin, and Lt. Thomas Little, both of the Thirty-first Infantry, got drunk and apparently had a serious disagreement over some issue or other. A scuffle ensued, with Little striking Rankin. Both officers subsequently preferred charges against each other but later withdrew them. However, the district commander, Col. Philippe Régis de Trobriand, at Fort Stevenson, refused to endorse the withdrawals, believing that to do so would be detrimental to military discipline. Accordingly, in December 1868, Rankin was replaced by Capt. Francis Clarke.[35]

Kelly spent his first few weeks at Buford cutting wood and hunting meat for the garrison. No doubt he also thoroughly explored the surrounding area just as he had done at Fort Berthold. By early February,

Fort Buford, Dakota. A young Luther Kelly arrived here in the late autumn of 1868. It was from here that Kelly set out to deliver dispatches to Fort Stevenson and had his famous duel with the two Sioux warriors on his return journey to Buford. This view taken in August 1988. *Author photo.*

however, he found himself looking for additional income. Probably his mustering-out pay was dwindling and his funds needed replenishment. And perhaps a little adventure would also be welcome. In any case, an opportunity that was to have a marked impact on his career soon presented itself.

Two military couriers, George Parshall and a man known only as "Dutch," who regularly carried the mail between Forts Stevenson and Buford, were long overdue and it was feared that they had fallen victim to a roving Sioux war party. The newly installed post commander, Captain Clarke, called for volunteers but, not surprisingly, there were no takers. Then Luther Kelly stepped forward and asked for the assignment. He recalled that there was some laughter from those present. And one can imagine their amusement at the naiveté of this youth with the cheek to imagine that he could do what far more experienced men recognized as much too risky, if not suicidal. Clarke undoubtedly appreciated the gesture but refused Kelly on the grounds of age. Once again, however, Kelly's persistence rose to the challenge and he pressed for the assignment. Eventually, Clarke acquiesced, probably out of desperation more than anything else. The mail had to get through and this young man was the only one who seemed willing to undertake the assignment. It was to be the only time in Kelly's career that he served as a mail carrier, but it proved a memorable occasion.[36]

With a roan mustang provided by the quartermaster, Kelly left Fort Buford at twilight on Friday, 5 February 1869. The roan, evidently filled with a surplus of pent-up energy, promptly took his head and tore off down the snow-packed trail for some distance before Kelly was able to slow him down. Around midnight he reached the Mandan camp where he had stopped on his way from Berthold to Buford. As he dismounted, the roan spooked and broke free, leaving the young courier horseless. On the brighter side, the Mandans made him welcome, and after food and good conversation, he discovered that his hosts had also managed to retrieve the wandering roan, a fact that undoubtedly contributed to the few hours of restful sleep that followed.[37]

The next morning he continued on his way, by and by reaching the camp of Red Mike Welsh, who welcomed him back and provided accommodations for another night. The following morning he resumed his journey, passing through Fort Berthold and finally reaching Fort Stevenson on Sunday, the seventh, where he presented his dispatches to Colonel de Trobriand, whom Kelly remembered as a "portly man with pleasant face."[38]

Kelly's downriver journey to Fort Stevenson had been free of incident and if anything, characterized by the hospitality accorded him. The return trip to Fort Buford was to prove far more eventful. Following a "day or two" of rest at Fort Stevenson, Kelly started his return trip to Fort Buford, spending the first night at Red Mike's. Here he found a party of Arikaras—Rees, as they were better known—under Bloody Knife, a warrior of some repute who would later lose his life at the Little Bighorn.

The next morning, the Rees headed out to hunt while Kelly continued on his way to Fort Buford. As he was rounding a turn in the trail, near a place called the Great Bend, some forty miles beyond Fort Berthold, he saw a pair of Indians on horseback moving toward him; only forty or so yards separated them. Spotting Kelly, the two Indians quickly dismounted. Kelly halted but remained in the saddle, withdrawing his Henry repeater from its scabbard. As he did so, the Indians moved into the brush alongside the trail. One, Kelly noted, was armed with a double-barreled shotgun, the other with a bow and arrows.

Suspicious of their behavior, Kelly asked for identification and was informed they were Mandans. However, their mode of dress and speech convinced him they were lying, and a moment later that belief was confirmed when the one Indian opened fire, hitting Kelly's horse. As the wounded animal began to pitch about, Kelly jumped off but lost control and hit the ground full length. As he started to rise, the Indian with the shotgun charged toward him and, at a distance of only a few feet, attempted to fire, but the weapon failed to discharge. Spared, Kelly promptly fired and killed the Indian.

The second Indian, meanwhile, had taken up station behind a tree that was not quite wide enough to entirely shield him. In the duel that followed, the adversaries fired at each other several times, with Kelly sustaining a knee wound during the exchange. Although he was without cover, having a sixteen-shot repeating rifle gave Kelly a decided advantage as he attempted to work his way into position for a better shot. Presently, he managed to hit the Indian in the arm. As his opponent slumped to the ground, Kelly approached and discovered he had scored other hits as well. The dying Indian informed Kelly that he belonged to a small party of Hunkpapas in the area, a concern that had been on the young courier's mind throughout this duel. If those other Sioux, drawn by the sound of the firing, arrived on the scene while he was still around, Kelly would be most apt to join his now dead adversary. Accordingly, with his own mount dead or dying, Kelly wasted no time heading back to Red Mike's on foot.

Reaching Mike's camp safely, Kelly had his knee attended to, all the while relating the story to Bloody Knife and his companions, back by this time from their hunt. The young courier's tale proved exciting news to the Rees who promptly headed back up the trail to the scene of Kelly's triumph, returning some time later with two scalps, "singing and waving coup sticks." After his knee had been taken care of, Kelly and Red Mike returned to the site to collect their own trophies, which consisted of a bow and quiver of arrows, a robe, moccasins, and the shotgun.[39]

The news spread rapidly. The next day some friendly Gros Ventres, having heard of Kelly's exploit, rode into Mike's camp to meet this young white man who had killed two Sioux warriors. These Gros Ventres and perhaps Bloody Knife and his Rees seem to have been the ones to christen Kelly "Little-Man-With-The-Strong (Big)-Heart." And when he returned to Fort Buford a couple of days later, Kelly discovered his reputation had preceded him. No longer was he a tenderfoot. He had suddenly become something of a hero and local celebrity. Indeed, Lt. Cornelius Cusick, Thirty-first Infantry, whom Kelly would have occasion to meet later on as a scout with Miles, was so impressed

Luther Kelly's duel with two Sioux warriors. Sketch by Charles M. Russell. *Luther S. Kelly Memoirs.*

with the young man's accomplishment, that he presented Kelly with a fine army overcoat.[40]

On the face of it, the incident seems to have attracted more attention than it merited. Had an older, more experienced frontiersman killed two Sioux warriors, the event would likely have passed with little fanfare. Undoubtedly, however, Kelly's age and "tenderfoot" status exaggerated the importance of the affair. Still, he found himself in a difficult situation and, despite his youth and lack of experience, acquitted himself well.

Kelly left no record of how he might have felt after having killed two Indians. He had never before taken a human life and it must have had some effect, though it may not have been felt until later, after the impact of the event had a chance to sink in. Generally speaking, though, killing in this frontier world, whether animal, Indian, or in some instances, even another white man, was an omnipresent reality—a fact of life, a matter of survival. One either learned to accept this as a condition of existence out here, or perished; it was that simple. And while Kelly never gave any indication that he enjoyed killing another man, he obviously learned quickly that it was sometimes necessary.

In the immediate aftermath of his fight, the adrenaline was surely pumping and his main concern was survival. He was "obsessed with the fear that there was a war party close by. . . . At last I turned and made for the stockade camp of Red Mike as fast as I could travel."[41]

The duel with the Sioux warriors earned Kelly his first full measure of respect, establishing the foundation for a reputation that was to grow in the ensuing years. Later, this duel would serve as the subject of a Charles M. Russell sketch that was eventually published in *Back-Trailing on the Old Frontiers*. Kelly liked Russell's sketch and thought it an accurate depiction of the event.[42]

Shortly after Kelly returned to Fort Buford, the two overdue mail carriers also arrived, having reportedly returned by a round-about way, presumably because of the Indian threat. The one, George Parshall, whom Kelly had come to know, took his celebrated young friend to meet the post interpreter, Ed Lambert.

Ed Lambert was one of those colorful Canadian voyageurs who were no strangers to this part of the American West. From the earliest days of European contact, the French had demonstrated a knack for mixing with the indigenous peoples and adapting to their culture, much more so than either the English or Spanish. Lambert served as a latter-day example of that ability to blend in. He was married to an Indian woman and had fathered two girls. He seems to have been in the area for some time, knew the Indians, and possessed considerable knowledge of the region. The Indians called him Chagashape, or "Worker-of-Wood," because of his skill with an axe.

Lambert was yet another of those fascinating and colorful characters that weaved in and out of Luther Kelly's life, unwittingly serving as tutors in the always chancy classroom of the frontier. But then Kelly was also an apt and willing pupil; the sort of likeable young man that makes older people want to take them under their wing. At any rate, during these early years in Dakota and Montana, Kelly probably learned as much or more from Ed Lambert as anyone. On one occasion, Kelly and Lambert had been hunting buffalo up around the Milk River. After returning to Fort Peck, Lambert was asked what he had killed. "I kill nosing," he replied, "but Kelly she killed a geese."[43]

Kelly remembered Lambert as a "man of great muscular strength [who] had once, on a wager, packed a heavy keg of pork around the stockade of old Fort Union."[44] On another occasion, when Lambert was post trader and interpreter at Fort Peck, Sitting Bull crossed the river with a party of Hunkpapas and strode into Lambert's store, declaring that he would "show you white men how to trade with Indians." So saying, he then proceeded to act as trader, doling out to his party various items such as cloth, sugar, coffee, powder caps, and ammunition, in return for what he considered a fair number of furs. All the while, Lambert, wise enough not to invite more trouble, strode back and forth, "past an open keg of powder, ready to blow

(left to right)
John George Brown,
Ed Lambert, and
Yellowstone Kelly,
in the early 1870s.
Luther S. Kelly Memoirs.

up the store if things went to extremes." The Hunkpapas finally got the message and departed after setting fire to some cordwood along the river; one way or another, it seems, they would have the last word.[45]

Kelly spent the five years or so following his arrival in the upper river country, ranging back and forth through the region. Sometimes he could be found at Fort Berthold, at other times, Fort Buford or Fort Peck, or somewhere in between. Like other nomadic white men on the frontier, his was a way of life that was tied to nothing but his own inclinations. He came and went as he pleased and answered to no one; it was perhaps about as free a life as one might imagine. He hunted, trapped, and, on occasion, cut wood for the river steamers, as during the fall of 1871, when he and a character named "Stub" Wilson had a wood yard on Porcupine Creek above Fort Peck.[46]

On one occasion during the winter of 1868–1869, Kelly wandered up a little valley near the junction of the Yellowstone and Missouri Rivers. Here he found and killed an elk and in doing so was struck by the fact that both he and the elk were alone in this place. After skinning the animal (and presumably dining on a portion of it), he passed a comfortable night with the elk skin between himself and the snow-covered ground. Out beyond the perimeter of his small camp, a pack of wolves howled through the night, but knowing they would not "harm a live man [he] lost no sleep on their account." The next day he returned to Fort Buford in a snowstorm. The incident evidently made a firm imprint on his memory because many years later, while composing his memoirs, he chanced to be reading an account of Lewis and Clark that described how they had discovered and explored what he was sure was this same little valley where he killed his elk sixty-odd years later.[47]

Luther Kelly and his generation of frontiersmen arrived in the West a little too late to qualify as true mountain men, if one limits the use of that term to those whose time in the sun lasted from Lewis and Clark to the beginnings of the great overland migration. Still, Kelly's way of life was not so different from that of the Jim Bridgers and the William Sublettes who had preceded him. One suspects that had he been of an earlier generation, Kelly would have had no difficulty "cutting it" as a mountain man.

But there was a price for this free existence: life itself; and those who failed to grasp that basic fact and hone their survival skills to a razor sharpness were most apt to find themselves beyond the pale of further worry. The scourge of the mountain men had been the Blackfeet. In Luther Kelly's world, it was the Sioux, for whom one always kept a wary eye posted. During the summer of 1870, for example, when Sioux war parties were unusually active, he and another individual known only as "Longhair Smith" reportedly braved "the gauntlet" to provide meat for the Fort Buford garrison.[48]

Winter along the Upper Missouri River arrives early and departs with great reluctance. The spring of 1869 "was long in coming," Kelly recalled, "and I became restless again; life at Fort Buford seemed unbearably humdrum. To the north lay Fort Peck,"[49] toward which place his roving eye was drawn, and little wonder that it was. The country about Fort Peck was a hunter's paradise, offering an abundance of wildlife, including plenty of buffalo. Indeed, the Milk River drainage was one of the best buffalo ranges in the northwest.[50] In his mind he imagined himself exploring the charred ruins of old Fort Union, and pictured daily life at Fort Peck. Having thus fired his imagination, he determined to press on, guided by the admonition from a poem he recalled:

> Keep not standing fix'd and rooted
> Briskly venture, briskly roam[51]

The thought typifies perfectly his personal philosophy, not just during these early years, but for much of the remainder of his life as well.

Before striking out for Fort Peck, Kelly turned his pony loose, feeling safer on foot, his only equipage being blankets and a rifle. A horse provided greater mobility but also increased a man's risk of being spotted, or revealing his presence to a passing Indian pony. Concealment was easier on foot.

A day out of Fort Buford, Kelly chanced upon a trio of Indian lodges, where the elderly occupant of one lodge extended his hospitality, offering the young traveler food and a place to sleep. The lodge also contained a squaw and three little girls, whom he feared were forced to yield their beds to accommodate their guest. In the morning, when Kelly was ready to depart, the old man gave him a pouch containing a mixture of tobacco and red willow bark together with one of the small stone pipes frequently used by traders in bartering with the Indians. In return, Kelly presented a red blanket to one of the girls. At his camp that night, Kelly tried a pipe full of his new mixture. The sampling proved to be the beginning of his tobacco habit.[52]

Keeping careful watch, for this was Hunkpapa country, he continued his journey, finding both antelope and buffalo plentiful. On the third day he came in sight of his objective. Situated on a high point above the Missouri at its confluence with the Big Dry, Fort Peck was stockaded and featured a heavy wooden gate, which, he would presently learn, was kept securely locked at night for obvious reasons.[53]

He seems to have remained in the Fort Peck area through the spring and summer anyway. The country was new and the hunting first rate, but the chance of a run-in with a Sioux war party was also high. In point of fact, shortly after arriving at Fort Peck, Kelly had what was probably his second encounter with the Sioux, or at least his second serious encounter. Little is known of this particular episode, but it evidently occurred while Kelly was hunting. He managed to escape, though not before he sustained a wound in his left hand that apparently shot away most of the little finger.

When Kelly returned to Fort Peck, there apparently was no surgeon to attend to his wound, so George Towne, a young man about his own age, newly arrived in the country and employed as a freighter, offered to amputate what remained of the digit. Necessity being the mother of invention, Towne used a small file to fashion a surgical tool out of an old harness knife, and proceeded to amputate what remained of Kelly's finger. The only anesthesia was "a little spirits of booze and a chew of tobacco." Afterward, Kelly and Towne teamed up to hunt and trap for a time.

Another photo of Yellowstone Kelly taken during the early 1870s. Note the missing little finger on the right hand. The weapon is the Springfield rifle he used while his Henry was out of commission. The Springfield would seem to have been the weapon he referred to as "Old Sweetness" (see Chapter Two, note 27). *John M. Carroll Collection.*

Nearly forty years later, Towne, then active in the Montana Pioneers Society, wrote to Kelly who was finishing up his tenure as agent at the San Carlos, Arizona, reservation, asking for recollections of the old days. Kelly promised to comply, adding that he clearly recalled Towne's surgery. "I remember the cutting business, Kelly replied. "Harness knife, was it not? Lord but it hurt, but I did not let on."[54]

It is interesting that of all the Indian encounters he had on the frontier, to say nothing of the tough fighting he experienced in the Philippines, Kelly was a casualty only twice, and neither instance was serious. Further, both wounds occurred during his first year in this Upper Missouri River country. Perhaps a charmed life, but something, it seems, also deserves to be said about learning how to take care of one's self.

Indian encounters were frequent and interesting; often, but not always, hostile. One way or another, though, the experience was educational. On one occasion, for example, he witnessed how Indians who might be unfriendly during the summer months, often moderated their position in the winter so as to take advantage of government annuities.

During what was likely his first winter, a band composed mainly of Yanktonais came into Fort Buford to trade and put on a show of sorts for the garrison. One of three tribes of the middle branch of the Dakota nation (the Santee being the eastern and the Lakota the western), the Yanktonais, while perhaps not as feared as their western brethren, could nevertheless be plenty troublesome when they were of a mind to do so.[55]

The event made an impression on young Kelly who recalled that despite cold weather, the dancers wore only breechclouts and leggings as they simulated the movements of a buffalo herd. "Counterfeit buffalo," he called them. Indeed, several years later, when Kelly and a partner were stalked by a war party whose movements were similar to those of the dancers, he had occasion to remember this moment.[56]

The fall of 1869 found Kelly in company with three men who had a cabin near the Big Muddy, a stream that flows into the Missouri near present-day Culbertson, Montana, perhaps forty or so miles west of Fort Buford. The trio cut wood for the river steamers and also hunted and trapped. Shortly after Kelly's arrival, the group apparently was joined by a fifth individual known only as "Missouri." As always, survival in these parts was a risky proposition, as Kelly continued to discover.

On one occasion—and very likely there were others as well—a strong war party, likely of Sioux, attacked them while they were near the river, probably cutting wood. Despite the perilous nature of their position, Kelly could not help but appreciate the scene. "On they came," he recalled, "in wild disorder, their ornaments of bright metal flashing in the rays of the morning sun, and there was such a flutter of waving plumes and feathers that the sight was altogether thrilling." Kelly and company could ill-afford to dally in admiration, however, exiting the scene as fast as they could run, pursued by their attackers who were mounted.

Taking cover in a marshy area near the river, the four fended off their attackers with careful fire. "Missouri" scored a hit, as did Kelly and at least one other man. Presently, Kelly noticed that some of the Indians had dismounted and were moving forward on foot. Suggesting that they take leave of the place, the five men plunged across the slough and into a stand of willows, all save for Ed—who had on boots—losing their moccasins in the process. The Indians chose not to follow the

men into the brambles and pulled out. Once their attackers had departed, the men were compelled to head back to their cabin, through cac-
tus, barefooted—all, that is, except for Ed. With no immediate
replacement for his moccasins, Kelly killed a couple of beaver and used
the hides to fashion some footwear that would last until he returned to
Fort Buford. One presumes his companions were equally resourceful.[57]

Chapter Three

THE YELLOWSTONE VALLEY AND THE JUDITH BASIN,
1870–1876

It was a beautiful place and view. The smooth bottom land was turfed to the edge of the timber, to which the bank, six feet higher than the bottom, sloped.[1]

To the French it was *la Roche Jauney*—River of Yellow Rock. Indians knew it as the Elk River, because of the large elk herds to be found along part of its course, but the label that has survived is that of the Yellowstone, a name that sings of history in a special way. Lewis and Clark knew this river, and before them the Verendryés, and before them, who knows? Along its storied course came countless Indians, mountain men, prospectors, traders, and soldiers. As an artery of travel and commerce in this region during much of the nineteenth century, it was second only to the Missouri. The history of the region cannot be told apart from it.[2]

It should be pointed out that the Yellowstone, like the Missouri, is really a river of two parts: upper and lower. The river rises in the

Absaroka Mountains of northwestern Wyoming, begets Yellowstone Lake in Yellowstone National Park, flows north into Montana, thence east by northeast across the state to its eventual union with the Missouri. From its fountainhead to, roughly, Billings or Miles City, depending exactly on where one wishes to mark the dividing line, it is the Upper Yellowstone. From that point to its confluence with the Missouri, it is the lower river. Along much of its course, the Lower Yellowstone is not especially wide or deep: three to four hundred yards across, with a depth ranging from two to eight feet, depending on the precise spot, the season, and the particular year. Along the way the Yellowstone accepts tribute from the smaller streams and rivers that feed it, including the Big Horn, Tongue, Powder, and Rosebud Rivers. By the time it junctions with the Missouri, it is the largest free-flowing river remaining in the United States.

In the late spring of 1870, Kelly, in company with Ed Lambert, made what was probably his first real penetration of the Yellowstone country he would eventually come to know so well. It was sometime during this period of his life that Kelly acquired the sobriquet "Yellowstone Kelly," though exactly how that came about is not at all clear. Kelly himself never talked about the origin of the name.[3]

Kelly had a skiff that he and Lambert put into the water at the junction of the Missouri and Yellowstone near old Fort Union. Nearby stood a rotting Indian burial scaffold. The place, Lambert explained, had once witnessed a fight between Sioux and Crow.[4] The duo moved on upriver several miles, maneuvering their craft around and through the numerous rapids and small, wooded islands that marked the course of the river. That night they enjoyed a pleasant camp. Nearby, a family of beavers was active enough to draw Kelly's attention. He watched them in the moonlight, seeing "their dark noses pointing swiftly up and down stream, leaving a v-shaped wake behind."[5]

The following morning they resumed their journey. Visible now was a vast prairie "covered with buffalo and bunch grass," stretching northward toward far, low-lying hills. Kelly was moved by the striking panorama that stretched away before his youthful gaze. In those days, the Yellowstone Valley was still a thing of pristine beauty; little had changed since the days of Lewis and Clark, John Colter, Antoine Larocque, and the Verendryés. Though its days were numbered, time enough remained for Luther Kelly to savor its sweetness. Indeed, one can easily imagine him composing some verse to express what he surely must have felt. As it was, he later wrote that this "was a beautiful place and view. The smooth bottom land [along the river] was turfed to

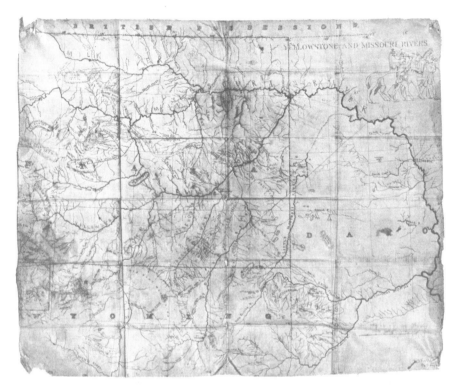

Map traced by Yellowstone Kelly while at Fort Buford, Dakota Territory, about 1870. Kelly apparently created this from a military map of the area, then added a number of features based on his discoveries while roaming through the region. The original of this map is in the Parmly Billings Public Library. *Luther S. Kelly Memoirs.*

the edge of the timber, to which the bank, six feet higher than the bottom, sloped."[6]

It was a leisurely sort of expedition. During the day they explored the surrounding area, with Kelly adding to his growing fund of knowledge about animal habits, in particular those of the buffalo and antelope. At night, after dining on fresh antelope meat, and potatoes from a supply that Lambert had apparently cached on an earlier trip, they sat around the fire, while Lambert regaled Kelly with stories about Indians, buffalo, Fort Peck, and the Milk River country.[7]

From here, the two men had decided to continue their journey on foot; how far would depend on whether or not they encountered Indians. Accordingly, after caching most of their supplies, they continued upriver, along the north shore of the Yellowstone, past the future site of Glendive, Montana, where they killed a bull buffalo and cow for meat and hides. The buffalo was very nearly as important to the commissary of the plainsmen as it was to the Plains Indians. Little was wasted. The meat was hung out to dry and the green hides were then stretched over willow frames. When dry, the hides could be used to construct bullboats, one of the most ingenious vessels for river travel ever devised.[8]

Of Indian origin, bullboats were quickly adopted by white frontiersmen. The boats were immensely practical, because they could carry a considerable cargo while drawing only a few inches of water. This shallow draft made them ideally suited to run rivers like the Yellowstone where the water level was often quite low, particularly late in the season. Moreover, construction was simple and materials were readily available, at least as long as the buffalo remained plentiful. The boats varied in size, depending on the number and size of the individual hides, but a typical boat might be about five feet in diameter.[9] Kelly described the technique of maneuvering one of these craft.

> You use a short paddle in propelling a bullboat and this is done by reaching straight out and pulling the paddle toward you. No great progress is made, but it is a safe craft, riding a few inches in the water and rolling around any obstruction it meets, unless it be a tree at right angles to the current.[10]

With the meat cached and the hides curing, Kelly and Lambert resumed their trek. Noting that the south bank afforded better cover than the north, Lambert skillfully constructed a raft that ferried them across the Yellowstone. Presently, however, the country began to open up and Indian sign grew plentiful—here, the framework of a recently used sweat lodge, there a trail revealing the passage of many horses. Then shortly, they spotted a party of five mounted Indians that Lambert soon identified as Oglala and they in turn were discovered by the Indians, who demanded to know what the pair was doing in this country. Lambert responded, saying that they were hunters. The answer apparently did not fully satisfy the Oglalas, who hollered some and launched a few insulting gestures at the two *wasityus* (a Lakota word for white man), but in the end elected not to press the issue and finally rode off.[11]

Concluding that it might be best to turn back, Kelly and Lambert first worked their way inland, paralleling the river from a distance before heading back to it. Locating their raft, they moved downstream to the bullboat camp, which, fortunately, had remained undiscovered.

However, the hides and meat had not yet cured sufficiently, so, it being a fine camp, they elected to remain there for a day or two, though extra care would have to be taken since the Lakotas were obviously aware of their presence in the area. Many years later, Kelly recalled that they were not terribly worried about the five Indians, who would be reluctant to attack two watchful white men; those were poor odds. Undoubtedly, however, they were concerned about the possibility of a larger war party coming after them. With this in mind, the bones and skulls of the two buffalo they had killed earlier were removed from the campsite and disposed of in the brush. At night, Kelly recalled, "we ate our supper by the light and warmth of the dying cottonwood coals that preserve their redness longer than most woods." They did not bother to stand watch, however, knowing the Sioux did not attack at night.[12]

Here on the north side of the river, the number of buffalo and antelope had greatly increased. Lambert speculated that the Indians had been hunting the buffalo south of the river and followed the herd across to the north side to replenish their meat supply and obtain new hides for their various and sundry needs.

Luther Kelly was certainly not the first to feel compelled to paint a word picture of a buffalo herd. To say that it must have been an impressive sight seems somehow to do an injustice to the experience. Lewis and Clark, Catlin, Parkman, and a host of others recorded their reaction to this grand sight. Kelly's description of the scene here along the Yellowstone, though brief, is clear and particularly vivid. "The scene was exhilarating," he wrote. "[T]he dark bodies of the buffaloes as they moved in clusters or singly, the combative bulls raising a dust cloud as they came together, contrasted with the light-colored antelopes on the outskirts, ready to give alarm at a moment's notice."[13]

When the hides had dried sufficiently, they loaded their supplies into two bullboats and continued downriver to the spot where Kelly's concealed skiff awaited them. Unable to manage the skiff and both bullboats, they were forced to cut one loose, presumably transferring its load to one of the other boats. Landing at Fort Buford, everything was loaded onto a Red River cart and wheeled up to Lambert's home where both men were welcomed by the latter's family. It had been a satisfying expedition.[14]

Outings such as this were a way of life for Kelly in the years that followed. His natural curiosity about the region, especially the country north of the Yellowstone, proved an irresistible lure. Many of his junkets took him back along the Yellowstone, while others took him north into the Milk River country or west into the Judith Basin. Sometimes he traveled with companions such as Ed Lambert, or Jack Mail, another young frontiersman like himself who had gained some familiarity with the country south of the Yellowstone. On other occasions, though, he was content to journey alone.

When not hunting or exploring, Kelly turned to the world of the written word. Fortunately, he was able to borrow books, sometimes from an officer at Fort Buford, or from a trader. It was an opportunity for him to become reacquainted with Scott, Poe, and Shakespeare, "whose works I had read when I was too young to appreciate fully their value." If he was regarded as something of a curiosity because of this fondness for books—not exactly a common or popular pastime among most of his contemporaries—the record does not show it. One suspects he had proved himself in the ways that counted and thereby earned the right to read if he chose to do so. Perhaps many of them were impressed with Kelly's capacity to do what they were either completely incapable of doing or had only the most rudimentary ability.[15]

Despite all of its wild, unsettled vastness, there was a community of sorts within the region. Not surprisingly, this community was predominantly Indian, some (but not all) of whom were hostile toward white men, though this behavior, too, ebbed and flowed with the mood of the moment. There was also a camaraderie that existed among the free hunters and trappers who worked the region. Not everyone was well acquainted with everyone else, perhaps, but if a man stayed in the territory for any length of time, he was known of, through interaction with traders, the military, and others like himself. And sometimes, two or more men might decide to throw in together for a season, then split up to go their separate ways when the season ended.

Kelly apparently had no difficulty blending into this community. He retained his own identity, but at the same time seems to have had no trouble interacting with others, white or Indian. He fought and killed Indians when that was necessary, but like many other frontiersmen, including Daniel Boone, he was not an Indian hater. Rather, he saw Indians as individuals: some were good, others bad. Some bore watching, others he found friendly and hospitable, as for example, the Arikaras and Mandans. To Kelly and many of his ilk, Indians were as much a part of the frontier milieu as the buffalo and the wolf. One respected them and accepted them on their terms. In point of fact, there was much about the Indian way of life that held great appeal for many white men, some of whom became white Indians in effect.[16]

When dealing with Indians of that time and place, tact and firmness were essential prerequisites. It was essential to understand their view of things—what they respected and what they did not, how their sense of humor worked, what they valued, and so forth—indeed, it was vital to one's survival. Kelly seems to have grasped this early on, his youth notwithstanding. He hunted with Indians and often accepted the hospitality of their lodges. His linguistic skills were, by his own admission, limited. He could speak a little Sioux, which, interestingly enough, was the tongue most used by traders because it was easiest to learn. And of course he was able to communicate through the universal language of "signing."[17]

Kelly also did business with Indians from time to time. Once he recalled trading a rifle and two mountain lion pelts to an Indian for a fast buffalo horse. The animal did indeed prove fast, but had been trained to stay on the right side of a herd, which created a problem for Kelly who was left-handed. Eventually, the horse slipped away from him and Kelly speculated that he had headed south across the Yellowstone to more familiar country.[18]

During what was probably one of his first winters in the region, Kelly paid a visit to an Indian hunting party composed of Mandans, Rees, and Gros Ventres. The hunters were camped along one of the tributaries of the Little Missouri, in what would today be southwestern North Dakota or southeastern Montana. It was an area rich in game, and not far from the buffalo range. The party, numbering about forty, of which only two or three were women, had set up shop in a likely spot, constructing several conical style huts out of poles and covered with green boughs. One hut, larger than the rest, apparently served as a sort of camp headquarters. Here, Kelly was made welcome, amid much conviviality. He offered his meager supply of coffee, tea, and sugar to the group who received it enthusiastically and quickly disposed of it, along with his stock of tobacco. Later, he retired to another lodge for sleep, but the singing and smoking continued well into the night.

The next day the hunt commenced. The camp itself was evidently located in prime hunting country. Deer and mountain sheep abounded. The hunters spread out, more or less in a huge circle, then proceeded to work toward the center, driving the animals before them. In this fashion those remaining in the camp had an opportunity to participate in the hunt and there was plenty of game for all. The hunters were not deprived. As it turned out, Kelly's hunting companion was a relative of the young Mandan who had earlier accompanied him on his journey to the Painted Woods. In short order, Kelly and his companions killed as many animals as they could handle. It had been a rich harvest, with much deer and elk being hauled to the main camps along the Missouri. That night there was, Kelly recalled, "great feasting and the air was tainted with the odor of burning bones."[19]

Sometimes these hunting expeditions were risky because of the Sioux. However, scouts had reported that the Sioux villages were well west of the Yellowstone and, accordingly, it was judged safe to hunt in the area. When Kelly saw some of the hunters returning from the west with buffalo meat, he sought permission to do the same, but was turned down. These young hunters were scouts, he was told, whose job it was to observe the enemy's movements, not to disturb the buffalo. However, if they found an animal separated from the herd, it was permissible to kill it with arrows and bring the meat back.[20]

Those living on the Great Plains, Indians as well as white men, subsisted mainly on a diet of red meat. Sometimes this would be supplemented with potatoes, squash, corn, or perhaps a canned delicacy such as oysters or fruit obtained from a post trader. But almost always the *pièce d'résistance* was meat: buffalo, deer, elk, or antelope. When one reads about these feasts of buffalo ribs sizzling over the campfire, or imagines a buffalo hump, specially seasoned, then wrapped in a green hide and left to cook overnight in a bed of coals, it sets the salivary juices to flowing. But an all-meat bill of fare usually left a craving for other foods. Kelly said he could handle a diet of straight meat for about a week, then began to feel a desire for bread and coffee. Frank Grouard, another well-known Indian scout of the same period, described the same craving for bread after a prolonged meat-only diet.[21]

A self-portrait provides us with an image of Kelly during this period of his life.

> I wore at this time a white blanket long coat with hood,
> and under this a soft buckskin shirt of well-smoked leather.
> There were no fringes or beads on this shirt, but it had a narrow
> strip of fur-edged collar and cuffs. I wore moccasins of elk-skin
> and dark jean trousers, which were encased below the knee.
> In winter I usually wore a fur cap of fox or beaver fur.[22]

In the fall of 1871, Kelly headed for the Milk River country, astride a fast new pony acquired in a trade with an Indian. En route, he came to the wreck of the *Amelia Poe*. The vessel, carrying one hundred tons of freight, including a considerable quantity of whiskey and a wide variety of other liquors, had been wrecked on a sand bar in the Missouri in May 1868. Since then, the wreck had attracted whites and Indians alike, all of whom sought to salvage the vessel's spirituous contents. One party of white salvagers on their way to the wreck had a fierce fight with an estimated three hundred Lakotas near Fort Peck in December 1868. Four whites and five Indians were reportedly killed.[23]

When Kelly arrived on the scene, a group was hard at work. He watched with some amusement as one man, armed with a grappling hook and line, stood in water up to his neck, using his feet to locate what he thought was a cask of whiskey. Once a cask was located, he attached the hook to it and the men on shore then attempted to reel in their catch. Sometimes their efforts paid dividends, but other times the hook would tear off the top of the cask allowing the contents to float away, "exhorting a general wail from the bystanders." Although he had never acquired a taste for strong spirits, he did sample some of the *Amelia Poe's* stock and concluded "that such whiskey could very well go into the river, though I did not claim to be a judge in that line."[24]

One of those on the scene was Maj. Alonzo S. Reed, the Indian agent at Milk River. Reed had no military background, but for some obscure reason, Indian agents carried the honorary title of major, even as Kelly himself would do while serving as agent at San Carlos, Arizona, thirty-three years later. Kelly remembered Reed as then being in "the prime of manhood, punctilious, dashing and brave, a gentleman of the old school and a fine type of frontiersman." Later, as a frequent visitor to the Reed and Bowles trading post in the Judith Basin, Kelly would come to know Reed well.[25]

In the spring of 1873, Kelly paid a visit to his friend Stub Wilson who had a cabin and wood yard on the south bank of the Missouri River, about twenty miles below Fort Buford. On this particular occasion, Kelly was mounted and offered the use of his horse to help Stub harvest wood, which he later sold to river steamers for fuel. When the horse disappeared one day, Kelly tracked him to a band of Indians from Fort Berthold. When he confronted the Indians, they finally agreed to return the animal, which they explained was found wandering alone in the woods.[26]

That same spring, the steamer *Key West*, piloted by Capt. Grant Marsh, stopped at Wilson's cabin on its way upriver. The stop here had a two-fold purpose: first, to take on a load of wood and, second, to arrange for Kelly's services. The *Key West* was temporarily under the military command of Lt. Col. George Alexander "Sandy" Forsyth, hero of the 1868 Battle of Beecher Island.

Forsyth, who was on the staff of Lt. Gen. Philip H. Sheridan, commanding the Military Division of the Missouri, had been directed by

In this Edwin Deming drawing, Yellowstone Kelly stands on the bank of the
Missouri River watching the steamer *Far West* as it rounds the bend. The time
could be the early 1870s. *Luther S. Kelly Memoirs.*

Sheridan to explore the Yellowstone River from its confluence with the
Missouri, to the mouth of the Powder River. No steamboat had ever
ascended the Yellowstone that far and Sheridan was desirous of knowing whether, in the event of military operations in that region, it would
be feasible to plan on having riverboats bring supplies that far
upstream, or possibly even farther. Accordingly, Sheridan engaged the
Key West and her veteran skipper to undertake the assignment.[27]

At that time, the *Key West* was the second-largest vessel on the
Upper Missouri. Owned by the Coulson Company, she was a stern-
wheel packet, measuring 200 feet from bow to stern and 33 feet in
width, with a depth of 4 1/2 feet from bottom timbers to the top of the
main deck. She weighed 422 tons. Her captain, Grant Marsh was even
then a near legendary figure, having been plying the often treacherous
waters of the upper river for two decades. "That incomparable river
man," Kelly called him.[28]

Asked by Forsyth to suggest a reliable guide, Marsh named Kelly,
who would turn twenty-four in July. Kelly had now been a resident of
this part of the world for five years and had obviously established
something of a reputation, at least enough for Grant Marsh to recom-

mend him. Kelly accepted the job. It was just the sort of enterprise he liked. "An adventure of this kind suited me very well," he later wrote, and we may well imagine that it did.[29]

At Fort Buford, the expedition added two companies of the Sixth Infantry, commanded by Capt. Montgomery Bryant, one three-inch rifled gun, together with horses and "abundant ammunition." Besides Kelly, Forsyth had fifteen Arikara scouts, bringing his total command to 160 men. Kelly observed that the infantrymen were excited about the prospect of this particular outing and evidently regarded it as a "much desired" assignment. Despite her rather full load—Kelly described it as being somewhat crowded—the *Key West* drew but twenty-six inches of water, which was well because, said Forsyth, "The usual spring run having not yet taken place, the river was at a very low stage of water, much lower than it had been for several years previous."[30]

The upriver voyage commenced at 1 PM on 6 May. Kelly watched with great interest as Marsh maneuvered the *Key West* around a difficult spot known as "Snaggy Bend." As the vessel worked its way up the Yellowstone, Forsyth pressed Kelly for information "as to the lay of land beyond the visible divide and the creeks and valleys that had living streams and springs." To some of these queries, Kelly was able to provide illumination, to others he was not, explaining to Forsyth that he had not yet "been far from the valley of the Yellowstone, but I pointed out great trails over the low divides made by buffaloes and traveled by Indians." Kelly likely told Forsyth that he was more familiar with the country north of the Yellowstone than that to the south and to a degree this would always be true, probably because there was an abundance of game to the north. Finally, the region was simply more appealing to him.[31]

At night the *Key West* pulled in to shore and tied up. Kelly's practice was to sleep on the bank until about 1 AM when he had the sentry awaken him. He would then move inland some distance, find a likely spot, and resume his sleep until dawn when he went off in search of game. The idea here was to move far enough inland so that the noise of the boat did not frighten away any game in the area. Often he would return to the *Key West* with an antelope or two. And of course, one always had to be alert for Indians. This experience may well have reminded him of his first journey up the Yellowstone with Ed Lambert.[32]

Each time the boat landed, infantry work parties went ashore to collect wood for fuel. These steamers had ravenous appetites and fuel was a high priority. However, there were no wood yards along the

Yellowstone such as the one Stub Wilson had on the Missouri. As a consequence, wood-gathering parties were out and about each time the boat put in to shore. "This was our invariable custom at night and at least once during the day," wrote Forsyth, "an abundance of wood, principally cottonwood and ash being found along the banks and upon the islands in the river."[33]

The journey was a mixture of relatively smooth going at times, difficult at others. Small islands and numerous rapids frequented the main channel. Some rapids posed no problem, while others proved difficult. Each bore the name given it by some river pilot: "Alone Rapids," "Monroe's Rapids," "Townsend's Rapids." On occasion, the vessel had to be hauled over sandbars and shoals by Forsyth's infantrymen strung out along the shore. And at times, heavy winds slowed the *Key West's* upstream progress to a crawl.[34]

At the mouth of Glendive Creek, supplies were put ashore in compliance with orders from department headquarters. Brig. Gen. Alfred Terry, commanding the Department of Dakota, had directed that a supply depot be established at this point to serve the forthcoming Northern Pacific Railroad surveying expedition, then assembling at Fort Rice on the Missouri River.[35]

While here at Glendive, Forsyth and a small party, including Kelly, climbed a nearby hill and scanned the countryside, with Kelly identifying such landmarks as he knew. He recalled that Forsyth was expecting some party traveling overland from the south. Using what he called "excellent field glasses," probably furnished by Forsyth, Kelly scanned the surrounding country on a clear night, but saw nothing save for grazing buffalo and an old road made by some former expedition. It was another of those moments that remained as crystal clear in his memory as the Montana night sky of which he wrote. "Having attained this elevation in the night, I rested in a depression of a ravine that ran to the summit. I remember the faint odors of sage and other herbs that made fragrant the still air as I lay on the ground looking up at the stars, waiting for the dawn."[36]

With first light, and having accomplished his mission, Kelly elected to rejoin Forsyth by daylight, rather than wait out another twenty-four hours for the cover of darkness, well aware, however, of the ever-present danger of Indians. He well recalled his return trip back down to the river:

[S]o I wormed my way slowly down ravines and gulches,
    scanning the ground for footprints of Indians and horses,

a part of my business for which I needed daylight on ground
that was much marked by the footprints of deer and buffaloes. In exposed places where there was no cover I literally
crawled from rock to rock or from one shrub to another, such
was my caution to avoid the sharp eyes of some prowling
Indian, for I knew that they thought nothing of lying concealed all day without water when on the lookout for some
enemy, or in a willow-covered eagle trap on a high point
motionless for hours waiting for the great bird to drop for
its bait, when it is seized by the legs with eager clutch
and deprived of the prized tail feathers.[37]

Three miles from their objective at the mouth of the Powder it was
judged best not to ascend the Yellowstone any farther, thereby risking
damage to the vessel. Not to be thwarted when he was this close, however, Forsyth marched his infantry overland to Sheridan Buttes near
the mouth of the Powder. Here, he found a large tableland, which he
described as being "a most beautiful location for a fort should the
Government desire to erect one at this point."[38]

His mission completed, Forsyth instructed Captain Marsh to return
to Fort Buford, which place they reached on 16 May, having traveled
some 470 miles in ten days. It had been a successful undertaking. Not
only had it been demonstrated that the river was navigable as far as the
Powder, but that with a little clearing of the channel and a higher water
level that would be available with the spring run-off, it would be possible to go even farther. Said Forsyth of Kelly's services, "Our guide,
known as 'Yellowstone' Kelly was another capable character, who gave
us much information of the country on each side of the river through
which we were passing, and he has since won a lasting reputation on
the old Western frontier as an able scout and a reliable guide."[39] Kelly,
for his part, recalled Forsyth as a "very pleasant gentleman, quiet and
reserved, not much given to recounting past deeds or events, never a
word of Beecher Island, or the stiff fight and defense made there."
Forsyth's 1873 Yellowstone expedition marked the first occasion of
Kelly's service as a government scout. It would not be his last. His reputation was growing.[40]

Where Kelly spent the summer and fall of 1873 is not known, but a
good bet would be in the neighborhood of Fort Buford, or somewhere
north of the Yellowstone. It seems unlikely that he would have
remained in the vicinity of the river itself, since that summer witnessed the arrival of the Northern Pacific Railroad survey, escorted by

Custer's Seventh Cavalry. None of the accounts of that expedition talk of meeting Kelly, nor does he mention such an encounter, and it seems highly probable that a meeting would have taken place had he been in the area.

In any case, as the year drew to a close—his fifth on the frontier—Kelly was again overtaken by a sense of restlessness. Accordingly, when an opportunity presented itself to offer his services as a guide for one of Charles Broadwater's bull teams (wagons hauled by oxen) en route from Fort Peck to Helena, he elected to give it a try.[41]

Kelly joined the train somewhere between Fort Peck and the Milk River. Buffalo were plentiful. Indeed, they were never out of sight of the shaggy beasts, which insured a plentiful supply of meat for the caravan. On one occasion, Kelly, using his Henry, shot and killed a two-year-old heifer, carried what meat he could back to camp, then returned with his horse for the remainder. He also retrieved the hide, which was covered with "dark, silky fur" that he judged would make a fine robe when cured.[42]

When he returned to the campsite, the cook had a roaring fire in progress, along with a kettle of coffee and "Dutch ovens of frying meats and hot biscuits." Shortly, two strangers, one a man named Bill Norris, with whom Kelly would later work during the Nez Perce War, arrived in camp and at Kelly's invitation began roasting some of the fresh buffalo ribs. The odor was stimulating in the "biting air" and soon everyone was gathered around the fire roasting ribs, much to the cook's chagrin.[43]

Where the old wagon road swung north around the western flank of the Bear's Paw Mountains,[44] Kelly bade farewell to the bull train, aiming to cross the Missouri above Carroll,[45] a new landing on the river that had set its sights on capturing the Fort Benton trade. Born in 1874, Carroll played an important role in the central Montana story for a decade, although its two peak years were 1874 and 1875. The town was the head of the Carroll Trail, an overland wagon route from the Missouri River to the territorial capital of Helena. Prior to the founding of the trail, freight was hauled by steamer up the river to Fort Benton, then off-loaded and transported by wagon 140 miles to Helena. Overland, the distance from Carroll was greater by seventy miles, but the route was easier and Carroll could still be reached for two months after Fort Benton was closed down for the year. Carroll offered the advantage of a low-water landing site for steamboats plying their way upriver. Here, a steamer could ease its way up against the four-foot-high bank, tie up to a handy cottonwood tree, and off-load its cargo to waiting wagons for the overland haul to Helena. Carroll never did reach a point where it seriously threatened Fort Benton's status as king of the Upper River, but it flexed its muscles, and while it lasted things hummed aplenty.[46]

The place took its name from one Matthew Carroll of the Diamond R Freight Line. Kelly recalled that Carroll was located in a "narrow strip of cottonwood timber" and included a "trade store, storehouse, and factor's residence, also a few shacks and cabins." The *Helena Herald* described it as a community of about "twenty log cabins, permanent population about 150, with two good stores, three restaurants, one hotel and two blacksmith shops, not so many saloons 'but one can generally find sufficient.'"[47]

To this motley collection of rough shacks and cabins that had materialized almost overnight, along the south bank of the Missouri,[48] came wandering hunters, trappers, traders, bull whackers, and itinerant travelers. Here, bustle and excitement were in abundant supply, what with steamers arriving, wagon trains departing, and the air filled with the bawling of men loading and unloading. With its colorful cast of characters, Carroll would have been just the sort of place to capture Luther Kelly's fancy.

South out of Carroll, the trail skirted the Judith Mountains, winding through the basin of that same name; it flowed around the western flank of the Big and Little Snowy Mountains, thence on through Judith Gap and around the Little Belt and Castle ranges into Helena. And lovely country it was. Indeed, if there was one spot in all of Montana that Luther Kelly found particularly fetching, it was this land of the Judith Basin. We can't know for certain when Kelly first laid eyes on the area, but by the mid-1870s it had become a favorite haunt for him. Kelly remembered it fondly. The basin proper was too exposed, but southeast of Judith Mountain, along the "slopes and cedar ridges extending to the Musselshell River and beyond to the breaks of the Yellowstone was a veritable hunters' paradise for game of all kinds, including elk, deer, and mountain sheep, and cinnamon, black and brown bear." He also recalled that "[t]he basin was then a borderland, a disputed ground where Sioux, Crows, and Blackfeet met and exchanged courtesies in the usual savage fashion with clash of arms."[49]

So travel along the trail was not free of hazards. First, one was apt to encounter the gluelike gumbo mud that had to be worked through after heavy rains. And then there was the omnipresent danger of Indians, who always made travel through their country a chancy dodge. The establishment of Camp Lewis, near present Lewistown, in the spring of 1874 by a company of the Seventh Infantry did provide some measure of security for travelers along the trail, but the risk remained high, nonetheless, because foot soldiers lacked the necessary mobility to pursue Indian raiding parties. At Camp Lewis in the spring of 1875, Kelly made the acquaintance of the noted ethnologist and naturalist George Bird Grinnell; their paths would cross more than once in the ensuing years.[50]

Not far from Camp Lewis and some sixty miles southwest of Carroll sat Reed and Bowles Trading Post. Established in 1874 by Alonzo S. Reed and John Bowles, the post became a noted stopping point on the Carroll Trail. From here, one could continue on to Helena or strike south to Bozeman and the mining camps of southwestern Montana.[51] Like Carroll, Reed and Bowles drew an adventurous cast of frontier types and enjoyed a brief but exciting life. In 1878 an English sportsman, Charles Alson Messiter, painted a word picture of Reed and Bowles.

> The ranche consisted of a square stockade with large
> entrance gates, inside which were four or five small log
> cabins, one of which was the trading store, another was for
> Bowles and his wife and Reed to live in, while the others
> were for eating rooms. The whole place was very untidy
> and dirty, a squaw having no ideas of cleanliness.[52]

Kelly was a frequent visitor to Reed and Bowles, as well as to Carroll, and as we have seen was often a participant in the goings-on at both places. In the autumn of 1875, for example, he was at Reed and Bowles when a Lakota war party, fifty or so strong, swooped down to run off a small herd of ponies belong to a party of Prairie Gros Ventres who were trading at the post. The Gros Ventres had let their ponies wander off to graze the hillside and so were nearly a mile distant when the Lakota struck. Kelly later described the incident for George Bird Grinnell.

> We had just finished eating dinner when one of the boys
> in the store yelled, 'Indians, boys! Hostiles!' At the cry we
> grabbed our rifles and cartridge belts and rushed out of the
> cabin. Along the foothills, stretched out in loose order, we
> saw about 18 or 20 Indians riding at an easy gallop in the
> direction of the pony herd, about three-quarters of a mile
> distant. Most of them had blankets wrapped closely about
> them, over or under the shoulders, and their every action

The remains of Reed and Bowles Trading Post near Lewistown, Montana.
Author photo.

was graceful as they rose and fell to the movement of their
swift and agile ponies. They were so near that we could see
their motions and could tell that their faces were turned
toward us. They seemed to be watching our movements with
an indifference that was very irritating. All this we saw at
a glance.

With us were two Prairie Gros Ventres—modest, unas-
suming young men, for Indians—who were stopping at the
trading post for a few days. They had seven or eight ponies
in that herd, and I suppose it flashed across their minds that
they would have to give an account of those ponies when
they returned to camp. Although our own ponies were safely
cached in a coulee, I knew that we—Jack Mail, John Lee, and
myself—were instantly siezed [sic] with a strong desire to
frustrate the purpose of the Sioux. We all raced madly to cut
them off. But running afoot at full speed just after eating is
very disastrous to [the] wind, and we never got closer than
about 500 yards to the war party, who watched us but kept
on their way.

As they bunched up a little before rounding up the herd, we threw ourselves on the ground and popped it to them with our rifles. It seemed as if some of the shots must have told, but the Indians paid no attention to us, and rounding up the herd struck for the foothills. Then we turned and plodded back to the cabin, but the Gros Ventres boys, who had followed our actions, rose from the ground and set out after the Sioux at full speed, and the last I saw of them they were rising a distant hill, still going along at the same steady dog trot.[53]

At Reed and Bowles he renewed acquaintances with several men he had come to know during the past five years, including his erstwhile companion of past trails, Red Mike Welsh, and a Georgian named Jim Cooper. It was during this period, too, that Kelly struck up a friendship with Sandy Morris, a "red-headed, freckle-faced man," who would become another of his Judith Basin hunting cronies. At Carroll, Kelly also cultivated the friendship of the trade store factor, who loaned him volumes of Edgar Allen Poe's prose works. Throughout his time on the Western frontier, Kelly always took advantage of any opportunity to stay in touch with the literary side of his nature.[54]

On one occasion, Kelly also organized a hunting party of four, which found a plentiful supply of elk in the neighborhood and presently returned with a nice supply of skins, including one particularly large animal. The member who had downed this elk took great pains and pleasure to leave as much meat on the hide as possible. However, when the group brought their batch of hides to the trader, he, being wise in the ways of such things, left this hide on the scale for several days. Kelly recalled checking it every few days to how much weight it had lost. "I will venture to say that there were over ten pounds of meat on that hide [said Kelly] that did not belong there and was only fit for a fertilizer," adding that "Indians never resorted to such practices as this. The skins they bring to the trader are clean, dry, well stretched, and neatly packed, as if for their own use."[55]

Carroll's life span was brief, but it seldom lacked for excitement and Kelly was frequently involved. Once, a Lakota war party raided Carroll, but then quickly withdrew, pursued by Kelly and a companion on foot. The pair ran into the hills where they found a fine, handsome black mare tied to a tree. Since he was the first to touch the animal, Kelly's companion claimed title. Thinking the owner might return, the two men hid nearby and waited. However, when in due course no one showed up, they returned to Carroll with the prize. It turned out that the black mare was also a swift animal and demonstrated her speed in many of the races held at Carroll. Kelly later bought the animal for his own use and eventually sold her to Capt. Cornelius Cusick, Twenty-second Infantry, whom he had first known at Fort Buford.[56]

But an encounter with Indians could sometimes take a surprisingly humorous twist, as on one occasion when Kelly was on foot, bound for Reed's fort. It was just past dawn, with the sun beginning to rise above the rim of the nearby hills. As he approached a flat stretch of ground, he suddenly spotted a file of Indians in the distance, moving in his direction. He recalled the moment with clarity and described it with his usual literary flourish.

> I saw coming over the crest of the rising ground beyond,
> each particular metal ornament or scheme of fluttering color
> illumined by the glorious sun, a considerable body of Indians,
> afoot, strung out in a line at right angles to my course.
> As they marched slowly down the grassy slope in irregular
> lines—for more were coming over the crest—with lances
> and feathers waving, the whole presented a spectacle most
> striking and war-like. But not for me.[57]

There was little to do but stand his ground. The timber that might have provided an escape was too far. He weighed the option of running for it, believing himself to be as fast as any Indian, but in the end decided to stand fast, preferring to die if necessary "rather than be chased like a wolf." To his immediate front was a large rock. Walking over to it, he took several cartridges out of his pocket and held them ready in one hand, watching as the Indians moved inexorably toward him, somewhat scattered now, but striding "with that easy, graceful motion of the moccasin wearer, alert and keenly noting, as I suspected, my every motion."

When the Indians approached to about 150 yards, Kelly, cradling his rifle in his right arm, raised his left hand, signaling the Indians to stop, which they obliged him by so doing. Presently, the leader advanced toward Kelly, who was suitably impressed with the approaching figure who came "fully armed, a dignified warrior, with a circlet of bears' claws about his neck and a coil of lariat in his belt."

Looking Kelly straight in the eye, he asked, "Does the Wasityu hold the road against the Yankton?" Relieved to discover they were not Lakota, Kelly bade them come ahead, which they in fact had already started to do even as he waved them on. Soon he was the center of attention, surrounded by a bevy of grinning faces. Kelly offered a plug of tobacco to the leader, who, noticing the cartridges in the young man's hand, expressed surprise, but seemed not to have been offended. The Yankton were in a conversing mood, explaining to Kelly that they were returning from an unsuccessful horse-stealing foray against the Crows. The little gathering came to a sudden end when the Yankton spotted a bear that had rambled into the timber and rushed off in pursuit.[58]

During the winter of 1874–1875, red-headed Sandy Morris invited Kelly to return to the Bear's Paw Mountains and help him harvest some wolf carcasses. Sandy and a former partner, George Horn, had set up a promising wolfing operation in that area before Sandy was wounded and Horn killed by Indians. Sandy was sure that the poisoned bait they had put out would have produced a large number of carcasses, so on the face of it, the proposition appeared financially attractive. If Kelly supplied the packhorse they'd need, he would be an equal partner. Kelly liked the idea and agreed.[59]

A good deal of Kelly's time in Montana, at least in the years prior to his service with Col. Nelson A. Miles during the Indian campaigns, found him actively engaged in "wolfing," i.e., hunting and trapping wolves. In those days wolves, like buffalo, flourished. Just as did the Indians, wolves followed the great herds, which provided subsistence for both. So the animals were in abundance and hunting, trapping, or poisoning them was a profitable occupation. A prime wolf pelt brought five dollars and a hunter or consortium of hunters could do right well during the course of a season. The wolves could be found in a variety of colors. Timber Wolves had "yellowish markings on the side, while the buffalo wolves "found north of the Missouri were coarse haired compared with the gray wolves found near Flat Willow Creek; some were pure white, others different shades of cream, the full-grown ones being of the very largest size." If the wolf was a noble beast in its own way and an attractive economic target, his cousin the coyote was a nuisance of the first order. They "were ki-hi-ing all hours of the night," Kelly recalled "and sometimes in daylight, we considered them hardly worth skinning."[60]

The way it worked in Kelly's Montana was that the hunters would kill a buffalo, deer, or elk. After removing any portions they wanted, such as the tongue of the buffalo which was considered rich eating and a delicacy, the carcass would then be laced with strychnine and frozen, then left alone to attract wolves. Freezing the carcass insured that the wolves would not devour it too quickly. It was not unusual for the hunter to find anywhere from ten to fifty dead wolves stretched out around the poisoned carcass. The dead wolves were allowed to freeze, then were covered with brush, to be skinned later after thawing. The hunter was advised to visit his bait periodically, to protect the wolf carcasses from assault by hungry magpies and ravens. It seems a gruesome and inhumane process by our standards, for we can imagine these animals dying a horrible death. Kelly, however, came to believe that those who reduced the wolf packs by poisoning actually provided a useful service to large animal herd management. "It was said," wrote Kelly,

> that wolves killed more buffalo than Indians and whites combined. I am convinced that the men engaged in poisoning wolves for their pelts rendered a good service in protection of herds of wild game. I have seen in the North bands of wolves numbering fifty or more traveling with noses up on the scent of buffaloes borne by the wind. They killed the young calves and hamstrung the cows and bulls.[61]

It is often pointed out how the buffalo was the mainstay of the Plains tribes; how virtually every part of the animal contributed to Indian society in some way. In contrast, white hunters slaughtered the herds, taking only the hide and delicacies of the animal. Kelly recalled, though, that the Indian could be as wasteful as the white man—for example, killing buffalo cows "for the unborn calves for the purpose of feasting, the cows being at that time of year poor in flesh and the robes by no means prime."[62]

En route to the Bear's Paw Mountains, Kelly and Morris found buffalo plentiful and were nearly charged on a couple of occasions. Somewhere near Cow Creek, which flows south out of the mountains and empties into the Missouri at Cow Island, the pair found an abandoned Indian war house. These were usually conical-shaped affairs, made out of whatever materials happened to be available. They were created by Indian war or hunting parties that passed through the region and often reused on the group's return journey. There was evidence that this particular hut had recently been occupied, but Kelly and Morris decided that the comfort it offered, considering the rocky, snow-covered terrain outside, was worth some risk.[63]

They were up and on the trail at dawn, after first locating the horse that had been left to fend for itself during the night. Along the way, Kelly shot a blacktail deer and set out the poisoned carcass to attract wolves. When they reached the area where Sandy and his erstwhile partner Horn had been attacked, they did not find as many wolves as Sandy had expected, but a few days' worth of work soon produced enough to make a fair load. After placing more bait, they cached some supplies and headed back to Carroll.[64]

After a week's respite at Carroll, Kelly and Morris returned to the Bear's Paw country to see how the wolves had responded to "the choice meats prepared for their palates." Retracing their steps, they found shelter once more in the same Indian war house they had used earlier. Stepping inside, they discovered it had since been occupied by Indians, who were thoughtful enough to leave behind strips of fat buffalo meat that they obviously intended to use on their return journey. The two young wolf hunters, however, had no qualms about consuming it themselves.[65]

Returning again to the locale where Sandy and Horn had previously worked, they enjoyed some success and were in the process of skinning out their wolf carcasses, when a gunshot alerted them to the presence of Indians, who turned out to be a hunting party of "Stonies" down from Canada. "They were as black as burnt wood," Kelly recalled, "the result of camping in the mountains and using pine for fuel. I could not talk to them to any advantage as they were as poor in the sign language as I was."[66]

Satisfied that they had tapped out this area, Kelly and Morris headed south in February, crossing the frozen Missouri on the ice. From their camp in some cedar breaks, the pair decided that the country thereabouts appeared promising enough to spend a few more days in search of more wolf pelts.[67] Accordingly, the next morning each sallied forth to examine the country and set out traps. As Kelly was passing along a narrow and "treacherous trail," he suddenly found himself face-to-face with a large bull buffalo that was lying down. It was a tense moment. Kelly recalled,

> I could not turn around or run without the risk of slipping and falling to the ice below. When I spied the animal he was about thirty feet away, but he proved to be a very lively bull, for he sprang to his feet instantly and with head down and tail up came for me. I shoot from the left shoulder, but there was no time for that operation, so, quickly shifting my little Henry rifle, I held it on that grisly ornament of his face, the forelock, heavy with sand and matted burrs, which hung between his eyes, and when he was about ten feet away let him have it. He dropped on the instant. I felt immensely

relieved, for you cannot always count on a successful issue in shooting at the forehead of a buffalo bull.[68]

After surveying his "unsought and unlovely prize, lying prone on the frozen ground," Kelly concluded the animal was too old and tough to skin and use as bait, "for your wolf is a discriminating animal unless starved."[69]

Later, as Kelly and Morris were collecting their wolf carcasses, Kelly spotted a party of Indians moving over a nearby ridge, striding toward them. When the leader confronted Morris, Sandy offered him a piece of tobacco, but he gruffly demanded all they had. Not to be bluffed, however, the two men, with rifles showing at the ready, stood firm and the Indian leader backed down. Kelly felt certain that if he had not been fortunate enough to notice them they would likely have attacked. Later, Kelly learned that they were Yanktonais from north of the Milk River who had been on a horse-stealing raid against the Crows.[70]

The Indian presence in the area was of more than passing concern. If the Indians managed to steal their horses, it would work a considerable hardship on them, what with their pelts and all. Accordingly, they wasted no time packing up, but after doing so discovered they had forgotten the traps and were obliged to undo everything and retrieve the traps before heading back to Carroll.[71]

After what was probably an idyllic summer of 1875 spent wandering around the Judith Basin area, now and again dropping in at Reed and Bowles, Kelly was ready for another trapping season. Accordingly, that autumn found him engaged in another wolfing operation, this time with a trio that included the Erwin brothers Jean and Sid together with Red Mike Welsh. It was a well-organized retinue that set out for the country southeast of the Judith Basin. The Erwins furnished a wagon and team, while Kelly and Mike Welsh each provided a packhorse in addition to their own mounts. They were well stocked, too, with Dutch ovens, grindstones, picks, and strychnine. In addition to using poisoned bait to catch wolves, traps would also be employed. Their reputations as hunters enabled them to secure the necessary credit from the trader.[72]

Near Cone Butte Pass, they put up a cabin to use as their base camp. With game plentiful, the next step was to provide enough meat for food and bait. The abundance of both the timber and buffalo wolf was the attraction that brought them to this remote and beautiful but disputed area where Sioux, Crows, and Blackfeet often clashed.[73] While one member of the party remained at camp, the other three set out to hunt. Two paired off, but Kelly preferred solitude. "I delighted to hunt alone, to wander through the open timber and grassy openings, not caring whether I saw a deer or not until it came time to return to camp. Then I got busy, for I could not go back empty-handed."[74]

One evening a group of Crows appeared at their camp, and in the honored fashion of the frontier, the visitors were offered something to eat and drink. Later, after the traditional pipe was passed, the occasion was given over to discussion. The Crows pointed out that Lakotas were only two sleeps away, but Kelly and his partners explained that while they were few in number they had bad medicine in their guns for those who trifled with them.[75]

Later, Kelly drew on his memory of this particular occasion to describe some of the characteristics of the Indians he had had an opportunity to observe during his years on the frontier.

> As a rule the wild Indians of the mountains and plains are well-bred in company and possess a natural politeness and decorum of manner well worth observing. Transport one of them to a crowded drawing-room, and though the change would be startling it is safe to say that he would rise to the occasion and in bearing, at least, would conduct himself with all the ease and nonchalance of a man of the world. Of course Indians differ as other peoples do, and there was a marked difference in the scale of intelligence, in early days, before the government established schools among them. The Crows differ from the Sioux in feature and dress, and very much in language. Within the border of Wyoming and Montana territories, there were eight or more tribes of Indians, each with a language of its own, differing from the others as much as English differs from Russian. Of these the Sioux, of which there are several dialects, is perhaps the most musical, affording a copious flow of words.[76]

By the middle of November, Kelly and his partners left the Cone Butte region and struck southeast for the Musselshell country, which subsequently proved to be prime wolf territory. The howling at night "was almost incessant," Kelly recalled. "One would start a prolonged howl, then another would take it up in a different key; others would join in quick succession, producing a medley of most satisfying discord."[77]

On one occasion, Kelly was out alone, placing bait. Presently, he spotted a buffalo cow lying down in an open area, where, if he killed her and poisoned the carcass, she would be in an excellent spot to draw wolves. As he proceeded to work himself into position for a good shot, a pair of wolves appeared, noted the buffalo, then approached Kelly. After observing him from a respectful distance for a few moments and having satisfied their curiosity, they turned back to the cow, who rose to defend herself. She was lame, Kelly could now see, and as the wolves prepared to attack, Kelly fired and killed the animal. The wolves quickly disappeared at the report of the rifle.

Later, when Kelly was preparing the carcass with strychnine, he noted an audience of wolves, some twenty or more, watching with great interest from a distance of a hundred yards. "They were lined up in a row as though they had been bidden to a feast and were not particular as to how it was served." Kelly imagined that they had probably observed this sort of ritual before as they followed Indians on the hunt. "Though uninvited, I would not allow their appreciation to pass unrewarded."[78]

The four wolf hunters fared well that autumn. Returning to the site of the poisoned buffalo cow, Kelly and Jean Erwin found twenty-two large wolves, and fine specimens they were. "Two were almost pure white, one was of a creamy color, and several had the tawny markings of the timber wolf; the rest were gray, but of finer hair than the buffalo wolf."[79]

As the autumn deepened, a two-day blizzard struck with typical suddenness, driving the hunters to the confines of an old war lodge they found in the area. With some patching here and there the lodge provided a relatively safe harbor, though the fierce wind kept their fire smoke from escaping through the hole at the top of the lodge, so that they passed a "most uncomfortable" forty-eight hours.[80]

When the storm had relented early on the third day, Kelly and Erwin searched for their ponies, whose tracks had been covered by the drifting snow. Eventually, they found the animals in a timbered hollow where they had taken refuge. Later, the four hunters were also reunited and after sharing stories of how each pair had survived the blizzard, they set about collecting and skinning a nice harvest of wolf carcasses, made possible by the thaw that had followed the storm. This done, they returned to their cabin at Cone Butte and collected the pelts they had cached there. "The skins of elk, deer, wolf, and fox soon covered the ground in process of airing and drying." When this was finished, the hunters set out for Carroll, where they found a St. Louis buyer amenable to their price. They had done well, so that even after the trader had been paid for the supplies given them on credit, "there was a snug little sum left to divide among the four hunters," Kelly recalled.[81]

For the moment at least, Kelly had had enough wolfing to satisfy him. He was ready to move on. "I had only to saddle my pony and lash my belongings on the pack horse and I was ready for the trail. I did not remain long in Carroll. The lovely hills and valleys called me."[82]

Chapter Four

THE SIOUX WAR OF
1876–1877

PART ONE

**The news these men had caused me to change my
mind about going to the Basin and to turn back with
them to the new camp, which I now learned was under
the command of General Miles.**[1]

With the arrival of the year 1876, the youthful United States could
reflect on a full century of independence and take pride in the
glorious success of the democratic experiment. However, from the
northern plains, nearly two thousand miles west of where the nation
would celebrate its birthday on July fourth, would come news of a most
distressing sort, unless of course one was a Lakota or Cheyenne, in
which event there was ample cause for jubilation. Out here, beyond
the hundredth meridian, 1876 and 1877 were watershed years. Once
they had passed into history, nothing in this part of the world would
ever be quite the same.

Even as eighteen-year-old Luther Kelly was working his way west in the beckoning spring of 1868, peace commissioners down at Fort Laramie were putting the finishing touches on a document known as the Laramie Treaty. As such things went, this particular agreement between the United State government and representatives from various bands of the North Plains tribes—Sioux, Northern Cheyenne, Crow, and Northern Arapaho— was one of the most significant instruments of its kind.

Mainly the agreement was intended to restore order to an unsettled region by bringing an end to a two-year conflict called Red Cloud's War, in which the Lakota Sioux forced closure of the Bozeman Trail and the three outposts that had been intended to provide protection for travelers along that trail. The new treaty provided agencies for each tribe in an area defined as the Great Sioux Reservation. The treaty also reserved, as an Indian hunting preserve, a huge tract of unceded territory, bounded, roughly, by the Black Hills on the east, the Big Horn Mountains on the west, and the Yellowstone and North Platte Rivers on the north and south, respectively.[2]

However well intentioned it may have been in some quarters, the Laramie Treaty was doomed to failure. Like so many of its predecessors, it sought a long-range solution to the Indian problem through acculturation, never mind that the Indians had no interest in shedding their culture for that of the white man's. But as noted, that was the distant vision. At the moment, the hard reality was that no treaty ever cut could possibly be expected to stand up to the advancing tide of civilization that was already pushing beyond the pale of the Missouri River. And if that wasn't enough, dissident voices among the plains tribes, notably the wild bands of Hunkpapa and Oglala Lakota in particular, who refused to even enter into discussions with government representatives, let alone agree to the treaty's provisions, made its true *de facto* value questionable at best.[3]

Luther Kelly's sojourn in the Montana Territory during the years following the signing of the Laramie Treaty was a hiatus, a time between old and new. It was the last gasp, so to speak, of a frontier that would still have been largely recognizable to Lewis and Clark and the mountain men: a region where immense herds of bison could still be found, along with the horseback Indians who hunted them. Kelly arrived just in time to be a participant in the twilight of an era; a decade later would have been too late. In 1868, the Union Pacific Railroad reached Cheyenne, and a year later steel rails joined the east and west coasts. By 1872, the Northern Pacific was poised at Bismarck, North Dakota, ready to push west across the northern plains.

In the eight troubled years that followed the signing of the Laramie Treaty, there were numerous clashes between whites and Indians: an army patrol here, a luckless rancher there. Sometimes the army struck back, but more often than not, there was little opportunity to do so. Col. David S. Stanley had a fight with the Sioux along the Yellowstone during the first Northern Pacific survey in 1872. And Lt. Col. George A. Custer also had a run-in with them on the second Northern Pacific Railroad survey, the following summer of 1873 (just a few weeks after Kelly and Sandy Forsyth had explored the river); but with these possible exceptions, there were no major Indian-white encounters in the region.[4]

The summer of 1874, however, witnessed an event of some considerable importance. Under orders from Gen. Philip Sheridan, commanding the Military Division of the Missouri, Custer led a large expedition from Fort Abraham Lincoln, near Bismarck, into the Black Hills of Dakota, a region that some argued was off limits to whites by virtue of the Laramie Treaty. But the army argued that the language of the treaty did not prohibit exploration and road-building, and they had a point. Despite this, the purpose of the expedition was to locate a suitable site for a military post, a location that would enable the army to better control the troublesome Sioux. An unofficial reason for the expedition was to confirm the suspected presence of gold in the Black Hills.[5]

Gold indeed was discovered and when the news got out, it triggered one of the great gold rushes of western history. At first the army made an effort to turn back the hordes of prospectors that flocked to the country, but eventually threw up its hands and so presently the once quiet and sedate Black Hills were soon alive with the sounds of pick and shovel. And names like Deadwood and Custer City were making headlines across the nation.

Since the white occupation of the Black Hills was now a *fait accompli*, the government next sought to buy the territory to make it all legal and proper, but the Indians weren't selling. Their refusal left the government on the horns of a dilemma. To try and force a withdrawal now would be political suicide. The nation would not stand for abandoning so rich a prize as the Black Hills—not now, at any rate. Question was, what then to do about the Indians? The solution, as worked out by President Grant, with the counsel of Senator Zachariah Chandler of Michigan, Secretary of War William Belknap, and Generals Sheridan and Crook, was an 1870s version of the Gulf of Tonkin: create a situation. Accordingly, a decree was issued ordering all Indians who had not already done so, to return to their agencies by 31 January 1876 or be considered hostile, in which case the army would be sent to bring them into the agencies, forcibly if necessary. No one believed the Indians would take the decree seriously, particularly since it wasn't issued until December and few of the non-reservation bands—the so-called "hostiles"—who received the word would have time to make such a journey even if they were inclined to try, which they were not.[6]

Not surprisingly, then, the deadline passed without compliance and the Indian Bureau turned matters over to the War Department for action. Accordingly, early in February Sheridan notified his field commanders, Gen. Alfred Terry, Department of Dakota (St. Paul), and Gen. George Crook, Department of the Platte (Omaha), to move against the "hostiles." Sheridan had been a proponent of winter campaigns ever since Custer's victory on the Washita in 1868. It was a simple matter of catching the hare. Indian mobility was limited in the winter, and the villages were easier to locate and attack. At any rate, Sheridan was anxious that Crook and Terry get underway quickly, especially since the winter was waning.[7]

Crook went first. Marching north out of Fort Fetterman (present Douglas, Wyoming) on 1 March, he attacked what was at first believed to be the village of Crazy Horse, along the desolate reaches of the upper Powder River in southeastern Montana. As it turned out, this was mainly a Cheyenne village—not that it made a great deal of difference, however. The attack was a stunning success...at first. Col. Joseph J. Reynolds—Crook's deputy—had victory in his grasp, only to see it slip away when the Indians counterattacked, recaptured their ponies, and sent Crook limping back to Fort Fetterman, overflowing with chagrin.[8]

Two months later, having regrouped and reinforced his expedition, Crook sallied forth once again, retracing his earlier route along the old Bozeman Trail. On 17 June, along the banks of the Rosebud River, some thirty miles from where the drama on the Little Bighorn would shortly be played out, Crook's powerful column—largest of three in the field— was suddenly struck by a good sized Indian war party, estimated at perhaps a thousand strong. In a savage encounter lasting several hours, Crook was fought to a standstill before the Indians finally withdrew. Crook might have retained the tactical initiative, but he chose to withdraw, await reinforcements, and recover a little lost poise. The decision, in any case, removed Crook's command from the campaign until late summer, by which time it was all too late.[9]

Meanwhile, as George Crook was twice engaging the Indians and having a decidedly miserable time in doing so, the other two prongs of Sheridan's grand design were setting forth to see what effect they might have on the situation. Early in March, Col. John Gibbon, commanding the District of Montana, started east from Fort Ellis (present Bozeman), along the north bank of the Yellowstone with a mixed force of cavalry and infantry. And finally, on 17 May, the Dakota Column, including Custer's Seventh Cavalry, and a complement of infantry, all under the command of General Terry, headed west from Fort Abraham Lincoln (present Bismarck, North Dakota).

After rendezvousing with Gibbon, the combined force reached the junction of the Rosebud and Yellowstone Rivers. Here, Custer was given his final orders and on 22 June, marched up the Rosebud, aiming to find what was believed to be a large Indian village. The remainder of the Terry-Gibbon force would meanwhile proceed west along the Yellowstone to the Big Horn River, then turn south. It was hoped that the Indians would be caught between the combined columns of Custer and Terry-Gibbon and driven in to the agencies.

That was the plan, but it fell on hard times, and the finis of this scenario rivaled that of any Greek tragedy. Four days after cutting loose from Terry and Gibbon, Custer and five companies of his regiment were annihilated on the slopes above the Little Bighorn—called Greasy Grass by the Indians. And the remainder of the regiment was bloodied pretty well besides. Sheridan's columns had not just failed to bag their quarry, they had fallen on their collective backsides...hard. Crook's twin setbacks had been embarrassing, but the loss of Custer and his command was a disaster of the first magnitude.[10]

In the immediate aftermath of the Little Bighorn, Sheridan promptly dispatched reinforcements to his field commanders. The Fifth Cavalry under Col. Wesley Merritt was sent to join Crook's expedition, then licking its wounds in camp on Goose Creek (present Sheridan, Wyoming). Merritt did so, though along the way he intercepted a band of Cheyennes en route to join their brethren, turning them back at a place called War Bonnet Creek in extreme northwestern Nebraska. Here Buffalo Bill Cody, in a dramatic display of valor, killed a Cheyenne leader named Yellow Hand or Yellow Hair, afterward lifting the Cheyenne's scalp and proclaiming it to be the "first scalp for Custer."[11]

In addition to sending the Fifth Cavalry into the breech, Sheridan also sent Col. Ranald Mackenzie's Fourth Cavalry to Crook's Department of the Platte, and to Alfred Terry went the infantry reinforcements. From its station at Fort Leavenworth, Kansas, came the veteran Fifth Infantry, commanded by the vain and ambitious, but extremely capable, Col. Nelson A. Miles. Miles and his regiment would be a key factor in the army's war against those Indian bands who still remained at large. Finally, six companies of the Twenty-second Infantry provided Terry with still more muscle.

Sheridan, who had long sought authorization for a military post in the Yellowstone Basin, renewed his request, and Congress, finally stirred to action by the Custer disaster, responded with authorization for not one, but two forts. One post was to be built at the confluence of the Yellowstone and Big Horn Rivers and named Fort Custer, while a second, to be located at the joining of the Tongue and Yellowstone, would eventually be called Fort Keogh. Thus, Sheridan's commitment of troops and resources to the North Plains conflict was major in scope and determination. In a very real sense, the Indian coalition that had destroyed Custer in effect hastened its own inevitable doom. For even as the dust and smoke above the Greasy Grass dissipated, the bell was tolling for the Lakota Sioux and their allies.[12]

Be that as it may, nothing much happened for the next month. Finally, reorganized and reinforced, both Crook and Terry resumed their individual movements in early August. After what turned out to be a surprise meeting of the two commanders on the tenth, the combined columns lumbered on in search of the Indian army that had destroyed nearly half of the Seventh Cavalry. But the huge village that Yellow Hair Custer attacked on 25 June had long since dissolved into smaller bands. And so the nature of the campaign had changed. There would be no one big fight that settled matters. It had now devolved into a matter of finding and rounding up the various bands wherever they had sought refuge. This was precisely what the army had hoped to avoid at the outset. And this was exactly what Custer had wanted to prevent when he struck on the twenty-fifth.[13]

The Terry-Crook column—now some four thousand strong—proved a short-lived arrangement. In this case, bigger was not better. After a week or so of plodding about, the two of them agreed to split up. Terry (the senior), concerned that some of the Indians would slip across the Yellowstone and find a haven in Canada, decided to concentrate his efforts on preventing that eventuality, while Crook continued to follow the Indian trails that led east. So Crook, dogged fellow that he was, pressed on. And then the rains came, and the mud. Rations ran out and the troops were reduced to subsisting on the flesh of their animals—"horsemeat march," they called it.

In early September, an advance force under Capt. Anson Mills, Third Cavalry, on a quest for provisions from the Black Hills settlements, stumbled across a Lakota village at a place called Slim Buttes on the northern fringe of the Hills. While it lasted, it was a pretty fair scrap, but then Crook arrived with the main body and secured the army's first victory in this ill-starred centennial summer. Following Slim Buttes, Crook withdrew from the field, to return later in the fall.[14]

Terry, meanwhile, had returned to the Yellowstone, where Miles was already patrolling the river line, in accordance with Terry's orders. Upon his arrival at the river, Terry found steamers with construction supplies for the new post to be built at the mouth of the Big Horn. And shortly, he received a communiqué from Sheridan directing him to also get underway with a cantonment at the mouth of the Tongue River. Fall was coming on and Sheridan wanted a post ready before winter set in. He wanted a strong military presence in the region on a year-round basis.[15]

The strategy had changed. Control of the Indian agencies had now become the province of the War Department, which meant that Sheridan's field commanders had a dual responsibility: to see that surrendering Indian bands were disarmed and returned to the agencies, and to conduct operations against those bands that refused to surrender. Sheridan saw the establishment of military posts in key locations throughout the troubled area as the key to winning this war. In his mind, the Yellowstone River figured prominently in this strategy. He wanted the pressure kept up on the hostile bands and the only way for that to happen was to have operating bases in the Yellowstone Valley. Thus, the new cantonment at Tongue River, particularly, assumed a key role in his strategy. It was hoped, too, that the aggressive Nelson Miles would prove to be the much-needed catalyst.[16]

Meanwhile, field operations against the hostile bands continued. On the twenty-seventh, Terry and Gibbon moved north from the Yellowstone through a bleak and largely unknown region hoping to cut off any hostile bands that might be headed north. The effort proved barren of results, however, and by the end of the month, they were back at the Yellowstone. Just prior to reaching the river, Terry learned of a Sioux movement near Glendive. Accordingly, Maj. Marcus Reno with the remnant of the Seventh Cavalry made a sweep in that direction but turned up nothing.[17]

With the arrival of September, Terry prepared to officially end the summer's campaign. Gibbon was directed to return to his district in western Montana on 6 September while Terry himself prepared to return to his headquarters in St. Paul by 15 October in accordance with Sheridan's order.[18]

Despite August's torrential downpours, the level of the Yellowstone had fallen and it became increasingly difficult for steamboats to ascend the river much beyond its confluence with the Powder River. This, in turn, presented a logistical problem for Terry and Miles, because at any one time there might be as many as four or five steamers loaded with supplies, equipment, and construction materials for the new posts. Terry's solution was to establish a supply depot near the present site of Glendive where steamers could off-load cargo that would then be hauled upriver to its final destination. Lt. Col. Elwell S. Otis, with six companies of the Twenty-second Infantry, was charged with the responsibility of protecting the depot and providing escorts for the supply trains that shuttled back and forth between the new posts.[19]

Meanwhile, as Terry and Gibbon were examining the country north of the Yellowstone, Miles's Fifth Infantry had gotten underway with construction of the new post along the west bank of the Tongue River at its junction with the Yellowstone. Cantonment at Tongue River it would initially be called, and Fort Keogh later when it became a permanent post. Like the regiment that built and garrisoned it, Fort Keogh was to play a prominent role in the events of the next twelve months, as would Luther Kelly.[20]

It is difficult to say exactly how much Luther Kelly knew of all that had happened during this momentous summer and of the events leading up to it. There are enough references in his memoirs and in later correspondence to suggest that he was at least somewhat informed. He had undoubtedly picked up stories early on of Red Cloud's War, Fort Phil Kearny, the Fetterman disaster, and the Bozeman Trail. Those events would have been recent news by the time he reached Fort Buford. And as the years passed, he probably learned of most happenings in the region that were of any real consequence. News had a way of circulating. It would be surprising, indeed, if Kelly did not know about the two Northern Pacific surveys along the Yellowstone in 1872 and 1873. It seems likely, too, that he would have gotten wind of Col. James Forsyth's further exploration of the Yellowstone in 1875, two years after Kelly and Sandy Forsyth (no relation to James) had journeyed up the same river on the *Key West*. And word must surely have reached him about the government directive requiring all Indians to report to their respective agencies and that this was probably going to lead eventually to military action.

By his own recounting, Kelly was mainly in the Judith Basin in 1875 and through most of the summer of 1876. He recalled that Sioux war parties were on the prowl throughout the area, especially during the weeks preceding the confrontation on the Little Bighorn. Clearly, a major clash with the Indians was close at hand and he could scarcely have escaped that realization. News of the Custer disaster had apparently reached him by way of the Gallatin Valley and he was soon to discover for himself the army's presence along the Yellowstone.[21]

In any event, during that wretched (for the army) summer of 1876, even as Crook and Terry were getting underway with their futile perambulations south of the Yellowstone, Luther Kelly was still savoring the good life up in the Judith Basin. But the times were changing. After learning of the events on the Little Bighorn from the occupant of a cabin in the Judith Basin, Kelly, who had caught a young antelope and thought to make a pet of it, left the animal with that individual and turned "his horse toward the Yellowstone country." We cannot say what his motives were at this point, but it may have been nothing more than curiosity, since he later said he intended to return to the basin.[22]

Along the way, Kelly chanced to fall in with a man named John Stanwix and two companions. We know nothing of Stanwix, or "Stan" as he seems to have been called, except that he was a member of that fraternity of plainsmen, of which Kelly was now a member in good standing. Stan and his companions were also bound for the Yellowstone to do a little prospecting and, since they were going in the same direction, Kelly opted to join them. By Kelly's account it was a pleasant enough journey, with the four travelers sharing the warmth of fire and the satisfaction of food, tobacco, and conversation, which was always welcome to men who spent long periods alone. The story of the Custer disaster was a topic of discussion around the campfire.[23]

In the vicinity of Pompey's Pillar, Stan and his companions headed west, upriver, bound for some spot where the "color" looked good. For his part Kelly turned east, traveling along what he called "a well-worn road." His downriver route did not precisely follow the "windings" of the river, but as he worked his way east it was through the same downpours that plagued the Terry-Custer column. Indeed, the creeks and rivers had risen noticeably. When it wasn't pouring rain, it was hailing, or blustery and cold. Indeed, the weather seemed as unsettled as life itself in this valley of *La Roche Jaune*.[24] Kelly discovered considerable traffic along the river, with wagons and detachments of troops moving in both directions, as well as several army bivouacs, all indicative of the activity spawned by the Custer disaster.[25]

Kelly reached the mouth of the Powder River between 17 and 23 August. Here, he found Crook's command preparing for its eastward pursuit of the Sioux. His old friend Grant Marsh was here as was Vic Smith, another plainsman of some repute and with whom he would soon be working as an army scout. Like Kelly, Smith, too, hailed from western New York State. The occasion also marked Kelly's first meeting ever with Col. Nelson Miles, a man who was to play a significant part in his life from then on. Kelly remembered Miles as then being "in the full vigor and flush of manhood."[26] How long Kelly remained here is not clear, nor is it clear exactly what he expected to do here. Perhaps he had thoughts of offering his services only to find they were not needed. In any event, he finally decided to return to the Judith Basin and, accordingly, started back upriver in company with a party of miners. Somewhere beyond Tongue River they learned of a new military post being built near the confluence of the Tongue and the Yellowstone and turned back to investigate.[27]

En route, Kelly and one of the miners, who had apparently decided to accompany him, elected to do a bit of hunting north of the river. After spotting a large cinnamon bear and downing him, Kelly removed one of the bear's exceptionally large paws and hung it on his saddle, after which he and his companion continued on their way to the Tongue River cantonment. Arriving at the site, they crossed the river on a small ferry operated by the soldiers and found only the quartermaster, Lt. Edward Locke Randall, Fifth Infantry, and a few others in camp. The main body of troops, Miles included, was out cutting timber. After introductions and a few pleasantries were exchanged, Randall suggested that Miles would probably want to talk to Kelly about the Sioux and the country thereabouts. The captain evidently could not help noticing the bear's paw and commented on its size (it was over a foot long), whereupon Kelly suggested it be sent to Miles as his calling card.[28]

In due course, Miles returned and, after being given the bear's paw, sent for Kelly. We do not know exactly what exchange took place on this, the second meeting of the two men, except that Kelly tells us Miles questioned him "about the country north of the Yellowstone and as far as the British line, its accessibility as a field of operations against hostile Indians, and the location and disposition of the Sioux toward the north." Kelly's response was that he had "roved for years in parts of that region, hunting, trapping, and 'standing off' bad Indians." Miles was evidently impressed with Kelly's knowledge, and probably with his forthrightness as well, because when their meeting adjourned Kelly returned to his camp carrying an appointment as chief scout for the District of the Yellowstone, at a pay rate of ninety dollars per month.[29]

With the return of General Terry to department headquarters in St. Paul, Colonel Miles became the ranking officer in the Yellowstone Valley and the one who now prepared to execute the kind of tough, hard-nosed winter campaign that Sheridan had envisioned at the outset of this war.

Col. Nelson A. Miles,
Fifth U.S. Infantry, 1877.
*Little Bighorn Battlefield
National Monument,
National Park Service.*

Terry thought winter campaigning on the Northern Plains an invitation
to disaster and tried to get Miles to rethink his strategy. Miles, however,
believed that with proper preparation, the thing could be brought off
successfully. And Sheridan, of course, needed no persuading.

Nelson Appleton Miles may have been the most ambitious soldier
ever to wear the uniform of the United States Army. Vain to a fault, he
never hesitated to sound the trumpet on his own behalf. And yet his
Indian-fighting record speaks for itself. He may, arguably, have been
the best of the lot. As a campaigner, George Crook is sometimes cited
for his persistence in pursuing an enemy (the summer of 1876 except-
ed), but he was never more dogged than was Nelson Miles during the
winter of 1876–1877.

By late September 1876, Miles had all ten companies of his Fifth
Infantry on hand, plus two companies of the Twenty-second Infantry,
and a contingent of white and Indian scouts. For artillery support, he
had one 3-inch ordinance rifle, a 12-pounder Napoleon gun, and 8
Gatling guns, though their usefulness in the forthcoming operations
would be minimal. The rough nature of the terrain over which the

western Indian campaigns were conducted usually rendered Gatling guns more a liability than an asset.[30]

All of the above would comprise the garrison of Cantonment Tongue River (later Fort Keogh). Originally, Miles had been advised that the cantonment would also house a regiment of cavalry, which would have raised the garrison's strength to nearly 1,500, but that had changed when Sheridan decided that the horse soldiers were needed to help control matters at the Missouri River agencies.[31] So now, Miles found himself with some 500 men in all, a force slightly smaller than Custer's column, but far fewer than had been with either Crook or Terry.[32] In addition, Miles also now had at his disposal four companies of the Twenty-second Infantry and two of the Seventeenth Infantry under Lt. Colonel Otis downriver at the Glendive supply depot.[33]

As the autumn deepened, good progress was being made on the cantonment. Buildings constructed of cottonwood logs were taking shape quickly, and Miles was able to advise Terry that quarters for the men would be ready by mid-October. Water level permitting, steamboats brought supplies upriver to the cantonment; otherwise, wagon trains, including some civilian consists, hauled supplies overland from Glendive and later Fort Buford as well. However, Miles estimated that by the end of October, all of the supplies stockpiled at the depot would be on hand at the cantonment, obviating the further need for wagon trains.[34]

If any member of Miles's command hoped or imagined they were going to hole-up for the winter in the new cantonment, they were disabused of that notion by the arrival, in late September, of a supply of buffalo overcoats and buffalo-hide overshoes. Clearly, the colonel had no notion of waiting for spring to take the field again.[35]

Although reduced army appropriations had forced Miles to cut back on the number of civilian scouts in his command, he was still able to assemble a coterie of able individuals. They were a typical cross-section of colorful frontier characters, including John "Liver-Eating" Johnson, Billy Cross, Vic Smith, and Tom Leforge among others. These were men who, like Kelly, had developed a unique set of skills for which there was an immediate need, although one that was to be short-lived. Aside from Vic Smith, it is not clear whether Kelly knew any of the other scouts in the detachment, though it seems reasonable to suppose he did. In any case, during the next two years he would have ample opportunity to work closely with several of them.

White, Native American, and mixed-blood scouts played a key role during the Indian wars. Indeed, such individuals were essential not only to the United States government, but to European powers in their colonial wars. Conducting military campaigns in a largely unknown territory and against a foe who operated on familiar ground called for an expertise beyond what military commanders could reasonably be expected to possess. A good scout was able to provide the field commander with the information necessary to carry out an effective campaign. To do this, the scout needed, above all, to be well acquainted with the area: where water could be found; where the river fords were located; where game was likely to be found. The scout needed to be skilled at following a trail and reading signs. The scout was expected to be familiar with the various tribes and their habits. Being able to communicate with Indians through "signing" or speaking their language was also a valuable asset. Finally, the scout must of necessity be a man who thrived on solitude, because much of the time he found himself operating either alone or with one or two others.[36]

Toward the end of September, Miles, in company with a small contingent of soldiers and scouts, crossed the Yellowstone and headed downriver to Fort Buford. The purpose was two-fold: first, to scout the country along the river to determine the best route for hauling supplies overland from Fort Buford to the new Yellowstone posts. Second, Miles was interested in seeing whether there was any recent evidence of Indian activity along the river that might suggest a movement toward the north.[37]

Meanwhile, Miles had wasted little time putting Kelly to work. Before departing for Buford, he directed Kelly to scout the country north to Fort Peck and the Milk River country for signs of Sitting Bull's Hunkpapas. As Kelly had explained to Miles, this was unknown territory, "a blank on any map available." Nearly all of the country to be traversed was great game country and choice buffalo range, dominated in part by the different bands of Hunkpapa, Teton, Oglala, and Yankton, who were jealous of encroachments by other Indians. "No white man in my time had gone through that region."[38]

Given the nature of the mission, Kelly wanted a second pair of eyes and asked for Vic Smith, for whom he had high regard as both comrade and scout.[39] Smith was then working for Colonel Otis out of the Glendive depot, but Miles consented to the request and Adj. Lt. Frank Baldwin issued an order for Smith to join Kelly, while Miles furnished his chief scout with authorization to draw whatever rations they might require from the Glendive depot.[40]

From the cantonment, Kelly journeyed downriver to the Glendive depot, where he presented his authorization for supplies to Colonel

Otis and picked up Smith. "I wish you a successful trip [Otis told them], but I have not the slightest idea where you are going."[41]

Kelly proposed to strike northwest across the Sheep Mountains and ford the Missouri River near Fort Peck. Beyond that point, their course would be determined by circumstances as they found them. In any event, it promised to be a "long, lonesome trip."[42]

Leaving behind the rough, broken country along the Yellowstone, the two riders eventually came to the divide that separates the flow of watercourses between the Missouri and Yellowstone. Kelly had recently traded a pony for a pair of fine field glasses, which he put to good use as he and Smith wended their way toward Fort Peck. As darkness came on, the duo moved steadily through a new land, filled with shapes made strange by the refracted light.

> It was now night [wrote Kelly], with no moon and the sky
> only partly clear. I had never before been in that part of the
> country. Nevertheless, we continued on far into the night,
> as long as we could see. We had encountered no timber since
> leaving the Yellowstone, excepting here and there a scraggly
> cottonwood, but now before us was a low plain dotted with
> shrubbery and a shimmer of water. Was this a mirage of the
> night? We stepped carefully toward it and the whole thing
> melted away as a band of buffaloes and their near friends,
> a cloud of white antelopes, slipped out of sight.[43]

Some distance beyond, they reached the edge of a slope whose steepness dictated they continue on foot. Dismounting and leading their horses, the pair picked their way down the slope and soon came to a level area, dotted with sagebrush that the night's eerily refracted light had distorted into big trees at a distance.

> Traveling across country over unfamiliar ground on a night not
> too clear is trying to the nerves [Kelly recalled], and we made
> our way slowly, routing out buffaloes that were invisible to us,
> but indicated by our horses pricking up their ears and chang-
> ing gait a trifle. They could see pretty well in the night, but for
> us the rumble of hoofs, the odor of warm bodies and the light
> skim of dust that held in the air was convincing enough.[44]

It seems odd that neither Kelly nor apparently any other white man of that day had been through this area. True, it was country frequented by the Lakota, but then was there any part of this region where one could safely expect not to find them? Besides, this was "great game country and choice buffalo range," which also meant plenty of wolves would be hovering around the flanks of the herds and the combination of plentiful game and pelts was usually inducement enough to attract men such as Kelly, Ed Lambert, Vic Smith, and others of that breed. There was also something to be said for simply seeing what was on the other side of the mountain. That, too, was part of the allure, after all. Yet despite the apparent attraction, the area was evidently avoided and that seems puzzling.[45]

Nevertheless, Kelly and Smith reached Fort Peck without incident. Here Kelly discovered that surprising changes had taken place since his last visit with Broadwater's ox train en route to Carroll back in 1874. Old friends like George Cooley, the master cook, were no longer around. Cooley, a consummate *artiste* with meat dishes, was particularly adept at concocting savory meals using pemmican. So good was he, in fact, that Indians would often trade furs for one of his meals, especially if it happened to include bread, a scarce commodity on the frontier.[46]

In addition to its more traditional function, Fort Peck now also served as a school of sorts for young Indians who were even then preparing for class under the tutelage of agent Thomas J. Mitchell, as Miles's two scouts arrived on the scene. Kelly found the changes at Peck nearly overwhelming. "Gone was the romance of the trader, trapper, hunter! Enter the new order of education!"[47]

After a discussion with the agent about the Indians and their future, Kelly and Smith learned that there were no permanent Indian camps in the area. A few individuals had perhaps crossed into Canada, but most were evidently around or below the Yellowstone. The two scouts were then provided with a bed, pointing up yet another change that had taken place. Heretofore, a man simply spread his blanket on the floor, or maybe had the loan of a buffalo robe. In the morning, having fulfilled their mission, they struck south and returned to Tongue River to report to Miles.[48]

Meanwhile, after returning to Cantonment Tongue River from Fort Buford early in October, Miles learned, through contacts at the various agencies, that Sitting Bull was primed to cross the Yellowstone and head north. Crazy Horse, so the reports went, was still to be found along the upper Tongue or Powder Rivers. If true, the report would seem to have left Miles with one of two choices since he lacked the resources to pursue both bands of Sioux simultaneously. As it turned out, the Indians made the choice for him.[49]

On 10 October, a wagon train left the Glendive depot bound for Cantonment Tongue River. Its course lay along the north bank of the Yellowstone. At Spring Creek (present Sand Creek), a short distance beyond the depot, the train was attacked by a mixed war party 300 to 400 strong, thought to be composed mainly of Sitting Bull's Hunkpapas. Despite the presence of an escort of four infantry companies, the train was forced to return to the depot.

On the fourteenth, the wagon train set out once more, this time with a slightly reinforced escort, including three Gatling guns, and under the personal command of Lt. Colonel Otis himself. An intellectual with a cherubic face and handsome muttonchops, Elwell Stephen Otis was a thoroughly capable officer who knew how to be tough when the occasion called for it, as subsequent events did. Twenty-four hours out of the supply depot, the wagon train again encountered Indians at Spring Creek, but this time skirmishers drove them back with a vigorous assault, allowing the train to continue its journey.[50]

Miles, in the meantime, had grown concerned over the failure of the supply train to put in an appearance and dispatched four scouts to ascertain what had happened, even if it meant sending them all the way to Glendive.[51] On the night of 14 October, the scouts ran into a war party, losing one of their number in the ensuing fight.[52] The following day, the three remaining scouts joined the supply train as it was under attack near Spring Creek.[53]

When his scouts failed to report in, Miles prepared to take the field. Crossing the Yellowstone on the seventeenth, he moved northeast, toward a hoped-for rendezvous with the supply train. Behind him marched all ten companies of the Fifth Infantry, more than 400 officers and men, marking the first time in nearly two decades that the entire regiment had taken the field together.[54]

On the eighteenth, following a tough two-day march, part of which was through "clouds of dust and burning sand," Miles met Otis and the supply train near Custer Creek. Otis brought him up to date on the events of the past two days, perhaps the most significant of which had been a message from no less than Sitting Bull himself. The message, thought to have been written by one John "Big Leggins" Bruguier, a mixed-blood wanted for murder and who had found a sanctuary in Sitting Bull's camp, enjoined the army to leave the area or expect a fight. The note also rather arrogantly demanded that Otis leave all his rations and some powder before departing. After dispatching a messenger to inform the Indians that if Sitting Bull wished to fight, he would be pleased to accommodate him, Otis pressed ahead.[55]

Shortly thereafter, Otis was approached by a pair of Indian emissaries from the Standing Rock Agency who informed him that they were on a mission to persuade Sitting Bull to surrender. They advised Otis that Sitting Bull's band was then either near Cabin Creek or on its way to Fort Peck. Would Otis meet with the Hunkpapa leader? Otis responded that he was unable to negotiate terms of any sort. Then, after leaving a supply of bacon and bread for the Indians, Otis and the supply train resumed their journey. In any event, after apprising Miles of these details, Otis continued on to the cantonment. After delivering the supplies, he returned to Glendive on the twenty-sixth without further incident. [56]

Satisfied that the supply train was safe, Miles determined to go after Sitting Bull, resuming his march on Thursday, 19 October, tramping some sixteen miles northeastward through the autumn cold. Kelly, who had expected an assignment from Miles when the regiment left the cantonment on the seventeenth, was not disabused of that notion. Miles needed information regarding the whereabouts of the Indians. Accordingly, late on the nineteenth, Miles directed Kelly to take two other scouts and ascertain whether the Indians were still near the Yellowstone, or had moved north.[57]

Kelly believed the Indians were still on the north side of the river, but it remained for the three scouts to confirm his supposition. In any case, the assignment involved a "night ride on a moonless night... across a rough country, some of it like the bad lands in character." Other than the mixed-blood, Billy Cross, whose skills proved particularly helpful in finding the way on this black night, Kelly does not identify his other companions, though Vic Smith was apparently a member of the party as well.[58]

They headed south toward the river, traveling "under the misty stars," Kelly recalled, pausing now and again to check for signs of Indian activity. Eventually, they picked up a trail that led them to the site of a deserted village near Chokecherry (or Cherry) Creek.[59] The village had been abandoned not long before, as the ground was still warm from the heat of lodge fires; indeed, some embers were still aglow. It had been a fair-sized encampment, too, as the scouts counted one hundred lodges, some of which had been arranged in a circular disposition and revealing that the encampment had included a party of Cheyennes. Here, the scouts also found the scalps of two white women. After a brief rest, they pushed on at first light, following the Indian trail that led north.[60]

Ironically, Miles found the Indians first. Even as Kelly and his scouts were picking up the trail, the Fifth Infantry had continued its northeastward march. After being approached by the same emissaries who had called on Otis and learning that Sitting Bull desired to parley with him, Miles pushed on to meet with the Hunkpapa leader near Cedar Creek on 20 October. Two face-to-face sessions in as many days, conducted under cold, windy conditions, proved frustrating and totally fruitless. Sitting Bull angrily refused to comply with Miles's ultimatum for unconditional surrender, while Miles patently refused Sitting Bull's demand to get out of the country.[61]

With the war of words over for the time being, Miles moved against the Indians on the afternoon of 21 October. The ensuing clash of arms was a spirited affair as the men of the Fifth Infantry pushed forward through the rough, broken country separating the Missouri River drainage from that of the Yellowstone. The Indians fired the grass in the ravines and hollows on the flanks of the advancing infantrymen. Aided by a strong wind, the fires burned fiercely. Great clouds of smoke billowed up, but the infantrymen advanced steadily, climbing the burning ridges through the choking smoke, drawing fire from the Indians in return. Throughout the afternoon, the boom of Miles's three-inch ordinance rifle added its resonant voice to the din of battle.[62]

Meanwhile, Kelly, Vic Smith, and Billy Cross had also pushed steadily on, following the Indian trail, which brought them by and by to Cedar Creek. As they approached the area, the bark of the ordinance rifle alerted them to the fact that a fight was in progress. Nearing the crest of the divide, they could see horsemen on the distant hills. Before them stretched "a wide, treeless valley of yellow grass, on the farther slope of which a small train of army wagons moved slowly toward the ridge, while on the other side a line of soldiers afforded protection against the Indians, who were darting and circling on two sides of the train and exchanging fire with the troops, who were firing at will whenever a mark presented itself."[63]

From their vantage point, Kelly judged the troops to be more than a mile distant. Unfortunately, the only way to rejoin the command, without resorting to a long, roundabout course, was straight ahead. Smith and Cross wanted to wait until dark, but "Kelly insisted on taking daylight for it," Smith recalled. "So, with almost a certainty of being shot, we started for the command."[64] Accordingly, the three scouts plunged down and across the now hazy, smoke-filled valley floor. At first they were paid little mind, but as they neared the rear guard, the Indians opened up on them, driving the scouts to safety, Smith and Cross taking to a ravine, while Kelly sought shelter beneath a creek bank. Tortured by thirst, Kelly, despite an advancing wall of prairie fire, sprinted out to a small pool of water, drank his fill, and dashed back to the sheltering bank. Meanwhile, the rear guard, having noticed the movement of the three men, advanced cautiously, believing them to be Indians, until Kelly called out their identity. Kelly apparently found the entire episode exciting. Smith and Cross, however, regarded their companion's behavior as rash. Fortunately, the rear guard discovered who they were in time. Otherwise, given the poor visibility, the soldiers almost certainly would not have recognized the three scouts and might well have dispatched them. Privately, Kelly was forced to agree and "blessed the gods that watch over careless folks."[65]

Eventually, the steady advance of the soldiers cleared the area and reached the now abandoned site of the Indian encampment. Although darkness terminated the action, scattered firing continued through the night, while the still-burning prairie fires created an eerie backdrop for the bivouacked troops. During the night, an orderly awakened Kelly with word that Miles wished to see him. Reporting, Kelly found the colonel and his staff lying on the ground and wrapped in blankets. The night was "clear and cold," recalled Kelly, "and while all around the ground was covered with sleeping bodies the commander was awake and taking measures for the coming day's work." Miles questioned Kelly at length about the distance to the Yellowstone, where the Indians might cross the river, and their most likely route.[66]

In the morning, Miles had his regiment in pursuit, moving east. The Indian trail was not difficult to follow, being marked by discarded pieces of equipment, some of which had once belonged to Custer's command. In an effort to discourage or at least deter pursuit, the Sioux attacked and were driven off, repeating the tactic throughout the day. The Indians also ignited more grass fires, which Miles was compelled to fight by lighting backfires.[67]

About midday on Monday the twenty-third, the advance of the Fifth Infantry—including Miles, some of his staff, and the scouts—reached the Yellowstone, following two days of tough marching down Bad Route Creek. Here they learned that Sitting Bull and company had already crossed to the south side of the river. Miles directed Kelly and Lt. Hobart Bailey to examine the river as a suitable crossing point. Kelly rode partway across to the deepest point to demonstrate that the "ford was feasible and easy if a fellow did not mind wading in cold water to his waistline, about forty feet on a gravelly bottom."[68]

When the main body of the Fifth Infantry arrived the next day, there was a lively exchange with the Sioux who were finally dispersed by a round from the three-inch ordinance rifle. Establishing camp here,

Miles took time to report to Terry, bringing him up to date on recent events. The Indians, Miles told Terry, were running short of food and ammunition and their stock was jaded.

Knowing that some of the Indian leaders had been disposed to surrender, but had refrained from doing so because of Sitting Bull's powerful presence, and sensing that this might be the right moment to make an offer, Miles sent word across the river suggesting another council. The Indians agreed and on 25 October—a grand and sunny Wednesday—a coterie of leaders splashed across the glistening waters of *la Roche Jaune* for yet another session with this soldier they had dubbed "Man with the Bear Coat."[69]

The moment was not devoid of drama. "Some [of the Indians] did not come direct to meet the officers," Kelly recalled, "but circled around like wild creatures suspicious of a trap. Finally, the leading men sat down in a half-circle on the yellow grass, facing General Miles and his officers. With the soldiers hovering in the background and the October sun above casting light and warmth, the group made an interesting and striking picture."[70]

Among the headmen confronting Miles and his staff on this golden autumn day were Gall, Bull Eagle, Red Skirt, and Small Bear, an amalgam of Hunkpapas, Minneconjous, and Sans Arcs; all hard-liners three months ago when the grass was tall and the medicine strong. But now that food and bullets were growing scarce and ponies lame, many were ready to listen to the words of Bear Coat.

Kelly especially remembered that

Gall, the cunning fellow, did not come in with the rest of the chiefs, but after the conference had started he crossed the river alone and took his seat with the rest in the circle. Hard-tack had been passed around, and Gall, taking four in his hand, took a big bite out of all four like a hungry man. Some point of interest being stated, he suddenly ceased munching with his jaws and listened intently, while a wild look shone in his eyes.

Indeed, the hard-eyed Gall, second only to Sitting Bull in his refusal to give in, would shortly slip away himself to rejoin the Hunkpapa leader.[71]

Miles had earlier decided to take advantage of the brief hiatus, sending his supply train downriver to the Glendive depot to stock up, so that he would be prepared to resume the chase, should the Indians again reject his demand to surrender. But Miles shortly learned that

Sitting Bull had gone him one better. During their retirement down Bad Route Creek, Sitting Bull and a small following had split off from the main body of Indians, circled around, and headed back north to the Missouri River.[72]

Disappointed, as he surely must have been to learn that Sitting Bull had slipped away, Miles could take some satisfaction in the knowledge that a very sizeable body of Indians seemed disposed to surrender, which, in point of fact, is what transpired after two days of negotiating. Ironically, their surrender presented Miles with a new problem. He could not resume his pursuit of Sitting Bull while shepherding the newly surrendered Indians to an agency. Neither had he sufficient provisions at the cantonment to feed them and his own command. Miles's solution was unusual. The Indians were released on their own recognizance with orders to report to the Cheyenne River Agency, while a group of their headmen were taken, under escort, to department headquarters in St. Paul as hostages. As it turned out, the arrangement, which probably exceeded Miles's authority to begin with, fell apart. Although a few of the Indians did actually reach one of the agencies, a number of others apparently had second thoughts about turning themselves in and instead joined up with Crazy Horse's Oglalas. Eventually, they would have to be dealt with again, but for now, as October played itself out, Miles returned to Cantonment Tongue River, from which point he intended to resume his pursuit of Sitting Bull in short order.[73]

Chapter Five

THE SIOUX WAR OF
1876–1877

PART TWO

We rode down the right bank of the Missouri while dark clouds gathered denoting a storm. Finally, it did snow heavily, covering all tracks, but we pushed on for there was no stopping until we had got beyond Wolf Point.[1]

Although Nelson Miles had some reason to feel pleased with his autumn campaign, the Indian problem in the Yellowstone Valley remained far from resolved. Sitting Bull and Crazy Horse were still on the loose and news of the sale of the Black Hills did little to encourage their followers to view surrender as the best course of action. And the army, for its part, had little hard evidence as to where exactly these Indians might be found.[2]

Then, from Col. William B. Hazen at Fort Buford, came word that Sitting Bull was reportedly on the Big Dry near Fort Peck, some twenty miles south of the Missouri. Armed with this information, Miles prepared to head off in pursuit. Accordingly, on 6 November, he crossed the Yellowstone with 10 companies of his Fifth Infantry—some 449 officers and men—two pieces of artillery, plus a coterie of ten white and two Indian scouts. A month's supply of provisions was hauled in wagons and aboard a string of pack mules. The thorough Miles also saw to it that his men were prepared for winter, being clothed in buffalo coats, leggings, overshoes, caps, and gloves.[3]

The land of the Big Dry was a great feeding ground for buffalo that moved south to find shelter among its ravines and draws. Not surprisingly, it also attracted traders and mixed-bloods who drifted down with the herds to hunt, fashion buffalo robes, and trade with the Indians who liked Red River rum when it could be gotten.[4]

Following an exhausting ten-day march through rugged country and in brutal winter weather, Miles bivouacked on the south side of the Missouri River, near Fort Peck, on about the sixteenth. Here he again encountered, and this time enlisted the services of, Johnny "Big Leggins" Bruguier, whom Kelly regarded as a "fine interpreter and man." Bruguier, called "Big Leggins" by the Indians because of the cowboy chaps he wore, had recent and first-hand knowledge of the hostiles and Miles was anxious to have his services. In return, Miles agreed to intercede on Bruguier's behalf with regard to the murder warrant that was outstanding on him.[5]

There were mixed reports of Indian bands here and there, and it was not always easy to determine whether a particular band was one of hostile intent or was out of the Fort Peck agency. On the nineteenth, having learned (incorrectly, as it turned out) that Sitting Bull was near Black Buttes, Miles divided his command. He would take five companies and strike directly for Sitting Bull's suspected camp, while Capt. Simon Snyder with four companies was to make a sweep up the Big Dry in search of other Indian bands, then rendezvous with Miles at Black Buttes eight to ten days later.[6]

Kelly's assignment was to move down the south bank of the Missouri with a small detachment of scouts and determine whether any hostile parties had managed to slip across the river and head northeast of Fort Peck. This done, the scouts were to join up with Captain Snyder's command.[7]

Kelly's companions on this mission were Jim Woods, Tom Newcomb, and Jack Johnson. Under threatening skies, the quartet headed east. Presently, heavy snow commenced falling and continued as far as Wolf Point, beyond which they found evidence of one small camp, though the snow had obliterated the trail.

Leaving his companions to establish camp, Kelly crossed the Missouri on thin ice to make an inquiry at a small trading post about Indian activity in the area. Here he learned that three families of Lakota, perhaps the same band whose campsite the scouts had just discovered, had crossed the river that day.[8] Concern over recrossing thin ice in the dark prompted Kelly to spend the night with the trader and his family, whom he found affable hosts. They looked forward to the day when the government would have the Indians reporting to established agencies where they could be properly cared for.[9]

In the morning, an Indian boy warned Kelly that the ice was *suta*, or soft, and offered to test it for the scout. Kelly declined, however, "thinking that I would rather encounter the danger alone than have a boy, even an Indian boy tackle it in my behalf." Accordingly, moving out on his own, he crossed the river alone, finding the ice to be stronger than expected.[10]

Rejoining his companions, they struck out across country to find Captain Snyder's battalion. Their route was over high ground so as to provide wide visibility. The weather had turned threatening once more. Again, Kelly's literate pen sketches a picture of the scene for us. "The gray sky gave a somber cast to the uplands, on which the antelopes trotting in a circle stood out clear and distinct against clay bank or drifted snow. We saw no other game, not even a slinking wolf or fox."[11]

They dined sumptuously that night, thanks to a buffalo shot by Jim Woods. After providing their horses with nutrient-rich green bark from yellow cottonwood trees, the scouts turned-to on the buffalo. In accordance with protocol, Woods was given the choice tongue, and the hide of the beast, on which he placed his bedroll for the night. There followed then a savory meal of roasted buffalo, washed down with hot coffee. Thus passed a comfortable night, with little fear of Indians or prowling wolves, either of whose scent would immediately be winded by the horses.[12]

The following day, on their way to rendezvous with Captain Snyder's battalion, the scouts had a brief brush with five Indians, who managed to escape into the rough, broken country with the scouts in hot pursuit, close enough to see the breechclouts trailing behind their quarry.[13]

As darkness fell on 24 November, Kelly and company rode into Snyder's bivouac area along Dry Creek, and the following day the battalion pressed on toward Black Buttes, which they reached as snow fell on the twenty-eighth.[14] Miles had not as yet put in an appearance and Snyder dispatched his scouts to try and make contact, but they found no sign of Miles. Neither did signal guns or fires produce results. At length, with supplies dwindling, Snyder decided to start back for Cantonment Keogh, with Kelly picking the route. Since their purpose in being there at all was to locate Indians, Kelly chose a way that would lead the column near likely sites for an encampment. It may, however, have been a little too roundabout for Snyder, who experienced frustration over the delays encountered. "Dollies wagon delayed us again today, but not through his fault this time. Yellowstone Kelly seems to be considerably out of his reckoning in regard to branch I am stryking [sic] for. He expected to reach it in 10 miles from last camp, but now reports it 12 or 15 miles further."[15]

It was an arduous trek as well. After four days en route, with his animals growing weaker, Snyder sent Kelly and Jack Johnson on ahead to the cantonment on the fifth, which place they reached without incident. By the eighth, a contingent of Crows met Snyder's battalion on the trail with a supply of corn for the starving animals. Kelly, meanwhile, accompanied by two other scouts and under orders from the cantonment commander to try and make contact with Miles, had turned about and headed back to Snyder's command along with the Crows. After preparing a dispatch for Lt. Frank Baldwin, which he then gave to Kelly to deliver, Snyder continued on to the cantonment, arriving on 10 December.[16]

Two days to the north, the scouts located Miles's battalion and checked in. Kelly learned that Miles had also undergone a rigorous march, covering some 600 miles over extremely rugged terrain, and in weather that had ranged from spring-like to bitter cold, which, as Kelly well knew, was perfectly typical for the region. It was especially galling to Miles, though, that it had all been for nothing. Sitting Bull had eluded him once again. And so it was back to the cantonment, chagrined at what had pretty much been a fruitless campaign. Four days behind Snyder's battalion, Miles's weary troopers tramped into the cantonment.[17]

One unit still remained in the field, however. Based on a report that Sitting Bull was going to cross the Missouri east of Fort Peck, Miles, on 29 November, sent Lieutenant Baldwin and three companies to investigate. Miles had, meanwhile, moved on to join Snyder, who by this time was on his way back to the Yellowstone. Baldwin subsequently located and attacked Sitting Bull's camp near Ash Creek on 18 December, capturing or destroying the precious winter stores. Outnumbered and harassed along the return march, Baldwin's command reached the Tongue River cantonment on 23 December, the last elements of the regiment to return.[18]

Although his quarry remained at large, Miles could take some comfort in the fact that Baldwin's destruction of those winter stores would
work a real hardship on Sitting Bull's Hunkpapas. Somehow, though,
the Indians had managed to avoid the loss of their ammunition supply,
which meant they were still a dangerous foe. After the loss of the village
at Ash Creek, Sitting Bull and his followers turned south to find succor
among the Oglalas.[19]

Work on the cantonment progressed despite the deepening winter.
Supplies and equipment, including forage for the animals, continued
to arrive. Nelson Miles was no fair-weather soldier. He intended to take
the field again before spring. Accordingly, in anticipation of further
cold-weather campaigning, the troops fashioned articles of clothing
out of blankets and canvas to supplement the buffalo coats they had
been issued.[20]

Although there were small signs that civilization was beginning to
work its way into the Yellowstone Valley, Indian troubles were far from
over. Raiding parties continued to harass mail carriers and strike beef
herds, this latter not surprising given that buffalo were becoming
noticeably scarce.[21]

For the time being anyway, Miles could concern himself with the
country south of the Yellowstone, where Crazy Horse was reported to
be in camp along the Tongue River with perhaps as many as 600
lodges. Sitting Bull, whose following had waned of late, had been
unable to unite with Crazy Horse after Baldwin's attack at Ash Creek,
due to deep snow and bitter cold. By early 1877, however, Sitting Bull's
lodges had again increased in number and the Hunkpapa leader
recrossed the Yellowstone once more and struck north to ultimately
find refuge in Canada.[22]

Meanwhile, Brig. Gen. George Crook had taken the field again. Late
in November, his cavalry, the Fourth U.S., under Col. Ranald
Mackenzie, devastated the Cheyenne village of Dull Knife and Little
Wolf on the Red Fork of Powder River, west of present Kaycee,
Wyoming. The survivors fled through snow and cold to find relief
among Crazy Horse's Oglalas. The arrival of the Cheyennes created a
subsistence problem for the combined village and may also have gen-
erated some hard feelings among the two peoples. The fact that some
Cheyennes had served as scouts for Mackenzie perhaps did not sit well
in these lean times.[23]

But a peace faction had developed among the Lakota and not long
after Miles's return to the cantonment, five of them approached under
a flag of truce to parley, only to be suddenly attacked and murdered by

Crows from a nearby village, who had first feigned friendship. Miles was furious. If he had entertained any possibility of ending hostilities without further campaigning, that hope now vanished. Still, there was little he could do other than to admonish the Crows and order the guilty parties disarmed. Kelly thought the incident "one of the minor tragedies of the war."[24]

In late December, Miles again took the field. Indian raiders had run off the cantonment's beef herd, most of which was subsequently recovered, but it was clear that the time had come to deal with the Lakotas and Cheyennes south of the Yellowstone.[25]

Under a cheerless, leaden sky, with the temperature standing at thirty degrees below zero and snow blanketing the ground, Miles marched his battalion south out of the cantonment, along the reaches of the Upper Tongue.[26] He had with him three reinforced companies, 436 officers and men, plus a three-inch ordinance rifle, a twelve-pounder Napoleon, and the omnipresent detachment of scouts, which included Kelly, Tom Leforge, Robert Jackson, "Liver-Eating" Johnson, Johnny "Big Leggins" Bruguier, and James Parker. Additionally, the group included two Crows and a Bannack named Buffalo Horn, whom Kelly regarded as the bravest Indian he ever "had anything to do with."[27]

On New Year's Day, the ever-changeable Montana weather did an about-face, as the temperature rose and rain began to fall, quickly turning the snow to slush. The following day, the scouts had a brief skirmish with a party of Indians and later came upon the remains of an Indian camp, which Kelly figured had been built by Dull Knife's Cheyennes after they had fled from Mackenzie's strike on the Powder back in November.[28]

On the third of January, Miles's main column pushed on, up the valley of the Tongue. The odor of Indian tobacco was heavy in the "still, cold air" and fresh pony tracks indicated that the troops were under observation. As the column moved out, a four-man detachment was left behind to recover several oxen that had wandered off. The four troopers were promptly attacked by watching Indians, who killed a man before being driven off by a relief party dispatched when the sound of gunfire reached the main column. After burying the soldier and obliterating signs of his grave, the troops resumed their forward movement, amid persistent rain and over the now muddy terrain. That night the scouts were sent on to examine the valley of the Rosebud for Indian sign.[29]

Twenty-four hours later, the scouts, having returned from their night survey of the Rosebud, were about a mile beyond the column

Scenes from
Harper's Weekly
illustrating Col.
Nelson Miles's
winter campaigns
against the Sioux,
1876–1877.
Yellowstone Kelly
is seen top, center.

proceeding cautiously up the narrowing Tongue valley. Tired from the previous day's efforts, they paused to rest in an inviting little place where, as Kelly recalled, "the winter sun shone warmly." Uncharacteristically, they neglected to post a lookout and as a consequence failed to note Indians secreted nearby, waiting to attack. Luckily, three Crow scouts in company with the redoubtable Buffalo Horn, riding up from the main column on a little hunting foray, stumbled on the waiting Indians. Having lost the advantage of surprise, the Indians fled up the valley, pursued by the scouts.[30]

On 7 January, as the column neared Wolf Mountains and prepared to bivouac, Miles directed Kelly to take the scouts and continue up the valley to look for Indian sign. Kelly, who was still in the saddle when Miles called, "was contemplating with a pained aspect, the appearance

Col. Nelson Miles and staff preparing to take the field against the Sioux. The temperature stood at nearly forty below zero on this January morning in 1877. (left to right) 2nd Lt. Oscar F. Long, Surgeon Henry R. Tilton, 2nd Lt. James W. Pope, Colonel Miles, 1st Lt. Frank D. Baldwin, 2nd Lt. Charles E. Hargous, 2nd Lt. Hobart K. Bailey. Yellowstone Kelly is seen mounted, directly behind Lieutenant Long. *National Archives photo.*

of the army wagon that contained the scouts' plunder and bedding, which as usual had been overturned in one of the numerous crossings of the Tongue River." Reaching the point of a high bluff, the scouts found some respite from a strong, cold wind, in the lee of a large cedar tree. Scanning the surrounding country with field glasses, Kelly spotted a party of Indians moving up the valley toward them.

As the Indians neared their position, it became clear that there were several women and a boy. After cautioning the Crows not to touch these Indians, Kelly and the others quietly approached the party. Seeing the scouts, the women began to cry, but the scouts signed to them not to be afraid. The scouts questioned them in Sioux, but got no response. Kelly figured them to be Cheyennes, returning from a visit to another village and perhaps mistaking the smoke from the army fires for their own camp. In any case, the scouts accompanied them back to the bivouac where they were given food and shelter.[31]

Barely had this happened, when more Indians were spotted down the valley, bringing the scouts flying back, through the waning afternoon light. Near the place where they encountered the Indian women, the scouts noted several Cheyenne warriors on high ground ahead and Kelly, driven by the excitement of the moment, foolishly decided to charge straight at them. The Indians, as it turned out, were resting their rifles on crossed sticks, so as to provide a stable firing platform and cut loose when the scouts got to within about fifty yards. Fortunately for the scouts, they were saved by poor Indian marksmanship.[32]

As it was, two horses were hit, including that of Tom Leforge. Many years later, Kelly could still see Leforge tumbling off his horse, Cheyennes all around them.[33] Taken aback by the hot reception accorded them, the scouts sought safety amid a bunch of scrub oak in a small hollow. To reach the spot, however, required them to jump their mounts "down a rocky shelf, five or six feet to solid ground," while Indian bullets zinged off the surrounding rocks, "raising little dust patches from the ground. It was miraculous," said Kelly, "that no one was seriously hurt."[34]

Once secreted among the scrub oaks, the scouts were able to return fire and give a good account of themselves. The Indian who revealed himself for longer than a moment was generally out of the play for keeps. Still, it was a brisk, spirited affair, with the Indians, who had the advantage of numbers, slowly but steadily surrounding the scouts.[35] Meanwhile, the Indian "friendlies" had advanced up the valley toward the scouts, halting some 300 yards back. Buffalo Horn, however, pushed on and joined the scouts, seemingly indifferent to the hazards.[36]

During a brief pause in the fighting, Kelly and Buffalo Horn managed to thwart an effort on the part of several Cheyennes to work their way around behind the scouts. Kelly described the moment.

> Our enemy now numbered more than a hundred. There was a
> lull in the firing, an ominous lull. Pointing to the high bank just
> above us, I nodded to Buffalo Horn and together we dashed up
> it just in time to intercept three Indians who were stealthily
> approaching our retreat. Almost before we could fire at them
> they had worked out of sight in the most wonderful way. They
> seemed to fly along the ground, but I am confident that I
> made a hit in that flying exit of feathers, legs, and arms.[37]

But it was a touch and go situation. "The Indians made it so hot for us here," said Kelly, "that I was forced to rejoin my companions in the oak grove. The 'Bannock,' however, concealed himself in the grass and did good execution during the engagement. This Indian did not know what fear was."[38]

In the meantime, sounds of the action had carried back to the troops, prompting Miles to move forward in support. Arriving, he found himself confronted by a mixed force of Lakota and Cheyennes numbering in excess of 200 warriors. Fighting was brisk in the thin light of the dissipating January afternoon, with the Indians finally dispersed by the army's field pieces. As darkness closed in, the soldiers withdrew, although the gutsy Buffalo Horn stayed behind and shot a pair of Cheyennes that attempted to follow the troops.[39]

That night, a few Cheyennes crept in close enough to the army bivouac to exchange a few words with the women prisoners. But the contact led to nothing, and aside from a few scattered shots with the sentries, the night passed, cold and snowy, but uneventfully.[40]

The next morning, 8 January, was pure winter, with the temperature standing at minus fourteen degrees. Not far from the bivouac area along the frozen Tongue River, amid timbered-studded hills and ridges some 700 yards distant, rose an eminence that would one day be suitably christened Battle Butte.[41] Halfway between the Butte and the army camp ran a high bench or mesa. Anticipating its tactical importance, Miles had had his men prepare positions here the night before, and at daylight he himself climbed to the top to glass the surrounding countryside. Kelly may have accompanied him, but if not joined Miles shortly thereafter.[42]

What greeted Bear Coat's studied scrutiny on this frigid Montana morning might have passed for a scene from some surrealistic painting. Through the mist, rising from the frozen Tongue River bottomlands below, could be seen a bevy of Indians—perhaps as many as 600, Miles estimated.[43] What's more, they seemed to be spoiling for a fight. From the tops of nearby ridges and knolls they gestured and taunted the soldiers. Kelly responded in Sioux, calling them "women."[44]

The war of words was brief. Miles wasted no time, deploying the infantry along the ridgeline as well as east and west of a small streambed that fed into the Tongue. The artillery section, consisting of the twelve-pounder Napoleon and three-inch Rodman gun, was posted on the mesa, from where Miles would direct the conduct of the battle. On this day, Kelly's role would be strictly that of an observer.

As this was a soldiers' fight, where the scout would find little freedom to exercise strategy in stealing upon the enemy without danger of being subjected to a cross fire from both sides, I became a mere spectator, so I took my place near the artillery on the bench, where General Miles stood with a little switch in his hand directing operations.[45]

The Indian attack was temporarily stymied by artillery fire, as the heavily garbed soldiers worked their way through the deep snow to take the fight to the Indians. Firing was heavy. At one point, the twelve-pounder Napoleon began to attract the fire of an Indian sniper. Kelly tried to locate his position, but was unable to spot the man. What he did spy, however, were Indians moving toward the crest of Battle Butte, which was within rifle range of the mesa from where Miles directed the battle. Kelly brought this to the attention of Miles, who promptly dispatched Capt. James Casey's company to counter the threat, but it was more easily ordered than obeyed, as Indian warriors fired on the advancing troops from nearby knolls.[46]

At one point Big Crow, a Cheyenne medicine man, danced out in front of the troops fully garbed in all of the magnificent attire appropriate to his high station. The ridge along which he danced was level and along it Big Crow in "full costume of feathered cloak and war bonnet danced for a space of forty yards in the most graceful and nonchalant manner. Here was a challenge of the first order. If Big Crow's medicine was strong, the soldier bullets would do him no harm and the warriors would emerge triumphant. And the soldiers blazed away, but the shuffling, ever-fluid medicine man managed to avoid being struck, until at length, a bullet found its mark, felling Big Crow."[47]

Meanwhile, Casey's company fought its way to the crest, where the Indian defenders, some without ammunition, used clubs to try and beat back the soldiers. After gaining the top, Casey was forced to repel an Indian counterattack, supported by a second company sent into the breech by Miles.[48]

Elsewhere, the fighting was equally hot and heavy, as Indians fired from timbered positions on other elements of Miles's command, attempting to secure control of additional pieces of high ground that dominated this frozen battlefield. Eventually, the support of the three-inch Rodman gun, coupled with the determination of the soldiers, managed to drive the Indians back from the ridgetops.[49]

By now it was nearing midday. Snow had begun to fall and quickly intensified into a full-blown blizzard. Miles pursued the retreating Indians for some three miles up the valley before returning to the bivouac area. That night the snow again turned to rain and Indian snipers harassed the troops. The next afternoon, Miles resumed the

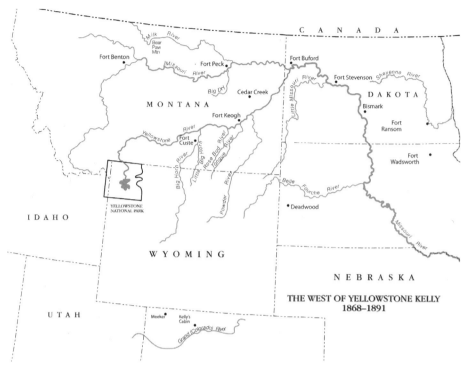

Map showing key sites of Colonel Miles's campaigns against the Sioux and Nez Perce and the area of Kelly's Colorado experiences. *Map by Tom Child.*

pursuit, but the Indians had managed to melt into the surrounding hills, leaving behind only the debris of their abandoned campsites.[50]

With dwindling supplies and an exhausted command, Miles began the long, cold return march to Cantonment Tongue River on 10 January. Plummeting temperatures, exacerbated by strong winds, made for a nightmarish trek, until at length on the eighteenth, the weary column trudged into the cantonment.[51]

Although there still remained a core of Lakota-Cheyenne resistance, the Wolf Mountains Campaign effectively ended the power of the Indian forces that had known their summer of triumph. How fleeting had been the taste of those victories. And then had followed the great diaspora. Of the two principal Indian leaders, Sitting Bull had gone north and Crazy Horse remained south of the Yellowstone. They would not again know the unity that had been theirs along the Greasy Grass.[52]

But if Miles had cause to feel a strong sense of accomplishment, he also had cause to know anger. Upon returning to the cantonment, he

Yellowstone Kelly in 1878. Photo by L. A. Huffman, Fort Keogh, Montana, photographer. *Montana State Historical Society, Helena.*

discovered that the War Department's budget had been slashed and that as a result he was directed to terminate all of his civilian employees, save for two scouts. Miles protested bitterly, but in the end agreed to undertake no further winter campaigns, a decision that was undoubtedly welcomed by the men of the Fifth Infantry.[53]

For Luther Kelly, the events of the past six months, culminating in the Wolf Mountains Campaign, stood as a transition period. The casual, rather free and easy manner of life he had known during the past eight years was giving way to something else. Kelly may or may not have had some sense of what was happening, but at any rate, he was changing—evolving is perhaps a better word. He was 28 and a different individual from the youth who had arrived at Fort Buford that long ago spring of 1868. He was older and seasoned now, with all of the finely honed wilderness skills of a man who had lived well beyond the pale of civilization and survived.

But there was more to it than that. The way of life Kelly had known since 1868 was, in and of itself, no longer enough to sustain his soul. Kelly had discovered a need for the companionship of educated men; men who knew of books and literature, art, and politics, and history; men who could converse intelligently on these and other topics of interest; the good life, so to speak. In any case, he found such men among the officers of Nelson Miles's command. It wasn't that he had lost a sense of appreciation for individuals such as Ed Lambert, but rather that he now needed more than what they could provide. For their part, Miles and his staff found Kelly a good companion. Indeed, they found him the best card player when it came to cutthroat euchre.[54]

Kelly's service with Miles had also filled his life with a stronger sense of purpose. Helping to bring about an end to the Indian problem in the Yellowstone country was putting his skills to a wider use than mere survival. He would never entirely lose his affinity for solitude and the lure of distant places. Indeed, half a century later, he could still describe, in mouth-watering detail, the aroma of buffalo ribs roasting over an open fire. But from this point forward, Luther Kelly's life would reflect his efforts to find the proper balance in his life—a balance where the hunger for adventure might live in a comfortable sort of peace with his growing need for the gentlemanly existence.

Chapter Six

AN EASTERN JOURNEY AND THE NEZ PERCE CAMPAIGN,
1877

**It was now about twelve years since I had left home
to enter the army in the closing year of the Civil War,
and as everything seemed quiet on the border,
I broached to General Miles the subject of
going east on a short trip.[1]**

Early in the spring of 1877, probably during the last half of March, Kelly found himself headed back to Fort Peck to investigate Indian movements in that region. Although most of Miles's attention had been focused south of the Yellowstone since December, he remained only too aware of the fact that Sitting Bull remained at large. And while it was true that the Hunkpapa leader no longer posed the same threat he had just a few months ago, it was a bit unsettling to know he was still on the loose. As a consequence, Miles directed Kelly to head north and evaluate the situation.[2]

For this expedition, Kelly took with him Red Mike Welsh and a young Fifth Infantry corporal named John Haddo, both of whom he knew well. Red Mike, of course, was his old friend of Fort Buford days and Haddo, a soon-to-be recipient of the Medal of Honor, whom Kelly described as "a fine fellow as well as a good shot," had accompanied him on other missions.[3]

They traveled over the same ground that Kelly and Vic Smith had covered the previous fall. Indian sign was absent during the early part of the journey, enabling the trio to ride at ease. Along the way, Red Mike shot an antelope that provided a fine meal. Afterward, they roasted bones "far into the night," which was chancy in hostile Indian country, Kelly recalled, because "a most appetizing odor arises from bones roasting before an open fire, an odor that promotes congeniality and fires expectation."[4]

The mission was largely uneventful. Along the way, there was contact with a party of friendly Assiniboins and some buffalo-hunting Yanktons, one of whom, Good Dog, Kelly had known in the old days. Good Dog later helped them to identify another band of Indians as having formerly been with the Hunkpapas in Canada, around Wood Mountain. Aside from this, though, the most excitement occurred in crossing the Big Dry, which was running unusually full. Red Mike's horse stumbled, forcing its rider to jump off. In the process, Mike's rifle slipped from its scabbard and was apparently swept away.[5]

By early April, the trio had completed its survey of the region, and from Wolf Point Kelly penned his report on the ninth. Sitting Bull, he had learned from reliable sources, had crossed the Missouri near Fort Peck on 17 March, but had suffered a considerable loss of supplies and equipment to high water. Kelly imagined they would move north as soon as conditions were favorable. Although he thought there were at present no hostile bands between the Yellowstone and the Missouri, he recommended that troops be stationed in the area to thwart further Indian movement. Kelly could not have known it at the time, of course, but the day after he prepared his report, 10 April, a council composed of Sitting Bull and other Lakota leaders convened on Beaver Creek, some sixty miles from Fort Peck, to discuss their future course of action. Some wished to pursue the struggle, but Sitting Bull declared he was going to Canada, which place he in fact reached in early May.[6]

Their mission completed, the three scouts returned to the cantonment. At this juncture, Kelly concluded it was time to visit home, which he had not seen in a dozen years. Miles had no objections, though he did alert Kelly to a forthcoming campaign he might not want to miss.[7]

But the scout had made up his mind and so Miles gave Kelly his blessing, along with "letters of introduction to prominent officials in Washington." Exactly what purpose these documents were intended to serve is not known, since Kelly offered no further explanation, nor did Miles. However, in the spring of 1877, with military appropriations about to be cut, or having recently been so, Miles, as always, was looking for support and, of course, recognition. At age 28, Luther Kelly was in the full flower of manhood and surely must have cut a handsome, romantic figure. He was, as well, an articulate man who could speak knowledgeably as to the situation in Miles's district. Taken all together, Kelly would have made a first-rate emissary.[8]

As to the trip east, Kelly says only that he departed when the ice was out of the Yellowstone. However, since his report from Wolf Point was dated April 9 and since he was carried on the roster of scouts through April, it seems likely that he departed about the first of May.[9]

In any event, he joined up with a party of soldiers headed downriver in an old boat and apparently volunteered to serve as pilot. The journey proved to be one of hair-raising proportions. One of the soldiers remembered, "That ride through the ice and uprooted treetops worried me more than all the Indian fighting I ever did." Kelly, too, had vivid recollections of the journey.

> Turning a bend near the mouth of the river, we came
> suddenly upon an ice jam extending high above the banks
> that blocked the channel from side to side and we made
> haste to reach the shore. In the night the ice gorge broke
> with much grinding and din, leaving a solid wall on each
> side of the channel, and next morning, after a survey to see
> if old *Minnishushu* was clear, we made our way through
> this forbidding avenue of thrashing water until the broad
> and swollen current of the Missouri received our battered
> craft and wafted us along a wooded bend for the space of
> a mile to a plain on the farther bank, where stood the
> military post of Fort Buford.[10]

An observant young woman traveler, bound for the cantonment aboard the steamboat *Josephine*, noted Kelly and company when they arrived at Fort Buford on 5 May and recorded an interesting impression of the scout in her journal. Clearly Kelly's reputation had grown. "There was a boat came down from Tongue River, with Yellowstone Kelly, one of the greatest scouts we have [*sic*] noted for his bravery, rather delicate looks something like an Indian, very modest looking, had on moccasins without socks." To have noticed that Kelly had no socks was indeed an interesting observation by a young woman of that era when proper ladies simply did not discuss such things. But then the observation was private, of course, and she never imagined that eyes other than her own would share these inner thoughts.[11]

By his own admission, Kelly's eastern sojourn was brief. After a dozen years in the West, he may well have felt somehow out of step. The contrast between frontier and urban life was undoubtedly quite dramatic, perhaps more so than he had imagined it would be. He found city life exciting in a way, but "not to his liking." The life he had known since 1868 was a basic, no-frills sort of existence. On the frontier a man cut it or didn't last. But here in the East, life may well have struck him as being somehow artificial and contrived. In later years he would find city life more attractive, but for now, here in 1877, Kelly was more than ready to return to the frontier. Accordingly, after seeing family and friends in New York and Washington, he set out again for the West.[12]

Exactly when Kelly commenced his return journey is not clear, but we do know that he boarded the Northern Pacific in St. Paul on 5 July. The long train ride across Minnesota and North Dakota did not lack for conversation. On board, Kelly chanced to meet a man named Stearns and his partner on their way to the Black Hills. For Stearns, at least, it was an impressionable meeting. Stearns would remember Luther Kelly for the rest of his life.

> This morning I met a noted scout who is said to have killed
> more Indians than any other man on the frontier of his age.
> He is a young man 27 years of age and has been a scout
> twelve years, and was formerly from Elmira, New York. He is
> called "Yellowstone Kelly." Is about five feet ten inches in
> heighth [*sic*], straight as an arrow, long black hair, and keen
> dark eyes. He is far from the Eastern idea of an 'Indian scout'
> as he is very modest and unassuming, uses fine language
> and no oaths.[13]

Reaching Bismarck on 11 July, Kelly borrowed a horse, on the back of which he placed his own saddle, and "set out for the lonely ride up the Missouri."[14]

Between Fort Berthold and the Yellowstone, a hunter informed Kelly that a solitary Indian was on the same trail, only a few hours ahead. Kelly caught up with him near Tobacco Gardens, one of several stage

Perhaps the best known Yellowstone Kelly photograph, this was taken in 1877 when Kelly served as Chief of Scouts for Col. Nelson Miles during the Great Sioux War of 1876–1877, and the Nez Perce War of 1877. *Photo by John H. Fouch, provided through the courtesy of Dr. James S. Brust.*

and way stations between Bismarck and the mouth of the Powder River. The lone Indian, it turned out, was a Northern Cheyenne, Two Moons, who had recently surrendered to Miles after the fight at Wolf Mountains. Two Moons was returning to Montana after a meeting with General Sheridan in Chicago, where he an several other Indians had lobbied on behalf of a Cheyenne reservation in the Yellowstone country.[15]

Although they had been adversaries at Wolf Mountains, Kelly recalled that he and Two Moons greeted each other in friendly fashion and rode on together "in perfect amity... as though we had always been the best of friends." Kelly thought the Northern Cheyenne weighed about two hundred pounds. He "wore a black felt hat with a feather and garnished band, a woolen shirt, leggings, moccasins, and a painted robe adorned with picture writing." At the crossing of the Yellowstone, Kelly shot a wildcat they spied in a tree and, after skinning the animal, he presented the pelt to Two Moons who was pleased to have the gift. As they ambled along toward Tongue River, Two Moons commented on the absence of buffalo and observed that "[p]lenty wagon tracks, buffaloes take to the high ground." And so it was, Kelly noted, that buffalo were indeed grazing on the hills beyond the valley.[16]

Meanwhile, the weeks following the Wolf Mountains campaign provided a welcome and much needed respite for the Fifth Infantry. As for its aggressive commander, Nelson Miles had demonstrated that he knew how to get results, and that realization was not lost on either Sherman or Sheridan. Both Crook and Terry had been a disappointment in their respective failures to act with the kind of determination and tough-mindedness that had characterized Miles's campaigns of the past fall and early winter. Granted, Miles, with his ceaseless pestering for more authority and promotion, was a real irritant, but despite that, it seemed clear that he was the one to finally end the Indian problem in the Yellowstone country.

Accordingly, in March 1877 Sheridan prepared to create the District of the Yellowstone. When finally authorized, it would give Miles official jurisdiction over his sphere of operations, which essentially embraced the Yellowstone Valley north to Fort Peck; in effect he would have an independent command. In addition, Miles was to receive reinforcements in the form of four companies of the Second Cavalry from Fort Ellis and two additional companies of the Twenty-second Infantry. Nor was this all. The reorganized Seventh Cavalry and four companies of the First Infantry were also tabbed for assignment to the District of the Yellowstone. Once all were on hand, Miles would command more than two thousand men, divided between the post on Tongue River and the second post, to be called Fort Custer, near the confluence of the Bighorn and Little Bighorn Rivers.[17]

All of this was promising enough, but for the moment the ambitious, ever-restless Miles lacked supplies enough to take the field again and was compelled to stifle his frustration. However, if active campaigning was on hold, efforts to encourage the Indian bands south of the Yellowstone to surrender were pursued with vigor through the winter and on into the spring. Indeed, the competition between Miles, operating out of Cantonment Tongue River and George Crook out of Fort Robinson, Nebraska, was highly competitive, with each seeking to reap the harvest of publicity that was sure to attend the victor. To say the two were rivals was to characterize it mildly. Each sent emissaries to the various bands. Johnny "Big Leggins" Bruguier represented Miles, while the influential Brulé leader Spotted Tail carried Crook's message. As it played out, Bruguier did pretty well on Miles's behalf, persuading some Lakota and a large body of Cheyennes to turn themselves in. Crook's efforts, however, paid the richer dividend when Crazy Horse and nine hundred of his followers surrendered at Fort Robinson in early May, about the time Luther Kelly's party was commencing its descent of the Yellowstone–Missouri Rivers.[18]

And, just as Miles had predicted, Kelly missed what turned out to be the final act of the drama begun in that now seemingly distant February of 1876 when the War Department received its directive to commence operations against Indian bands still in the region who refused to surrender. On 29 April 1877, finally resupplied, Miles took the field with nearly 500 men and a contingent of white and Cheyenne scouts, the latter having volunteered to serve following their surrender in the aftermath of Wolf Mountains. On 7 May, Miles struck the Minneconjou Lakota village of Lame Deer lying along what is today Lame Deer Creek, a tributary of the Rosebud, effectively shattering the last pocket of organized Indian resistance in the Yellowstone Valley. For all intents and purposes, the Lame Deer fight brought an end to the Great Sioux War. Aside from a few small bands of Indians who refused to acquiesce, there was now little to impede the advance of civilization across southern Montana. There was, however, a postscript yet to be written, one that was to be forever remembered as an American epic. Luther Kelly may have missed the final battle of the Great Sioux War, but he would be on hand when Chief Joseph of the Nez Perce surrendered at Bear's Paw Mountain.[19]

After his return from the East in mid-July 1877, Kelly spent the summer scouting the country between the Yellowstone and Missouri Rivers, looking for signs of Sitting Bull, which were much in evidence, enough so to keep Nelson Miles in the field for most of the summer. However, his labors on the sun-seared plains of central and northern Montana, notwithstanding, the frustrated colonel of the Fifth Infantry could do little more than chase the exiles back across the border.[20]

In any case, on one of these outings, Kelly seems to have been accompanied by an Englishman named John Howard. An adventurer and army veteran, Howard, like many others from Great Britain, had come to the United States in search of diversion and excitement. Whether he found excitement cannot be said for certain, but life in Montana during these years was seldom dull, so one suspects he was not disappointed. And although Kelly does not elaborate on their time together, he evidently found it not an unpleasant experience, later recalling how they "brewed tea from wild cherry bark, in a region where there was no good water to drink."[21]

That summer of 1877 also found him back at Carroll, where he renewed his acquaintance with Maj. Alonzo Reed. On one of these visits, he chanced to join a party of civilians, who may have been involved in unloading a steamboat at Carroll. At any rate, it proved an amicable group, boasting a supply of freshly killed buffalo. That night's camp served as yet another illustration of how frontier life, though always demanding and often dangerous, was not without reward for those who marched to the beat of her drum.

After feasting on roasted tongue and ribs, the group's reigning expert on such culinary delicacies took charge of preparing the hump. Wrapping the hump in a piece of green hide, it was placed in the fire pit, then covered with live coals and finally overall with dirt. In the morning, it provided a royal feast, enough, said Kelly, "to make one wish for absent friends to be present and enjoy." Moments such as these imprinted themselves on the face of Luther Kelly's memory, to be savored and recalled many years later by an old man in the twilight of a life most men only dream of.[22]

Meanwhile, even as Kelly and his companions were savoring their baked hump, a storm that was brewing far to the west would presently spawn a great American odyssey. Like virtually all Indian-white conflicts, the Nez Perce War, as it came to be known, had its origin in a land treaty dispute. The so-called "nontreaty" Nez Perce refused to abide by the terms of an 1863 treaty, which reduced land set aside for them in Oregon and Idaho by virtue of an earlier treaty signed in 1855, though not ratified until 1859. But, gold was discovered here in 1860, you see, and in order to open up that territory to mining, the government sought to revise the reservation boundaries. Some bands of Nez Perce agreed to the realignment, but others, the nontreaty bands, did not, and thus was planted the seeds of the Nez Perce War.[23]

The issue did not become serious, however, until the mid 1870s, when Gen. Oliver Otis Howard, newly installed commander of the

Department of Columbia, took steps to compel the nontreaty bands to relocate. As the *de facto* head (or at least spokesman) of the nontreaty bands, Joseph, who would go down as one of the great Indian leaders, played a pivotal role in the drama about to unfold. During the period November 1876–May 1877, efforts to persuade Joseph and the other nontreaty headmen to move failed. Frustrated, General Howard gave them thirty days to comply, or he would force them to do so.[24]

The situation was tinder dry and little provocation was needed to set it aflame. The spark was struck in mid-June 1877, when a trio of young Nez Perce warriors, fired with the passion of youth and angry over the situation, killed four white settlers. Not surprisingly, near panic swept the countryside. Rumors abounded. Responding to the threat, an army column was attacked in White Bird Canyon, Idaho, and roughly handled. It was a harbinger of things to come. Fearful and confused, the nontreaty Nez Perce bands, consisting of 300 warriors, together with some 500 women and children, elected to cross the mountains to the buffalo country where their hunting parties traveled annually in search of meat.[25]

Meanwhile, learning of the setback at Whitebird Canyon, Howard promptly issued a call for reinforcements and, five days later, took the field himself from Fort Lapwai, Idaho, with a mixed force of some 227 cavalry and infantry, a number that would eventually swell to nearly 600. When Howard departed Fort Lapwai, he initiated a pursuit that lasted four months and which would culminate, in late October, in the Bear's Paw Mountains of northern Montana, some 1,700 miles from the Nez Perce's ancestral homeland.[26]

En route to their date with destiny in the Bear's Paws, the Nez Perce fashioned the stuff of legend, beating their pursuers often enough to become more than a little embarrassing to the U.S. Army. The marksmanship of these *Nee Mee Poo* was superb, their courage and determination of the highest order.

At Cottonwood, Idaho, on the fourth and fifth of July, they took the measure of a hastily assembled volunteer force and a few days later held off Howard's regular troops on the Clearwater River. Crossing the Bitterroot Mountains they camped along the Big Hole River in southwestern Montana, where they themselves were surprised by a column under Col. John Gibbon, moving from Fort Shaw to intercept. But the Nez Perce rallied, and after bloodying the army's nose once more, slipped eastward through Yellowstone Park, where they killed two tourists and might well have captured General of the Army William Tecumseh Sherman, had his visit to the park been a bit later.[27]

Meanwhile, the army had been busy ordering in units to try and corral the Nez Perce and bring this thing to an end. The Fifth Cavalry was on its way to seal off one of the exits from Yellowstone Park, while a second regiment, the rebuilt Seventh Cavalry ordered into the breech by Nelson Miles, to whose command it had recently been assigned, blocked the other route.

Miles, for his part, had been carefully monitoring the unfolding drama. At the same time, though, he was also keeping a wary eye on the Canadian border, concerned as always about the movements of Sitting Bull, who for the moment at least was his number one priority. Still, Miles figured the Nez Perce were most likely to head northeast from Yellowstone Park, toward Luther Kelly's old haunts in the Judith Basin. Accordingly, with this in mind, on 10 August he dispatched six companies of the Seventh, now under its true commander, Col. Samuel D. Sturgis, whose son had perished with Custer on the Greasy Grass the year before.[28]

On 27 August, Miles telegraphed Sturgis to "strike the Nez Perce a severe blow if possible before sending any word to them to surrender." In this, Miles's expectations were due for a setback.[29] There were two principal eastern exits from the park: Clark's Fork and the Stinking Water. Learning that the Nez Perce were headed toward the latter, Sturgis moved to intercept them, but they doubled back and eluded him. So for a time, the Seventh Cavalry actually found itself behind Howard's troops, on the tail end of this pursuit. Recovering, an embarrassed Sturgis pushed on and caught up with his quarry at a place called Canyon Creek near present Billings, but the Nez Perce parried Sturgis's efforts and continued their northward journey, once more demonstrating their evasive skills.[30]

Near mid-September, Miles sent Lt. Hobart K. Bailey and a small detachment of cavalry to look after a cache of ammunition stored at Carroll, so as to prevent it from falling into the hands of the Nez Perce. Kelly was directed to accompany. With no apparent need for urgency, the detachment rode in leisurely fashion to the Musselshell River and from there down Crooked Creek to a ridge overlooking the Missouri. Again, Kelly's sense of time and place are reflected in his perception of the moment. From this particular vantage point, they gazed down on the historic Minnishushu, "where the wild Indians may have looked down in wonder at the boats of Lewis and Clark as they ascended the stream two generations earlier."[31]

Arriving at Carroll, they located the ammunition that was stored in a small log building that was locked. Unable to gain entrance, they were in the process of breaking in when the owner, Alonzo Reed, happened along. The former partner of Reed and Bowles was amused at the soldiers' predicament. He and Kelly discussed the Nez Perce situation, though Reed could provide them with no new information.[32]

The picture soon changed, however, because late that afternoon, scout Bill Norris arrived with orders for Kelly to join Miles at the mouth of the Musselshell. When Bailey's detachment had headed north on its assignment, there had been no expedition in the offing. Thus, the message surprised Kelly, who had no idea that Miles had taken the field.[33]

What had happened was that on 17 September General Howard telegraphed Miles requesting his assistance in cutting off the Nez Perce. For Miles, the door of opportunity had opened wide. He could hardly have ignored Howard's request, even had he chosen to do so, which thought never entered his mind anyway. Accordingly, he wasted no time answering the summons and by first light on the eighteenth was swinging north with five companies of infantry and two of cavalry. Five days later, on 23 September, he was in bivouac near the Musselshell's confluence with the Missouri, from whence he sent courier Norris, to fetch his chief scout.[34]

Moving mostly by dark, Kelly wended his way cross-country beneath a sky "luminous with stars," and presently arrived at the bivouac area near midnight on the twenty-fourth. After finding some forage for his horse, he located Miles aboard the steamer *Fontenelle*[35] having a friendly tussle with Capt. Frank Baldwin over who had first choice of the two available beds. The pair laughed when Kelly approached. After presumably bringing him up to date on the Nez Perce situation, Miles directed Kelly to collect his scouts and in the morning see if they could pick up the Nez Perce trail.[36]

The Nez Perce, as it turned out, were closer than anyone realized. In the morning, a small boat arrived with news that the Nez Perce had crossed the Missouri the previous day at Cow Island, some sixty miles upriver. After skirmishing with a small army detachment at that place and burning a large quantity of freight, the Indians pushed on and were camped only some thirty miles from the army bivouac even as Kelly and Miles were discussing the situation on board the *Fontenelle*. As Kelly later observed, a small thing sometimes "makes or mars an enterprise."[37]

The steamer had, meantime, started downriver, but was caught and brought back to the bivouac area where Kelly and four scouts promptly crossed to the north bank of the river, followed soon thereafter by the troops. Riding hard toward the northwest, the five scouts reached the

Little Rockies, some thirty-five miles distant. From a high point they glassed the surrounding countryside for sign of the Nez Perce.

> Below our point of observation [wrote Kelly] lay People's Creek, its course being traced a long way in the direction of Milk River. Beyond People's Creek to the left extended a broken plain to the foot of the Bear Paw Mountains, hazy and dim in the distance. From the Bear Paw to the Missouri every ridge was scrutinized for signs of travelers, for it was apparent that no great company of people with a multitude of live stock could conceal from view their movement on that open plain, nor would they try, expecting pursuit only from the rear. We looked long and earnestly, but no object appeared to move, not even buffaloes where one might expect plenty.[38]

With daylight fading, Kelly now reasoned that in as much as they were now across the Missouri River, the Nez Perce might well pause a day or two to rest, but if not their trail could be cut by pushing on to the Bear's Paw Mountains. However, before putting his reasoning to the test, it would be wise to determine what Miles had in mind. By this time, Kelly figured the army bivouac would be at the northeast end of the Little Rockies, as indeed it was. Riding cross-country, through the day's waning light, the scouts soon reached the camp, which was located only a mile or two distant. As Kelly suspected he would, Miles pushed on toward the Bear's Paws in search of the Nez Perce trail, directing him to report to Lt. Marion P. Maus who had already gone on ahead with a small detachment of mounted infantry.[39]

Kelly wanted to get started while some light yet remained, for the weather looked threatening and rain seemed imminent. For this mission, Kelly again chose Cpl. John Haddo and a new man named Milan Tripp, who had been recommended to him, along with one other man.[40] Wasting little time, the quartet started out for the Bear's Paw Mountains, in what by this time must have been the twilight of 26 September, joining Lieutenant Maus's detachment en route.[41]

Fearing that they might miss the Nez Perce trail in the darkness, especially as it was a cloudy night and misting, Kelly recommended to Lieutenant Maus that they camp for the night and Maus agreed. After picketing the horses, each man sought out as decent a spot as could be found. For his part, Kelly found a smooth spot, wrapped himself in his saddle blanket and eventually drifted off to sleep, to be awakened at dawn by Haddo.[42]

As they went about preparing coffee, the scouts suddenly spied Miles's column in the distance. And of course it would not do at all to have the main body out in front of the scouts, so after abandoning coffee plans, Kelly soon had them back on the trail for the Bear's Paws. Weather conditions had improved. The overcast had cleared and as they rode, Kelly recalled how the rain-freshened air "made beautiful the mountains, partly shrouded in clouds and mist that wasted slowly under the rays of the morning sun."[43]

Trotting across the stone-covered ground that marked the approach to the Bear's Paw foothills, Kelly noted for the first time the natural, cone-shaped "rock monuments that occur at regular intervals along their face." Arriving at a high point, Kelly spotted a pair of Indians driving their ponies. Not expecting pursuit from this quarter, the Indians were unaware of the scouts who promptly pressed on. As the detachment drew closer, however, the Indians, who had become aware of their presence, soon took to scrambling up a rocky, brush-covered hillside across the small valley that separated them from Maus and his scouts. The steepness of the hillside prevented the scouts from resuming the pursuit until a trail could be found.[44]

Impatient, some of the scouts opened fire on their own volition, but were quickly directed to stop. As Kelly observed, their job was to find the Indians, not fight them. As a consequence, he was content to let them go. "I was satisfied," he later wrote, "that they were not near enough to us to perceive the military character of our party, and our object was to find the trail, or camp, of the Nez Perce."[45]

In any case, about the same time the shots were fired, it was observed that the main Nez Perce trail was visible on the floor of the small valley below them, and along which could also be seen the remains of the recent Indian campsite. Locating a way down, the scouts descended into the valley, and after examining the ground, determined that one trail led through the mountains, though it was impossible to tell if it was the main trail because of the heavy horse traffic that obliterated much of the other sign.[46]

Lieutenant Maus was anxious to follow the Nez Perce trail, but Kelly counseled caution and suggested they sit tight and await the arrival of the column. He reasoned that inasmuch as the weather had once again turned rainy, it offered ideal conditions in which to surprise the Indians. Maus evidently saw the wisdom in this idea, prepared a dispatch for Miles, and gave it to Milan Tripp to deliver, as he had the freshest horse. That done, the detachment settled down to await the arrival of Miles and the main body.[47]

When, however, Miles failed to put in an appearance after what seemed a reasonable time, Kelly suggested that they move along the base of the Bear's Paws in search of the troops. Striking out toward the east, they soon discovered the army trail, estimated to be no more than a mile ahead. Despite the fact that they trotted along at a brisk pace, the scouts failed to catch up with Miles until the morning of 30 September, by which time he had already attacked the Nez Perce encampment.[48]

Miles, meanwhile, had pushed hard on the twenty-seventh, moving along the eastern apron of the Little Rockies, reaching the Bear's Paw Mountains on the evening of 29 September. The lowering clouds and misty conditions masked the approach of the troops as they moved into position to strike the Nez Perce camp. Indeed, conditions were dreadful; visibility was so poor that Maus's party failed to spot the troops when they passed them.[49]

Early on a cold 30 September, Miles attacked the Indian camp, which had been located along Snake Creek. The Nez Perce, though, had taken a cue from their experience at the Battle of the Big Hole and created a strong defensive position with entrenchments, and it paid off. After the bloody repulse of a battalion of the Seventh Cavalry, Miles was forced to lay siege to the camp, concerned all the while that Sitting Bull might show up to aid the Nez Perce.[50]

Although the fear of Indian reinforcements from across the border was a real enough threat, it never materialized and the next several days witnessed an unusual sort of battle, at least insofar as these Indian-white clashes went. Here in these Bear's Paw Mountains, in the often wet, bone-cold autumn of 1877, the soldiers and Indians spent five days, exchanging sporadic, but often deadly sniper fire, punctuated now and again by a blast from Miles's Hotchkiss rifle, "which was vomiting shot at intervals into the center of the Indian stronghold." It was a deadly affair, with casualties heavy on both sides. To make matters worse, snow had commenced and a bitter wind whipped across the battlefield.[51]

The Nez Perce were located in a gulch, around which they had constructed rock rifle pits that afforded excellent protection from incoming fire and made their own fire hazardous in the extreme for any attacker who was careless enough to expose himself. One Indian auxiliary, however, proved particularly adept at slithering across the ground until he found a spot from which to take the measure of some Nez Perce.

> I saw an Indian named Hump [Kelly recalled], a bold and
> picturesque fellow, crawling along the ground toward a rifle
> pit that held a warrior who had taken heavy toll of the

soldiers. I watched Hump as he wormed his way skilfully [*sic*] from one little depression to another. He could travel flat on the ground with the greatest ease, but I did not envy him his present quest. Another Indian had started with him, perhaps to give him encouragement and support, but he had stopped halfway and from his vantage point, which was as close to mother earth as an Indian could get, lay watching Hump's farther advance.

Others were watching too, as well as myself, among them several Sioux and Cheyenne scouts, who were friends of Hump. Suddenly, Hump came to a stop, and shifting his position slightly, pulled his rifle slowly to the front and carefully sighted it toward an object at an angle to his line of advance. He fired, gazed a moment, then crooned a war-note which was heard by his waiting friends, and edged along the course he had pursued. He had killed his man, for when the Nez Perce surrendered, we found a rifle pit in the direction of his fire, and in it, cold and stiff, a warrior bowed over his rifle.[52]

But the fearless Hump, not satisfied with this score, sought yet another and this time was himself hit. Fortunately for Hump, the wound seems not to have been serious. Not all were so lucky, however. Kelly had several times urged his friend Haddo to keep low, but the young soldier was careless just once too often, and when Kelly returned from having coffee, he found Haddo shot through the heart. "I missed him much," said Kelly. "Cool and fearless, he had been my companion on many trips."[53]

On 4 October, the long-suffering Oliver Otis Howard finally arrived on the scene, but graciously refused to assume overall command from Miles, though his rank entitled him to do so. If nothing else, however, Howard's timing was perfect, showing up just in time for the final act of this drama. Having concluded, finally, that his people had suffered enough, Joseph surrendered to Miles and Howard, and in the process of so doing, uttered his famous "From where the sun now stands" speech, a profound and fitting tribute to an event of epic stature. Surrender perhaps they had, but with those words, Joseph and his followers became something more than captive tatterdemalion fugitives. Refusing to give up, some of the Nez Perce did make their way across the border into Canada.

And so this four-month odyssey was finally finished, and costly it had been…to both pursued and pursuer. Estimates of Nez Perce casualties range from 125 to 200 killed, and some 90 wounded. Miles suffered 177 killed, including 50 civilians, together with 147 wounded.[54]

Meanwhile, on the night 30 September, Kelly was awakened and, in company with another scout, headed out to bring in the expedition's wagon train. The night was "gloomy and starless," Kelly recalled, and they several times lost the trail in the darkness before calling a halt to await the dawn. With first light, they quickly picked up the trail of the wagon train and would have overtaken it had not Kelly noticed a large number of horses grazing on a nearby hill. Concerned that they might be Sioux Indian ponies, which meant that a war party had come down from Canada to aid the Nez Perce, Kelly investigated and found they were army horses.

Returning to the bivouac, Kelly reported his discovery to Miles and learned that a large number of horses, including the colonel's own personal mount, had stampeded during a snowstorm, causing some alarm, inasmuch as it was feared they might be picked up by a band of roving Sioux. Accordingly, Kelly found himself another scout and the pair returned to gather up the horses, numbering more than a hundred, and drove them back to camp. Still at large, however, was the colonel's mount.[55]

With the surrender terms complete, Miles, shepherding the Indians, marched to the Missouri River, where all wounded soldiers and Indians were placed aboard a pair of steamers, while the remainder of the expedition and the nonwounded Nez Perce moved south to Cantonment Tongue River, all except Kelly, however, who had a new assignment.[56]

Chapter Seven

THE CANADIAN BORDER TO YELLOWSTONE PARK AND ANOTHER EASTERN SOJOURN, 1877–1878

> When we got around the spur of the mountain I laid a course due north and we traveled on over a rolling prairie all the afternoon. About dusk we saw a light straight ahead which seemed near but was afar, for we traveled hours before it loomed as a camp fire, in whose light we passed around a considerable camp of infantry and cavalry to a group of tents, where we dismounted and asked the guard if General Terry occupied the large tent.[1]

In late August 1877, the administration of President Rutherford B. Hayes agreed to send a commission to Canada to see what might be done to resolve the thorny political issue of Sitting Bull and his followers. As it filtered down from the White House, General of the Army

Sherman appointed Gen. Alfred Terry, commanding the Department of Dakota, to head up said commission. With his legal background and gentlemanly demeanor, Terry was probably the ideal person to carry out the mission.[2]

The Sioux problem had gotten to be a real embarrassment for both governments. Miles reported that the Indians moved back and forth across the border at will, mainly to hunt, but occasionally on a horse-raiding foray, too, so where they might be found at any one point in time was a good question. At any rate, Terry's instructions were to offer peace to the bands if they were then located on Canadian territory. If not, he was to prepare a military campaign against them. Clearly the intent here was political. In order to avoid further embarrassment with the Canadian government, the United States government was willing to extend the hand of peace to Sitting Bull and his followers in order to entice them out of Canada. However, in the event the Indians were to be found south of the border, military action was in order. In part, this was fueled by some considerable fear—promoted largely by unfounded newspaper stories—that another Indian war would erupt, with the Sioux reinforced by Blackfeet and Nez Perce and armed with weapons supplied by Canadian traders.[3]

Thus, against this backdrop and in company with his secretary, Capt. Henry Clarke Corbin, Twenty-fourth Infantry, Terry left St. Paul on 13 September and arrived at Fort Benton on 6 October, his journey having been interrupted by the Nez Perce trouble. However, with Miles's victory at Bear's Paw on the fifth, Terry was free to resume his journey and did so, leaving Fort Benton on 10 October. Along the way, he rendezvoused with the escort provided by Miles and proceeded to the border, which he reached on the fifteenth.[4]

Meanwhile, before starting south with his Nez Perce charges, Miles asked Kelly to carry some dispatches to Terry. Miles's message was contained in a large envelope, which Kelly stuck in his belt. A companion was needed and this time Kelly chose Tom Newcomb, something of a newcomer and who was particularly "noticeable on this occasion as he had on leggings made of red blanket stuff."[5]

Starting out on 11 October, Kelly and Newcomb met a lone rider who informed them that Terry's party had left Fort Benton on the tenth and advised them as to the location of the general's camp. The directions were good and the two scouts found Terry's camp with no difficulty. Kelly was impressed with the size of Terry's personal tent, which, he thought, "seemed a very large one, even for a headquarters, and was comfortably furnished."[6] After handing his dispatches to Terry and answering the general's questions about the Nez Perce campaign, Kelly and Newcomb were provided with a meal of hardtack, bacon, beans, and coffee. The next morning, Terry asked Kelly to ride to the Canadian line and deliver a letter to the English commissioners and return with their response.

Accordingly, the two scouts headed north over a rolling countryside that Kelly knew well, with "dry lakes on one side of the Milk River and many, many antelopes, beautiful creatures." The weather was cold, though hardly unseasonable for mid-October in that far northern clime.[7] North of the Milk they encountered three young Sioux, well armed but not with hostile intent. Their presence here, nevertheless, seemed to support Miles's contention that the Sioux continued to roam freely between the two countries. After a brief exchange, the scouts continued their journey until, presently, in the distance they could see a lone horseman and could make out the "mounds marking the international line."[8]

The rider turned out to be a member of Canada's Northwest Mounted Police force, who directed Kelly and Newcomb to the camp of the commissioners, which featured "only one light untopped wagon, one tent fly for cover, and a half dozen troopers for escort," in marked contrast to the "imposing establishment maintained by General Terry." Seeing the general's camp here reminded Kelly that Terry's habits had not changed since he first viewed the latter's entourage south of the Yellowstone back in the late summer of 1876. Kelly had decided then that Terry was "too fond of his own comfort to get far away from a wagon train and steamboat on any old Indian trail."[9] Still, Kelly was not above making allowances. "The hero of Fort Fisher believed in traveling in comfort as well as in state. And why not, when you have the command and opportunity?"[10]

After delivering his message and receiving a reply, Kelly and Newcomb turned back to meet Terry and his party, who had camped near Wild Horse Lake, a shallow body of water but a short distance from the border, where they were presently joined by the British commissioners.[11] In the morning Terry and the commissioners, accompanied by a small detail, started for the border. Kelly and Newcomb followed, only to be stopped by a member of Terry's staff who informed the scouts that only those specifically appointed by Terry would be permitted to cross the border. Kelly was disappointed, as he had wanted to sit in on the talks and report the decisions to Miles. He was not at all sure the officer who turned them back had fully understood Terry's instructions, either, but elected not to argue the point.[12]

So, after returning to the camp on Wild Horse Lake, the two scouts awaited further instructions from Terry and when none were forthcoming, headed south. Once this had been a game-rich region, but recent events had left it drained and limp. For his part, Kelly was happy enough

to leave these cheerless plains, which had charmed in former years when they were thronged with buffaloes and antelopes, and elk in great bands were found along the wooded streams and mountain slopes nearby. Now the elk had wandered or been frightened away by the many bands of hostile Indians camped along the border, whose hunting parties had cleared the plains of buffaloes.

Kelly had discovered a hard truth here, that this land of seemingly inexhaustible abundance was, despite its toughness and hard-shelled exterior, a fragile system, whose balance could easily be interrupted and forever altered.[13]

As they rode through the Bear's Paw battleground, where Kelly's old comrade John Haddo had earned the Medal of Honor at the expense of his life, the scouts unexpectedly met up with a well-armed band of Prairie Gros Ventres (Big Bellies) who had unearthed a large cache of weapons, along with cooking utensils, clothing, and much more, that had been captured by the Nez Perce when they raided Cow Island on the Missouri River just prior to the Bear's Paw fight. The battlefield itself, empty now of life but well marked with signs of death, "looked gruesome enough," Kelly recalled, "with its scattered bones of cavalry horses and mounds of freshly piled earth that covered the remains of soldiers and warriors who had answered their last roll call."[14]

Continuing on their way, the scouts chanced to come upon a small band of horses that had been stampeded during the Bear's Paw fight and which had escaped the earlier roundup and included Miles's personal mount. After catching the animal, Kelly transferred his own saddle and trappings to the animal for the remainder of the ride back to the cantonment, apparently with his other mount in tow.[15]

Upon reaching the Missouri River, Kelly and Newcomb found a river steamer tied up at the bank. The passenger list included Capt. Frederick. W. Benteen of the Seventh Cavalry, together with three companies of his regiment. Benteen, a survivor of the Little Bighorn debacle, chatted with Kelly for a time. It also turned out that one of Miles's aides was on board and Kelly turned the colonel's horse over to him before the steamer ferried him and Newcomb across the river to resume their southward journey.

Meanwhile, after leaving the Bear's Paw battlefield, Miles, escorting some four hundred Nez Perces, and in company with General Howard and staff, had moved slowly south. At the Missouri River, they parted company, with Howard boarding one of two waiting steamboats for his journey east, while Miles continued south to the cantonment with the Nez Perce. Before leaving the Bear's Paws, Howard, being the senior officer, had instructed Miles to hold the Nez Perce at the Tongue River cantonment until spring, owing to the lateness of the season and what Howard judged would be the high cost of transporting the Indians back to their northwest homeland by rail. Howard's order was to have unfortunate repercussions.[16]

Miles reached the cantonment on 23 October. Howard's issuance of the order to Miles, coupled with newspaper stories largely crediting Miles with the victory over the Nez Perce while ignoring Howard's role, ignited a nasty feud between the two men, as well as harsh words from Sherman, Sheridan, and Terry. Howard was later judged by the adjutant general as having exceeded his sphere of authority in issuing the order to Miles.[17]

In any event, on 29 October, Miles was directed to send the Nez Perce downriver to Bismarck and Fort Lincoln, where it had been decided they could be cared for through the winter at less expense than at Tongue River. Due to the lateness of the season, however, steamers were no longer plying the river, so Miles sent about half of the Nez Perce downriver on a flotilla of flatboats. The remainder was loaded aboard wagons for an overland journey to Bismarck, accompanied by Miles, Kelly, and an escort. It seems not to have been a particularly pleasant journey, as Kelly later recalled that he had to follow the ambulance on horseback and few things annoyed him more than trailing an ambulance in this fashion.[18]

On 19 November Miles was feted with a lavish banquet at the Sheridan House in Bismarck. Kelly was numbered among the guests. Shortly thereafter, his assignment completed, Miles, Kelly, and the escort started back to the cantonment. In Bismarck, the Nez Perce were subjected to yet another change of plans. From here they were shipped by rail to Fort Leavenworth, then on to the hated Indian Territory.[19]

By the time Miles and Kelly returned to the Tongue River, the new post, located two miles west of the cantonment, was largely finished, and on 1 December was officially named Fort Keogh in honor of Capt. Myles Keogh, who had perished with the Custer battalion at the Little Bighorn.[20]

   The spring of 1878 marked Kelly's tenth year on the Plains. On 25 April Miles asked him to take a three-man detachment and investigate the feasibility of establishing a wagon road and mail route between Tongue River and Deadwood, Dakota Territory. This would be new territory for Kelly and we may imagine that he looked forward to the assignment with some excitement the way he always did when given an opportunity to see the other side of the mountain.[21]

   Kelly's detachment consisted of a sergeant named Gilbert, together with two privates, all of the Second Cavalry. The most direct route between the Tongue and Deadwood was cross-country, where wagons seldom traveled, but the idea was to see if the terrain would accommodate wagon traffic. The men carried their supplies aboard a light wagon, driven by one of the privates. Kelly and Gilbert rode ahead, while the third member of their party acted as rear guard.[22]

   Their course took them up the Tongue and across Pumpkin and Mizpah Creeks. Antelope and buffalo abounded on the rolling countryside, which Kelly thought showed good promise for farming and stock raising. His ever-inquisitive mind led the quartet to examine some petrifactions of marine life. Otherwise, the journey was uneventful, save for a problem with one loose wheel on the wagon, which was corrected by removing the wheel each night and soaking it in water. As it dried, the wood expanded and tightened. The country revealed no sign of recent Indian activity, though old campsites were found.[23]

   Notorious Deadwood was then at the zenith of its frontier reputation. Gold had been discovered here by the Custer expedition just four years earlier, and it was but two years ago this month that Wild Bill Hickok had been killed in the Number Ten Saloon by Broken Nose Jack McCall. What really impressed Kelly and his companions, though, was the great hydraulic hoses used to wash hillsides away and in the process reveal whatever gold deposits lay buried beneath the surface.[24]

   While in Deadwood, Kelly was interviewed by a young reporter about the purpose of his trip and the country through which he and his companions had traveled. In addition to providing a succinct and lucid description of the journey, the article revealed that Kelly's reputation was firmly grounded, indeed. "From a frontier acquaintance with 'Yellowstone Kelly,' the scout, which has traversed nearly a dozen years and has been mingled with many Indian experiences on the Missouri, the writer attests his bravery, intelligence, and courtesy."[25]

   Their mission completed, the four men set out on the return trip to Fort Keogh. Kelly opted to try a different route, probably just to see the country, but possibly to report on its suitability for wagon travel as well. After crossing the Belle Fourche River, they turned west. In the distance rose Devil's Tower, which proved another object worthy of Kelly's facile pen.

> [W]e turned to the left and entered that great plain that gives a view of the Devil's Tower, that black rock, or collection of rocks, that stands out from the mountain, of gloomy aspect when in shadow, but often fantastical under sunlight and heat waves from the plain. Buffalo bulls were in evidence, but skittish. Antelope were plentiful, too, and easier to bring down, so we had our usual feasts.[26]

The spring runoff had the Powder River running high, and with a wagon to think of, the men were forced to travel upstream (south) for some distance in search of a suitable crossing site. Evidently, the north or downstream route offered no possibilities, so Kelly elected to look for a crossing to the south, since it would be necessary to cross the Powder at some point in order to return to Fort Keogh. At any rate, the detour was a long one, taking them as far as old Fort Reno, east of present Kaycee, Wyoming, where they found a rope ferry operated by the fort's garrison.[27]

Established by Col. Henry B. Carrington in 1866 as one of three military posts on the old Bozeman Trail, Fort Reno had been abandoned two years later in keeping with the provisions of the Laramie Treaty of 1868. However, during the Sioux War of 1876, the site, renamed Cantonment Reno, was reestablished by Capt. Edwin Pollock, Ninth Infantry, and served as an advance base and supply post for Gen. George Crook's campaigns into the Powder River country.[28]

When Kelly briefed Pollock on his mission, he learned that Col. Wesley Merritt and the Fifth Cavalry were scheduled to arrive shortly, with orders to create a new post in the region. In view of this, Kelly and his companions promptly resumed their journey, fearing that otherwise their horses might be appropriated by Merritt's cavalry.[29]

Turning north now along the old Bozeman Trail, the quartet came to the site of old Fort Phil Kearny. Sergeant Gilbert had traveled over the trail previously and was able to identify landmarks. Like Fort Reno, Fort Phil Kearny had been abandoned in 1868, then burned. Kelly was underwhelmed and thought it a dreadful spot for a military post, dreary and wind-swept, the only surviving remnant being a half-decayed flagstaff.[30]

Beyond Fort Kearny, they camped near a "rushing mountain torrent," and Kelly couldn't help but think that if Indians had been roaming about as they had been a year earlier, "they might have walked into camp without our hearing them." But as it was, there was little to fear from Indians south of the Yellowstone any longer and not a great deal to be concerned with north of the river for that matter, so for Kelly and company it had been a sort of idyllic, largely uneventful journey, the final stage of which was down the Tongue to Fort Keogh, where Kelly turned in his report.[31]

In July 1878 Miles presented Kelly with a two-fold assignment. He was to take two soldiers and check out reports that a party of miners were trespassing on the Crow reservation, a portion of which was then located between the Yellowstone River and the forty-fifth parallel (the present northern boundary of Wyoming). The second part of the mission called for Kelly to try and determine whether the Bannock Indians, who had become restless this summer, were attempting to move east. Kelly's instructions authorized him to procure supplies at Fort Custer and at Fort Ellis out of Bozeman. [32]

Exactly where the prospectors might be found, or where they were bound, was not clear, though it seemed it might be Yellowstone Park, an area then unknown to Kelly, save by reputation. The first and one of the largest of our national parks, Yellowstone had been created only six years earlier. It was a region whose great scenic beauty and remarkable features had already forged for it a reputation of mystery and grandeur, and Kelly undoubtedly welcomed an opportunity to see it for himself.[33]

One of Kelly's companions on this outing was the same Sergeant Gilbert who had been on the Deadwood expedition and perhaps other expeditions as well. Like Kelly, Gilbert was quiet, but friendly and a "skilled hunter." We know nothing about the third member of the party, other than that he seems to have been a friend of Gilbert's and was a disciple of Isaac Walton who "kept the camp supplied with trout when we were near a mountain stream."[34]

Leading three pack horses carrying blankets and supplies, the trio left Fort Keogh about 10 July. The most direct route to their first stop, Fort Custer on the Big Horn River, would have been to strike out cross-country. However, inasmuch as Kelly was curious to see what changes had taken place in the Yellowstone Valley since the military had established two permanent reservations in the area, they followed the Yellowstone to its confluence with the Big Horn, before turning south to Fort Custer. He was surprised to find very little in the way of settlement along the river east of the Big Horn, although west of that point towns and farms were beginning to emerge.

Built atop a high bluff, Fort Custer offered a striking view of the Big Horn Mountains to the south and west, which stood out in "clear and rugged outline like stately sentinels of the landscape." Here, the three men replenished their stock of supplies and rested up a day before resuming their journey, riding along the foothills of the Big Horns, through grassy meadows filled with wildflowers, whose colors "harmonized with the brown rocks," as did the ubiquitous antelope.[35]

The odyssey that lay ahead of these three was special indeed, the taste of which one never forgets. It would be a memorable journey today, but in 1878, when the region was still largely unknown, its experience may only be imagined. Their course took them southwest, through Pryor Pass and into the basin dominated by the Wind River and Absaroka Mountains. Stunning vistas stretched out from all points of the compass. To the west could be seen a towering wall of peaks that reached north, clear to the valley of the Yellowstone. To the south, their eyes beheld "Washakie's Needles, a group of slender peaks named after a Shoshone chief; to the east, the dark, gloomy entrance to the Black Canyon, and above it, Cloud Peak with its cap of perpetual snow."[36]

Continuing on, they passed down the Stinking River—or Stinking Water River (today's Shoshone River)—probably entering the park by today's east entrance. Shortly, they chanced upon "a couple of gentlemanly prospectors" who informed them that there was a small prospectors camp not far ahead, which Kelly saw fit to investigate. While the third member of the trio stayed behind to build camp, Kelly, accompanied by Gilbert, rode on ahead to locate the camp of the prospectors, which they found in a ravine near Heart Butte, south of Yellowstone Lake. There was little left of the camp, however, most of it having been washed away in a heavy rain, leaving the occupants glum and discouraged. Since the prospectors were nowhere near the Crow reservation, Kelly judged there was no reason to disturb them.[37]

Having satisfied himself about the prospectors, Kelly and Gilbert set out to do a bit of exploring in the mountains before returning to their camp. Their course proved tough for the horses to negotiate, but it seems to have been a satisfying detour. Along the way, they paused to observe a black bear on a snow bank, gorging itself on grasshoppers, washed down by melting snows. Later, they met up with a cavalry detachment from Fort Washakie, searching for deserters. After exchanging the details of their respective missions, Kelly and Gilbert crossed the mountains to their campsite, which they reached the following morning.[38]

From here, the trio aimed for Yellowstone Lake, following game trails ever higher, through pine and aspen forests, camping that afternoon "in a little park of grass and flowers and feasted on coffee, trout, and venison, flanked by cans of condensed milk and currant jelly."[39] "Oh, Wilderness, were Paradise, enow!"[40]

After their repast, Kelly left his two companions in camp and struck out to locate the trail to Yellowstone Lake. One suspects, too, that he was after some time alone as much as anything. Climbing steadily upward, he at length gained the summit from which could be seen the lake, and a memorable sight it was. Clearly, the park made a deep impression on Kelly, just as would Alaska twenty years later—an evergreen moment, as reprised in his memory many years later. Breathless, he threw himself on the ground and

> gazed long at the beautiful view spread out before me. Below
> was the lake at a distance of ten or twelve miles, like a gem
> of silver in an emerald setting; beyond the continental divide,
> with the Three Tetons looming dark and misty to the left in
> the distance, jagged and capped with snow. With my glasses
> I could see whitecaps on the lake, snow-white flocks of peli-
> cans, and steam rising from some geysers on the east shore
> of the lake.[41]

From this spellbound moment, Kelly hated to detach himself, but eventually had to do so. Returning to camp, he "shot a noble buck whose horns were in velvet"[42] and later collected a fine otter pelt. Their journey through the park appears not to have been hurried, though they were ever watchful for signs of Bannock movement. From a camp near the foot of Mount Sheridan, Kelly ascended the rocky, ten-thousand-foot summit, but the surrounding countryside revealed no sign of Indian activity.[43]

Their course now turned northward to Baronette's Bridge, built by Yellowstone Jack Baronette during the winter of 1870–1871. The bridge was the only crossing of the Yellowstone River within the confines of the park, thence on to Old Faithful where Superintendent Philetus W. Norris had his headquarters.[44] Here, their arrival was graced by eerie overtones. "In the chill mist of the early morning we passed like ghosts along a rude road into the geyser basin. The steam rising from the pent waters seemed a part of the mist." The mist prevented them witnessing the geysers in action, but the roar was clearly audible and the unstable nature of the ground suggested cautious passage. Kelly dismounted and led his horse "around the thin places for fear he would break through and scald his legs."[45]

The sights and sounds and the general ambience of the park experience created an indelible memory for Kelly and his companions, just as they have for later generations. They found themselves

> charmed by the sights on either hand, the morning sun shining over the tops of the pines pierced the mist and disclosed to our gaze Old Faithful, a tall rugged mound gleaming in grays and whites from a recent display of its spouting column.[46]

From here, the trio continued on north through the park and on to Fort Ellis and Bozeman, perhaps following the route blazed by Capt. William A. Jones five years earlier.[47] How long the three men remained in Bozeman is not clear, but in any case it was long enough for Kelly, whose reputation had preceded him, to be recognized as the famous Yellowstone Kelly.[48]

They returned to the park via a different route only to discover that while they were in Bozeman, the Bannocks had managed to slip through the park unobserved—not difficult to do, Kelly noted, when there were but three men watching 100 miles of wilderness. But the Bannocks were not to fare as well as the Nez Perce did, if in fact, one can say the Nez Perce fared well, though they did manage to get some distance beyond the park before their string played out.

While this small drama was working its way to a finale, Nelson Miles was bound for Yellowstone Park on a vacation outing with 100 men in company with a small party of civilians, including his family. The so-called Bannock uprising had flowered back in May in Idaho, again in Oliver O. Howard's military department. Mostly the trouble had been contained, but a band of these Indians had splintered off and headed east to join Sitting Bull, so once again it was Miles into the breech. Upon learning of the development, Miles sent his noncombatants off to Fort Ellis, then divided his meager force to cover the park's two eastern exits. As it came down to the finis, Miles himself, with 35 men and a Crow contingent, surprised the Bannock camp at Clark's Fork on 4 September, capturing or killing most of the inhabitants. Ironically, the brief Bannock War also saw the death, on 5 June, of the brave Bannock leader, Buffalo Horn, who had rendered such valuable service to Miles at Wolf Mountains and whom Kelly had so admired.[49]

When Kelly and company returned to the park, they found Miles and his party camped near the Lower Falls of the Yellowstone, where they learned of the attack on the Bannock village. Their arrival would have been sometime after the fight of 4 September because the non-combatants had by this time rejoined the group, though the mood was somewhat somber given that they had lost one of their members, Capt. Andrew Bennett, Fifth Infantry, in the fight.[50]

The campsite was an idyllic one, but eventually Kelly grew restless again and, with his two soldier companions, left Miles and his party to enjoy the rest of their sojourn in the park and struck off on a little independent exploring before eventually returning to Fort Keogh. The assignment to Yellowstone Park had proved a rich and rewarding experience. Kelly would return to savor its offerings the following year.[51]

December 1878 found Kelly again passing through Bismarck on his way east, reportedly to get married, according to the *Bismarck Tribune*, although Kelly himself makes no mention of any intended nuptials, nor does the *Geneva* (NY) *Courier*, which does, however, report his arrival in that town on Saturday, 25 January 1879.

According to the story in the *Courier*, Kelly came to visit friends, including a former teacher. As he had the year before, Kelly made good copy. The hometown hero was back from the Wild West, preceded by his exploits. The *Courier* painted a Davy Crockett-type picture of its own frontier hero. He was "tall and well shaped, straight as an arrow, and showing great strength in every movement. It is hard to believe that this gentlemanly appearing, quiet and reserved man is the hero of so many battles, a dead shot, and the destroyer of numerous Indians and wild animals." In his fringed buckskin jacket and long black hair, he was easy to spot on the streets of Geneva. Kelly's stay in town was brief, however, and he soon moved on to Elmira, New York, where his mother and brothers had moved by that time.[52]

Exactly how long Kelly remained in the East, or whether he visited places other than Geneva and Elmira, is not known. In any case, by mid-April he was back in Bismarck, waiting for Miles and the next boat upriver, reportedly with the intention of going into the cattle business on the headwaters of the Big Horn River.[53]

Nor is there a clear picture of Kelly's activities that spring and summer of 1879. He may well have ridden north with Miles when the latter was ordered by General Terry to drive Sitting Bull's people back across the Canadian border in June. If so, however, Kelly accompanied Miles on his own, as he is not carried on Fort Keogh's roster of scouts at any time during the year 1879. What seems more likely is that Kelly, intrigued by Yellowstone Park, whose wonders he had only begun to sample the previous year, returned for a second visit in 1879.[54]

Kelly may have spent the entire summer in the park, and at any rate was there in the fall when Park Superintendent Philetus Norris asked him to serve as guide for a troop of cavalry from Camp Brown, near present Lander, Wyoming. The cavalrymen had been assigned as escort for the R. J. Reeve boundary survey, which was then surveying the western boundary of Wyoming Territory.[55]

Kelly was camped on the west side of Stinking River Pass[56] when he chanced to meet a trapper named George Towne, who carried Norris's request. Kelly had seen the trapper a few days earlier at Mammoth Hot Springs. Towne had in tow a New York artist named Seymour, who apparently had come out to sketch the region's wonders.[57]

Norris's instructions as to where exactly the cavalry escort might be found were vague, but Kelly reasoned that upon arriving at the park from the south, they would naturally follow the Yellowstone River to Yellowstone Lake, to which place Kelly, accordingly, set a course. It was rugged traveling, too—thickly forested, marked by only thin game trails. Not only was the going tough, but it was slower than necessary. Kelly had to be especially vigilant because Seymour, without saying anything, had a habit of stopping to sketch a scene whenever the inspiration happened to strike him, forcing Kelly to turn back and retrieve the dilatory artist lest he become lost.[58]

Eventually, the cavalry escort was located near the lake as Kelly had suspected. The officer in charge, a captain, welcomed him, delighted to at last have someone with more savvy than he himself possessed, to lead them through this wilderness. The surveying party was understood to be in Geyser Basin, which Kelly knew would be a tough trek. Their course lay around the south end of Yellowstone Lake, and would take them near Heart Lake and Mount Sheridan, through country he knew from the previous year's sojourn in the park. They moved through a dark forest, where little sunlight penetrated, through an area that might well have seemed grim and foreboding to a sensitive spirit. Kelly penned a moving description of their passage, one that not only painted a vivid portrait of their surroundings, but revealed, once again, a window into his adventurous soul.

> The somber forest lay all about. Early in the day we came to
> the spot on the west side of the lake, of dubious repute, where
> a man might throw for a trout, still on the hook, to a spot
> where it is cooked in the boiling water of a hot spring issuing

from the shallow bottom. From this point we were to leave the lake and penetrate an untraveled and unknown forest to reach the geyser basin. I was confident that we could make it, but expected to strike very rough going. That piece of country had an evil reputation. Alone or with a companion, I should have liked nothing better than to attempt it.[59]

The heavily timbered area was covered by numerous deadfalls, so that progress was slow and difficult. To make matters worse, the mules belonging to the escort's pack train would stop to graze, then charge ahead to close back up on the bell mare at the head of the train. The mare's clanging bell, which Kelly referred to as a "brazen appendage," managed to frighten off any game in the vicinity.[60]

Despite this, Kelly managed to kill an elk and the fresh meat was well received by the soldiers, who had dined mainly on fish since leaving Camp Brown. After a welcome meal of elk, the cooks, using the last of their flour, prepared loaves of bread for baking. The loaves were first placed in pans, then in a trench, covered first with coals and hot ashes, and finally with turf. Kelly was not on hand when the bread was removed in the morning, having gone on ahead to check the route, but he apparently returned in time for breakfast and saw the results, which he described as being "light and beautiful bread, crisp to the touch when broken, sweet and wholesome as any that ever came out of an oven, with a nutty flavor born of the compressed steam that enveloped them in their earth prison."[61]

Continuing on, Kelly and his charges crossed the Continental Divide at what is now known as Norris Pass, witnessed an erupting "Old Faithful," then moved across Firehole River, and on into Upper Geyser Basin, where a rendezvous was made with the surveying party.[62] Here, they also found Superintendent Norris.

Something of an eccentric and apparently possessed of boundless energy, Norris was a man who had dedicated himself to the preservation and protection of this the nation's first national park. Kelly found him amiable enough and Norris apparently took a liking to the scout. Together they would often go for an evening stroll around the camp on the pretext of savoring the area's great natural beauty, though Kelly guessed it was as much to "wear off some of his nervous temper" as anything else.[63]

Learning that Kelly's party had come across the Divide at a previously unknown pass, Norris promptly dispatched a work crew to establish a roadway at that point before it should be forgotten. Even then, tourists were beginning to visit the park, and Norris, Kelly speculated, saw the pass as a valuable portal. Interestingly, Norris later claimed that Kelly had named it Norris Pass, but only after Norris himself had discovered it.[64]

Sometime that fall of 1879, it is not clear exactly when, Kelly returned to eastern Montana. Perhaps he spent that autumn and early winter hunting and trapping in the Judith Basin, or somewhere along the Upper Missouri. Certainly, he was fond enough of that part of the world, so that it would hardly have been surprising if he had elected to return to those old haunts. In any event, we do know that by February 1880, if not earlier, he was back at Fort Keogh, or at least in the general vicinity of the post. Since he was no longer on the army payroll as a scout, we can only speculate as to why. Possibly he anticipated other assignments from Miles, or simply chose to return to a familiar environment while he pondered his next adventure.[65]

In February 1880, Kelly witnessed one of the last big gatherings of buffalo north of the Yellowstone River. Extreme cold had driven the animals south from the Milk River region to the Yellowstone Valley, near the mouth of the Powder River, thereby working a real hardship on Sitting Bull's people, who were deprived of their meat source.

However, the Lakota's loss proved the army's gain in this instance. The presence of the herd brought out a hunting party from Fort Keogh, which included Luther Kelly. The great plain was covered with the shaggy animals, perhaps half a million, Kelly estimated. The cold was so intense, remembered Kelly, that "the smoke from a campfire rose in a slender black thread high into the air."[66] The cold had virtually numbed the animals, who refused to move, even as the hunters were systematically killing them. Kelly's party found a cluster of young bulls gathered in a river bottom and killed enough to fill three wagons. Years later, Kelly recalled the experience for an old friend. "The buffalo were massed along the Yellowstone in very cold weather, so cold that the buffalo were stupid. We approached within forty yards of them and they would scarcely run when we commenced firing."[67]

If killing the buffalo proved easy, skinning and cleaning was not. Removing the warm innards of the animals was easy enough, but in the intense cold—it was fifty below on the post thermometer at Fort Keogh—the men were forced to use mittens to skin the animals. Probably because they were simply too cold to bother, the men failed to quarter the carcasses after skinning and gutting them. And this, said Kelly, was a big mistake, because the next morning when they prepared to load the carcasses aboard their wagons, they were frozen so hard "that an axe in the hands of a soldier made little impression on it, and meat and hide slivered off like ice."[68]

During this same period, Kelly met up with his old friend Sandy Morris, who, along with a partner, one Samuel Stone, was then trapping along the Powder River. Sandy and his partner had a run-in with a party of Sitting Bull's Hunkpapas down from Canada, as it turned out, on a horse-stealing foray against their old enemy, the Crows. In a skirmish that followed, one of the Indians was wounded, but Sandy and his partner managed to escape and reach the safety of Fort Keogh. Upon learning of the incident, Miles sent out an eight-man detachment from the post under the command of Sgt. T. B. Glover. The party included Kelly, Sandy, and another civilian, together with half a dozen now friendly Cheyenne scouts and at least one friendly Sioux.[69]

They tracked the Sioux up the valley of the Powder, then through the rough breaks around Mizpah Creek, while the "raw February wind swept down from the gulches with chilling force." Eventually the Hunkpapas were brought to bay in an ice cave, but not before one soldier was killed and another seriously wounded. Surrounded, the three Indians could not escape, but nevertheless remained a dangerous foe to anyone careless enough to venture too close. The friendly Sioux warrior, meanwhile, volunteered to carry word to Fort Keogh and guide a relief party back with a doctor to attend to the wounded soldier.

Believing the Indians would attempt to escape in the dark, Kelly's party took up station to watch and wait. Camp that night was cold and cheerless: "a raw, cutting wind prevailed and the night was dark, the moon showing but dimly through the drifting clouds." Still, the soldiers were far better off than the three Hunkpapas huddling in their small, cold ice cave. Under cover of darkness, Kelly made an attempt to retrieve the body of the dead soldier. His plan was to loop a rope around the soldier's foot, then drag him back. Worming his way over the ground close to where the body lay, he found that the rope was too short, which meant that the only way to retrieve the body would be to pick it up and drag it back and that meant exposure to fire from the Hunkpapas. Inching forward a bit more, Kelly was finally able to grasp the man's boot. Then, lifting himself up ever so slightly, he studied, as best he could in the cold darkness, the lay of the land over which he would be dragging the corpse. The picture was not encouraging. "All was silent as the grave," Kelly recalled, "save the wind sighing through the cedars." Being close enough to the Indians' place of concealment to hit it with a rock, he concluded, finally, that the risk was not worth the gain and returned to camp.

In the morning, following a quick breakfast, Kelly and the others had determined to simply rush the cave and force the Indians out, killing them if they resisted. Before they could implement their strategy, however, a column from Fort Keogh under Capt. Simon Snyder arrived and the Hunkpapas were subsequently persuaded to surrender.[70]

A dozen years earlier, a young 19-year-old Luther Kelly, fresh from a three-year stint in the Tenth Infantry, had taken his discharge and headed west for the land of the Upper Missouri River, little dreaming of what the future held in store for him. Now, here in this nascent spring of 1880, Yellowstone Kelly, scout and frontiersman *par excellence*, looked about and with discerning eye saw that the day of the scout had passed, at least in the land of the Yellowstone and Missouri River valleys. As he himself put it,

> The great blank spaces on the map of this extensive region had now been filled with trails and wagon routes; hunters, stockmen, and prospective settlers roamed at will looking for locations. Even the red men who had fought us at Wolf Mountain and had surrendered in good faith to the military were contented in their camps under the observation of competent officers; while the hostile and turbulent element, under the leadership of Sitting Bull and other chiefs, were safe—as we then judged—across the border to the north, under the observation of Dominion officers.[71]

It was time to move on.

Chapter Eight

COLORADO,
1880–1891

**On the north fork, near the head of Bill Williams' Fork of
Bear River, I found a beautiful little lake hidden in the
forest, called Trappers' Lake, that was swarming with trout.
There was not a sign of a trail leading to this lake,
nor was there any grass for camping purposes.[1]**

In the spring of 1880, Kelly concluded that it was time to seek adventure elsewhere. Montana was growing up and the challenges once presented by a wild, free land were now as scarce as the great buffalo herds. Accordingly, with nothing more than his rifle and duffle bag, he boarded a downriver steamer and bade farewell to the region that had been his home for more than a decade. He would be thirty-one in July.[2]

We can't say exactly what route Kelly followed, but he seems to have been bound for Colorado, so a reasonable guess would be that he traveled down the Yellowstone and Missouri Rivers to Omaha, thence by train to Denver, because when next we pick up his trail he is aboard a stagecoach bound for the high country, "crawling ever upward through the cooling pines."[3]

After spending the night in Leadville, enjoying the company of some mining people, he purchased a horse and continued his journey to Aspen, now and then killing a deer for meat as needed. The region abounded in game and he had little difficulty providing for himself.[4] Near Grand Mesa he met the Ute chief Colorow. Colorful and testy, the then seventy-year-old Colorow weighed nearly 300 pounds and had figured prominently in the recent Meeker troubles. But this day, the blustering old chief lusted after Kelly's knife, offering a pair of horses in exchange for the blade. Politely but firmly, Kelly turned him down.[5] Kelly arrived in Colorado less than a year after the tragic Meeker Massacre, and it may well have been news of the unsettled conditions in northwestern Colorado that drew him to that part of the state to begin with, just as news of the Custer disaster brought him down to the Yellowstone in the summer of 1876. Although the situation in Colorado had pretty well been defused by the summer of 1880, things were still a bit tense.

Like so many other Indian-white troubles, this one was not born overnight. By the 1870s, there was a general population movement across the Rockies into Colorado's Middle Park. As well, the issue of statehood was a powerful motive for Indian removal. In 1878–1879, the discovery of silver in the mountains around Leadville and beyond had proven irresistible to prospectors who, not surprisingly, paid little heed to the Ute reservation boundaries. Although Ouray, prominent leader of the Southern Utes, counseled peace and acceptance of the white ways, not all Utes agreed with him, particularly up at White River (near present Meeker), where an agency had been established for the Yampa and Grand River bands in 1868. These Utes, under their leaders Douglas, Jack, and Colorow, were less tolerant of white transgressions.[6]

Notwithstanding the relentless advance of white settlers and miners, the real key to the Ute troubles was bound up in the person of agent Nathan Meeker, a sixty-one-year-old religious zealot and social reformer, who was appointed agent at White River in the spring of 1878. Meeker was followed a few weeks later by his wife, Arvilla, and daughter Josephine.[7]

A more unsuitable choice than Nathan Meeker could scarcely be imagined. He arrived on the scene bearing the misguided philosophy that the Utes must change their way of living; they must set aside the ways of the hunter and become instant farmers. His ideas were to bear bitter fruit.[8]

During the summer of 1878, Meeker elected to move the agency downriver a dozen or so miles to a place known as Powell Park. Here, land was more fertile and lent itself to the agricultural pursuits Meeker had in mind. The problem, however, was that the great flat expanse of Powell Park had long been favored by the Utes as a grazing area and racetrack for their ponies, and they did not take kindly to Meeker's seizure of the land for his purposes.[9]

As the summer progressed, tensions rose. Nathan Meeker grew increasingly concerned. Believing that the Utes were out of control, he requested military assistance. In response, an army column under Maj. Thomas T. Thornburg arrived in the area in late September. The army's presence angered the Utes, who attacked Thornburg's column, killing the major and laying siege to his command. Their blood up, the Utes then attacked the agency, killing Meeker and nine employees. Arvilla and Josephine Meeker, together with another woman and two children, were taken captive. Through negotiation, the women were eventually released, but the deaths of Meeker and his employees and the seizure of the women, coupled with the stunning victory over Thornburg's command, brought the Ute question into sharp focus.[10]

Unfortunately for the Utes, while their understandable response to Meeker's behavior undoubtedly provided momentary satisfaction, in the long run it hurt their cause. Coloradans, particularly those on the state's Western Slope, demanded the Utes' punishment and removal. Military units poured into western Colorado. The army, angered over Thornburg's death and defeat, was ready to undertake punitive action; fortunately, cooler heads prevailed. Through the efforts of Interior Secretary Carl Schurz, Charles Francis Adams, former agent at Los Pinos, and Ouray himself, the Ute problem was resolved without need for further military action. Discussions and negotiations continued through the ensuing year and in June 1880, Ute leaders agreed to terms that included relocating the White River Utes to the Unitah Reservation in Utah. Eventually, the Southern Utes would also move. The Ute leaders had further agreed to see that a dozen members of the White River band who had been charged with murder in the killing of Agent Meeker and his employees would be surrendered to white authorities, but this never came to pass.[11]

With the expulsion of the White River Utes, northwestern Colorado eventually became available for settlement by whites, although the Indians' departure did not occur overnight. Some Utes could still be found in the area as late as 1882, because of which the army was directed to maintain a presence in the area for the time being. To this end, a cantonment was built at White River. Col. Wesley Merritt, Fifth Cavalry, who had led the relief column that rescued Thornburg's beleaguered command, returned to Fort D. A. Russell in November, but a

The White River Museum, Meeker, Colorado, was originally the headquarters building for Cantonment White River, where Kelly served as a scout from 1880–1883. *Author photo.*

portion of his command remained at the cantonment through the winter of 1879–1880, to be replaced in July by half a dozen companies of the Sixth Infantry.[12]

Northwestern Colorado was thus still a rather tentative area when Luther Kelly arrived that summer of 1880. Memories of Nathan Meeker and Milk Creek were plenty fresh as he rode past the now blackened and charred ruins of the agency buildings. Despite the grim scene, his immediate reaction appears to have been one of exuberance for the beauty of this new country. At the head of Plateau Creek, near Grand River (now the Colorado River), he found a fine spot for gold, but was not at all interested: "What did I care? Being heart and mind free, I gave myself up to the joy of living and camped in the shadow of aspens in lovely spots where deer and elk were abundant." He obviously was caught up in the excitement of exploring a new country, probably with a zest he hadn't experienced since his sojourn in Yellowstone Park.[13]

From here he drifted on down to the burgeoning new community of Grand Junction, located "on a sagebrush flat, devoid of timber or shrubbery, another tent city, garnished with a multitude of wells with long wooden sweeps for raising water." The country thereabouts

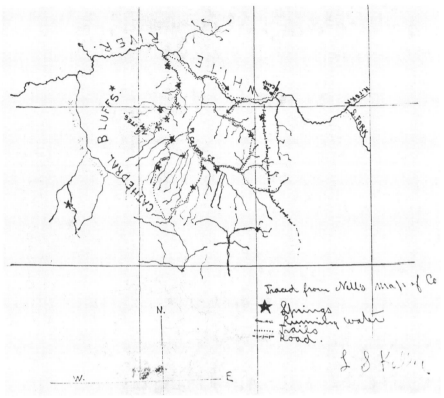

Map of northwestern Colorado as sketched by Luther Kelly. The map accompanied the reports prepared for the adjutant at Cantonment White River.

impressed him with its good soil, favorable climate, and availability of water.[14]

From Grand Junction, Kelly may have explored the country as far south as Cantonment Uncompahgre, near present Montrose, Colorado, before heading back north. Exactly when he arrived at Cantonment White River is not clear, but it was at least as early as the summer of 1881, by which time the original garrison had moved west to Utah, there to build Fort Thornburgh on the Green River, so as to be in a better position to monitor Ute activities on the Unitah Reservation. Replacing them was a detachment of the Fourteenth Infantry under Maj. William Drum.[15]

Kelly's duties as a scout at White River were considerably less demanding than those he had known at Fort Keogh. Here he found himself with plenty of time to hunt and to discover places like Trapper's Lake, which swarmed with trout. Trapper's Lake, as beautiful a spot as any in Colorado—or the West, for that matter—would later be chosen to introduce the concept of a wilderness area by the U.S. Forest Service. In the 1880s the area was rich in game, and he would often bring groups of officers from the cantonment to Trapper's Lake on hunting or fishing expeditions. While here at White River, Kelly also had the opportunity to shake hands with legendary Jim Bridger, "Old Gabe" of mountain man days. Here were two scouts whose careers had spanned the West from the fur trade to the Indian wars.[16]

During the fall of 1882, Kelly was sent to ascertain whether there were any Ute camps remaining in the area and if so, whether this might be a potential source of trouble. Mostly, the Utes had moved on, but a few camps were still to be found. Insofar as he could determine, settlers who had moved into the area were experiencing no problem with those Utes who remained. However, Kelly pointed out, "should the Utes camp on grazing grounds now held by the settlers, grounds for complaint would arise."[17]

Kelly found the Ute people to be "rather moody and silent in disposition." And, as Major Thornburg's command quickly discovered, they were first-rate fighters. After a dozen years of close involvement with the tribes of the North Plains, Kelly's observations here are noteworthy. He had learned something of how to deal with Indians. You were straightforward and truthful, and above all, you didn't waffle. Once he was sent to advise old Colorow that he must move his camp of a dozen or so lodges on Piceance (pronounced Pee-ants) Creek to the Unitah Reservation, as the Utes had agreed to do after the Meeker troubles. There is no record of exactly what was said, but Colorow promised to relocate and it would be reasonable to assume that Kelly's negotiating skills helped the old chief to see the wisdom of compliance. One wonders whether Colorow remembered and tried once again to talk Kelly out of his knife.[18]

On three occasions between December 1882 and March 1883, Kelly was sent out from White River to examine the country between the cantonment and Grand River, and from the latter as far as Grand Junction to determine the feasibility of establishing a wagon route between the cantonment and Grand Junction. Kelly's mission was to report on winter conditions, including the depth of snow and the feasibility of year-round travel, as well as the most suitable route for a permanent road. An examination of the country in December, and then again in February and March, would provide a clear picture of winter conditions.

Kelly's reports not only contain essential information, they stand as models of lucid reporting. Few indeed were those frontiersmen who combined wilderness skills and knowledge of Indians with the kind of literary ability to report on their findings the way Luther Kelly was able to do. Little wonder that he was so highly regarded by Nelson Miles and other officers who had occasion to avail themselves of his services.

The first of Kelly's three reports, written on 27 December 1882, provided an early winter view of the region. In addition, his recommendations for the roadway, especially the bridges, together with the work already done by the early settlers in the area, paved the way for that stretch of the future interstate highway I-70 that currently traverses Colorado from east to west.

Camp on White River
Dec. 27–1882
To the Camp Adjutant- Sir:

In compliance with orders No.192 Extract II dated Camp on White River Dec. 4, 1882, I have to state that a single reconnaissance cannot determine the character of the road from White River to Grand Junction as applied to winter travel, as the greatest snow fall occurs later in the season.

Up to Dec. 19 the ground was bare of snow along the road from this point to Grand Junction, with the exception of about two miles near the divide between White and Grand River, and three miles near the foot of the "Grand Mesa," where the snows lay respectively, 2 and 4 inches deep.

During the winter preceding this, there was no time at which this road was impassable to travel.

The greater portion of the road has a southern or western exposure, and the snow does not remain for any length of time, except on the higher points.

A fairly good road has been ~~built~~ made from the mouth of Rifle creek down Grand River for a distance of ten miles, and over a heavy grade, this work has been carried on by the settlers along Grand River. I have made as careful an examination of the "Hog Back" cañon as the time and season would permit, having been enabled (by doing some work) to traverse the entire canon with our horses and pack animals. I find that it is the most natural way for a road, and the way that it will eventually be built. At the entrance to the canon a bridge will be required about 200 feet in length across one channel of Grand River onto an island, and at the lower end of the island a bridge or ferry back to the north bank of Grand

River, timber for building accessible and at hand. The cañon proper is about ten miles in length, the principal work heavy side grading in loose rock and earth (sandstone) with very little blasting. The advantages of this route are: in shortening the distance to Grand Junction about six miles, avoiding some high ascents and possible snow drifts & reducing the work in bridges. It will require however three or four times as much work to construct the road by this route.

The point of divergence of the two roads would be about five miles above the mouth of Roan Creek. With the exception of about one half mile at the entrance of the canon, the road would follow the right bank of Grand River from the mouth of Rifle Creek to Grand Junction. The soil of Grand Valley is light and dry and is packed solid by the rains in summer. The work in the cañon can be carried on during the winter season.

The cañon is approached from the Grand Junction end by a wagon road which extends up Grand River 18 miles.[19]

Kelly's report of 23 February 1883 further elaborated on midwinter conditions, reporting on snow depths at various locations along the route. Although the winter season of 1882–1883 had been especially severe in terms of snow, he reported that the "road can be traveled by wagons during the entire season."[20]

His final survey of the region took place during the last half of March and paid particular attention to the feasibility of building the two bridges across the river that had been suggested in his December survey. The report also commented on Indian presence in the area, as well as the area's suitability for further development. Departing on 13 March 1883, his route took him along the wagon road

to the mouth of Rifle Creek, thence down the Grand River valley to the "Hog Back" Cañon, and after making some observations at that point, returned by way of Parachute Creek. The road is open to travel along the entire route, the snow having wholly disappeared except on the high points. Grand River at this season is very low. At the point in the "Hog Back" Cañon where it will be necessary to make two crossings of the river, I examined carefully, and do not think there will be any great difficulty or expense in building two bridges at the points described in a previous report, the necessary timber being within two hundred yards. I think the two crossings of the river can be avoided by about one half mile of blasting in soft sandstone.

Work in the cañon can be pursued to better advantage during the season of low water, which occurs from about July 30 to the middle of April.

From the mouth of Rifle Creek, down Grand River to Salt Creek, below Grand Junction, there are but two points where Indian trails lead north to the hunting grounds. These are at Parachute Creek, and Roan Creek, and could not be made available for wagon travel. This is owing to the precipitous nature of the bluffs and canons, which line the north bank of Grand River. And although a constant search has been made by the people near Grand Junction for a way of reaching the divide north, I do not learn that they have been successful in doing so, except by difficult and precipitous game trails, nor do I think it is possible, although I have not examined the country closely enough to determine positively. Since the establishment of this military camp on White River, the Utes have in no case formed a camp east of this position but have confined themselves in most part to the region drained by Douglas and Pice-Ance Creeks [Piceance]. I have found signs of their summer camps on the bluffs, which immediately overlook Grand River, this is a grass and timber region well watered in the early summer. The region drained Douglas and Pice-Ance Creeks can be entered by wagons only on two routes, (from Grand River side) one by the road which connects at mouth of Rifle Creek, the other by the trail up the east fork of Salt creek below Grand Junction, the latter route requiring much work to make it a wagon road.

The region spoken of is easiest entered from the White River side as the country is more rolling. Grand River valley is gradually being settled up, there are many large bottoms favorable for town sites.[21]

In August 1883, Kelly resigned his position as scout. The decision was not a surprising one. As he had pointed out in his final report, settlers were beginning to move into the area and the need for a man with his particular skills was fast disappearing. Besides, the military had decided to abandon the White River Cantonment and although he was encouraged to find another army post where his skills might be put to use, Kelly wished to remain in the region. Since arriving in northwest

Kelly's Colorado homestead cabin was located in this general area. The railroad maintenance shed in the foreground stands on the site of Una, some five miles west of Parachute, Colorado. The Grand (Colorado) River is directly ahead. *Author photo.*

Colorado he had been very favorably impressed with the area's climate and agricultural potential. His wagon route survey of the region introduced him to the country adjacent to the Grand River, which he found to his liking. A thousand feet lower in elevation than the cantonment, its winters would have been a little milder and hence more favorable to agricultural pursuits. In any event, he acquired about sixty acres of land on the north side of Grand River, just west of Parachute, where he planned to do a little farming and run some cattle.[22]

Although the Ute troubles had officially ended, dissatisfaction remained among many of the Indians, prompting concern over future outbreaks. In a July 1884 letter to now General Nelson Miles, Kelly commented on the situation. The letter reveals something of his understanding as to how Indian-white troubles often began. Almost certainly he had Major Thornburgh and the Milk Creek disaster in mind when he referred to the Indian reaction to a military force.

> I do not think that the White River Utes have any grounds for
> dissatisfaction that could not be adjusted by firmness and

tact. The trouble is the settlers often precipitate matters by needless alarm, which places the Indians on the alert and defensive, and as they always regard the approach of a military force as a menace, they usually commence the attack from the advantage of well chosen positions. . . . If the White River Utes should go on the war path I think the headwaters of Evacuation Creek would be their point of retreat.[23]

In the late summer of 1885—probably September—Kelly journeyed east for the third time since the advent of his frontier experience. On this occasion, however, his destination was Detroit, Michigan, to visit an old boyhood friend, John Murray. Of Murray we know little, save that he was originally from the Geneva area and moved to Detroit in 1866, later establishing himself in the advertising business in that city. Despite the gulf of physical distance that had come to separate them, Murray and his old chum "Lute" Kelly had managed to stay in touch over the years.[24]

Whether the visit had another purpose to begin with is not entirely clear. What we do know is that he arrived a single man and left with a wife. The relationship may have been initiated by his friend Murray and perhaps it then flowered through correspondence. In any case, Luther Kelly and Alice May Morrison were married on 23 September 1885. He was 36, she was 29. The ceremony was performed in the Morrison home by the Rev. Dr. W. W. Ramsay. Kelly listed his address as Grand Junction, Colorado, and his occupation as that of farmer.[25]

In retrospect, it seems something of a curious match. Kelly had spent his entire adult life on the frontier, while she, the daughter of a jeweler, had grown to adulthood in an urban environment. Both may have felt a sense of urgency and perhaps seen in each other one last chance to marry before the advancing years found them alone in middle age. It is also possible that Alice—May, as she was known to family and close friends—was captivated by the aura that surrounded Kelly, the romantic Indian fighter and quintessential strong, silent type. May's father, John, had died recently; she would have been in mourning, and Kelly may have provided strength in an hour of emotional need. But there was certainly more depth to the relationship than that; there had to have been for the marriage to last forty-two years, and under some fairly trying circumstances at that. Unfortunately, no diaries or personal correspondence that might have revealed the depth of their feeling for each other have survived, but from what is known, it seems clear that theirs was a relationship about which both cared deeply.

Alice May (Morrison) Kelly. Undated photo, but possibly taken about the time of her marriage to Luther S. Kelly. *George Bille Collection.*

May Morrison must have had a certain inner toughness, and perhaps this was something Luther saw or sensed in her that appealed to him. In any event, she agreed to return to the West with her new husband, an act calling for more than a little courage. In 1885, northwestern Colorado was still very much in a frontier condition and living there meant making a drastic adjustment for a city lady, but adjust she did and in the years that followed accompanied her husband to other remote locales.

Many years later, in a talk prepared for the Women's Improvement Club of Paradise, California, May described the experience of traveling to her new home in the West. And what an adventure it must have been for this city-bred girl, who gazed upon her first Indian in Meeker, Colorado. En route to Colorado, May recalled how she and Luther frequently slept in the open, under starry skies, forded numerous streams, and how she was introduced to her first settler's cabin, a one-room affair for two people, where they accepted lodging for the night. Happily, she was to find her own home somewhat more spacious.

At the time of his departure for Detroit, Kelly made arrangements with a local man to look after the ranch in his absence. May recalled with amusement that when the ranch-sitter spied Kelly and his new bride approaching on horseback, there was a great flurry of activity, including much sweeping and the rapid departure of a friend. Her new home, complete with two rooms and fireplace, provided a welcome contrast to the one-room affairs she had seen along the way. Although nearly half a century later, May was to recall with fondness this first of her marriage homes, one imagines said fondness to have grown in proportion to the passing years, which have a way of glossing over what must have been a hard, demanding life.[26]

If May had a major adjustment to make in adapting to a life beyond the pale of the social amenities she had known, Luther, too, had to deal with a change in the way of life he had known. For the past seventeen years he had lived a solitary existence that was free of worry or responsibility for any other human being, save perhaps an occasional hunting partner. His had been a fluid sort of lifestyle, in which he was as free to come and go as the shifting winds, but now the picture had changed. From here on out, all plans would have to include May, and judging by what we now know of their life together, Kelly did exactly that, although one cannot help but wonder how May felt about the long absences that would touch her life in the years ahead.

It would not be surprising to learn that a man who had lived as he had lived subsequently found marital responsibilities to be more of a burden than he was prepared to shoulder; but as far as we can tell, Kelly never expressed any regret, nor is there any evidence that May ever regretted her choice. At the same time, it must also be pointed out that, periodically, Kelly's restless spirit did intrude on their domestic life. For example, May recalled the years in their Colorado ranch home as a pleasant experience, except for those long lonely hours when Kelly was absent and which we might imagine were often a little frightening for a young woman unaccustomed to living under such conditions. Nevertheless, she persevered and it stands as testimony to her toughness that she did not bail out.[27]

An interesting part of this picture is that in the spring of 1886, legal title of the ranch property, including horses, cattle, and whatever money he had, was transferred to May "for her own use and disposal." This was not done as part of a last will and testament, but as a here-and-now transfer of assets, which suggests that perhaps Kelly, recognizing that his activities often put him in harm's way, thought

A posed shot of Luther S. Kelly taken during his Colorado years, probably between 1880 and 1883. Kelly is standing. The seated figure is thought to be the artist/scout Charles S. Stobie. The figure reclining is unidentified. *Denver Public Library, Western History Collection.*

it best for May to have control of everything. He was taking no chances with her welfare in the event something happened to him.[28]

Of Kelly's absences during these years we know virtually nothing. The period from 1885–1891 is almost totally lacking in any sort of evidence that would provide clues as to his activities. The lonely hours May Kelly refers to may well have been nothing more than extended hunting excursions to provide meat for the table, or to simply explore the country. Until he settled in California during the final years of his life, Kelly never lost the urge to examine new ground.

Another intriguing possibility, however, is that he took on assignments as a hunting and fishing guide. During his tenure at White River Cantonment, he had often taken officers to pristine spots such as Trapper's Lake, so he had developed some experience as a guide. By 1885, the Indian problem had been largely resolved. The West was beginning to fill up, and men like Kelly could put their wilderness skills to good use showing hunters where the game was to be found. The ranch seemed not to be doing especially well and guide services would have fit in nicely, providing an opportunity to enjoy the old ways while at the same time earning needed money. Moreover, he would not have had to confine his guide services to Colorado. He was certainly familiar enough with Montana and Wyoming to have acted as a guide in those areas. And indeed it might well have been on such a junket that he first met Theodore Roosevelt, who later referred to Kelly as one of his "old-time Western friends."[29]

Luther and May were highly regarded citizens of northwestern Colorado. When the first settlers began arriving in the Parachute area, Kelly often provided advice on where to locate a homestead, particularly with a view to winter conditions. In 1942, the Rev. Charles P. Hiller, who had been a minister in the area during the 1880s, recalled the Kellys in a letter to the area's current minister. "He and his wife were lovely folks and I ate many meals at their hospitable home." By the time of his 1942 letter, Hiller had read Kelly's published memoirs and, as exciting as he had found them to be, Hiller thought that to hear Kelly talk of his adventures was "even better than to read what he has written."[30]

Late summer brought news of the death of Kelly's mother, Jeannette Eliza Sage Kelly, who passed away in Germantown, Pennsylvania, at age seventy-four on 30 August 1890. Luther had been only eight when his father died and it had been his mother who had seen him through his boyhood until he joined the army in 1865. Luther has left no record of his maternal feelings, but knowing that he made at least two trips east to see her in the 1870s, we might assume he harbored fond memories of her and undoubtedly experienced a sense of loss upon learning of her death.

Jeannette Kelly had moved from Geneva to Elmira, New York, sometime in the 1870s and from that place eventually to Germantown, where the rest of her children had settled. All had done well, too. William Dunham, three years younger than Luther, was an officer in the Clearfield Bituminous Coal Company, as was the youngest brother, Albert Frederick, who was Luther's junior by eight years. Anna, the only surviving sister, ranked between William and Albert in age.[31]

In 1891 Kelly was appointed Parachute's first justice of the peace and notary public. Nearly two decades later he would hold a similar position in Nevada.[32] He enjoyed the role of arbiter in legal disputes, and being justice of the peace also provided needed income. In an 1891 letter, he described his life to Capt. Frank D. Baldwin, formerly of the Fifth Infantry and with whom he had served in the Fort Keogh days.

As you perhaps know, I am leading the peaceful life which
surrounds farmer hayseed. I am also a justice of the peace
and once in a great while, I have a case and a passage at arms
with the lawyers.... I have a very pretty ranch, bounded on
one side by Grand River, and on the other by the Rio Grand [*sic*]
Junction R.R. which is now a continental thoroughfare.
Nevertheless though I like the life it is not profitable, and if I
could sell out I would like to take up the study of law in some
place where I could have access to courts and libraries.[33]

During his time at Fort Keogh, Luther Kelly developed a great
respect for Nelson Miles's philosophy of dealing with vanquished
Indians. Kelly himself had always counseled firm but fair treatment.
Above all, one avoided sudden movements where Indians were concerned; being too quick with a show of force, for example, often precipitated unnecessary conflict. Kelly had personally witnessed Miles's
treatment of the Nez Perce after their surrender at Bear's Paw
Mountains and regarded it as exactly the right course of action.
Thirteen years later he again had occasion to admire Miles's tactics,
this time at a place called Wounded Knee.[34]

On 15 September 1890 Miles received his promotion to major general and along with that second star, command of the huge Military
Division of the Missouri, with headquarters in Chicago. The Missouri
Division included both the departments of Platte and Dakota, where
Miles had once waged his tough winter campaigns against the Lakota
and accepted the surrender of Joseph and the Nez Perce. His home-
coming, if it can be thought of as such, would shortly prove to be nothing if not eventful.[35]

Barely had Miles assumed the reins of his new command when the
last gasp of Indian resistance erupted in the form of a new religious fervor that spread across the Lakota reservations in South Dakota. The
Ghost Dance movement was inspired by the mystical teaching of a
Paiute shaman named Wovoka, who preached a glorious new life for all
Indians; a nirvana wherein the dead would be reunited with their living brethren, in a world free of suffering...and the white man. Those
Indians who participated in the Ghost Dance would be accorded a brief
view of this heaven-to-come. Although Wovoka preached nonviolence,
the Lakotas, disillusioned by failed treaties and broken promises,
rejected this particular aspect of the new messianic religion. The
shamans among them preached that those who wore ghost shirts
would be impervious to bullets.[36]

On 13 November, the fear of a general Indian uprising such as hadn't been felt in twenty years prompted the authorities to order military action. Miles sent troops into the area with orders to prevent a coalescing of the militant factions, including the arrest of Sitting Bull, whom Miles feared might inspire and unite the discontented as he had in 1876. Ironically, on 15 December, while Indian police attempted to arrest Sitting Bull, a melee ensued in which the Lakota leader and his son were killed, along with several Indian policemen.[37]

In the aftermath of Sitting Bull's murder, militant Indian factions gathered along Wounded Knee Creek. Here, on 29 December 1890, the Indians were surrounded by Custer's old regiment, the Seventh Cavalry. While attempting to disarm the Indians, a scuffle ensued that quickly turned into a nightmare, with 150 Lakotas killed and another 50 wounded. The Seventh Cavalry suffered 64 casualties.[38]

In the wake of a disaster that, by some standards, rivaled Sand Creek, Miles moved quickly to avoid further tragedy. At a place called Drexel Church, some four miles from Pine Ridge, angry warriors torched the mission church. Fortunately, a second bloodbath was averted by Miles, who defused an explosive situation through negotiation and a judicious demonstration of military presence.[39]

Meanwhile, back in Colorado, Kelly, who had naturally followed the events surrounding Wounded Knee with great interest, commented on Miles's wisdom in dealing with Indians to Frank Baldwin in his July 1891 letter.

> I presume last winter's campaign against the Indians revived
> in some measure the memory of the Yellowstone operations,
> though of course, superior conditions nowadays serve to
> bring hostilities to a speedy close. I could read between the
> lines however, in the newspaper accounts, and had a pretty
> accurate idea of the whole proceedings, I have never ceased
> to admire the system inaugurated by Gen. Miles in his treat-
> ment of surrendered Indians, and the confidence and pros-
> perity which such treatment engendered.[40]

By the end of the decade, the Colorado experience was drawing to a close. The ranch had not been a financial success and Kelly had begun to consider other possibilities. In this, he was perhaps encouraged by May, who might well have had her fill of frontier ranch life with its lack of amenities. Mostly, however, it would appear to have been the constant press for money that prompted a change. In the old days on the Upper Missouri, money wasn't that crucial to him; game was plentiful and peltries provided cash or served as a medium of exchange and a young man on his own hook needed little else. But times had changed and the lifestyle that had once fit him so perfectly no longer met his needs.

In a dozen years, the West itself had changed dramatically. No longer was it possible to live the idyllic sort of life that Kelly had once experienced, because he, no less than the West, had also changed. The brash nineteen-year-old lad who had once carried dispatches from Fort Buford to Fort Stevenson was now a wiser, more mature man of forty-two. His own needs were different now and there was a second person to provide for as well.

Passage of the Indian Depredation Act of 1891 held promise of a little financial relief. Kelly hoped to take advantage of the act to be reimbursed for his services as mail carrier at Fort Buford back in 1869. At the time he had been promised full pay—$150—for carrying dispatches to Fort Stevenson, but he had received only half that amount and was now trying to recoup the balance of $75. The Bureau of Claims, however, thought it too paltry a sum for him to bother with, but obviously he regarded it otherwise, which says something about his financial position.[41]

Within four months after writing to Frank Baldwin, the Kellys had moved to Chicago, where Luther took a position as general services clerk at army headquarters, Department of the Missouri.[42] Whether he had asked Miles and/or Baldwin to see what sort of position might be available for a man with his particular skills, or whether they offered to be of service in this regard, is not clear. Possibly, Miles extended an invitation to Kelly and used his influence to help his former scout find a position.[43]

For the next six years, Kelly's lifestyle would be far removed from the rough frontier existence he had known for the past quarter-century. Indeed, his life from here on would reflect his continuing effort to find a niche within the affluent upper middle class. From time to time this proclivity for culture and the finer things of life would take a back seat to the yen for adventure and wild places that would always be a part of who he was.

Chapter Nine

THE WAR DEPARTMENT,
1891–1898

**My army friends found a place for me in the
War Department and I returned once more to the
peaceful life on which while still a mere boy
I had turned my back.[1]**

By late fall 1891, the Kellys were settled in at 634 Monroe Street in downtown Chicago. The headquarters of the Military Division of the Missouri, where Luther began his War Department clerical career, was located on the corner of Washington and LaSalle Streets near the present County Building, perhaps a mile to the east of his home and certainly within walking distance of it.[2]

If Kelly had any difficulty adapting to city life, he left no evidence of such. Indeed, he appears to have adjusted quite nicely. The following year, 1892, found him a member of the George H. Thomas Post, No. 5, Grand Army of the Republic. We don't know about May's educational history, but considering her middle-class background, it was, like Luther's, probably above average. Given Luther's fondness for books and literature, and perhaps hers as well, they both likely

Luther S. Kelly during his
government years. Photo
taken in Chicago between
1891 and 1896.
Denver Public Library,
Western History Collection.

found outlets for their interests that had not been available to either
for some time.

Although as the Missouri Division commander, Gen. Nelson Miles
would have operated on a different plane than Kelly, both officially as
well as socially, the two men undoubtedly found moments in which to
reminisce about the old days and to generally discuss issues that were
of interest to both men. Miles, for example, was also a member of the
George H. Thomas Post, so he and Kelly would have had an opportunity to visit at post meetings.[3]

Although the nation was in the throes of a recession, the Chicago
economy was thriving. Life in 1890s Chicago must have seemed exciting to a pair fresh from the frontier of western Colorado. This was the
"Gay Nineties." Movies were being introduced in New York. People were
reading Oscar Wilde, Rudyard Kipling, Thomas Hardy, and George
Bernard Shaw. Idaho and Wyoming were added to the Union, and
Grover Cleveland was elected president for the second time. On the
other hand, Kelly probably lamented the passing of James Russell

Lowell, Herman Melville, and especially Robert Louis Stevenson, whose work he particularly admired.

The Columbian World's Exposition, which opened in May 1893, would surely have attracted the Kellys. An outgrowth of the 1876 Centennial Exposition held in Philadelphia, the Columbian Exposition was created to honor the 400th anniversary of Columbus sailing to the New World. A stunning event, the Exposition attracted more than 27 million people during the course of its six-month run. Visitors could see such varied attractions as Little Egypt, the Eiffel Tower, a Lapland Village, and South Sea Islanders. "One of my pleasant recollections," Kelly recalled, "was to wander along the midway with its myrid [sic] lights and noisy music." On one occasion, he met a cousin, who had in tow his Samoan wife, together with a number of other Samoans, who performed their picturesque dances and songs. And on still another occasion, he had the opportunity to meet the noted African explorer Paul Du Chaillu, who brought back the first gorillas ever seen in America.[4]

One of the featured attractions of the Columbian Exposition was William F. "Buffalo Bill" Cody's Wild West Show, the presence of which allowed Kelly an opportunity to renew his friendship with the famous scout turned showman. At one of their meetings, Cody introduced him to Gen. Charles King, who had served with Cody in the Fifth Cavalry and whose novels depicted army life in the nineteenth century.[5]

We don't know exactly when Kelly and Cody first met, but it almost certainly was in August 1876 when the forces of Crook and Terry united in their pursuit of the Indian coalition that had wiped out Custer and his immediate command at the Little Bighorn. In recalling their meeting at the Columbian Exposition, Kelly remembered Cody as still being in his prime and "whether afoot or on horseback cut a graceful figure for strength and self possession, especially when at the head of his rough riders of the World he burst into the ring stopping instantly with hat in hand and bowing said: 'Ladies and gentlemen, you see before you the rough riders of the world!'" Kelly contrasted Cody's stylish grace with that of a band of buffalo being driven around the arena. Kelly thought they seemed "mistreated by civilization and tho in the throes of slavery had as yet, poor things, to resist commerce with comb and brush."[6]

Another twenty years would pass before the two old scouts would again meet. Sometime soon after the Kellys retired to Paradise, California, Kelly chanced to be staying at a hotel in the Sacramento Valley where he learned that Cody, who was then performing for the

Sells Bros. Circus, was due to arrive in town within a few days. Kelly's business apparently kept him in town long enough for a get-together with Cody and the two chatted for an hour. Kelly noted that Cody's long hair had thinned and whitened noticeably in the twenty years that had passed since their Chicago meeting. That evening, Cody brought a rig around to Kelly's hotel, intending for the duo to take a tour around the city, but Kelly had already returned to Paradise. The two scouts would not meet again. In Luther Kelly's estimation, Buffalo Bill Cody was the "premier scout and plainsman of his time."[7]

Chicago in the 1890s was also the scene of the nasty Pullman strike, during which railroad workers rioted against management. Workmen, gathering in front of the Pullman Building, obstructed traffic and were being forced back by police armed with clubs. Watching the goings-on from one of the upper windows of the Pullman Building, Kelly found his mind wandering beyond the trouble and turmoil below to the peaceful vastness of Lake Michigan and from there to his home town of Geneva, "nestling at the foot of one of the slender lakes of the Empire State, where I had 'my being,' when, like a gasping catfish, I entered this world. And I wished I were back there again, if only for a day."[8]

To deal with the crisis, President Grover Cleveland ordered federal troops to assist U.S. marshals in maintaining peace. Kelly was on duty the night that President Cleveland's directive arrived. As the duty clerk it was his responsibility to see that General Miles received the order. Miles was dining with his family that evening at the Auditorium Hotel. "When I entered the dining room," Kelly recalled, "alight with electric lamps of that period, ever new to me and with a warmer color than the present white light, I quickly spied General Miles at his table and gave him the papers which he received with a smile."[9] Miles was opposed to using the army in such situations, but was overruled by the President and General of the Army John Schofield. The confrontation, which included mob violence, lasted through the summer of 1894.[10]

Kelly's tenure as a general service clerk, employed by the army, lasted just under three years. The Army Appropriation Act of 5 August 1894 repealed a provision in the law that allowed for the army to hire clerical personnel directly, just as any private sector business would do now, requiring, instead, that such clerks be hired under the civil service system. However, on the same day he was discharged from his position with Headquarters, Division of the Missouri— 6 August—he was hired as a civil service clerk in the Bureau of Records and Pensions.[11]

In November 1894, Nelson Miles, continuing his ascent up the army's hierarchical ladder, was appointed to command the prestigious Department of the East, with headquarters on Governor's Island, New York.[12]

Soon after Miles moved to New York, Kelly requested and received a transfer to Governor's Island as well, where he was employed as a clerk with the Records and Pension Bureau at an annual salary of $1,000. Whether Kelly's request for a transfer was based entirely on his wish to serve close to Miles is not entirely clear. However, Luther—and perhaps May as well—was apparently not all that enamored of Chicago's weather. "I found the salt air of the port of New York more congenial than the chill fog of the great city by the lakes."[13]

While Luther was stationed on Governor's Island, he and May occupied a small, crowded apartment in Brooklyn, where old photographer friend L. A. Huffman paid them a visit. Huffman had been one of the early post photographers at Fort Keogh and later in Miles City. In those long-ago days, Kelly liked to relax in Huffman's studio, sometimes taking a nap on a pile of buffalo robes, or reading a book. Kelly reminisced about those times in a letter to Huffman fifteen years later. "I remember your visit to our rooms in Brooklyn, and that our cramped quarters did not allow of prolonging your visit as we could have wished. There have been a good many changes in the world since that time. Many whom we knew have passed away."[14]

During the summer of 1897, an undisclosed illness forced May to have surgery. Then, soon after affecting a recovery, she learned that her brother had also been taken ill and this, combined with the death of their mother, required her temporary presence in Detroit.[15]

Kelly was comfortable in New York, perhaps more so than in Chicago, though he left no record contrasting the two experiences. But the office hours on Governor's Island were relaxed and easy, allowing Kelly ample time to seek out new acquaintances. The editor of *Recreation*, a publication for which he would later write, introduced him to the Campfire Club, an organization composed of men who had either "killed or painted big game," men such as Dan Beard, of Boy Scout fame, and the naturalist writer Ernest Thompson Seton. On one occasion, at the Madison Square Garden Sportsman's Show, he renewed his friendship with George Bird Grinnell, now owner and editor of *Forest & Stream*. Grinnell invited Kelly to his home on the Hudson River. By this time, Kelly had tried his hand at writing a few things. He brought along a scrapbook and watched as Grinnell "read one of his yarns, smoking his pipe furiously the while."[16]

One day, while strolling down Broadway, Kelly met another old acquaintance in the person of Thomas Elwood "Uncle Billy" Hofer, a Yellowstone Park guide, who had just arrived in town from the park. Hofer suggested they pay a visit to Theodore Roosevelt, who was then New York City Police Commissioner. Roosevelt was delighted to see both men, and after a nice visit about the West, Roosevelt invited them to join him for lunch. Accordingly, at noon, the trio rendezvoused outside Roosevelt's office and walked down to Five Points to "Beefsteak John's." Here, Kelly recalled, "we found a considerable company at the different tables, and I judged by the greetings and nods exchanged, that Mr. Roosevelt was not an infrequent visitor at this excellent eating house."

On another occasion, Kelly toured the Sportsman's Show with Roosevelt, who had his children in tow, and a pleasant afternoon was enjoyed by all. Kelly was impressed by Roosevelt's devotion in explaining the many details of various objects that aroused the curiosity of his children. Kelly liked the ebullient Roosevelt, who shared many of his own ideas regarding hunting, conservation, and the treatment of Indians. He was, Kelly thought, an "impulsive noble gentleman."[17]

Meantime, with the retirement of Gen. John M. Schofield in October 1895, Miles finally reached the apex of his career when he was named commanding general of the army. The promotion took him to Washington, D.C., and it is interesting to note that within two years Kelly had relocated there as well. On the face of it, the Kelly–Miles relationship seems odd and difficult to explain. The two personalities could not have been more dissimilar. Miles, the senior by ten years, was vain, ambitious to a fault, and often contentious with his superiors. Kelly, on the other hand, was the soul of self-effacement; quiet and reserved, yet a good conversationalist when in the company of the right partner, but definitely not the garrulous sort. Indeed, some of the soldiers around Fort Keogh dubbed him "Kelly the Silent" and "Kelly the Sphinx." This tendency to say little was, apparently, not a contrived trait. He was, by nature, simply a shy man.[18]

It would be an exaggeration to say that Luther Kelly and Nelson Miles were the closest of friends, but the two men had enjoyed a certain camaraderie during their campaigning days and that bond remained long after their frontier experience had passed. Once the Fort Keogh days had ended, contact between the two men was infrequent, sometimes amounting to nothing more than a letter, but the bond survived. To an extent, what they had gone through during those campaigns against the Sioux and Nez Perce provides a partial explanation.

After all, the shared experiences of combat and perilous times do indeed forge a special kind of relationship, but there was something deeper than that at work here.

A closer comparison of their individual personas suggests that both men had more in common than would at first meet the eye. Each had reached about the same level of education and shared a thirst for knowledge. Each, in his own way, was self-made. Each was fueled by confidence in his own ability. Each man stepped to the sound of his own drummer, but did so to a distinctly different cadence. If Luther Kelly and Nelson Miles shared certain traits, they remained diametrically different personalities.

Whether Miles was unable to pursue a higher education due to family circumstances is not entirely clear. Neither is it clear why he did not seek an appointment to the United States Military Academy, since he obviously had a taste for the soldier's life. It may be that he simply sought to find success in his own way. But whatever the reason or reasons that kept Miles out of a college classroom, it evidently had nothing to do with his desire to learn.[19] While working as a crockery store clerk, he attended night school and read voraciously. He was, thus, a self-made man in all respects: Civil War hero; Medal of Honor winner; brevet major general by age twenty-seven, and commanding general of the army by age fifty-nine. Yet notwithstanding his distinguished military career, Nelson Miles apparently came to regret not having pursued a formal education and remained self-conscious about it for the remainder of his life.[20]

It is not particularly surprising that Miles should have felt this way. Many if not most of the officers with whom he served had attended college or were West Point graduates, and Miles would understandably have been sensitive about not having had this experience. The whole idea was not so much about learning as it was about having experienced this rite of passage. When others talked of their college days, there was nothing for Miles to contribute. He did not belong to that fraternity and came to regret not being a member.

As he grew older, Kelly, too, may well have come to regret that he had not continued his own formal schooling. Like Miles, he was not a member of the college fraternity, which was unfortunate because he had the soul of a scholar, albeit blended with the instincts of a frontiersman—a curious mix indeed. He was drawn to learned people and enjoyed stimulating conversation. It was said, for example, that he was mightily impressed with Capt. Eli Huggins of the Second Cavalry, who reportedly was able to "read several foreign languages."[21]

Although Kelly was widely read and well informed, he was not really prepared to fill any role beyond the frontier existence he had known all of his adult life. Whereas Nelson Miles had learned about soldiering on the battlefields of the Civil War, Luther Kelly's wilderness skills had, by the 1890s, become largely useless. While those skills were in demand, he felt comfortable and secure, but as the frontier world he had known gradually diminished, Kelly began to feel that he had become something of an anachronism. It is difficult to pinpoint exactly when this feeling began to take hold, but it was probably during the latter part of his Colorado sojourn, and in any case would have been firmly in place by the time he and May moved to Chicago.

Perhaps the glue that cemented the Kelly–Miles relationship, then, was this sense of self-consciousness they both felt. While they were campaigning together, the two men talked freely and, we might imagine, discussed a wide range of topics and were comfortable in each other's company. In Nelson Miles, Luther Kelly found a man who shared his own intellectual curiosity and Miles found the same to be true of Kelly. Back then, both Kelly and Miles had been robust physical specimens in the prime of their manhood. Now, in their middle years, those days surely beckoned from a bourn beyond reach, save in memory.[22]

As we have seen, Kelly had great respect for Miles's firm but fair treatment of Indians, and undoubtedly for his skill as a military commander. How he felt about Miles's arrogance and vanity, especially his posturing for advancement, is not known. If privately he deplored such behavior, he left no record of such.[23]

Chapter Ten

ALASKA:
The Glenn Expedition, February–October, 1898

The Lapps were picturesque looking fellows being clad in reindeer skins made into shirts and trousers, their headgear consisting of stuffed pillows of the same material and made to withstand the attack of the deer that have a fashion of striking with the front hoofs.[1]

In 1898, Luther Kelly prepared to embark on a series of new adventures that, in many respects, would prove to be the most interesting and challenging of his rather remarkable life. Alaska (twice), the Philippines, and the American Southwest, were yet to provide nearly two decades filled with the kind of experiences that most men only read about. Although he had been living a sedentary existence for some five years and would turn fifty-one in July, an age when most men begin to think of tapering off a bit, Kelly seems to have welcomed a fresh opportunity to once more pit himself against tough, often dangerous physical challenges. Indeed, if anything, it seems more than a little surprising that for nearly seven years he had been able to remain apart from the active, vigorous sort of existence that had so characterized his life before the move to Chicago.

Alaska called first. Although the territory was not unknown to Americans, it had remained largely ignored during the two decades since its purchase from Russia in 1867. Most Americans perceived Alaska as a cold, inhospitable sort of place that drew but few intrepid souls to its bosom. The picture changed dramatically, however, when the discovery of gold along the Klondike River, near Dawson in British-controlled Yukon Territory in 1896, catapulted Alaska to the forefront of public attention and imagination. Soon the Klondike was very nearly a household name. Like earlier strikes in the lower forty-eight states, the Klondike quickly became a magnet for prospectors, opportunists, and riffraff. Where earlier Congress had been disinclined to fund exploration of a largely empty region, it now found itself faced with controlling the sudden influx of prospectors and others drawn to this far-off northern wilderness.[2]

When Gen. Nelson Miles assumed command of the Department of the Columbia in 1881, he interpreted his sphere of command as including the territory of Alaska and regarded it as his responsibility to learn something of the region. Unfortunately, he received little support for exploration either from the army or from Congress, which was opposed to spending money to explore such a sparsely populated region. So Miles did what any resourceful commander would do: he improvised. During the 1880s he sent three small parties up to take a look at the interior of Alaska: Lt. Frederick Schwatka, Eighth Cavalry, in 1881; Capt. William R. Abercrombie, Second Infantry, in 1884; and Lt. Henry T. Allen, Second Cavalry, the following year. Despite their small size, these parties did provide a base of information that would prove useful to later groups.[3]

With no authority to restrain the frenzied miners who flocked to the new gold camps, it was soon a situation that was out of hand. In the Yukon, the Royal Canadian Mounted Police did an admirable job of maintaining order, but in U.S. territory no such force existed. Accordingly, in August 1897 Capt. Patrick Henry Ray and Lt. Wilds Preston Richardson, both of the Eighth Infantry, were ordered to Alaska to provide a firsthand assessment of the situation.[4]

Their subsequent report to the War Department substantiated rumors of lawlessness and disorder in the new gold country. As well, there were reports of starving and destitute miners. Ray's report emphasized the need for law and order, exploration, mapping, and roads, as well as relief for the starving miners. Ray also recommended construction of an overland route from either Cook Inlet or Prince William Sound to the mouth of the Tanana River, so as to avoid reliance on a British railroad to access the Yukon Territory.[5]

At the urging of a Presbyterian missionary, Dr. Sheldon Jackson, who had spent considerable time in Alaska, the War Department agreed to mount an expedition to relieve the destitute miners, using reindeer as a means of transportation. Accordingly, Jackson was authorized to journey to Scandinavia, there to purchase a herd of reindeer, together with all necessary equipage and a party of Lapp herders to care for the animals.[6] But even as Dr. Jackson and his reindeer were en route to New York, new reports from the gold fields suggested that perhaps the destitute miners were not quite as bad off as was originally feared, in view of which the relief expedition was cancelled. However, owing to Captain Ray's report, recommending a scientific survey of the Alaskan interior, the War Department decided to send three military expeditions into Alaska, using some of the reindeer, intended for the now-abandoned relief mission, to haul supplies and equipment.[7]

On 5 March 1898, the War Department cut orders authorizing three Alaskan exploring expeditions. Number One, commanded by Capt. Bogardus Eldridge, Fourteenth Infantry, was directed to map a route from the Yukon to the Tanana River via Forty-mile Creek. Expedition number two, under Capt. William Ralph Abercrombie, was to explore the Copper River Valley north from Valdez. The third expedition was headed up by Capt. Edwin Forbes Glenn, Twenty-fifth Infantry, who was charged with the mission of exploring the region from Prince William Sound to the Susitna and Copper Rivers to Cook Inlet, then north to the Tanana River.[8]

On Saturday, 19 February 1898, four days after the destruction of the battleship *Maine* in Havana harbor, General Miles sent for Kelly, who had only been employed in the Bureau of Records and Pensions in Washington since early that month. When he arrived at Miles's office, the general informed him that he [Kelly] had been transferred to his department as the first step in assigning him to one of the three Alaskan expeditions then being formed. After studying some maps of the Cook Inlet area, Miles and Kelly walked over to the offices of the Secretary of War, where they were ushered in to see the assistant secretary, George D. Meiklejohn. Kelly recalled the moment quite clearly.

> I walked through a number of offices each resplendent in rich furnishings and portraits of eminent men. Arrived at the red

curtain I entered and the Assistant Secretary of War greeted
me in kind manner saying 'there is no reason why you should
not join one of the exploring parties soon to be on the way to
Alaska [*sic*] as your experiences and services will be of value
and I will make necessary arrangements to that end.'

The following day, Sunday, Kelly again met with Miles, this time at the
latter's home, where a reception was in progress. Adjourning to the
library, the general presented Kelly with a pair of rifles to take to Alaska,
a .32-calibre Ballard and a Sharps.[9]

Shortly thereafter, May arrived from Germantown, Pennsylvania,
where she had been staying with Kelly's brother William and his family. Miles had earlier directed Kelly to report to Lt. Daniel Bradford
Devore, Twenty-third Infantry, who had been assigned to work with
Dr. Jackson in procuring the reindeer, then en route to New York; but
while those orders were being processed, Luther and May had a few
days together. Since leaving Colorado they had not been apart for any
length of time. Undoubtedly, May had enjoyed their time together in
Chicago and New York and we may reasonably assume she was not all
that happy about facing the prospect of being separated from her husband for what promised to be an extended period.[10]

May had apparently taken up residence in Germantown when
Luther was transferred from Governor's Island to Washington on
3 February, but it was undoubtedly intended as a temporary arrangement until Luther located a permanent D.C. residence. Germantown
was a logical choice, having become the Kelly family home. Both
William and Albert were here with their families, along with their mother, Jeannette, until her death in 1890. Indeed, the Germantown address
(120 Cliveden Avenue), became Luther's more or less official residence
beginning with his assignment to the Glenn Expedition in 1898 and
continued as such until his return from the Philippines in 1904. As president of the Clearfield Bituminous Coal Corporation, William D. Kelly
was in comfortable circumstances and certainly able to provide living
quarters for his sister-in-law.[11]

The orders came through on Wednesday, 23 February, at which time
May returned to Germantown. Which one of the three expeditions Kelly
was to be assigned to was yet to be determined, but in the interim he
was assigned to the reindeer relief expedition. Accordingly, in company with two other civilians appointed by Secretary Meiklejohn, Kelly
departed for New York. At Governor's Island, they boarded a
Quartermaster Department boat and steamed over to the New Jersey

side to await the arrival of the ship bearing Dr. Jackson, Lieutenant Devore, and the reindeer party. Nearby sat the waiting cars of the Pennsylvania Railroad, with whom prior arrangements had been made to transport the reindeer and their handlers to Seattle.

If Kelly and his companions expected a brief wait, they were destined for disappointment and wound up cooling their heels for four days. Finally, on 27 February, the steamer *Manitoba* appeared on the horizon and docked shortly, bearing a herd of 538 castrated male reindeer, together with 418 sleds, 411 sets of harnesses, and a large supply of reindeer moss, the animals' principal diet. Accompanying the reindeer were some 113 Lapp herders and a Norwegian overseer, Mr. Kjellman, and a few assistants. Kelly found these Laplanders a colorful and interesting group. They were, he recalled, "picturesque looking fellows being clad in reindeer skins made into shirts and trousers, their headgear consisting of stuffed pillows of the same material and made to withstand the attack of the deer that have a fashion of striking with the front hoofs."[12]

The Laplanders may have been colorful to view, but up close they apparently emitted a strong, unwashed odor. Lt. Joseph Castner, Fourth Infantry, a member of Glenn's party, later recalled the stench that greeted him after locating the Lapp herders near Haines Mission, Alaska.

> On a nearer approach to these blonde people of the fjords and glaciers, we detected odors that did not come from Araby the blest, nor the Vale of Cashmere. A short experience with these people caused us to arrive at the conclusion that they must be as frightened about the external use of water as a Kentucky Colonel is reported to be over its introduction internally.[13]

The reindeer were promptly unloaded and transferred, in groups of four or five, to the waiting cars of the Pennsylvania Railroad. The cross-country rail journey lasted eight days, bringing the party into Seattle on 7 March. En route, the Lapps climbed atop the stock cars and fed the reindeer by dropping bundles of moss down to the animals. Saturated with moisture as it was, the moss provided the reindeer with sufficient water. While in Seattle, the reindeer were kept in a park on the outskirts of the city, where their presence made them something of a local attraction.[14]

On 16 March, the reindeer and their Lapp handlers sailed from Seattle on the steamship *Seminole*, reaching Haines Mission on the twenty-ninth. Kelly, meanwhile, headed down to Vancouver Barracks, just outside Portland. After reporting in to headquarters, he took a room at a small hotel near the post. Here he met Lieutenants Joseph Castner, Fourth Infantry, and Percival Lowe, Eighteenth Infantry, both of whom were awaiting assignment to one of the three exploring parties then be organized. Both officers expected to be named to the Glenn party and believed Kelly would join them.

In speculating about his future assignment, Kelly thought all three expeditions looked interesting and promised much adventure, making it a difficult choice to hope for one over the other. Shortly, however, it became a moot point when Captain Glenn arrived at Vancouver Barracks and selected Kelly to be a member of his party, along with Lieutenant Castner, while Lieutenant Lowe was assigned to the Abercrombie expedition. With the assignments set, the men now returned to Seattle in preparation for their journey to Alaska.[15]

While still at Vancouver Barracks Kelly wrote to his old friend, George Bird Grinnell, whom he knew would be most interested in the reindeer experiment as indeed he was. "It is interesting that they pack on the reindeer," Grinnell responded, "and I should like to know, if you have time to make a memorandum of it, how the packs are put on, that is, what sort of saddles they use and how lashes are put on and tied."[16]

Three weeks later, Grinnell wrote again, in answer to Kelly's letter of the eleventh, commenting on how the war with Spain had captured everyone's attention. Suddenly, the nation was interested in Cuba, not Alaska. Grinnell himself had been against war, but now that it was here he was thinking of what he might contribute to the effort.

> The newspapers are full of talk about what we are going to do and what the Spaniards are going to do and there is no room in their columns for any other subject. I do not imagine that there will be any important landing of troops in Cuba before autumn, and it is very uncertain how matters will turn out.
>
> I have been bitterly opposed to the war, but now that it has come we must accept it and simply say the country right or wrong. I had a notion of getting up a regiment of southern Indians for scout and outpost work, but inquiry at Washington seems to show that this would require special authority by Congress, and as a large part of the population of the United States seem to want to be generals and colonels, and as I could only go to the war at the cost of great personal inconvenience, I shall probably remain at home.[17]

In that spring of 1898, Seattle was boiling over with excitement and gold fever.

> Hundreds if not thousands of young men thronged the city of Seattle [Kelly recalled] waiting for the first boats to carry them to Alaska. Camps were formed along the waterfront and in different parts of the city. Near the docks I noted one camp in particular where some ingenious devices for mining and separating gold and other precious metals were exhibited.
>
> Clothiers and other outfitters did a rushing business and tailors worked night and day fitting and putting together garments for the would be miners. I myself invested in a pair of trousers of fabricated leather which I found very comfortable and serviceable on the long hike from the head of the Knick-arm of Cook inlet to within a day's march of the Tanana river and back.[18]

Before boarding ship, Kelly had agreed to an interview with a reporter from the *Seattle Times-Intelligencer*, but the frantic last-minute rush to finish up with details of freight and baggage compelled him to forego the meeting. He regretted missing the appointment, but there was nothing to be done about it. At 10 PM on 7 April, the *Valencia* got underway, steaming up the Inside Passage. Kelly and Lieutenant Castner shared a small cabin with someone known only as "young Robe." The scenery through the Passage was fine, Kelly recalled, "the dark water set off by the green hills on either side with high mountains in the background." A number of California miners were aboard, along with a number of tenderfeet. The odd appearing characters provided Kelly with a source of some amusement.[19]

If steaming through the Passage that first night was pleasant, they awoke to a wet day on the morning of the eighth and as the *Valencia* moved into open water, it encountered heavy swells. Kelly's party lined up on the forward deck and there "sucked lemons in order to stave off that set look of determination that agitates the frame when the sea comes up and the ship goes down." Although some were seasick, Kelly evidently was not bothered.[20]

On 12 April, a dismal foggy day punctuated by a sporadic cold rain, the ship moved into the Lynn Canal and anchored off Haines Mission, featuring a row of weather-beaten frame houses—holdovers from the Russian era—contrasting with some of more modern vintage. Behind them, the heavy, fir-clad hills swept upward. As soon as the *Valencia* had anchored, Captain Glenn and Kelly went ashore and received a distressing report about the reindeer.

The experiment had not panned out well. From the Norwegian interpreter, Mr. Kjellman, and Captain Eldridge, leader of Expedition Number One, which had reached Haines ahead of his own party, Glenn learned that thirty-six of the reindeer had already perished and that the remainder of the herd was in poor condition. The problem was that the supply of reindeer moss that had been brought over with the herd from Lapland had evidently been exhausted and was apparently not available in or around Haines Mission. The moss was the natural diet of the reindeer; without it, the animals were forced to subsist on alfalfa grass and did not fare well. Indeed, Lieutenant Castner described these "'mules of the northland' to be in a deplorable state, from want of their principal food, reindeer moss. Many had died and those left were scarcely able to pack themselves, much less be packed."[21]

The reindeers' suitability for further service was questionable at best. Nevertheless, with the cancellation of the relief expedition, some 100 of the animals were tabbed for service with Expeditions Two and Three. A portion of the surviving herd was subsequently turned over to the Department of the Interior for use by the U.S. Geological Survey. The War Department had paid $65,893 for the reindeer herd, to which was added $10,418 to transport the animals to Alaska, in all, a total of approximately $76,312, or $141 per animal, a rather stiff price for an experiment that yielded little if anything in the way of positive results.[22]

With the reindeer seemingly unsuited for further service, Glenn, accompanied by Captains Abercrombie and Eldridge, steamed up the Lynn Canal to the Fourteenth Infantry camp at Dyea, where Glenn had learned that a mule pack train might be available, and if so, this promised a better alternative to hauling supplies than did the reindeer. However, the colonel in command of the camp advised them that he had been ordered to return the pack animals to Seattle, probably because it was expected the animals would soon be needed in Cuba, as war with Spain appeared imminent. So, after taking on board several enlisted men and three officers that had been assigned to the various expeditions, the trio returned to Haines sans pack animals.[23]

Before departing Haines, Glenn—who was in overall charge of Expeditions Two and Three until they reached the jump-off point for each expedition—had left orders for some of the reindeer to be made available in the event pack mules could not be obtained at Dyea. However, the handlers were unsuccessful in rounding up the animals and as a consequence, Glenn, undoubtedly exasperated, elected to get underway with their mission anyway, requesting that pack mules be sent on the next steamer.

Accordingly, on 16 April, Expeditions Two and Three boarded the *Valencia* and steamed through Icy Straits and Cross Sound to the Gulf of Alaska. The crossing was rough and all hands suffered through an eighteen-hour bout of seasickness, until calm waters were reached at Nuchek. On the morning of the eighteenth, they reached Orca and that evening anchored at Swanport, across the inlet from what is now Valdez, but was then known as Copper City.[24]

At this point, the supplies and equipment for Abercrombie's Expedition Number Two were off-loaded onto flat-bottomed, stern-wheeled vessels, known as lighters, which carried the supplies in close to shore before running aground when the tide moved out. Glenn, meanwhile, directed that the supplies for his expedition be transferred to the steamer *Salmo* and sent on ahead to Portage Bay. And the following morning, a detachment of fourteen men under Lieutenant Castner was directed to proceed to Portage Bay, select a campsite and unload the supplies. Glenn and the rest of his party completed the off-loading of Abercrombie's supplies by the twenty-first, after which they sailed to join Castner's detachment, leaving Abercrombie's expedition to proceed on its own particular mission.[25]

In addition to Glenn, Expedition Number Three consisted of First Lt. Henry G. Learnard [Learned], Twenty-fifth Infantry; Second Lt. Joseph C. Castner, Fourth Infantry; First Lt. John S. Kulp, assistant surgeon; Acting Hospital Steward George Howe; two Hospital Corps privates; nineteen enlisted men of the Fourteenth Infantry; and geologist Walter Curran Mendenhall, on assignment to the army from the U.S. Geological Survey. Kelly was carried on the expedition's roster as guide and interpreter.[26]

Meanwhile, unbeknownst to them, some 5,000 miles to the east, President William McKinley asked the U.S. Congress to declare war against Spain on 23 April. Congress readily complied with the President's request, passing the resolution of war on the twenty-fifth but making it retroactive to the twenty-first.[27]

The long-anticipated war with Spain caught no one by surprise. As a consequence of that conflict, Captain Eldridge's Expedition Number One was no longer deemed a high enough priority to pursue and was cancelled, its members sent east for war service. When word of the war reached Glenn and Abercrombie, some in those two expeditions expected—indeed wanted—to rejoin their regiments in the fight against Spain. The Glenn–Abercrombie parties, however, remained intact; their missions would continue as planned.[28]

Luther Kelly was opposed to war with Spain for two reasons: first, he believed the United States to be unprepared for war with anyone, and second, he saw no just cause for military action. The war, he believed, had come about because President McKinley had succumbed to public pressure. There was, however, another side of this coin, insofar as Kelly was concerned. Regardless of whether he thought the war justified, it did offer him a window of opportunity that would not have been available in peacetime, viz., an opportunity to serve as an officer in one of the volunteer regiments soon to be formed.

Just how actively Kelly pursued a commission is not clear, but apparently it was enough so that in May, Miles recommended that he be given a commission in one of the new immune regiments.[29] Kelly surely was aware of Miles's action, but he may not have imagined that anything would come of it, since the consensus among senior military commanders was that the war with Spain would be primarily a navy show, with little for the army to do. Indeed, shortly after being assigned to the reindeer expedition, Kelly chanced one day to meet the assistant adjutant general, Col. John Curtis Gilmore, who expressed surprise that Kelly was going off to Alaska with war just around the corner, to which Kelly replied that "if there is any scrapping, I recon [sic] it will be mostly on the water."[30]

So it appears that Kelly, though ready and willing to accept a commission, was doubtful, at least, of an immediate appointment, while Alaska was the bird in the hand. But he did want that commission out on the table as an option. A commission, after all, would open the door for him to be a professional soldier, a career he seemed increasingly drawn to, but was disqualified for because of age. The age requirement, however, would be waived for service in the volunteers. As an officer, Kelly would be on the same plane as the men whose camaraderie he had come to value.

Probably sooner than most of his frontier contemporaries, Luther Kelly had seen the handwriting on the wall; he knew that what he had been had now become passé. The nation had moved on. To a new generation of Americans, Indians were no longer a threat—they were a curiosity, something to be ogled in Buffalo Bill's Wild West Show. His own life had reached something of a dead end, too. Aging frontiersmen, like himself, were becoming as quaint and picturesque as the Indians they once pursued. In a way, Kelly had come to regret having failed to pursue the kind of career he now hungered for, rather than answering the call of the wild as a young man. Perhaps, but if so, one has only to read his memoirs and personal correspondence to realize that he never really regretted his frontier experience. He may well have felt less accomplished than his younger siblings, William and Albert, who had become eminently successful in the coal business. But now, approaching the half-century mark in age, older brother Luther had little to show in terms of worldly success except for a lot of grand adventures, which were always good for the telling but added little to a man's affluence or resume of professional achievement. Besides, those adventures were dimming rapidly. After all, more than two decades had passed since he fought at Wolf Mountains and pursued the Nez Perce.

Luther Kelly does not come across as one who may have spent a lot of time brooding about what was or what might have been, though it has to have been something that flitted across his mind occasionally, as his young manhood receded further into the past. But he was not yet ready to simply sit back and play out the string. The yen to seek out and to improve his lot remained strong. Question was, just how to manage that? Undoubtedly, he could have joined his brothers in the coal business and perhaps come to experience the same degree of success they enjoyed, but a business executive Luther Kelly was not. For him, the road did not lead to bowlers and broadcloth and conference rooms. But an army commission with a chance for field service might be just the thing to rescue him from the staidness that touches so many men in mid-life.

Though it did not come equipped with a military commission, the Alaskan opportunity did promise something fresh and unique. The fact that Kelly may have perceived his life as being at something of a standstill, did not by any means indicate that he had lost his zest for adventure. The discovery of gold in Alaska had captured the public's fancy and offered him an opportunity to test those old wilderness skills in a totally new and exciting frontier setting. And perhaps his Alaskan service would demonstrate his physical fitness for field duty, thereby enhancing his chances for a commission in the increasing likelihood that war with Spain did become a reality. In any event, at the end of June 1898 he would be appointed a captain in the Tenth U.S. Volunteers, although word of the appointment did not reach him for some time. Not that it mattered, since his present Alaskan duties precluded him from accepting that commission anyway.[31]

Meanwhile, Glenn and the remainder of his own expedition reached Castner's camp on the south side of Portage Bay on 24 April 1898.

It was set up, reported Glenn, in a "nice grove of spruce timber...and had been well selected, as we had a stream of nice, clear, running water within easy reach on each side of us, plenty of fuel, and were well protected from the severe winds that blew across the glacier either up or down this arm of the sea." Geologist Walter Curran Mendenhall described the day as "clear and the scenery superb. The mountains rise steeply from the water's edge, and at this season were snow-covered to the very base." Fifty feet back of the camp rose a solid wall of ice that served as their fresh water supply.[32]

As noted, the first mission of Glenn's Number Three Expedition was to explore northeastward from Prince William Sound, looking for suitable routes of travel to the Copper and Susitna Rivers. The expedition was then to change starting points, moving to Cook Inlet, from where the objective was to seek out the most direct and practicable route from tidewater to the Tanana River. The idea, Castner later recalled, was to "find some place on the coast, where the sea did not freeze over at any time during the year, and from which a trail suitable at least for pack animals could be made into the interior." At any rate, the next four months were to involve a series of mini-expeditions and surveys conducted by various members of the Glenn party. On these outings, Kelly would often find himself in company with a man we know only as Lampe, a Norwegian sailor and mountaineer, and sometimes with the geologist Mendenhall, or on occasion with both men.[33]

Two days were spent examining the head of Port Wells Inlet, where Glenn and company encountered the very formidable Barry Glacier, named after the assistant adjutant general, U.S. Army. From this truly awesome and impressive spectacle of nature, they noted the breaking off of immense icebergs, many from "ten to twenty times as large as our boat." That evening they steamed back and set up camp in a well-protected little bay on the east shore, into which flowed a "creek of beautiful, clear water."[34]

The following day, 26 April, two hours of steaming brought them to the head of Port Wells Inlet, where they were treated to yet another grand spectacle, one that the expedition dubbed the Twin Glaciers. Glenn described the scene that met their eyes.

Directly in my front was the most imposing sight we had yet seen—I might add more imposing than any we saw during the season. Glistening in the sun were two large glaciers, which we named "Twin Glaciers," the pair being separated by a short ridge or hogback that runs down to salt water. In front

Luther S. Kelly in camp with the Glenn Expedition, Alaska. Photo was taken on wash day, 9 May 1898. *Walter C. Mendenhall photo, USGS.*

of the one on our right the sea ice extended for over 3 miles, while in front of the other this sea ice extended at least twice that distance. The ice was covered with snow several feet in depth. We soon discovered that it would bear up the weight of a man and that we could make no headway against it with a boat. Each of these glaciers is what is termed "live" or work-ing glaciers. The front of each was an almost perpendicular mass of ice, from which immense pieces were constantly breaking off and falling into the sea with a great roaring noise, due principally to the action of the tides.[35]

A valuable, if painful, lesson was learned during this explo-ration of the "Twins." The shorter, Canadian-style snowshoe was found to be wholly impracticable for use on Alaskan snows. They were, said Glenn, "too short, too broad, and too flat." Lieutenant

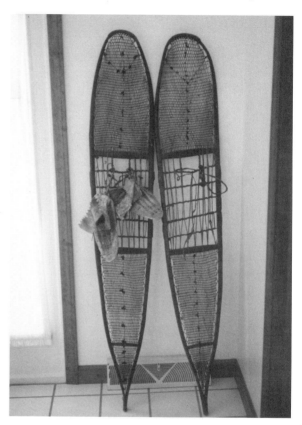

Kelly's snowshoes and
moccasins. *W. D. Kelly
Family Collection,
Author photo.*

Castner tried to wear rubber wading boots with his snowshoes
and wound up "rubbing off a good part of the great toe on each
foot." The brilliance of the sun reflecting off the snow and ice also
caused everyone in the party to be severely sunburned. Though
Glenn judged they were at least fifteen miles distant from Barry
Glacier, they could hear snow slides, and ice floes breaking away
from the glacier that could be heard two or three times an hour,
"like the rumblings of distant thunder, and which seemed to shake
the mountains on either side of us." That evening they returned to
the previous night's camp.[36]

The next morning, Tuesday, 26 April, Glenn dispatched a party of
six, including Castner, Kelly, Mendenhall, Howe, and Lampe, to explore
the glacier at the head of Port Wells.[37] On the following day, Kelly,
Mendenhall, and Lampe were given a day's rations and sent off to
explore the small creek in hopes of finding an outlet to the north.
During the course of this Alaskan summer, Kelly often found himself in

Walter C. Mendenhall, the geologist with the Glenn Expedition to Alaska, was also the unofficial photographer. Mendenhall accompanied Kelly on several treks. *USGS.*

company with Walter Mendenhall, whom he remembered as a "most companionable fellow." Long legged and a stronger walker than Kelly, Mendenhall generally took the lead on these outings.[38]

The trio set out in the face of a blinding snowstorm that reduced visibility to near zero. Why Glenn chose to send Kelly and company off on this mission in the midst of a blizzard is puzzling. Nonetheless, despite the storm, the three managed to proceed some three miles, until they found that the stream emanated from a frozen lake, at which point they concluded that it was pointless to continue farther and returned to the boat. Kelly suggested naming the body of water "Lake Cecilia," in honor of General Miles's daughter. The outing had otherwise been largely fruitless. "For our disagreeable day's work we secured no satisfactory results," reported Mendenhall.[39]

While Kelly and his companions were slugging their way up the small creek and finding nothing that made the effort worth the candle, the rest of Glenn's party spent the day hunting ducks and geese, which they found on Portage Bay in great numbers. The gravel in the creek looked promising, too, Glenn noted, but their efforts in panning produced no color.[40]

Since the storm showed no sign of slackening, Glenn, having learned that the steamer *Excelsior* had arrived at Portage Bay with mail, decided to return to base camp. A detachment under Lieutenant Learnard [Learned][41] was ordered to cross Portage Glacier and ascend Twenty-mile River to determine the practicality of a route from Portage Bay to the Knik Arm, an extension of Cook Inlet. After dispatching Learnard's party, Glenn decided to steam back to Valdez and make arrangements with the Pacific Whaling Company for further use of these vessels. The journey across Prince William Sound was a stormy one, with heavy snows falling during the night of the twenty-eighth and on into the twenty-ninth. Engine trouble slowed the crossing, but Valdez was finally reached at 3 PM Here, Glenn learned that Expedition Number One had been cancelled, an "action [he] fully expected."[42]

On 5 May, Kelly joined Lieutenant Castner's party in boarding the *Pacific* and steaming down to Port Wells to investigate a small stream (which Castner had named Whale Creek during an earlier visit) thought to provide a possible corridor into the interior. However, heavy fog prevented a detailed examination of the area. But on this occasion a brilliant sun quickly revealed that this effort was to lead nowhere. "Long before we reached Whale Creek," Castner recalled, "we saw that our mission would be fruitless. Great snow-capped mountains, 8,000 to 10,000 feet high, inclosed [sic] the head and sides of Port Wells. No trail could be made into or through such a region." By the evening of the sixth, Castner's party was back at the base camp on Portage Bay.[43]

On the tenth, Glenn sent Kelly and Lampe across the bay with a day's provisions to examine yet another outlet, Cabin Creek, which also gave promise of providing access to the interior. Up a ravine and over a hill, the trio wended its way through snow and a fine stand of spruce trees to the base of a mountain, where a beautiful waterfall debouched from the mountain pass. When their aneroid barometer read 2,500 feet, the wind picked up and it began to snow. So, stopping in a "sheltered place [we] ate our lunch of hard bread and cheese," Kelly wrote. "After a while it became bright again and we went on to the 2,800 foot elevation when the snow and wind became so thick that after waiting under a rock for nearly an hour, we were compelled, reluctantly, to turn back after all our labor." Here was yet another example of how unyielding this Alaska country could be; time and again throughout the life of this expedition, they would find it so.[44]

Before departing the States, Glenn's expedition had been outfitted with a sectional steel boat manufactured in Tacoma, Washington. The craft was designed to be used to haul supplies up inland waterways, but it lacked stability in rough water on the open sea. As a consequence, Glenn had to borrow boats from some of the locals in order to ferry Kelly and Lampe across the bay. Upon his return, Kelly told Glenn that he had discovered an abundance of reindeer moss on the tidal flat across the bay. The report must have chagrined Glenn because it revealed that there would have been plenty of feed for the reindeer had they been brought along.[45]

While here, news of the war with Spain reached them through a paper from Sunrise, which told of President McKinley's call for volunteers. The news undoubtedly dampened their spirits, as did the weather which continued wet and depressing. Rainfall was constant for the better part of two weeks and many of the men were afflicted with rheumatism. But conditions were about to change.

> On the morning of May 19 [wrote Glenn], the spirits of everyone rose with the sun which we had scarcely seen for two weeks. It was a glorious day. We had seventeen hours of sunshine without a cloud in the sky. Mr. Kelly took advantage of it to signal across the bay to us by means of an improvised heliograph. He used a small pocket looking-glass about 1 1/2 inches in diameter. Although he was five miles from us, on level ground, we had no trouble seeing the flashes or in understanding that he wished to be sent for.[46]

Indeed, the clarity of the Alaskan atmosphere was not something Kelly ever forgot. Field glasses extended his range of vision thirty miles. Directly ahead stretched the verdant green valleys of the Matunuska River, while off to the left was the Knik River, emptying into the great outlet of the same name, a continuation of a mighty glacier.[47]

Upon his return, Kelly reported finding at least 100 acres of pine forest that would provide an excellent source of timber for buildings that would be needed if the area proved to be an entryway to the interior, as it seemed to. Encouraged by the report, Glenn decided to have Kelly take a closer look at the area. Accordingly, on Friday, 20 May, Kelly and Lampe set out from Cabin Creek with four days' rations. Not expecting to find any game, Kelly elected to take his axe rather than a rifle. Kelly described the experience in his report.

We proceeded in a northerly direction a distance of 6 miles
to the summit of the pass, which was ascended with some
difficulty on account of having to break a trail through the
soft snow. The descent on the farther side was gradual.
Leaving our packs we traveled on snowshoes 4 miles to a
beautiful lake.... The ascent and descent of the pass
through the range from Portage Bay does not present any
great difficulty for establishing a pack or wagon route, and I
believe a railroad could be built over this route. The rock is
a slate, and easily worked, and there are no glaciers to
interfere with a route over this pass.[48]

Save for the snow and the mosquitoes, the experience may have
reminded Kelly of his Colorado days, when he surveyed a wagon
route from White River to Grand Junction.

Kelly and Lampe returned on the evening of the twenty-second[49]
having completed a twenty-six-mile round-trip journey from Portage
Bay. At one of the highest points, and with wonderfully clear visibility, they were able to see Turnagain Arm and two mountain divides,
which Kelly believed could be negotiated to the Knik Arm and possibly even Copper River. While on this assignment, Kelly also exper-
imented with smoke signals to determine whether Alaskan Indians
employed smoke to communicate and found that the various signals
corresponded with those of the Plains tribes he had known.[50]

On Monday, 23 May, Kelly and Lampe, this time in company with
Mendenhall, crossed Turnagain Arm in a small boat and proceeded
to the summit of Crow Creek, finding there a favorable pass, leading
north some seven miles to valley of the Yukla-hitna River. The country through which they passed on this particular outing impressed
Kelly as much as anything he'd seen in Alaska thus far.

At the foot the valley opened broad and smooth, bordered
with numerous parks and groves along its edge.

A magnificent glacier blocks the upper part of the valley, at a distance of 2 miles, rising to a height of several
thousand feet in 10 miles, and changes its direction to the
right behind a ragged range of mountains. The contrast of
green verdure close to this glittering mass of snow and ice
is very pleasing.

For several miles the riverbed, split into its numerous
channels fills the valley of the Yukla-hitna, but is easily

forded. The course of the stream is nearly northwest to the Knik Arm, the total distance being 33 miles.

This valley is one of great beauty, well timbered, and walled in at its upper extremity by bold and precipitous mountains that round off gradually into a low, flat country as the arm is approached.[51]

Meanwhile, that evening, the steamer *Wolcott* arrived from Valdez, bearing mail but bringing no word of the much needed transportation. Neither was there anything in the way of an official order directing the soldiers of the expedition to report to their regiments for duty in the war with Spain. The failure of such an order to be forthcoming "augmented very much this universal feeling of despondency," wrote Glenn.[52]

During these last days of May, the question of transportation continued to plague Glenn, as did the need to establish a permanent base camp on Cook Inlet. Without horses or mules, they could not hope to accomplish their mission in Alaska. As a consequence, on the twenty-seventh, Captain Abercrombie and Assistant Surgeon Kulp sailed back to Seattle where it was hoped mules could be obtained. This attended to, Glenn steamed back to Portage Bay, where, in his absence, a detachment under Lieutenant Learnard, including Kelly, had constructed a cabin on the north side of the Bay. After loading Learnard's detachment, the *Wolcott* steamed on to Resurrection Bay, where, on 30 May, Mendenhall and a small party were given rations for ten days along with instructions to travel overland to Sunrise City on Turnagain Arm. It was Decoration Day, which Mendenhall described as "beautifully bright and clear."[53]

While Mendenhall and company were crossing the peninsula to Sunrise, Glenn steamed on to Cook's Inlet, where it had been intended to establish their permanent base camp. Near Tyoonok an unexpected surprise awaited. "The first and most gratifying sight that met our eyes on the following morning," wrote Glenn, "was some pack animals (one horse and four mules), in charge of Sergt. Wm. Yanert, for duty with the expedition." So things were looking up. Since Tyoonok was home to a trading station and hundreds of prospectors, as well as Indians, Glenn decided to find a quieter spot for his base camp and selected Ladds Station, some five miles up the inlet.[54]

Meanwhile, on 29 May, Kelly, again with Lampe and four enlisted men, hauled supplies to the vicinity of Lake Glenn from the north side of Portage Bay. From here, the enlisted men returned to camp, while

Kelly and Lampe constructed a raft and transported their supplies to the foot of the lake. By 2 June, after hacking their way through heavy ice that had collected at the edge of the lake, they managed to establish a base camp near the foot of a dead glacier. From here, Kelly hoped to examine an opening in the mountains that he thought might provide a shortcut to the north. The following morning, with packs on their backs, they started across the glacier, only to find the early going to be more than a bit treacherous before smoothing out.

> The course we followed [Kelly wrote] soon became so per-
> ilous, by reason of clear ice and crevasses, that we were com-
> pelled to drop everything except our snowshoes. We then
> proceeded via the spruce ridge to the middle fork, or main
> stream, of the Twenty-Mile River, up which we had fine walk-
> ing on the gravel bars, and which brought us in 9 or 10 miles
> to the canyon at the foot of another glacier and, so far as we
> could observe, forms a solid glacier in the system to the north
> of Portage Bay, and probably beyond. We were unable to get a
> satisfactory view of the pass, although we climbed well up on
> the mountains, so we returned late at night to our camp.[55]

On 4 June, Kelly and Lampe shifted base camp to the mouth of the canyon to be better located to carry out their assignment, but rain, snow, and heavy fog precluded doing much of anything. By the ninth, however, the weather had improved sufficiently to allow them to reach the summit of the pass, though with difficulty. Here, they found a gla-cier, around which they were able to move easily some two miles to a rocky promontory, "which gave us a splendid view of the country beyond," wrote Kelly, who continued to be impressed with Alaska's stunning vistas.

> Due north about ten miles lay an immense basin, very low,
> fringed and shut in by a high range of jagged peaks. This
> basin was nearly filled by a flat glacier, which formed a lake at
> its southwest extremity. The outlet to it appeared to be on the
> west side of the basin, which was 15 or 20 miles in width. With
> the glass a wooded gulch appeared on the north side, about
> 20 miles away, and this was the only sign of timber in this
> region of bare rock, ice, and snow.
>   Observing a rocky ridge to the left of the summit which
> extended toward the lake below, I determined to examine

the west branch of Twenty-Mile River, as it appeared to have a favorable pass opening upon this ridge. The country to the northeast of the summit to Twenty-Mile River, as seen from that point and the higher points en route, is of the most forbidding aspect, forming an impassable barrier of glaciers and high mountains, with their peaks protruding through the ice. Fresh trails of so-called glacial bear and wolves were seen there, but no other sign of life except marmots and a few ptarmigan.[56]

Kelly and Lampe spent the next several days working their way up the west branch of Twenty-mile River. High water in the streams that fed that river forced them to move through tag-alder bogs and to pass dangerously close to slide areas. As a consequence, progress was limited to 3–4 miles per day. But at last, after battling brush, willows, and mosquitoes, they found themselves on the edge of a cliff, from where they gazed down on a great cavity of basin that Kelly judged was twenty miles wide, surrounded on one side by steep cliffs and towering peaks, while on the other rose a mighty glacier. "As I looked down," Kelly wrote, "the play of misty sunlight made it seem unreal, unsubstantial, as of some fabulous monster distorted and dissolving under the ardent rays of the sun, instead of a great force of nature yielding to a greater force."[57]

The incongruity of Alaska is that the presence of so much ice and snow does not prevent the onset of summer. With the June sun directly overhead for nearly a full twenty-four hours, the days were long and summer heat was upon them, as was the ubiquitous tormentor of residents and visitors alike, the mosquito pest, which "in all its fury assailed us and added very greatly to our discomfort," wrote Kelly.[58]

To those who have not been subjected to the assaults of Alaskan mosquitoes, it is quite impossible to appreciate their vigor and voraciousness. In his 1883 report, Lt. Frederick Schwatka wrote that next to nearly starving to death, the "mosquito 'pest was the worst discomfort' we had to endure. From this day, June 9, until August 25th we wore mosquito netting sewed to our hat brims, and tucked tightly under the collars of our shirts. On our hands were gloves or gauntlets. We ate and slept in small mosquito proof tents. Asleep or awake, these blood-thirsty visitors find a way through all covering to sting and annoy you."[59]

Their exploration did yield positive results in that it revealed an overland route from Portage Bay to Knik Arm, after which, having nearly exhausted their supplies, they returned to the main camp at Ladd's.

From Lake Glenn [Kelly wrote] the proper course is westerly
across the main stream [the Twenty-Mile River], thence up
the right bank of the west branch to the pass, over a compar-
atively level ground, which required the cutting of some
brush. By means of a winding trail the ascent and descent of
the pass is easy, as timber extends nearly to the top, and
while the snow was very deep on the summit, we found no
glaciers nearer than two miles. The valley of Winner Creek
falls gradually to California Creek, a distance of about 8 miles,
from which point I saw a favorable pass up Snow Creek, but
which I was unable to pursue at this time by reason of a
shortage of provisions, which compelled me to return to the
main camp at Ladd's Station.[60]

On 8 June Glenn detached Castner and a party of ten to explore
the interior by way of the Matanuska River Valley. Moving northeast
along the west side of Knik Arm, Castner's first stop was the Knik Indian
village, where the inhabitants were amused at the white men's intention to move into the interior, which they regarded as dangerous
beyond imagination. It was, they told Castner,

peopled with blood-thirsty savages ready to kill or make
slaves of all visitors. There were bears too large for bullets
to stop, and impassable snow mountains and glaciers.
There were unfordable mountain torrents, great barrens
devoid of all game and sustenance, and swarms of poisonous
insects. Worst of all were the legendary monsters with
the shape of men, leaving footprints in the mud of
riverbanks 12 feet long.[61]

Ten days after Castner's departure, Lieutenant Learnard, with a
small party, advanced up the Sushitna River to explore that area, with
Glenn intending to follow a few days later. The plan called for both
Castner and Learnard to eventually use Vasili's cabin on the Talkeetno
River as a base, where supplies could be hauled upriver by steamer to
that point. However, a message from Castner, received about 1 July,
stating that he would be unable to make contact with Learnard after all,
caused Glenn to revise his plan.

Since Learnard had supplies for two months and Castner did not,
Glenn felt it imperative that he make personal contact with Castner
and immediately prepared to set out after the lieutenant. However,

planning to take the field and actually doing so proved to be two entirely dissimilar animals. It took nearly a month before Glenn's party was finally able to move inland in pursuit of Castner. The delay was necessitated by first steaming to Knik Inlet to load supplies, then returning to Ladd's. On top of that, the whole process was further held up by a combination of tides, weather, and the procurement of livestock at Sunrise City. Accordingly, it was not until 23 July that Glenn finally got underway.[62]

In the meantime, though, Glenn had detached Kelly and sent him on ahead to make contact with Castner, whom he joined up with a week later on Boulder Creek. Castner recalled the moment.

> On the morning of July 7 we had the pleasure of greeting our chief of scouts, Mr. Luther S. Kelly, who had come into camp before we were up, *carefully guarding a package of oatmeal* [italics added]. He had come along the trail from Knik camp by easy stages. He was invited to make himself at home, as not making any report to me, and stating that Captain Glenn was to send him with six mules to Copper River, I concluded he was not part of the detachment under my command.[63]

Four days later, Castner's party, Kelly included, established a campsite on a high, grassy plateau, where on a clear day, large numbers of Bighorn sheep could be seen on the slopes of the nearby Talkeetno (Talkeetna) Mountains. Sheep Camp, as it was appropriately christened, was to be their home for some time.[64]

Sustaining a food supply en route proved a real challenge, necessitating an almost continuous supply line. Packer Dillon's arrival with a small stock would provide rations for only a short time. Accordingly, on 12 July, all of the group save Castner, Kelly, and a veteran Alaskan guide named Harry Hicks, were sent back to Knik to procure additional supplies. Having heard nothing to the contrary from Glenn, Castner was operating under the assumption that he was to continue with his assignment. But the season was marching along and by his calculations he would need to be back on the trail by 25 July if the mission was to be completed before the onset of cold weather. However, heavy rains made it seem unlikely that fresh supplies would arrive in time for them to be underway again by that date.

While awaiting the supply train, the men spent the days fixing a trail, mapping their future course, and examining the region's mineral potential, then returning to camp each evening. The day's

effort produced a hearty appetite, second only to that of the mosquitoes. Kelly recalled the challenge of trying to prepare a meal in
their presence.

> [A] brush fire was built and we endeavored to make some
> pancakes in an open frying pan. The pot of tea was simmer-
> ing alongside the fire, which had to be replenished with
> dry brush to make light, as candles would not stand in the
> light breeze that stirred, and each time the pan was advanced
> to the coals, a cloud of mosquitoes would fly over the fire,
> the heat of which would cause hundreds to fall into the
> batter and ruin our supper. Twice we had to throw away the
> batter, but the third effort under a protecting screen of a
> piece of light canvas was a success and we had our meal
> in some comfort.[65]

Much to Castner's pleasant surprise, Corporal Young arrived on the
twenty-fourth with 800 pounds of supplies, but with no further word
from Glenn.[66] In any event, Castner determined to move ahead as
planned. There was a fair piece of ground yet to cover before reaching
the Tanana and Yukon Rivers. Accordingly, on 26 July, the expedition hit
the trail once more. Since Kelly was not officially a member of the party,
Castner decided to leave him here at Sheep Camp with fourteen days
rations and complete freedom of movement. "He [Kelly] had orders
from me to do about as he pleased. To explore toward the Sushitna if he
so desired, to return to the coast, or to await the doubtful arrival of
Captain Glenn." Kelly was also given an additional stock of five days'
rations for two members of the party whom Castner anticipated sending back to the coast with worn-out livestock once they reached the
Indian villages on the Matanuska. Castner was to later regret having
been so generous with Kelly's rations.[67]

Glenn, meanwhile, leading a party of eight men and fifteen animals, was about five days behind, and on 1 August reached Kelly's
camp near Boulder Creek, where they learned that Castner had moved
on inland.

While awaiting Glenn's arrival, Kelly spent his days hunting mountain sheep in the nearby mountains. Glenn did not linger long here,
but set out immediately to overtake Castner. Glenn's string of pack animals was fresh, compared to those of Castner, but even at that it was to
take three weeks of hard slogging, often over rugged terrain and in dismal weather before the two parties were reunited on the Delta River on

25 August, nearly 300 miles from Knik Inlet. Many years later, in a letter to Theodore Roosevelt, Kelly painted a vivid picture of the region through which they passed on their journey to catch up with Castner, likening it to Montana in some respects.[68]

> With the arrival of Captain Glenn and party, we proceeded northerly through a wonderful park country of lakes, swamps and wooded hills and ridges. There were meadows of tall red top. Little prairies that were covered with short bunch grass and bordered with fur and spruce, just as you find in Montana. It was not all plain sailing tho, for we had roaring glacier streams to cross and some of our traveling was down the shallow beds of streams and over hills covered with moss. . . . The lakes hills and valleys of this region, are a marvel of beauty as far as the Delta river and beyond. Along the route, we could look back for a hundred miles or more and see the vast ice-cap that protrudes from the Matanuska to the Copper river. To the north, the McKinley group appears, and beyond Copper river, Mount St. Elias shows. When we could, we camped under the lovely spruce trees or on the shores of lakes.[69]

The combined parties remained together until the thirtieth, at which time Castner was supplied with rations for a month and sent on to, it was hoped, reach the Tanana and the Yukon, while Glenn turned back to Cook's Inlet with the remainder of the expedition. Kelly and a small party followed behind Glenn's main group to hunt sheep Along the way, Kelly observed that the character of the country was changing. They were moving into a dryer region. But there was something that he found even more interesting: gravel wash, which showed promise of gold. "I would have given anything for an opportunity to sink for bedrock gravel," Kelly wrote. But there was no time to investigate.[70]

For Glenn and company, the return journey, much of which parallels the current "Glenn Highway," was a mixture of travel over tough terrain and weather that ranged from heavy rain and hard freezes to days of sheer delight. The "cold raw wind and sleet blew in our faces during the whole day," Glenn wrote on 4 September. On this same day, they reached "Camp Discouragement," where geologist Mendenhall reported that "[m]any of the men were almost barefoot; everyone was worn out despondent and ill tempered." Glenn wrote that the

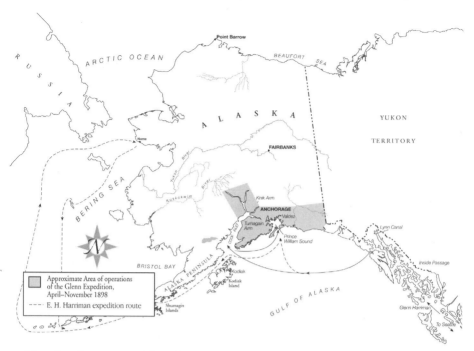

Map showing routes of the Glenn and Harriman Expeditions, Alaska, 1898–1899. *Map by Tom Child.*

moss was thick and underlaid with water, which, combined with the rain from overhead, thoroughly soaked all hands. In addition to the other discomforts, our trail was the most dreaded of any on the trip for the stock on account of one slope of the divide being covered with granite bowlders [*sic*] that were concealed by the moss, rendering the breaking of a leg by stepping into the crevices between them a constant and ever present danger."[71]

But two weeks later, Glenn could also write that "[w]ith the exception of cold nights, no better weather could be asked for than what we had for the past two or three days." And geologist Mendenhall described it as "most beautiful September weather. Cold frosty nights and hot days. Gets very warm in middle of days."[72]

The war with Spain had begun just as the expeditions of Glenn and Abercrombie were arriving in Alaska and ended a fortnight before the parties of Glenn and Castner were reunited. Occasionally, news of the war's progress would reach them by one means or another. The thought

Members of the Glenn Expedition, Alaska, 1898. Luther S. Kelly is standing far left. *National Archives photo.*

of their comrades bound for the Philippines and stopping en route at Honolulu and Japan "riled these soldiers detached for Alaskan duty," Kelly recalled. Then at one point, they chanced to meet a party of prospectors moving inland who gave Glenn a copy of the *Seattle Post-Intelligencer*, dated 29 July, reporting that Spain had sued for peace.[73]

On 24 September, they reached Melishe's Cabin on the west shore of Knik Arm, where they had made their first camp when setting out to reach the Castner party two months and two days earlier, having traveled 670 miles, and "mapped topographically and geologically, some 400 miles of hitherto unexplored territory." After a day's rest they moved on to Knik Station, where, on the twenty-eighth, it was "mail call" when the steamer *Perry* arrived. From here it was on to Tyoonok, where it was learned that in their absence, the Sushitna River had risen unexpectedly and washed away most of the cabins at Ladd's Station.[74]

While they had been off in pursuit of Castner, Kelly had received his second volunteer commission. Back in June, largely upon the recommendation of Nelson Miles and the political influence of his brother William, a member of the powerful Union League of Philadelphia, he had been appointed a captain in the Tenth Volunteers, but because he was in the midst of his work with Glenn, Kelly was unable to accept the

William Dunham Kelly I,
younger brother of Luther S.
Kelly and successful
Pennsylvania business-
man. William twice used
his prestige and influence
as an active supporting
member of the Republican
party to write Presidents
William McKinley and
Theodore Roosevelt on
behalf of his older brother.
George Bille Collection.

appointment. Now he was about to receive a second commission, this
time as captain in the Seventh Volunteers. Glenn had been directed to
see that Kelly departed at the first available opportunity and so, accordingly, on 9 October, he boarded the *Dora*, and steamed south to Seattle,
in company with Walter Mendenhall and a twelve-man detachment of
soldiers, which Glenn put in Kelly's charge.[75]

Glenn remained in Alaska until the end of the month, finishing up
expedition business, and by 10 November was back at Vancouver
Barracks, from where he had started seven months earlier. Castner,
meanwhile, with two companions and a pair of mules, had been directed by Glenn to head for Circle City and from there, by steamer, to
St. Michael, Seattle, and Vancouver Barracks. As it turned out, the Castner
party narrowly averted disaster. Unable to ascend the Volkmar River
due to the rugged terrain and a lack of supplies, they had to retrace
their steps. The two mules were killed and eaten, after which there was
little on which to subsist, and with their clothing in tatters, it was only
through the kindness and "never-failing hospitality" of the Tanana

Indians that the three men survived their ordeal. From the Tanana, Castner and his companions slogged their way on to Circle City, thence on to Dawson, White Horse, and Skagway in the Yukon. Not until 1 March 1899 would Castner's party again set foot in the United States.[76]

In retrospect, the work of the Glenn–Abercrombie expeditions is not regarded as having been notably fruitful, although geologist Mendenhall's work was certainly a contribution to his field of endeavor. But it can be said that the excursions of Kelly, Lampe, Learnard, and others of the expedition certainly added to the growing fund of knowledge about Alaska's Indians and some of its interior trail system. Both Glenn and Kelly believed that their surveys proved the feasibility of an Alaskan railroad route. Nine years after the Glenn expedition, Kelly, responding to an article on the subject of railroads in Alaska that appeared in the *National Geographic*, wrote to Alfred Hulse Brooks, author of the piece, pointing out what he [Kelly] regarded as a feasible railroad route to the Tanana River.

> The route would start from Resurrection Bay to Sunrise City, thence across or around Turnagain Arm, thence up glacier creek to Hitna Creek and down to Knik Arm and along [the] coast to the Matanuska river and up that river to the head, near which are indications of hard coal. You enter now a pleasant country of diversified parks and lakes with plenty of timber. The country at this point apparently slopes to the Copper river. Through this pleasant country, no great obstacles present themselves in reaching Delta river, down which the Tanana is reached.

Kelly and Glenn would both have the satisfaction of knowing that the Alaska Railroad, completed in 1923, followed much of the route they had recommended.[77]

Of Kelly's contribution in particular, Glenn wrote, "The results of the excellent work done by Mr. (now Captain) Luther S. Kelly in discovering the trail from Portage Bay to the Knik Arm, ... will, it is hoped, prove of lasting benefit to the people of the district through which he passed."[78]

Chapter Eleven

ALASKA AGAIN:
The Harriman Expedition,
1899

**It is difficult to convey in simple language the charm
of traveling in that region of Alaska. R. L. S. might do it
but even he would require more adjectives than he
used in his journey of the Cevennes.[1]**

En route to Seattle, the *Dora* put in at Juneau. Kelly and Mendenhall took the opportunity ashore to dine at the Occidental Hotel, which Kelly regarded as a fine hostelry, considering the fact that this was Alaska. Later, Kelly met an old Colorado friend, Dall Dewees, who invited him and three others to attend the *Varieties*. Kelly found the experience less than satisfying, but remained until he could tolerate no more. "The usher paraded up and down the aisle in his shirt sleeves, crying: 'cigars and beer, same price as at the bar!' the allusions were rather broad, so were the illusions. When the queen of the tragedy, in the 2nd act, began to sing 'Come back to Erin,' I fled."[2]

At Juneau they changed ships and prepared to board the *Alki*. First, though, one of Kelly's men had got himself in a bit of a scrape with the law when he was charged with smuggling whiskey. Kelly went to bat for the man, however, and arranged with the U.S. Commissioner to have the man released, ending, as Kelly said, "a vexatious matter."[3]

From Vancouver Barracks on 25 October, Kelly wired the adjutant general's office that he had returned from Alaska ready for duty and was subsequently ordered to report to Washington immediately. After some difficulty arranging for his transportation east, Kelly boarded the Northern Pacific on 2 November 1898. He purposely took a later train in order to see his old haunts along the Yellowstone Valley. Most such returns are a disappointment to the beholder, and so they were for Luther Kelly. "It was not the same old landscape of former years," he wrote, "no buffalo or game of any kind nor Indians, buildings in unlooked for places. Nor did I see anyone whom I knew. I was a stranger in a new old country."[4]

Upon arriving in Washington, Kelly took up temporary quarters at 1119 E. Capitol Street, near Lincoln Park. Since orders assigning him to duty with his regiment had not yet come through, we might imagine that during the hiatus he traveled to Germantown for a reunion with May and the family. And what stories there would have been to relate about great glaciers, mighty bears, hordes of mosquitoes, and a land where in the summer the sun scarcely set. One pictures nephews and nieces ranging in age from three-year-old namesake Luther Wrentmore Kelly to twenty-year-old Gregory Cook Kelly, both sons of brother William, listening transfixed to these tales of far-off Alaska. How exciting it must have been to have an uncle such as this![5]

Reporting to the adjutant general's office, Kelly learned that his original commission as captain in the Tenth U.S.V. had lapsed because he was in Alaska and unavailable. He was then given the option of accepting a lieutenancy in a white regiment or a captaincy in a black unit. After some deliberation, he accepted the latter and on 19 November he received his commission as captain in the Seventh U.S.V. and was duly sworn in. By virtue of Special Order Number 281, Kelly was directed to report to his regiment at Camp Haskell, Macon, Georgia, on 29 November.[6]

Following the swearing-in ceremony at the War Department, Kelly called on Miles, who offered his personal congratulations, which we may imagine were tendered with great satisfaction. Then it was on to New York, where he was a guest at the Camp Fire Club and presented with a fine "dress sword, gold mounted, with turquoise handle."

On 1 December, an old comrade from Fifth Infantry days at Fort Keogh, now Col. Marion P. Maus, invited him to lunch at the Army-Navy Club where he was introduced to naval Lt. Richmond Pearson Hobson, a hero of the Spanish-American War. It is not clear whether May returned to Washington with Kelly, though it seems likely that she would have done so and certainly shared in these heady moments with her husband.[7]

For May, who had been without her husband for the better part of a year, these pleasant hours must have passed all too swiftly and soon it was time for her to return to Germantown, while Luther boarded the Southern Railroad on 2 December to join his regiment at Camp Haskell, arriving in a rainstorm on the fifth, a week later than the date specified in his orders. Since his service record reveals nothing about an extension, nor a reprimand for the delay, we may assume that he was granted a further delay in orders. On 6 December, he officially took command of Company K.[8]

The Seventh U.S. Volunteers to which Kelly had been assigned was a short-lived War Department experiment. During the mobilization period back in the spring, President McKinley, responding to a strong cry from black Americans to participate in the war, accepted several black regiments from the South and Midwest. Congress had also authorized the creation of ten regiments of U.S. volunteer infantry (as opposed to state volunteers) from the southern states. Owing to their southern heritage it was thought that these men were immune to tropical fevers and would therefore render more effective service in areas where such fevers were prevalent. As a result, they came to be called "Immunes," thus the Seventh "Immunes." Of the ten regiments so authorized, six were to be composed of white troops, while four—the Seventh through the Tenth—were to be made up of black soldiers and white officers.[9]

The Seventh had been mustered into service during July at Jefferson Barracks, Missouri, then transferred to Lexington, Kentucky, in September, where the regiment was assigned to the First Corps. On 22 November, the Seventh was again reassigned, this time to Macon, Georgia, as part of the Second Separate Brigade, Second Army Corps, where it would remain until mustered out.[10]

At Camp Haskell, Kelly met yet another old friend from his Montana days, Col. Frank D. Baldwin, with whom he had campaigned during the Sioux and Nez Perce Wars. Baldwin introduced him to Maj. Gen. James Harrison Wilson, Union cavalry hero of the Civil War, whose command had captured the escaping Confederate President Jefferson

Davis in the spring of 1865. Baldwin thought Kelly belonged in a white regiment and stood ready to arrange for Kelly to join him [Baldwin] and Gen. Wilson when they transferred to Cuba. Kelly's role would be to take charge of the pack trains, but Kelly declined, believing it offered him no particular advantage to leave his new regiment. Besides, said Kelly, although "I love adventure and travel [I] do not want to risk fever and a hospital." Interestingly, he had no objection to later serving in the Philippines, perhaps because Cuba then had a reputation as an island of tropical fevers during the summer months.[11]

Christmas Day 1898 "opened fair and mirth reined," Kelly recalled. In a gathering at headquarters, there were speeches and a few rounds of "Tom and Jerrys," after which all adjourned to a circus tent, erected for the purpose, to listen to the chaplain expound on the significance of the day. The seats were all taken by the time they arrived and Kelly was forced to stand by the stove, where the combination of the heat and the punch caused him to faint. When he was carried outside, the cool air quickly revived him, but he was thoroughly mortified.[12]

Beyond organizational duties and close-order drill, there was little for Kelly's regiment to do except to possibly prepare for occupation duty in Cuba or the Philippines. Moreover, the area had recently been converted from farmland; the ground was soft and became a sea of mud when it rained. Kelly thought he suffered more at low temperatures here than in Alaska. Indeed, Alaska seems to have been much on his mind these days. Once during battalion drill Kelly drifted off into a reverie. Recalling Alaska, he contrasted those days to the present and wondered if he would ever enjoy a quiet life again. Here were the two sides of Luther Kelly, each vying for the dominant role in his life. Here was the quiet, introspective soul, the lover of words and music and solitude, as contrasted with that other self, that lover of the excitement bound up in high adventure. For most of his adult life it was this second self that held sway, though the margin at times was thin.[13]

Kelly seems not to have had any difficulty commanding black troops, though resentment toward blacks on the part of Macon's white community made Camp Haskell a less than ideal environment for a military installation with black troops. Interestingly, however, this racial bias did not cause Kelly to alter his views of Southerners, whom he liked because [he said] there was "so little of the foreign element in their makeup. They are Americans pure and simple. You will allow that a well bred southern man or woman is the peer of any on deck."[14]

Kelly left no record of how he felt about the soldierly qualities of black soldiers, though apparently he thought blacks made better enlisted men than they did officers. He found black lieutenants, for example, to be "fairly bright, active and intelligent soldiers, polite to a fault. When given a certain thing to do, it is necessary to stand by, until it is done. They are willing enouf [*sic*] but there appears to be a lack of stability in their make-up, and in an emergency they either side with the enlisted men or are helplessly dependent upon their white officers." Kelly believed, however, that the "rank and file would follow their superior officer to the death."[15]

The fighting between Spain and the United States had ended in August, and even as Kelly was taking command of his company at Camp Haskell, representatives of the two nations were in Paris, negotiating the terms of a permanent peace. As it turned out, the Seventh Immunes survived slightly less than three months, being mustered out of service on 28 February 1899. Kelly's tenure as a line officer had been short-lived.[16]

On the same day that the regiment was mustered out, Kelly took the train to Washington with a group of other officers, now unassigned. In the capital, Kelly took up quarters at the Ebbitt House. Here, he met and chatted with Brig. Gen. Anson Mills, another veteran of the Great Sioux War of 1876–1877. Here, too, was Col. Jesse Matlock Lee, who, as a young lieutenant twenty years earlier, had served as the court recorder at the Reno Court of Inquiry, established to investigate Maj. Marcus Reno's conduct at the Battle of the Little Bighorn. In the near future, Kelly and Lee would have an opportunity to work together in the Philippines.[17]

The Treaty of Paris, signed on 10 December 1898 (but not ratified by the U.S. Congress until the following February and by Spain in March) officially ended the Spanish-American War. Along with Puerto Rico and Guam, the United States acquired the Philippines, a sprawling archipelago of some 7,000 islands, covering about 500,000 square miles in the far western Pacific Ocean. With the acquisition of the Philippines, the United States became—for the first and only time in its history—a colonial power, and not since secession had an issue spawned such controversy and debate within the nation.

In the Philippines themselves, tension had existed between the U.S. military and the Filipino Nationalist forces of Emilio Aguinaldo virtually from day one, and had worsened right through the Spanish surrender of Manila on 14 August (two days after the signing of the Protocol of Peace, of which U.S. forces in the Philippines were unaware), during which U.S. troops had denied Aguinaldo's army access to the city and, thereby, participation in the Paris peace talks that followed.

During that autumn of 1898, while Luther Kelly was taking command of Company K, Seventh Immunes, and negotiators were ham-
mering out the final terms of the Treaty of Paris, Maj. Gen. Elwell
Stephen Otis, commanding U.S. troops in the Philippines, faced a vexing problem: manpower. Otis had assumed command of the Eighth
Corps following the departure of Maj. Gen. Wesley Merritt on 25 August.
The composition of the Eighth Corps—which had now become an
army of occupation—was a mixture of regular army troops and state
volunteers, of which the latter amounted to about seventy-five percent. As autumn progressed, some of these troops were rotated home,
but replacements proved to be poorly trained regulars. Most troublesome for Otis, though, were the state volunteers, who agitated to return
home now that the war with Spain was over and the yoke of tyranny
had been removed from Cuba's back; that had been the cause for which
they took up arms against the Spaniards in the first place. But these volunteers had not the same feeling for the Philippines that they had for
Cuba. They cared little enough for soldiering anyway, and now that the
war was over they clamored to go home. However, the strained and
chaotic situation in the Islands necessitated the need for a continuing
U.S. military presence here even though the war itself had ended.[18]

If the situation confronting Otis during that fall of 1898 was vexing,
it became a far more serious issue early in February 1899. The tension
between the U.S. Army and Aguinaldo's Nationalist forces that had
been building for months burst into the bright flame of war on the
fourth of February, just two days before the U.S. Congress ratified the
Treaty of Paris. Unlike the war with Spain, the United States soon found
itself embroiled in a much costlier war with the Filipinos, one that
would drag on for three long years. Because the state volunteers were,
by that time, more experienced and battle hardened than the regulars,
the burden of fighting this new war fell on their shoulders and intensified their desire to return to the States.[19]

As a means of resolving the army's manpower problem in the
Philippines, now exacerbated by the outbreak of war with Aguinaldo's
Nationalists, the U.S. Congress, on 2 March 1899, authorized an
increase in the regular army and the mobilization of up to 35,000 two-
year federal (as opposed to state) volunteers specifically to serve in
the Philippines. There was nothing at all haphazard about the organization of these U.S. Volunteers. Rather an experiment, it was, nevertheless, intended that these troops be well trained, disciplined, and
exhibit in every way the highest standards of the citizen soldier.
Officers were to be carefully selected, with regimental commanders

being chosen from among those who had served as line officers in the regular army. Company-level commanders were frequently West Point graduates, or had demonstrated effective leadership qualities as an officer of volunteers.[20]

Surprisingly, perhaps, in view of the state volunteers' lack of motivation to serve in the far-off Philippines, there was no shortage of men to sign-up for the new volunteer regiments, including Luther Kelly, who wasted no time applying for a commission. On 1 March he spoke with Brig. Gen. Henry Corbin, the adjutant general, about a captaincy in one of the new regiments—either cavalry or infantry, he had no preference. His request was endorsed by an impressive bevy of supporters, including Gen. Nelson Miles, Col. Edwin Alison Godwin, his former commander in the Seventh Immunes, along with his old Chicago comrades in the George H. Thomas Post of the GAR. Finally, New York Governor Theodore Roosevelt, whom Kelly described as a "kind, impulsive, gentleman, soldier and statesman," added his weight to the ranks of Kelly supporters.[21]

The coterie of unassigned officers from the Seventh Immunes, Kelly included, hung their hats at the well-known Willard Hotel in Washington, while awaiting news of their hoped-for appointments to one of the new USV regiments. The consensus among the senior officers was that vacancies in the regular army regiments would be filled first, then the volunteer units as needed.[22]

Meantime, Alaska had risen to the surface again. When Miles broached the subject to him, Kelly indicated he would be glad to return to Alaska, providing it did not interfere with his chances for active field service. Miles, however, seemed doubtful about Kelly's chances for the volunteers and asked his former scout what influence he could bring to bear on behalf of his commission, whereupon Kelly told the general who had written recommendations. Miles then suggested that his own and Roosevelt's endorsements would likely not help much, but Kelly might hang on to them as souvenirs.[23]

While Kelly was waiting for something to happen with his appointment to the volunteers, he and May, who had again joined him from Germantown for a brief reunion, toured the Bureau of Engraving and Printing, after which May returned to Germantown. Kelly also took the opportunity to get together with old friend George Bird Grinnell, who suggested he [Kelly] apply for the agent's post at the Blackfoot Agency in Montana. Kelly was interested and got a letter of endorsement from Miles to pursue it should he elect to do so.[24]

But the siren wail of Alaska was sounding stronger. Armed with a letter of introduction from the editor of *Recreation*, Kelly called on

G. Hart Merriam, head of the Biological Survey at the Department of Agriculture. The subject of their conversation, of course, was Alaska. Merriam had recently been approached by railroad magnate Edward H. Harriman about the idea of assembling a grand expedition to explore Alaska. Kelly was interested... and more than a little, we may imagine. Harriman's vision would result in what was perhaps the most unusual scientific expedition of its kind ever assembled. Whether Kelly had any sense of this at the moment is not known; perhaps he did, perhaps he didn't, but he was clearly interested in returning to Alaska, which place had captured his fancy.[25]

In late March 1899, fifty-year-old railroad magnate Edward H. Harriman decided on a most unusual adventure-vacation for himself and his family: an Alaskan cruise, but not just any cruise. What he had in mind was to see Alaska in the most luxurious style then possible. Only a few could afford such an undertaking and Harriman was one of them. He had made a fortune developing the Illinois Central Railroad, and then in 1898 moved on to even greater wealth and power as chairman of the board of the Union Pacific Railroad.

An intense, restless man, Harriman may well have decided that he simply needed a vacation. Clearly, though, it appears he was also intrigued by Alaska's great untapped commercial potential, especially with regard to the possibility of a railroad connecting Siberia and Alaska beneath the Bering Strait. Whatever the motivation, Harriman moved ahead with plans to completely refurbish the steamer *George W. Elder* in a most luxurious style.[26]

While these preparations were afoot, Harriman decided that, given the size of the *Elder* and its accommodations, it would be a shame to limit the passengers to only himself and his family. Accordingly, on 25 March, Harriman approached Merriam, proposing that a group of pre-eminent scientists join the cruise as his guests. Merriam was at first skeptical, but after learning that Harriman did indeed have the resources and was utterly serious about this undertaking, he agreed to act as coordinator for the scientific party.[27]

It was Harriman's idea to include the two top authorities from each appropriate scientific field, which eventually resulted in a party of 25 scientists, 2 photographers, 3 artists, 2 taxidermists, and a scout. To this group, Harriman added a surgeon, nurse, and chaplain. The Harriman family and servants numbered 14. Two secretaries and a group of 11 hunters and packers rounded out the passenger list. Adding a crew of 65 brought the total to 126.[28]

As finally constituted, the scientific party was like a who's-who of American science of that era and included, among others, paleontologist, William Healy Dall, geologist Grove Karl Gilbert, and Frederick Coville, Curator of the National Herbarium. George Bird Grinnell, authority on the American Indians and editor of *Forest and Stream*, lent his expertise to the party, as did famed ornithologist John Burroughs, along with John Muir, the beloved old man of the mountains.

Although several members would record their photographic impressions of the voyage, the then largely unknown Edward Sheriff Curtis was cast as the official photographer of the expedition and Grinnell though Kelly ought to be a member as well. Accordingly, on 3 May, Kelly again visited Merriam, who evidently agreed that Kelly would indeed be an asset to the expedition and broached the subject to Harriman, probably pointing out Kelly's background as a scout, adding that he had been in Alaska with the Glenn Expedition just the year before and that a man of his experience would make a real contribution to their effort.[29]

While things were developing with the Harriman outing, friends at the War Department provided Kelly with a letter to Assistant Secretary Meiklejohn, recommending that he again be employed as a guide on Captain Glenn's second foray to Alaska, also scheduled for that summer. That idea did not appeal to Kelly, however. Perhaps for reason or reasons unstated, he did not again wish to serve under Glenn. It proved academic in any case, because Glenn's party had already sailed from Seattle.[30]

On 9 May, Kelly joined Merriam and other members of the Alaska party at a Harriman-sponsored dinner at the New York Metropolitan Club. Kelly enjoyed the evening and found the members of the expedition to be "a jolly, interesting, as well as dignified crowd." As the evening drew to a close, Harriman asked Kelly to call at his office the following morning for a chat. The subsequent meeting proved amicable, with Kelly observing that Harriman fulfilled his reputation as an alert businessman. On his coat lapel that morning, Kelly chanced to be wearing a button honoring the War of 1812. Noting this Harriman asked if he had been a participant, to wit Kelly replied "only indirectly, sir; I am one of those who like to keep alive the traditions of one's ancestors."[31]

Harriman evidently liked the idea of including Kelly in his party and directed him to proceed immediately to Portland, stopping en route in Salt Lake City, where additional instructions would be forwarded by mail. Returning to Washington, Kelly found no new developments at the War Department and so on 12 May he entrained for Portland, which place he reached on the seventeenth. Here, he had an opportunity to take an advance look at the *George W. Elder*, then being refitted and refurbished to accommodate the Harriman party. Here, too, he met a young Edward Sheriff Curtis, who was to be the official photographer of the expedition. After checking in at Vancouver Barracks once again for an update on the volunteer regiments, he returned to Portland and presented himself to A. L. Mohler, president of the Oregon Railroad and Navigation Company to whom Harriman had given him [Kelly] a letter of introduction. For lunch, Kelly accompanied Mohler aboard a vessel of Japanese registry, then preparing to sail for the Far East. Kelly left no record of the lunch itself, but did recall that they were served an "apricot brandy or cordial of exquisite flavor."[32]

Meanwhile, the Harriman party boarded a special train at Grand Central Station on the afternoon of 23 May, and after a leisurely cross-country journey in grand style, reached Seattle on the thirty-first, where they found Capt. Peter Doran and the *Elder* patiently awaiting their arrival. Kelly's assignment as an advance man was to arrange for a group of packers, but Curtis apparently had already seen to it. Mostly, Kelly found, the packers were young college students with no experience whatever in the fine and tricky art of mule packing.[33]

One of the many perks Harriman provided for his gentleman guests was a supply of fine cigars, which was readily available. However, as they boarded the *Elder*, Kelly informed George Bird Grinnell that he planned to abstain from smoking on this trip. Last year, while with Glenn, he had found it "beneficial" to avoid the use of tobacco while traveling in the interior of Alaska and decided to do so again on this expedition.[34]

Word of the expedition had spread and a great crowd was on hand when they steamed up Puget Sound to Victoria for a brief stop. Kelly met the two "Johnnies," Muir and Burroughs, as the pair was affectionately known, on their way to the local museum. He yearned to join them, but elected not to, not wishing to intrude on this together time for two old friends. Later, he regretted not joining them. From Victoria it was on to Vancouver Island. On 2 June, the *Elder* steamed through the Strait of Georgia to New Metlakahtla, reaching Annette Island on the fourth and Wrangell on the fifth. These first days out of Seattle, the weather was overcast and often rainy, with the sun putting in only brief appearances. The *Elder's* course was over much of the same water as the Glenn expedition had followed, undoubtedly refreshing Kelly's recollections of a year ago.[35]

If the weather had been overcast and depressing between Seattle and Wrangell, it apparently changed for the better, even if briefly, after leaving the latter port. On 5 June, John Burroughs wrote to his son Julian, waxing eloquent about the sunset.

> Last night at nine-thirty we had such a sun-set; snow white peaks seven or eight thousand feet high riding slowly along the horizon behind dark purple walls of near mountain ranges all aflame with the setting sun. Such depths of blue and purple, such glory of flame and gold, such vistas of luminous bays and sounds I had never dreamed of.[36]

From Wrangell, the *Elder* steamed up the Lynn Canal to Skagway, arriving on 6 June, a date that was to take on a special meaning forty-five years hence, but here and now it was simply a drizzly sixth day of the sixth month. A boom town born out of the great Klondike gold rush two years earlier, Skagway still retained much of its gold rush flavor. Here the expedition was greeted by a welcome mail boat that brought letters and news from home. Later they boarded a special train belonging to the White Pass and Yukon Railroad. As the little narrow-gauge consist worked its way up the steep grade, the members of the expedition were moved by the visible debris of equipage and dead horses still littering the infamous trail that had claimed the lives of more than a few questing prospectors and pack animals. At White Pass summit, where the United States and British Empire joined, all hands enjoyed a grand picnic feast, courtesy of the White Pass Railroad. Edward S. Curtis recorded the scene for posterity.[37]

Delightful weather was theirs to savor upon arriving in Glacier Bay on the tenth. Here, the *Elder* anchored in some eighty fathoms of water, near the mass of Muir Glacier, where they found, still standing, the cabin John Muir had built twenty years earlier. Great glaciers seemed to rise up in every direction, stunning and crisp in the lucid atmosphere.[38]

Edward Harriman wanted a grizzly. Badly. If killing one of the big bears was not the primary reason Harriman was here, it surely ranked near the top. As a consequence, when John Muir described a place called Howling Valley, but a few miles away and supposedly filled with an abundance of wild game, especially wolves, from which the valley took its name, Harriman's ears picked up. The opportunity seemed too good to pass up and Harriman promptly organized a hunting party composed of himself, Kelly, Merriam, and Grinnell, plus physicians Edward Trudeau and Lewis Morris. It was an ill-fated outing from the start that saw the party mushing on through deep snow and freezing rain. After a torturous day and bone-freezing night, Kelly finally turned back. It seemed pointless to pursue the thing any further, but Harriman pushed on to Muir's Howling Valley, which proved as bereft of game as the day had been of warmth. Reluctantly, Harriman turned back.[39]

The eleventh of June came on, robed in brilliant northern splendor. Before them rose the eminence of Hugh Miller Glacier. Despite being thoroughly sore and aching in every joint from yesterday's strenuous trek to Howling Valley, the day's beauty did not go unappreciated by Merriam, who recorded that it was "[c]lear and fine all day—superb day." Sore or not, it was too splendid a day to ignore, though it was spent in a more leisurely fashion, cruising around North and South Marble Islands in a steam launch with a group that included Mrs. Harriman and children, Kelly, George Bird Grinnell, Walter Devereux, and William Averell, brother of Mrs. Harriman. After depositing Kelly et al. on the beach, Merriam dined with Mrs. Harriman and the children on one of the islands. Later, Kelly climbed one of the many peaks in the area and at Merriam's request brought down several alder and spruce branches for examination by the latter.[40]

On 12 June, the *Elder* docked at Sitka, where they were greeted by the governor, in company with a group of prominent local citizenry. The occasion was celebrated with a fine dinner on board ship complete with champagne toasts. The expedition remained here for five days, hunting, visiting hot springs, and gathering various marine specimens.[41]

From Sitka, the *Elder* steamed north, visiting Yakutat and Disenchantment Bays, and Malaspina Glacier before turning west across the Gulf of Alaska to Prince William Sound and Port Wells. Kelly surely experienced a sense of *dèjá vu*, although the weather here in late June was noticeably better than what it had been in April and May during last year's Glenn Expedition.

> This region in April [he recalled] was snow bound and afforded a magnificent spectacle. To the right of the entrance to Portage Bay is Port Wells, an inlet that has its head at right angles with the former bay, and is lost in the ice mass that extends to Copper River; the entire region forming a wild and glittering spectacle, worthy of the gods that dominate boreal zones. In our travels up and down these waterways, the scenery was a never ending delight.[42]

Being familiar with this area, Kelly extolled its delights to Harriman, who then decided that a little exploration was in order. Accordingly, the *Elder* steamed slowly up Port Wells, thence some dozen miles up a new waterway, unknown to the pilot. After a time, a small party put into shore on the ship's yawl or small boat. For this excursion, Kelly joined Henry Gannett of the U.S. Geological Survey; Grove Karl Gilbert, scientist and explorer; John Muir; mineralogist Charles Palache; Frederick V. Colville, U.S. Department of Agriculture; E. S. Curtis's assistant, D. J. Inverarity; and Indian Jim, a Tlingit Indian with a patch over his left eye, a fellow to whom Harriman had taken a fancy. A cook and a pair of packers completed the group.[43]

The group selected a campsite on the bank, some thirty feet above the water, amid a copse of spruce trees. Kelly thought the scenery magnificent, "tho it was a most desolate region; no sign of life, not even a bird!" Enormous dead glaciers that towered nearly to the peaks of surrounding mountains, and extending as far as the eye could see, suggested to Kelly that here was glacier bear country and he determined to try his luck at finding one of these elusive beasts.

Detaching himself from the others, Kelly headed out to try his luck. Harriman had loaned him a late-model .40-caliber Winchester, which he reckoned would be heavy enough. Finding no sign along the shoreline, he moved inland. And then, up ahead, in the fading half-light of the Arctic day he spied a pair of brown bears. Carefully, he worked his way toward them, but the terrain did not offer a clear shot and in the dim misty light he did not wish to chance just wounding one of the unsuspecting bruins, who, apparently, were oblivious to his approach. Retiring cautiously into the nearby timber, he found a likely spruce tree with a thick mantle of dry needles beneath. Standing his rifle against the trunk he sat down and, back to the tree, made himself quite comfortable.

This was vintage Luther Kelly, alone in the wilderness. Nowhere was he ever more content than in such surroundings as he presently enjoyed. Solitude always seemed to beckon. A year earlier he had found his time alone when Glenn sent him on ahead to locate Castner's party. Now he had found another such interlude. Surely this moment recalled other younger days in a hundred spots in the Judith Basin, or along the Upper Missouri and Yellowstone Rivers.

After building a small fire, he finished the remains of the lunch he had brought along, imagining how tasty it would have been to dine on one of the plump brown ptarmigans he had seen earlier in the day; but, he reminded himself, one did not waste ammunition on small game while on a quest for larger prey. Reflecting further on the hunt itself, it would, he thought, be one thing to shoot a glacier bear for his own satisfaction but quite another to kill a larger brown bear, whose pelt would be too much for him to handle alone. It occurred to him, as well, that the party he had come ashore with was somewhat vulnerable. After his party left the ship, the *Elder* had put back to sea and should something happen to the ship, no one would have any idea as to the whereabouts of Kelly and his companions. In his reverie, he dozed off, back against the spruce tree, head cushioned by the soft felt hat, warmed by the small fire in his front.

When he awoke, perhaps an hour later, the fire had burned down to a few small glowing embers. Gathering his belongings, he returned to the vantage point he had abandoned before his interlude. In short order, he picked up the trail of the two bears, following carefully. The tracks were plainly visible and presently he heard them thrashing through the brush up ahead, once being afforded a glimpse of their brown, furry bodies, though not clear enough for a clean, killing shot. But in any event, time was pressing and as there was no way to know when the *Elder* would return, he concluded it was time to rejoin the others. So, there had been no kill on this occasion, but he had had "good sport and enjoyed every moment of it."[44]

The morning of 1 July found the ship in Uyak Bay on the north shore of Kadiak Island. John Burroughs was enchanted, steaming along the coast over glassy seas, with great ermine peaks on the horizon.

> The sky was clear and the prospect most inviting. Smooth, treeless green hills and mountains surrounded us, pleasing to the eye and alluring to the feet...hills as green and tender to the eye as well-kept lawns...natural sheep ranges such as one sees in the north of England, but with not a sign of life upon them.[45]

Best of all was the balmy weather. "How welcome, the warmth, too! We had stepped from April into June; the mercury was in the seventies and our spirits rose accordingly."[46]

Perhaps it was just as well that Harriman had not bagged his bear in Howling Valley, for here dwelled the great Kodiak bear, which might prove an even greater prize. Harriman, accordingly, wasted no time assembling a three-man hunting party that included himself, Kelly, and Stepan Kandarkof, a Russian from one of the nearby villages who reportedly had once killed a Kodiak bear with nothing more than a knife. Kelly thought such intimacy too close for comfort. Unlike the futile effort at Howling Valley, this outing proved successful. Harriman dispatched a smallish female bear with one shot while Kelly shot the cub. Though far from a record trophy, Harriman was delighted. Viewing Harriman's bear in the slanted sunlight obscured by the gathered onlookers, Kelly observed that the kill was now "merely poor clay in a garment of brown fur." The following morning the two bears were sketched by one of the expedition's artists and afterward skinned by the taxidermist.[47]

Now in high spirits, E. H. Harriman had a second reason to participate in the next day's Fourth of July celebration. In honor of the nation's birthday, a small cannon was fired from the deck of the *Elder*, while the ship's gramophone played "Stars and Stripes Forever." It was, wrote John Burroughs, a day "overflowing with bunting and gunpowder hilarity." Ashore, members of the expedition enjoyed a picnic and watched a baseball game between the villagers. When the *Elder* resumed its journey north on the morning of 5 July, Burroughs recorded that "Kadiak, I think, won a place in the hearts of us all. Here our spirits probably touched the highest point."[48]

On the morning of 7 July, Kelly joined a scientific party which the *Elder* dropped off at Sand Point in the Shumagin Islands on its way north. The group, consisting of botanist Alton Saunders, entomologist Trevor Kincaid, zoologist William Ritter, and mineralogist Charles Palache, had decided it would be more profitable for them to spend time here, exploring and gathering specimens, than to continue north with the main expedition.[49]

After dropping off the party, the *Elder* steamed on to Dutch Harbor, Unalaska. From there it was around the Aleutians and out into the Bering Sea, thence north to Plover Bay, Siberia. On 12 July, the *Elder* docked at Port Clarence, Alaska, northernmost point of the expedition's adventure. Their stay here was brief and the return voyage commenced the following day.[50]

On 21 July, they picked up the Sand Point party and the southward journey was resumed. Two days later the ship anchored off the north shore of Yakutat Bay. Later Harriman gathered another hunting party that included Doctors Lewis Morris and Edward Trudeau, William Devereux, George Bird Grinnell, and Kelly. Ten Indians accompanied the party whose objective was to bag yet another bear. "About 11 o'clock they all returned," wrote Merriam, "having failed to land on account of the surf."[51]

The adventure was winding down. Mostly the members were anxious to return home, but none more so than Harriman himself, who was growing increasingly restless to be back in active touch with his corporate affairs. He'd gotten his bear and seen enough to satisfy him. Indeed, when one day they were steaming south and Merriam pointed out the beauty of the Fairweather Mountains, Harriman told him he didn't "give a damn if I never see any more scenery."[52]

The return voyage was not without its high spots. Champagne flowed as the expedition celebrated young Cornelia Harriman's fifteenth birthday, followed on the twenty-second by a celebration honoring Mrs. Harriman's birthday. Dancing and story-telling filled the ship. B. K. Emerson made "an excellent humorous speech" and Kelly performed a little Indian war dance, one which George Bird Grinnell probably appreciated more than the others. And a few days later, as the *Elder* steamed toward Juneau, there were toasts to Harriman and his generosity. And so if all hands were happy with the prospect of soon being back in the States, no one would deny that it had been a grand, exhilarating adventure, indeed, unique; one whose like would not be seen again.[53]

En route to Seattle, the *Elder* paid a call at Cape Fox, where members of the expedition went ashore to view the remains of a now deserted Indian village, where mighty, artistic totem poles stood tall and mute. "This picturesque village," Kelly observed, "ensconced as it were amid a forest of stately totem poles of native yellow cedar, skillfully and elaborately carved was built by native Alaskans." At Harriman's order, the poles—all nineteen of them—were dug up and hauled out to the *Elder*, much to the chagrin of some members, notably John Muir who was outraged. The poles would later be dispersed to several institutions in the United States.[54]

The *Elder* reached Juneau on 25 July and, following a brief layover there, resumed its southward voyage. On Sunday, 30 July, the ship docked in Seattle. Following a farewell dinner for all hands, Kelly bade farewell to his companions and traveled down to Vancouver Barracks, where, as he had done a year earlier, he wired the adjutant general's to the effect that he had returned from Alaska and was ready for service if there be a spot in one of the volunteer regiments. This attended to, he boarded an eastbound train.[55]

For Kelly, Alaska had proven to be a memorable experience. His memories of the Glenn and Harriman adventures would remain as vivid in his memory as the clarity of the Alaskan air. He had seen it twice now and each time under a different set of circumstances. Unquestionably, the Harriman expedition had been memorable for its luxury and convivial companionship. The Glenn expedition had been,

by far, more physically demanding; a year ago he returned with a hardened body. He contrasted the two experiences. "Constant traveling
toward the north, thru a little known wilderness brot [*sic*] me sinews of
iron, and the simple fare (we were always hungry) no doubt was good
for health. On board ship there was little chance for exercise, and the
food was of the best, yet I felt in pretty good trim for service."[56]

The region had impressed Kelly with its vastness, its towering glaciers, and the clarity of its atmosphere. These were not things easily
forgotten. Fifteen years later his enthusiasm for Alaska had not waned.
He might well have been preparing a chamber of commerce brochure
when he encouraged Theodore Roosevelt to visit Alaska.

> And I must tell you of the splendid opportunity you have to
> explore a new region in Alaska. I believe that Alaska, at least
> the part over which I traveled, and in summer time is the
> most healthy and salubrious in the world.... It is difficult
> to convey in simple language the charm of traveling in that
> region of Alaska. R.L.S. might do it but even he would
> require more adjectives than he used in his journey of
> the Cevennes."[57]

If Kelly regarded Alaska as the world's healthiest locale, he was soon
to find that the Philippines offered an entirely different sort of climate,
one far less salubrious than that he had experienced in the "Land of the
Midnight Sun."

Chapter Twelve

THE PHILIPPINES,
1899–1903

**When we were ready to go out, found that the party
had already landed and were marching up the main
throfare [*sic*], escorted by Dapitan's bare-footed brass band,
Mr. Taft towering in the lead like a band master. I met the
party, introduced myself, and invited them to enter
my Headquarters, which they did.[1]**

When Kelly wired the adjutant general's office and headed east, he was undoubtedly ever hopeful that a billet had opened up for him in one of the new regiments. Two weeks earlier, brother William had written President McKinley, lobbying once again on Luther's behalf. As far as we know, Luther was unaware of the effort, though it is entirely possible, perhaps even likely, that he had asked his brother to put in a good word for him. William's letter to the President was dated 12 July, when Luther was at Sand Point in the Shumagin Islands and out of touch. However, he could have wired his brother from some other place along the route—say, Sitka, for instance—indicating

Capt. Luther S. Kelly,
Co. A, Fortieth USV.
Taken while Kelly
commanded the post
at Dapitan, Mindanao,
Philippine Islands,
April 1900. *National
Archives photo.*

that he would probably be home in another month and asking for a
letter of recommendation.[2]

In any event, by mid-August Kelly was back in Washington. On the
nineteenth he was appointed a captain in the Fortieth U.S. Volunteers
and accepted his commission two days later. What is interesting here is
that War Department requirements for selecting officers, rather rigid as
they were, did not prevent Kelly from receiving an appointment.
Company commanders, for example, were generally either West Point
trained or had demonstrated leadership skills as a volunteer officer.
Noncommissioned officers who had shown promise were also considered. Kelly, however, did not qualify on any of the above counts. True,
he had commanded a company in the Seventh Immunes, but his term
of service had scarcely been long enough to judge his soldiering skills.

This is not to suggest, then, that his appointment was based solely on political influence. On the contrary, it underscores the confidence that professional soldiers such as Gen. Nelson Miles and Gen. Jesse M. Lee had in Kelly. They knew what he was capable of, either because they had actually worked with him in the past, as had Miles, or knew of him by reputation, as did General Lee. This is further borne out by the fact that he was appointed a captain, when a lieutenancy would surely have satisfied a purely politically motivated endorsement.[3]

As yet another illustration of the confidence Kelly inspired in others, on 24 August Col. Edwin Allison Godwin, his former commander in the Seventh Immunes, requested that Kelly be assigned to his regiment, the Fortieth USV, and the request was promptly honored.[4]

The appointment left Kelly little time for any family business, as he was ordered to report to the recruiting station at 104 West Fayette Street, Baltimore, on a ten-day assignment to recruit men for the new regiment. After becoming acquainted with recruiting procedures, he was ordered out to Des Moines, Iowa, which he recalled as a warm place in August that made him "feel like the Irishman who was 'Down with the faver six weeks in the hot month of August, and all my cry was, wather, wather.'" Des Moines proved something less than a fertile ground for new recruits, however, and after only a dozen men had signed on, the office was closed and Kelly took his detail to join the regiment at Fort Riley, Kansas, on 4 September and within a week had been given command of Company A, which he then promptly set to work to organize.[5]

After some six weeks of training, the regiment departed Fort Riley, traveling via the Union Pacific and Santa Fe Railroads to the Presidio at San Francisco, where, on 6 November, they joined Companies I and K, which had mustered at that post. Two weeks of additional training and preparation took place here at the Presidio before the regiment finally embarked for the Philippines. Kelly's Company A, together with Companies B, C, D, L, and M, loaded aboard the USC Transport *Ohio*, while the rest of the regiment boarded the *Indiana*. Following a two-day stop in Honolulu for provisions and coal, the *Ohio* reached Manila the day after Christmas, followed by the *Indiana* on the twenty-seventh. "Darkness shut off our view of the city," Kelly recalled, "and when the ship stayed at anchor off Manila, the sailing breeze which had attended us across the Pacific vanished. We were in the tropics."[6]

The Fortieth Volunteers remained on board ship until 28 December, at which time it was disembarked and took up positions east of Manila. Companies A, B, C, and D were assigned positions in the Pedrillo-San Felipe sector. Here, they performed outpost and patrol duty along the

Pasig and Marakina Rivers and valley region between San Mateo and Antipolo, in an area that had largely been cleared of Filipino forces, albeit very recently.[7]

For these volunteers, most of whom had likely barely heard of the Philippines until the war with Spain had splashed its name across headlines from coast to coast, this was undoubtedly a moment they would never forget. Luther Kelly, initially, at least, thought the Philippines a delightful country and recorded his impressions in a daily journal that later served as the basis for the unpublished portion of his memoirs.

> I remember the scene about us, typically oriental, filipino women with huge cigars in mouth and wares or bundles on head, moving indifferently by in the stately step burden carriers acquire, and all the picturesque throng garbed in colors of the east, *piña* and wraps of silk and native weave and lace of purest texture, but all barefooted they passed taking no heed of their surroundings.
>
> The people are modest neat and industrious. They need watching all the same. At our outposts troops of men women and children are daily searched to prevent smuggling to the insurrectos. Firing is heard on our lines at night, for the natives try to slip thru between the outposts.
>
> When we walk thru the villages the children greet us merrily and the villagers invite us into their quaint thatched bamboo houses and regale us with cigarettes fruit and sweetmeats.[8]

Following the outbreak of the Philippine-American War in February 1899, the U.S. Eighth Corps had waged a series of tough campaigns against Emilio Aguinaldo's Army of Liberation, forcing it back into northern Luzon. And although these campaigns had been largely successful in clearing out the northern and central sectors of Luzon Island, these areas were by no means entirely free of nationalist forces. While Maj. Gen. Arthur MacArthur (father of Douglas) moved against Aguinaldo's main force in northern Luzon, the colorful and dynamic Brig. Gen. Henry Ware Lawton, who had served with distinction in the Apache wars and in Cuba, was charged with the responsibility of cleaning up southern Luzon.[9]

Accordingly, on 19 December, just a few days before the Fortieth's arrival, a mixed force of infantry and cavalry from General Lawton's command had a stiff fight with a strong Filipino column under General

Pio del Pilar at San Mateo some twenty miles northeast of Manila. Tactically, the fight was a flop. U.S. forces did eventually emerge triumphant, but it proved a Pyrrhic victory, one that resulted in the unnecessary death of the tall, white-haired Lawton, who recklessly exposed himself to enemy fire and was shot down, the only American soldier to die on this dreary, rain-soaked day.[10]

As the new century began, the effects of the now nearly year-long Philippine War could be felt not only in the political arena, where disagreement between imperialists and anti-imperialists continued hot and heavy, but in other more subtle ways as well, such as with the war's impact on the hemp trade. The world's finest hemp, used in the manufacture of rope and cord, was produced in the provinces of Albay and North and South Camarine on the Bicol Peninsula in southeastern Luzon, as well as the islands of Leyte, Samar, and northern Mindanao.[11]

As a means of shutting down the flow of supplies and the movement of insurgent troops from one island to another, the U.S. Army, working in harmony with the navy in an uncharacteristic spirit of cooperation, had done a most effective job of blockading Philippine ports, especially those on the Bicol Peninsula. This, in turn, resulted in a growing shortage of hemp, so much so that agricultural lobbyists persuaded President William McKinley to take action lest the shortage seriously impact the nation's agricultural production.[12]

It was, the President decided, a situation that demanded prompt attention. Accordingly, War Department orders went out to open the hemp ports. Simple enough in Washington, but in the Philippines it presented a thorny problem to General Otis: how to manage this, while at the same time continue to apply pressure on Aguinaldo's army in Luzon. Otis believed that the heart of the "insurrection" (as it was then termed) was Aguinaldo and his Tagalog[13] followers. Crush Aguinaldo and the insurrection was over, or so the thinking went. Thus, when Otis was ordered to open the hemp ports, he found himself in the position of having to carry out a directive, which he really lacked the resources to execute. There was barely enough manpower as it was, and now to expand his sphere of operations into the hemp-growing regions of the archipelago would really be stretching troop strength to a dangerously thin level.[14]

But there was more to it than that. American commanders in the Philippines had yet to recognize that nationalism was not a goal pursued by all Filipinos; many did of course support Aguinaldo, but others had little or no interest in the independence movement. Aguinaldo's vision of a unified Philippines—undoubtedly with him as its head—was unrealistic and overlooked the traditional animosity that existed between many of the tribal groups—Aguinaldo's own Tagalogs and the Macabebes, for example. To the U.S. military, Aguinaldo and his followers may well have represented the most visible body of *insurrectos* in the archipelago, but to imagine that once Aguinaldo was disposed of resistance would collapse was an oversimplification of the first order.

Aguinaldo's sphere of influence, while strong in his Tagalog homeland, was shaky in the hemp-producing Bicol Peninsula, where Otis had been ordered to move. Aguinaldo, it would seem, made a mistake in the way he went about bringing these outlying areas under the aegis of the liberation movement. Instead of treating the population of these areas as he would his own Tagalogs, viz., as equal Filipinos, he seemed to regard them as subjects and appointed his own lieutenants to run the show. Sometimes the extraordinary charisma and ability of an installed leader was enough to bring it off, but in other instances it failed to forge an effective response. In a left-handed sort of way, what Aguinaldo was attempting here was not entirely unlike what the United States itself was up to in the Philippines, namely establishing a form of government, or rule if one prefers, in an area beyond the pale of one's own control.[15]

Filipino guerrillas and American forces vied for control of these outlying areas, but Otis lacked the troop strength to do more than secure the key hemp ports, while the guerrilla forces proved unable to rally the kind of local support that would have presented a unified front. Both sides sought to win backing of a native population that was composed of affluent merchants and planters on the one hand and a poor class of farmers on the other. The economic disparity between the two groups was great and it was all but impossible to gain the support of one without somehow alienating the other.[16]

So it was that, saddled with such constraints, General Otis prepared to carry out President McKinley's directive to open the hemp ports. Field command of the expedition was given to Lawton's successor, Maj. Gen. John Coalter Bates, whose First Division, Eighth Corps, was composed of two brigades under Brigadier Generals William August Kobbé and James Montgomery Bell.[17]

Kobbé's brigade was the first to see action. Composed of the Forty-third and Forty-seventh USV, plus a section of the Third Artillery (Kobbé's old outfit), the brigade sailed from Manila on 18 January and arrived at Legaspi, Albay Province, five days later. Here, on the Bicol Peninsula, the leader of the opposition, Vito Belarmino, was, fortunately for the

Americans, perhaps the least effective of Aguinaldo's lieutenants. Belarmino had organized a force of some 1,000 to oppose Kobbé, but they were poorly positioned and promptly overrun in a flanking movement by Kobbé, who subsequently secured the town. After detaching the Forty-seventh USV to occupy Albay province, Kobbé moved with the remainder of his brigade to secure the ports on the islands of Samar and Leyete, and despite a hard fight at Calbayog on Samar, was largely successful in achieving his objective.[18]

Phase two of Bates's hemp expedition got underway on 28 January, as the units comprising Brig. Gen. James M. Bell's Provisional Brigade were withdrawn from their outposts in the Pedrillo-San Felipe sector and sent back to the Lunetta at Manila, there to board transports for movement to the Bicol Peninsula.

An 1874 graduate of West Point, James M. Bell had risen through the ranks as an officer of cavalry and engineers. He had been appointed colonel USV in July 1899 and brigadier general in December. He had recently been awarded the Medal of Honor for gallantry in action near Porac, Luzon. The hemp campaign would be his first major responsibility since receiving his brigadier's star. Kelly and Bell may well have known each other during the Nez Perce Campaign, when Bell had been captain, Company F, Seventh Cavalry, at the Battle of Bear's Paw Mountains.[19]

Bell's Brigade consisted of two battalions of Col. Edwin A. Godwin's Fortieth USV, numbering some 842 officers and men, together with Col. Joseph Dorst's Forty-fifth USV, Companies G and H of the Thirty-seventh USV, plus detachments from the signal and engineers corps, two field pieces, and a hospital detachment. Godwin's second battalion, under Maj. William Craighill, had departed two weeks earlier and was currently occupying the port of Legaspi.[20]

Kelly's Company A was aboard the transport *Venus* when Bell's flotilla of five transports and a launch, escorted by the U.S.S. *Marietta*, weighed anchor and steamed out of Manila harbor at 7 PM on the evening of 15 February 1900. After five days at sea, the expedition reached San Miguel Bay, on the eastern shore of the Bicol Peninsula, early on the morning of 20 February. They were close enough to shore so that some of the natives could be seen running through the cocoanut trees to keep pace. Others, it was noted, were armed with spears and crossbows. Meanwhile, a brass band in a pavilion gave forth with a celebratory concert.

Landing the battalion, however, proved something of an ordeal. The troops had to be towed in as close to shore as possible by a launch from the *Marietta*. Unfortunately, because of the falling tide the launch had to disembark Godwin's men while still some distance off-shore, leaving the men to wade in across the tidal flats through waist-deep mud. As a consequence, disembarking took most of the day, but by mid-afternoon the mud-caked first battalion of Godwin's regiment under Maj. Michael Mark McNamee, plus Capt. Benjamin M. Koehler's two-gun battery, was ashore at Barcelonetta (Barcelonia), some eight miles west of the mouth of the Bicol River. Meanwhile, Godwin's third battalion, commanded by Maj. James F. Case, landed on the southeast corner of San Miguel Bay, from where it would march to Calabanga, detach two companies, then move on to Carolina.[21]

When Luther Kelly arrived in the Philippines, he must have found the climate and scenery a dramatic change from what he had been accustomed to. Less than a year earlier he had been tramping through a land of glaciers and near perpetual daylight. Now, as he led his volunteers ashore through the waist-deep mud, he found himself in a region far removed from anything he had known in the past. These Camarine Provinces of the Bicol Peninsula were lush and drought-free, with a rich and fertile volcanic soil that supported bumper rice crops and a bananalike tree known as Abaca, from which was produced Manila hemp, the reason for which these United States Volunteers had come to this place halfway around the world.[22]

After securing the village of Barcelonetta, Kelly's company captured a number of natives who had been hiding in the woods on the outskirts of the village. Kelly then directed one of the villagers to climb a tree and twist off some cocoanuts, "which he did very deftly digging into the bark with his toes until he had reached a cluster of nuts which he twisted off as each one fell at our feet. Another native with his bolo chopped off the top of a nut and then with the point of the bolo cut out one of the eyes and presented it to me." Kelly found the milk of the cocoanut to be palatable, especially where the water was poor.[23]

With Major McNamee in tactical command, Colonel Godwin accompanied the first battalion as it moved inland, with orders to pick up the main road from Nueva Caceres (present day Naga) at or near Libmanan and prevent the insurgents from escaping to the north. If possible, Godwin was also directed to occupy Libmanan.[24]

Before departing Barcelonetta, Godwin had enlisted the services of four native guides. Some two and a half miles from Libmanan, Godwin sent one of the four on ahead to inform the inhabitants that they would be spared injury if there was no resistance, but the guide soon returned with a report that the guerrillas were prepared to fight.

A half-mile from the village, the battalion reached a rice field, through the center of which ran the road. McNamee advanced his battalion, with skirmishers along both sides of the road. Progress was slow but steady. The terrain was rough and the guerrillas were determined in their resistance, using rifle fire and bolo charges to turn back the Americans, whose accurate fire inflicted heavy casualties on the defenders. By dark the guerrillas had been driven into the surrounding hills and Libmanan was in U.S. hands.

McNamee's casualties numbered one killed and eight wounded, while the guerrillas lost sixty-four of their number killed in the day's fighting, together with eleven wounded who were treated by the battalion's medical staff in a makeshift hospital set up in the local church. McNamee's battalion also released ten Spanish soldiers, who had been held prisoner by the guerrillas, and captured a small number of arms and ammunition. Libmanan, though minor compared to some battles in this insurrection—read war—was nevertheless tough and gritty, yet another illustration of Asian fanaticism that the United States was to experience in the decades ahead.[25]

After dark, Colonel Godwin ordered Kelly to examine the upper reaches of the church where Filipino sharpshooters were reportedly concealed. Taking with him a sergeant and one candle, they climbed the stairs into the belfry. "I did not relish the job," Kelly admitted, "but found nothing and soon returned to make my report."[26]

On the following morning, 21 February, Kelly's company was assigned the task of collecting and burying the dead. As his men went about the grisly task, it occurred to Kelly that it would have been a "wise and humane act to notify some of the crying and mourning relatives killed in battle." His men would, thus, have been relieved of this burden and the victims could then have received a Christian burial. "But war is war,' he said, "and it was no part of my duty to make suggestions—only to obey orders." On the face of it, there was no apparent reason why Kelly could not have made a suggestion to his commanding officer. One suspects there was something more to the incident than was revealed in his memoirs. Kelly tells us that he said nothing, but the tenor of his remarks in his memoirs suggests otherwise.[27]

Having secured the village and driven the insurgents into the hills, McNamee's battalion pulled out of Libmanan on the morning of 22 February and was ferried across the Bicol River on a steamer, then marched to Nueva Caceres (Naga), arriving that afternoon. Here, the battalion remained for seventy-two hours, before being ordered to march east to San Jose on the Gulf of Lagonoy. The battalion movement would be composed of two squadrons. Kelly's Company A, together with Capt. William J. Kendrick's Company B—4 officers and 142 men—under Kendrick's overall command, would march by way of Calabanga, while McNamee, himself, with Companies C and D—6 officers and 163 men—moved by way of Palestrina and Mabatobato. The expectation was that the two squadrons would rendezvous at San Jose on 28 February.[28]

The movement got underway on the twenty-sixth. Initially, McNamee's march was largely uneventful. The squadron reached Mabatobato on the following day, having encountered little opposition. Thereafter, however, the terrain grew increasingly difficult. Narrow trails wound through heavy timber, which insurgents took advantage of, firing into the column. By late afternoon on 27 February, McNamee had managed to reach Tiggon, having sustained four casualties. McNamee resumed his march to San Jose on the following morning. Again, guerrillas harassed his movement, at one point attacking the rear guard with a three-man mounted charge; all three riders perished in the attempt.[29]

By dark, McNamee's squadron had reached San Jose and established a bivouac. Guerrilla forces under the command of Lt. Colonel Legaspi, persistent in their efforts, continued to fire on McNamee's outposts throughout the night. On the morning of 1 March, McNamee proceeded to Logonoy Bay, where he put his wounded aboard the *Venus*, then turned about and headed back to see what had happened to Kendrick's squadron, which he feared had run into trouble.[30]

Meanwhile, Kendrick's squadron had indeed found trouble. Nearing the village of LaLud on 2 March, McNamee found Kendrick approaching the village from the opposite direction. Unlike McNamee, who had picked up a former Spanish prisoner at Nueva Caceres who knew the country, Kendrick had no local guide, which was unfortunate, because the terrain was atrocious. Writing of it two days later, McNamee called it the most difficult he had ever seen. "The trails on either side of this mountain [Mt. Isarog] are something that language can not describe. In all my experience in the mountains of Colorado, in the Bad Lands of Montana, in Cuba, and other parts of the world where I have traveled, I have never seen worse."[31]

The trails were narrow, single-file passages, flanked by dense undergrowth, mud, and mire. Periodically, it was necessary to descend banks forty to seventy feet deep in order to ford fast-flowing mountain streams. Visibility was extremely limited ahead and behind. "The enemy has only to construct his [ambush] at one of these crossings and lie in wait, sure that he can not be discovered until closely approached."

Fortunately for Kendrick, the guerrilla forces did not avail themselves of the opportunity to bushwhack the U.S. column, perhaps imagining that the terrain itself might dissuade any further advance. It didn't, but it did slow Kendrick down considerably and might have slowed his progress to an even greater extent had it not been for Luther Kelly, whose wilderness skills were never put to a tougher test than on this trek.[32]

For two days the Kendrick squadron had to hew its own trail through the jungle. "This was done," reported McNamee, "under the direction of Captain Kelly. An old frontiersman and scout, who knew that, the guides and trails failing him, it was the only resource."[33] And Kelly, calling forth all of his wilderness skills, was successful in guiding the squadron through this maze of brush and timber, but he felt the burden.

> The country was hilly and covered with dense timber and brush [he reported in his journal], but open in places. Being in the extreme advance I carried my revolver in hand not knowing what we would run into. About noon we had gained a bare grassy hill and had stopped to rest and look about. A lot of natives were on another hill watching our movements. Some trails trending in their direction I believe now were ones we should have taken, there were other trails in the direction I wished to pursue. The one I decided upon led into the timber and finally petered out. Our mode of travel was now in single file as I struck thru the timber in an endeavor to find an available road which I now believed to be at some distance. The strain of responsibility was rather heavy as there was no one else in the command who had had experience in traversing unknown ways; we were in a wilderness; our former guides were prisoners and forced to carry the burden of distressed soldiers. Cutting our way thru in places we came to a trail in the woods which we followed until dark and camped on it.[34]

Finally emerging from their nightmare of tangle and mud on 1 March, Kendrick's command had come upon a strong insurgent position not far from LaLud. The guerrillas were positioned behind breastworks on the far side of a wide gulch, across which ran the trail. Fortunately, Kendrick's advance spotted the enemy and the squadron quickly deployed for action. As it moved forward, the guerrillas, well-entrenched and concealed by banana plants and other heavy growth, opened up with two field pieces and small arms.

Accurate fire on the part of the Americans soon silenced the field pieces. Kelly commanded on the left flank, Kendrick on the right. Recognizing that the insurgent position would have to be taken head-on, Kelly volunteered and led a storming party of twenty men against the guerrilla ramparts and "drove them from the village.... After disposing my men, I entered a stone building and pulled eleven Spaniards out of a trap door in the floor." Reporting on the fight later, Major McNamee said, "Captain Kelly deserves much credit also in his part in the fight, where he volunteered to charge the works, and only waited until he had permission to do so."[35]

Kelly himself always believed he had earned a medal for this action, and apparently some of his friends—he does not identify them—later visited Colonel Godwin, recommending a Medal of Honor for Kelly. The colonel, however, rejected the recommendation, saying that Kelly had done no more than his duty. Kelly accepted Godwin's ruling, but he later told Earl Brininstool that Colonel Godwin was either incorrectly informed as to what had taken place, or was simply not inclined to recommend him [Kelly]. No medal, perhaps, but Kelly did come away from LaLud with the insurgent Colonel Legaspi's fine Toledo sword, which he had apparently abandoned in his flight from the village.[36]

Following the fight at LaLud, the reunited battalion marched back to Lagonoy Bay and boarded the *Venus*. An eruption from Mount Mayon volcano brought down a shower of ashes and imposing a darkness over the land that made it impossible for the *Venus* to depart. By 3 March the eruption had subsided and the skies had cleared enough for the ship to steam out of the bay, through the Maqueda Channel and out into the Philippine Sea. Reaching San Miguel Bay in the early hours of 4 March, the *Venus* landed McNamee's battalion at Mercedes, in the port of Daet, then deposited the remainder of Godwin's regiment down the coast at Mambulao. The two battalions were then to unite at Daet and return overland to Libmanan.[37]

From Mambulao, the troops moved on toward Daet, through woods dressed in "gorgeous orchids of fine and coarse texture hanging in clumps and festoons from trunk and limb." Natives fled in advance of their approach. On 3 March they reached Daet, where the late José Rizal, erstwhile champion of Filipino independence, was executed by the Spanish in 1896.[38] That evening, Major McNamee and his officers called on the *presidente* and were introduced to some

elegantly gowned ladies (Spanish half-bloods) who entertained us with piano and singing. In the middle of the room

two rows of chairs were placed facing inward at a distance of
about six or eight feet, the ladies occupying one row, the gentlemen facing them in the other row. Fancy the embarrassment [recalled Kelly] of a man who was born shy and
continued shy thru life.

The incident is notable in that it provides us with a personal admission
of his modesty.[39]

On another occasion, while still at Daet, Kelly, in company with
two other officers, visited a home of some means. They were welcomed
by the lady of the house who ushered them into a living room "frescoed
in gold and furnished with fine mahogany furniture." Later, the daughter of the house, "crowned with a mass of wavy, fluffy hair rendered
our national air, which is here interpreted as 'A Hot Time in the Old
Town Tonight.'" From the garden, the officers were presented with "fragrant yellow flowers," which Kelly remembered "exude[d] a subtle per-
fume of distracting sweetness."[40]

By 8 March, General Bates reported that no organized resistance
remained in either North or South Camarines. Of Colonel Godwin's
Fortieth regiment, McNamee's battalion came in for special commen-
dation by Bates, and rightly so, since it had borne the brunt of the
action in the Camarines. During the campaign, Bell's brigade fought
half a dozen sharp fights in Albay Province and an equal number in
the Camarines, including Libmanan and LaLud. The brigade had also
freed from captivity some 160 Spanish prisoners, including priests;
buried 101 insurgents; and treated 36 wounded. They had also captured
a number of small arms and ammunition, plus bows and arrows,
spears, and $2,300 in Mexican currency, of all things.[41]

During the next two weeks, Godwin's Fortieth Infantry was dispersed so as to complete any mopping-up that needed doing in Albay
and the Camarines. Case's battalion was at Nueva Caceres; McNamee's
divided between Libmanan and Daet, and Craighill's battalion at
Legaspi, Albay, and Daraga. An example of the kind of duty performed
by these detachments during this period is illustrated by Kelly's journal
entry for 15 March 1900.

Daet, South Camarines, Luzon, P.I., March 15, 1900

Got up at 4 a.m., and took 30 men as far as Basod, 4 miles
where it was reported insurgents with 30 rifles were lurking.
Found nothing. On return presently came General Bell,

from the boat. (Daet is six miles from the coast) He reports
Colonel Legaspi as surrendered and much frightened after
the repulse at La Lud and says they lost 24 in that action.
The General much gratified at the display made by our
troops on that occasion.[42]

The next phase of the hemp operation involved a movement to
Mindanao. On 20 March, General Bates was ordered to collect all
detachments of Colonel Godwin's Fortieth Infantry and establish several military posts along Mindanao's north coast. As newly appointed
commander of the District of Mindanao and Jolo Archipelago,
General Kobbé would assume overall responsibility for this phase of
the operation. Ships to transport the troops first had to turn back to
Manila and load stores before returning to San Miguel Bay to pick up
troops for the movement to Mindanao.[43]

On 31 March Kelly's Company A, together with Colonel Godwin
and staff, embarked on the *Castellano* and at 9 PM steamed to Dapitan,
Mindanao, arriving early the following day. On 1 April Kelly assumed
command of the new station, a billet he was to retain for the next
year. The remainder of the Fortieth Infantry was dispersed at various
points along the northern coast of Mindanao: Company B at Surigao;
Companies C and D at Misamis; E, F, G, and H at Iligan and headquarters; plus Companies I, K, L, and M at Cagayan.[44]

The islands of Mindanao, Jolo, and the Sulu Archipelago presented the United States with perhaps the most formidable challenge in
imposing its will throughout the Philippines. The region numbered
among its inhabitants a large population of Moros, who were of the
Muslim faith and avowed enemies of Christianity. The name "Moro"
originated with the early Spanish arrivals who thought the people
resembled the Moors of North Africa. When confrontations did occur,
Americans found Moros to be fierce and fanatical fighters.[45]

Although Moros could be found throughout the region, there was
more intertribal bickering and often fierce fighting on Mindanao than
in the Sulu Archipelago. On Mindanao there was no one *datu* (chief)
who exercised overall authority. Consequently, opposition to U.S.
presence was expressed through the whim and dictates of various
datus, some of whom were not altogether unfriendly to U.S. troops
when it was in their best interests to be accommodating. The unsettled conditions on Mindanao led to a proliferation of banditry.
Brigands—often called *ladrones*—posed a real threat to law and order
on the island.

The earliest of American policy-makers in the region, General Bates had negotiated a more or less successful agreement with various tribal leaders in August of 1899. The Bates Treaty, as it was known, embodied a number of provisions, including U.S. recognition of the sultan's authority, regulation of trade, and a joint effort to suppress the area's rampant piracy. In return, the Moro datus agreed to recognize United States sovereignty, to free any slaves, and to resolve all tribal disputes peacefully. In essence, it was an agreement that sought to establish at least a vestige of U.S. authority with a minimum commitment, and it accomplished exactly that for several years.[46]

The leader of the insurgent forces in the Dapitan area was one Vincente Alvarez, who had formerly been at Zamboanga on the extreme western end of Mindanao. Following the American occupation of Zamboanga, Alvarez had escaped to Basilan Island and from there had worked his way over to the Dapitan area where he was attempting to regroup his political and military fortunes. In the words of General Bates, Kelly was to "use every endeavor to capture him [Alvarez]."[47]

The Fortieth's tour of duty in Mindanao was to prove an active one. On 7 April, just a few days after landing on the island, a strong insurrecto force attacked Cagayan, which, along with the post at Iligan, stood as one of the regiment's two strong points. The strike at Cagayan ushered in a year-long campaign against the "gu-gu" insurrectos of Mindanao, during which the various companies of the regiment, sometimes alone and at other times in battalion-size force, sallied forth in pursuit of insurrecto bands. Save for Kelly's command at Dapitan, all companies of the regiment participated in these various operations at one time or another. Probably because it was one of only two single-company stations on Mindanao and owing to its distance from the other posts, Company A was not deemed strong enough to participate.[48]

The post at Dapitan was new, though the town itself had a history dating back to 1515. Kelly and his company, numbering 4 officers and 100 men, were the first American soldiers to take station here. Following their arrival here in 1531, the Spanish had built a fort atop a huge rock overlooking the town and had gone to considerable trouble to mount several brass and iron field pieces, "the placing of which," Kelly noted, "must have required a strong force of men and tackle. Kelly thought that with these cannons, Dapitan looked like Gibraltar.[49]

On Palm Sunday, 8 April 1900, Kelly and his officers attended Mass, accompanied by the presidente and town officials. For Kelly, at least, it proved a moving experience. With the presidente leading the way, they processed into the church, where chairs had been placed for them in front of the altar. Both sexes were well represented. The men, Kelly observed, were dressed mainly in white, while the women wore "dark gowns with exquisite lace *camisa* and *pannela*; cream, white and black were the colors."[50]

To his surprise, Kelly discovered that they were expected to take part in the service.

> The priest handed us long wands of flowers decorated with little paper flags and emblems. Then we formed a procession with the *presidente* behind the priest, who with his boys and chanters marched around the outside of the church and halted at the door, where some more singing and music by the band and the organ inside the church. After a good deal of this we entered and resumed our seats. There is a fine harmony in their music and singing which resembles the Swedish chants and hymns.[51]

Six months after assuming command at Dapitan, Kelly penned a brief but positive report of the area.

> The natives are satisfied with American rule, the civil and military government runs smoothly, schools are well attended, and the people are as prosperous as any people disinclined to exert themselves can be.
>
> The province contains 13,484 native Christians, and it is estimated that there are between 10,000 and 20,000 Lubanos or unbelievers.
>
> The climate for the last eight months has been superb, the rainfall not exceeding that of Washington, D.C.
>
> The land is rich and productive, with considerably fine hard timber.[52]

While at Dapitan, Kelly also wrote to Theodore Roosevelt, offering his congratulations on Roosevelt's nomination for vice-president and commenting briefly on the situation in the islands from his perspective.

> I am in command of this station and province, and since our arrival in April, the people have been peaceful and contented. They seem pleased to see the Americans.

Schools are flourishing. Bugbee [Fred William] of the Rough Riders is my second lieutenant. He makes a very good officer.

I have two black deer of the species found on this island that I intend to send to the New York Park if I can arrange for the transportation. They are peculiar and interesting.[53]

Roosevelt responded in his usual hearty manner, welcoming Kelly's letter, remarking that he [Roosevelt] had "always taken a good deal of enjoyment out of your career."[54]

In January 1901, Kelly led a reconnaissance force into an area known to be home to insurrectos. Following lunch at one of the villages, they resumed their journey in three boats equipped with outriggers, which had been provided by the local chief of police. Kelly recorded in his journal, "It was intensely interesting and exciting. We were entering a new region; the scenery was wild and grand, such as the mountain lands of the tropic's afford in wildest exuberance." On their return journey down the river, he noted what he thought was a half-submerged log, only to discover it was a crocodile. Before he was able to react and fire at the creature, however, it had glided out of sight. "The power for mischief and evil centered in that soft gliding motion tended to give me the unease." The command returned to Dapitan having had, in Kelly's word, "an enjoyable outing amid pleasing scenery and among friendly natives who received us with none of the distrustful and hostile manifestations that greet Americans in near-by coast towns."[55]

During the Philippine-American War, the U.S. army authorized the establishment of a Philippine Constabulary to assume the role of a civilian law enforcement body. At the same time, units of native scouts were also authorized as a native military force to work with the U.S. Army in suppressing the insurrection. In February 1901, in accordance with this directive, Kelly organized a company of 106 scouts, assigning command of the unit to Lt. William E. Utterback, who also served as inspector of customs, port captain, and collector of internal revenue for the post.[56]

Regardless of whether he was hunting and trapping in frontier Montana, exploring the interior of Alaska, or working his way through the Philippine jungles, Kelly was ever the keen observer, not only of indigenous peoples, but of native flora and fauna. Like Alaska, the Philippines offered him an excellent opportunity to observe and study, as time and circumstances permitted, some of the unusual species he found there. On one outing, for instance, he noted a tree that resembled the cottonwood, with which he was well acquainted

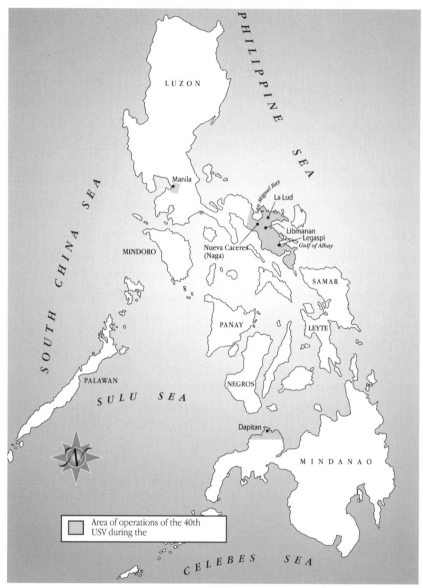

LUZON

PHILIPPINE

SEA

SOUTH CHINA SEA

Manila

San Miguel Bay

La Lud

Libmanan

Legaspi

Gulf of Albay

MINDORO

Nueva Caceres
(Naga)

SAMAR

PANAY

LEYTE

PALAWAN

NEGROS

SULU SEA

Dapitan

MINDANAO

CELEBES SEA

Area of operations of the 40th
USV during the

Map showing the movements of the Fortieth USV in the Philippines. *Map by Tom Child.*

from his days in the American West. Because of its thickly massed root system, Kelly thought this particular Philippine tree would prove of great value for preventing erosion, along the banks of a river, for example, providing it could survive in a temperate, rather than tropical, climate. Another time he spotted a species of tree cacti, which he thought unique and regretted not taking a specimen at the time, which proved his only opportunity.[57]

When Kelly discovered, or was presented with, a dead bird that had been killed near the post, he sent the carcass on to George Bird Grinnell, evidently suspecting it was an unusual specimen. His suspicion proved correct, too, because some time later he received a letter from Grinnell advising him that it was indeed a rare species of hornbill found only on the islands of Mindanao and Camagain. Grinnell said he had presented the skin to the Smithsonian Institution in Kelly's name.[58]

Later, while serving as treasurer of Surigao Province, Kelly joined a company of scouts on an outing to one of the villages in the interior. Their route wound through great forests of mahogany and other species of hardwood. Huge vines grew between the trees, running upward a hundred feet or more. The vines were exceptionally strong and were often used as shrouds and stays on schooners. They also provided a source of drinking water. One of the scouts whacked off a section of vine and held a tin cup beneath it to catch the water that soon began to ooze forth. Presenting the cup to his captain, Kelly soon had a "draught of cool limpid water that was highly refreshing."[59]

In May 1901, the Fortieth's tour of duty in the Philippines expired and the regiment moved to Cagayan, there to board the chartered steamer *Pennsylvania*. Kelly's tenure as commandant of the post at Dapitan appears to have been orderly and trouble-free. And insofar as we are able to judge, he seems to have been well liked by the residents of the community. Before taking his leave of Dapitan, he was presented with a small bronze cannon that was mounted on a "rude carriage."[60]

The *Pennsylvania* stopped in Manila for two days before beginning the long but euphoric voyage to San Francisco. At Manila, Kelly bade farewell to his company and comrades, having been ordered to report to headquarters for further orders. Two years of military service, particularly in a combat zone, gives birth to and nurtures a powerful sense of camaraderie. He had experienced this comradeship during his days with Miles and the Fifth Infantry, but not to the degree he had come to know it in the Philippines. In Montana, he had been a part of Miles's operations, yet apart from it. Here in the islands, the bond had been of a different sort. Of those who served under him, only one recollection of his leadership has survived. James C. Keeler, a private in Company A remembered that "Capt. Kelly was a real man. I was always up next to him."[61]

As an officer Kelly had performed his duties ably. In preparing his efficiency report for June 1900, Colonel Godwin described his duty as "well done," his general conduct as "excellent," along with his professional zeal and ability. He received slightly lesser marks—"good"—for the discipline of his men and capacity for command. All in all, it was a report that surely justified the faith that had been expressed in him.[62]

How Kelly came to remain in the Philippines is an interesting story. In February 1900, President William McKinley appointed William Howard Taft chairman of the second Philippine Commission. Although a jurist of some repute—he served on the U.S. Court of Appeals for the Sixth Circuit—Taft was perhaps an odd appointee. He knew nothing about the islands and had been opposed to U.S. acquisition of the Philippines to begin with, though he had not voiced his opposition in particularly strident tones. Still, the President rather liked the idea of having a man in Manila who was not out of the ardent expansionist crowd.[63]

For President McKinley and the Republican party, 1900 was an election year. And much like Vietnam would prove to be seventy years later, the Philippine issue had become something of a political liability. The euphoria that had propelled the nation into the war with Spain had largely subsided. The American public was sated with war, and polarized over the question of U.S. annexation of the Philippine Islands. McKinley believed that the solution to the Philippine problem was to create a self-governing infrastructure as quickly as possible. Thus it was that Taft and his fellow commissioners arrived in the Philippines in June 1900 prepared to get underway with the transition from military to civil government.[64]

At the time of Taft's appointment, the Philippine-American War had been ongoing for a year, with no real end in sight, and threatened to seriously jeopardize the President's chances for reelection come November. McKinley, perhaps having been erroneously influenced by the former military commander in the Philippines, General Otis, believed the United States to be closer to military victory than was actually the case and seems to have imparted this attitude to Taft and his commissioners.[65]

Of ponderous physical size, weighing well in excess of 300 pounds, "Big Bill" Taft and his fellows arrived in the Philippines prepared to carry out their mission of establishing a civil government, only to soon find themselves at odds with army leaders, specifically Maj. Gen. Arthur MacArthur, whose ego was perhaps second only to that of Nelson Miles, but he quite correctly knew that militarily the Philippine situation was far from being resolved. As would his son, Douglas, half a century later, Arthur MacArthur also found it nearly impossible to acquiesce to civilian authority, making the commission's job all the more difficult. Not until peremptory orders came through from Washington did MacArthur grudgingly yield to Taft, and finally in September 1900 civil authority became the ruling body in the Philippines, with Taft replacing MacArthur as the new civil governor.

On a subsequent tour of the Islands, Taft paid a visit to Dapitan. The ship carrying the governor and his party reached the harbor about dusk. Early the following morning, Kelly and his acting revenue officer, Lieutenant Utterback, went out to the ship in a small boat, but as no one appeared to yet be up and about, they returned to the post for breakfast. They had barely finished, however, when they learned that the governor's party had come ashore. Kelly's description of his first glimpse of Taft sounds like a scene cut from Meredith Willson's *The Music Man*. "We found that the party had already landed and were marching up the main throfare [sic], escorted by Dapitan's bare-footed brass band, Mr. Taft towering in the lead like a band master. I met the party, introduced myself, and invited them to enter my Headquarters, which they did."[66]

There followed, then, a conference between Taft and Dapitan's presidente and head men. Kelly listened in from the shadows, as he was wont to do, impressed with Taft's knowledge of affairs in the area. However, when Taft began to compliment the presidente on having a military officer present "who took an interest in the uplifting and prosperity of the people," Kelly, with characteristic modesty, excused himself and left. Later, he and Taft strolled around the town plaza and the governor offered him the position of treasurer of the large Mindanao province of Surigao, which Kelly accepted.[67]

Taft's offer of a civilian position to Kelly, an army officer, was the exception rather than the rule. Since his arrival in the Philippines, Taft had grown steadily less tolerant of the military figures with whom he had to contend. It had begun on a sour note with MacArthur and gone downhill from there. The army resented civilian interference and politicking and regarded the commission's view that the majority of Filipinos welcomed American rule as being pure rubbish. Taft and his fellow commissioners, of course, refused to recognize that conditions in the Philippines were not as trouble-free as they wanted to believe.

Thus, when Taft offered a responsible civilian position to Kelly, it made a clear statement to the effect that he did not regard Kelly as one of the typical officers he had grown to have so little use for. Taft had found a few other officers with whom he had developed a rapport, but they were in the minority. Apparently, Taft had been sufficiently impressed with conditions at Dapitan to see in Kelly the kind of individual whose views were entirely compatible with the objectives of the Commission.[68]

We know little about Luther Kelly's politics; how, for instance, he felt about a U.S. presence in the Islands. He had been opposed to war with Spain, but on the other hand he did volunteer for service in the Philippines, so one suspects that once his country had made the commitment, he was prepared to do his part to back it up. Like many of his generation, Kelly was an avowed patriot. We recall that he appreciated the pure Americanism to be found among well-bred Southerners and how he told E. H. Harriman that he liked to keep alive the tradition of his ancestors. Accordingly, it seems fair to suggest that Kelly believed the U.S. mission in the Philippines was a just and fitting extension of Manifest Destiny.

Insofar as his attitude toward the Filipino people was concerned, it mirrored his feelings about Native Americans: one needed to be fair, but straightforward and tactful, and always firm. This philosophy of dealing with native peoples had been evident throughout his frontier experience and there is no reason to suspect that it changed in the Philippines. It was an attitude perhaps best summarized by Kelly himself in a letter written to Theodore Roosevelt some years later. Here he was talking specifically about the Mexican people at the time of the revolution, but I think we may safely assume that this viewpoint would apply equally to all native peoples. "The people of that country [Mexico]," wrote Kelly, "are mostly of Indian blood and require a different course of treatment than a civilized people."[69]

Although he had great respect for the culture and traditions of native peoples and believed that they deserved fair and responsible treatment, this paternalistic philosophy stopped short of declaring outright equality. At the outset of American involvement in the Philippines, President William McKinley established the tenet of "benevolent assimilation," whereby the Filipino people were to be treated with firmness, but at the same time with kindness and respect. It was a policy that had as its objective the gradual absorption of those people into the American culture and way of life; it was, quite simply, an extension of the American Indian policy.

This "Americanization" of native peoples stood as the finest example of *noblesse oblige*; what better way to spread the strengths of a great and growing nation than by imbuing its principles in the souls and spirits of those less fortunate. And if today this strikes us as perhaps the aristocracy of arrogance, it must be remembered that in 1900, this was regarded as the genteel, and to many the Christian way, of dealing with ignorance and savagery.

As it would prove to be in Vietnam, the Philippine conflict had a very dark and grim side to it. Cruelty begat cruelty. American soldiers often adopted a fire-with-fire policy of retaliation. Some, such as Kelly's former Alaska comrade Capt. Edwin Forbes Glenn, were well known for their harsh treatment of Filipino guerrillas. Luther Kelly, however, seems to have avoided falling into that mindset and apparently impressed "Big Bill" Taft as a shining example of "benevolent assimilation" at work.[70]

On 12 May 1901, Kelly was detached from the Fortieth USV and reported to headquarters for reassignment, and on the twenty-third received orders to proceed to the Province of Surigao, there to assume the post of Provincial Treasurer, a position he was to hold for the next two years. Although technically still an officer in the USV, he now functioned as an employee of the Division of Insular Affairs, a new subdivision of the War Department that had been created to administer colonial affairs.[71]

Anxious to begin his new assignment, Kelly opted to travel to Surigao aboard a Spanish ship that plied the inland waterways of the Islands, rather than wait for a government boat. When approaching Surigao, the vessel seemed aimed directly at the shore, but then turned to coast smoothly "along the beautiful forested shore until arriving in front of an ancient wharf of rough timbers, came to anchor for the visit of the Customs and Health Officers, for all along this coast there is a rage and horror of cholera." When finally he stepped ashore, Kelly found no barefooted brass band to greet him as had welcomed Big Bill Taft at Dapitan.[72]

He found Surigao to possess a certain charm and beauty. From the wharf, the main street extended through an avenue of shade trees and orchids, past a short street known for its lovely "fire or flame" trees, to the provincial building that would serve as Kelly's headquarters. The row of fire trees, wrote Kelly, "sounded the depth of benevolent intention on the part of a native gentleman, desirous perhaps, to leave some testimonial fronting the portal of the church, and what better than living flame and grateful shade."[73]

At one time, the Spanish had worked the area for gold, which apparently could still be found by industrious seekers, which Kelly found these natives to be.

> I have observed [that while] the men with bars and
> picks loosened the sand and pay gravel from around rocks
> and boulders; the women and girls of the family washed
> the gravel and sand in wooden bowls; water for the purpose
> being brot [sic] several hundred feet in split bamboo troughs
> and piping. It is astonishing how much gold a family of
> four or five will work out in two or three days.[74]

In his early days as treasurer, Kelly found that if life at Surigao lacked the excitement of campaigning through the Philippine jungle, the routine of official business was nevertheless arduous enough to "make a stranger of monotony." In the wake of monthly paydays, either the provincial governor or secretary would host an official dinner, followed by dancing, all being on a "scale of munificence actuated by the glitter of Uncle Sam's gold coin, which was a never ending surprise to these native officials—expecting only pesos."[75]

Now that his active military service was over and his new assignment promised something closer to a relatively trouble-free and regular routine, Kelly took steps to have May join him early in 1902. Evidently, at some point after his departure for the Philippines, she had returned to Detroit, taking up residence with her brother George at 161 Forest Avenue. May's health was apparently not all that good, because Kelly requested passage for both his wife and his sister Anna, who, he claimed, was needed to assist May. In any case, Kelly's request touched off an exchange of letters between Rep. M. E. Olmstead of Pennsylvania, William D. Kelly, and the Division of Insular Affairs. The problem was that regulations authorized passage for only dependent family members which, of course, Anna was not and was therefore ineligible for government-funded passage. The problem was resolved, however, when John T. Macleod, president of *La Compania Maratima*, largest steamship company in the Philippines, granted the ladies complimentary passage from San Francisco to the Islands. Passage from Detroit to San Francisco remained their own responsibility.[76]

It is not clear exactly when May and Anna arrived in the Philippines, but it was probably sometime in May 1902. Whether their sojourn in the Islands was intended to be temporary is not clear. Although President Theodore Roosevelt would declare the Philippine Insurrection officially over on the Fourth of July, 1902, considerable unrest still existed on Mindanao. In Surigao, banditry was still rife and some of the pueblos in the province had been hit hard by a plague of cholera. Consequently, after a few months Kelly may have decided that

Capt. Luther S. Kelly, flanked by May Kelly on the left and an unidentified woman on the right. The location is unknown but could be Mindanao, Philippine Islands, in which case the woman on the right could possibly be Kelly's sister Anna. *George Bille Collection.*

it was in the ladies' best interest to move them out of harm's way. Accordingly, they booked passage back to the States, enjoying a leisurely voyage home by way of China and Japan.[77]

Kelly seems to have justified Taft's faith in him by performing his duties as provincial treasurer in exemplary fashion. Reporting on conditions in Surigao in January 1903, Provincial Governor Prudencio García requested that a steam launch be provided in order to enable the officials of his government to travel throughout the province, collecting taxes and attending to other matters of business. Kelly himself was on the road much of the time, demonstrating "energy, probity, and zeal... in the compliance of official duties."[78]

On 23 March 1903 a band of sixty to eighty prisoners, who had been convicted of ladronism (banditry) managed to escape their captors. Returning to Surigao, they surprised the constabulary barracks where, after killing Chief Inspector Clark and seizing arms and ammunition, they laid siege to the town. Kelly, who had been resting at his residence during the noon hour, heard shots, and was soon advised of what had transpired at the barracks. Gathering a small party of nine Americans, including four members of the constabulary and two women, Kelly directed them to the provincial building, where they took refuge and prepared to defend themselves with but a few shotguns and a limited supply of ammunition.

Presently, the ladrones sent emissaries to demand the group's weapons. While the men presented their demands, Kelly sat quietly, smoking a cigar. Then, through an interpreter, he rejected the demand, advising them that not a single firearm would be surrendered and that any prisoner within range would be shot. Having thus stated his position, Kelly rose to his feet and motioned for them to leave. Escorted by the guard, they moved down the broad stairway and "into the gathering darkness, the heavy doors being bolted behind them, and the guard released to other and more important points of approach."[79]

Kelly, meanwhile, had managed to get off a telegram to Brig. Gen. Jesse M. Lee at Iloilo, informing him of their peril. Lee promptly started help on the way, but Kelly and his party were compelled to hold out for eighteen hours until the relief column arrived. General Lee himself with additional troops arrived a few days later. Interestingly, Lee was one of those who had earlier written a strong letter of recommendation urging Kelly's appointment as a volunteer officer.[80]

In the aftermath of the affair at Surigao, General Lee, in reporting the incident to his superior, Gen. George Whitefield Davis, had the highest of praise for Kelly, saying that "Provincial Treasurer Kelly, ex-captain volunteers, has rendered me most valuable assistance. He is a tower of strength and in full accord with us."[81]

Governor Taft cabled a report of the affair at Surigao and of Kelly's role in conducting the defense of the provincial building. President Roosevelt and his family read Taft's cable at breakfast the following morning and Roosevelt promptly fired off a bully letter to Kelly, saying how the news made them all feel so pleased and proud. Roosevelt also asked to be remembered to his old Rough Rider comrade, Lt. Fred Bugbee, now serving in Kelly's company.[82]

The story of Kelly's eventual reassignment to the next chapter in his life, San Carlos, Arizona, reads like a page out of the bureaucratic manual for spinning red tape. While at Dapitan, probably in early 1901 but before his appointment as provincial treasurer, Kelly apparently sought then Vice-President Roosevelt's assistance in securing a position in either the Quartermaster's or Subsistence (Commissary) Departments. The Fortieth's term of service was drawing to a close and Kelly was no doubt thinking about a future billet. Roosevelt was delighted to help and penned a letter of support to the Secretary of War.

> Captain Kelly has a really remarkable record. I knew him in the early days of the West when he was one of the most daring scouts in all the Indian campaigns. He was then almost universally called "Yellowstone Kelly," but this nickname must not give the impression that he was in any way a rough character. He is emphatically a gentleman, comes from first class Revolutionary stock, and is a brother of Mr. William D. Kelly, President of the Clearfield Bituminous Coal Corporation of Philadelphia. He was appointed to his present position on the recommendation of the army officers who have served with him. He has not only served with gallantry and success in the engagements in the Philippines but has shown a high order of ability as an administrator. I venture to refer you to the reports of his superior officers on this account. It is a pleasure to send this word in his behalf.[83]

Despite the strength of Roosevelt's recommendation, no action appears to have been taken at that time. Kelly remained at Dapitan and, as we have seen, was subsequently appointed treasurer at Surigao. Then in 1903 Senator Boies Penrose and Representative M. E. Olmstead, both of Pennsylvania, renewed efforts to secure a quartermaster or commissary appointment for Kelly. This time the adjutant-general's office responded with the explanation that Kelly was no longer eligible for such a position. The Congressional Act of 2 February 1901 stipulated that a captain's billet in either quartermaster or subsistence departments could only be filled from the line of the regular army, and Kelly was beyond the maximum age (twenty-seven) for a lieutenancy in the regulars.[84]

Although unsuccessful in securing an army billet for Kelly, Theodore Roosevelt was able to offer Kelly a position as Indian agent, but inasmuch as that position paid less than his annual salary as provincial treasurer, Kelly declined the appointment, only to find himself wishing later that he had not done so. In January 1903 he wrote to George Bird Grinnell expressing his regret at not having accepted Roosevelt's offer. He was much too embarrassed to return to the now President of the United States, asking again for assistance. Old friend Grinnell might act as intermediary and he of course was glad to do so, writing to the President on 24 March 1903.

A short time ago I received a letter from him [Kelly] dated
January 18th, in which he said: 'I have been in the Philippines
so long now that I am getting tired of it. I am sorry that I did
not accept the offer that the President made me of an Indian
agency. Yet I have much respect for the man and his office
that I cannot ask him for anything without running the risk of
losing his regard, for I know he is pestered unmercifully for
office. *This country is a wearing one and I fear for my health*
[italics added]. As Treasurer I have the burden of the entire
Province on my shoulders. My health has been excellent, but
three years is the limit.'[85]

It is interesting that Kelly here makes a point of expressing concern for his health, *if he remains in the Islands*. This is a first. Never has
health been a reason for terminating an assignment or an adventure.
Clearly, he is tired and ready to return to the States.

Grinnell's letter to Roosevelt opened the door to an Indian agency
appointment a second time. And once again, brother William D. Kelly
exerted a little influence on Luther's behalf, working through E. A.
Hitchcock, Secretary of the Interior. Apparently, the San Carlos Apache
Agency in Arizona was on the table. Early in May, Hitchcock advised
William D. that when he [Hitchcock] returned to Washington in two
weeks, he would see about Luther's appointment to San Carlos. William
responded on 11 May, applying subtle pressure, saying, "I trust it will be
possible for the appointment to be made, and as requested in my previous letter, I will be greatly indebted to you if you will kindly advise me
of your action in this matter."[86]

On 4 June, Hitchcock wrote to Secretary of War Elihu Root, requesting that Kelly be relieved of his duties in the Philippines in order that
he might take up his new post at San Carlos in accordance with the
President's wishes. Within twenty-four hours the appointment was
made. On 5 June 1903 Governor Taft was advised by cablegram that

The President desires to appoint Captain ~~Arthur~~ Luther S.
Kelly, Treasurer of Province of Surigao, Indian Agent at
San Carlos Agency. If he accepts the President would be
glad to have his resignation from his present position
accepted with a leave of absence to enable his arrival
here prior to resignation taking effect if your regulations
and customs permit. Transportation from Manila to
San Francisco will be furnished.[87]

The policy of the Philippine Commission, under whose aegis Kelly was employed, was amenable to this arrangement and when presented with the appointment Kelly accepted, though as he was to discover, much to his chagrin, it was one thing to have an offer extended and accepted, and quite another for the details to be timely executed. Not until a month later did the Government of the Philippines acknowledge receipt of these directives. By mid-October, nothing had happened, although Kelly had twice applied to department headquarters in Manila for his leave of absence. Again Secretary Hitchcock wrote to Secretary Root pleading for action. The following day the Secretary of War again fired off a cable to Manila directing that the Kelly matter be taken care of promptly. At long last, effective 15 November, Kelly was finally granted fifty-nine days' leave of absence, to expire 27 January 1904, at a prorated compensation based on an annual salary of $2,300. His tour of duty in the Philippines had come to an end. Within a few weeks he would once more find himself overseeing the treatment and behavior of native peoples.[88]

Chapter Thirteen

SAN CARLOS, ARIZONA,
1904–1909

**It is a genial climate, quiet retired place, with fine
quail and turkey hunting. Quail are found in walking
distance, turkey two days ride in the mountains.[1]**

Exactly when Kelly left the Philippines is not clear, but it was likely
between 15 November and 1 December 1903, when his annual leave
commenced. En route to the East Coast, he stopped in Chicago,
spending a couple of nights at the Palmer House, just barely missing
the fire that destroyed that historic structure for the second time in its
history. It had been four years since he had tasted winter, and with
his system still acclimated to the tropics, one might imagine that he
felt the cold more than usual. Perhaps he wondered, in fact, how he
had ever managed to survive those winter expeditions with Miles and
the Fifth Infantry.

Kelly probably reached Germantown in time to celebrate the holidays with May, his brothers, and their families (Albert, the youngest
son, had married in 1896 and was also living in Germantown, or Mount
Airy as it was sometimes called).[2] Three years earlier Luther had

returned from Alaska with tales of reindeer, great glaciers, and perpetual daylight. Now he had come back from a distant land halfway around the world, as different from Alaska as Germantown was from the dark side of the moon. Given Luther's tales of the Philippines, combined with May and Anna's own descriptions of the Orient sights they had experienced on their own return voyage from the Philippines, it must have been a fascinating, if not at times a spellbinding, holiday season for the Kelly family.[3]

In late December or early January, Kelly traveled to Washington, where he arranged for his bond as agent at San Carlos and undoubtedly called on his new boss, the Commissioner of Indian Affairs, William A. Jones.[4] While in Washington, he also lunched with President Theodore Roosevelt. Whether it was a private or group luncheon is not known, although Roosevelt was frequently joined by old friends and cronies, of which Luther Kelly was regarded as one. At any rate, the President very likely asked to hear all about how Kelly stood up to those bandits at Surigao, for such was exactly the sort of conduct that Roosevelt thoroughly appreciated.

One cannot help but wonder if anything was said regarding General Miles, whose personal inspection tour of the Philippines in late 1902 and 1903, to investigate rumors of atrocities committed by the U.S. Army, had angered and embarrassed both President Roosevelt and his Secretary of War, Elihu Root. It is not clear if Roosevelt knew of the relationship that Kelly and Miles enjoyed, though surely he knew that the two had campaigned together during the Indian wars. Roosevelt, who was not averse to putting people on the spot and never met a subtlety he liked, may well have asked Kelly what if anything he knew about this atrocity business in the Philippines. After all, Kelly had just returned from the Islands and what did he think of Miles's accusations? An election loomed in November, and all of this talk about atrocities committed by the U.S. Army had become a major issue.[5]

Before departing the capital city, Kelly visited his old comrade from the Fifth Infantry days, now Brig. Gen. Oscar Long. If he also called on General Miles, there is no record of such a visit, but it seems likely that he would not have left Washington without seeing his old commander. And if so, we might further speculate about these issues from Miles's perspective. Like the President himself, Miles never pulled punches. And at the moment, he still seethed over Roosevelt's rebuke for his [Miles's] public criticism of a naval court's decision regarding the naval battle of Santiago de Cuba during the Spanish-American War. So, if Kelly did indeed call on his old commander it would not be surprising to learn that Miles minced no words about Roosevelt and the Philippine question.[6]

Luther and May arrived at San Carlos in late January 1904 and Kelly formally took charge of the agency from his predecessor, S. L. Taggart, on 1 February. San Carlos would be their home for nearly five years. Kelly left no record of what his expectations for the new position might have been, but he was definitely glad to be out of the Philippines and back on American soil. On the face of it at least, San Carlos might seem like a pretty decent slot for a man nearing age fifty-five with Luther Kelly's background, but as the years unfolded, they would reveal a different set of responsibilities and challenges than any he had previously known. Whether he was to emerge from this experience with any sense of accomplishment remained to be seen.

The San Carlos Reservation for which Kelly assumed responsibility was part of the Indian reservation system, administered by the Office (Bureau) of Indian Affairs, Department of the Interior, headquartered in Washington. Overall responsibility for Indian affairs was vested in a commissioner, to whom Kelly and other field agents submitted their reports and accountings and made requests for everything from medical supplies and machinery to paper and pencils. It was the agent's responsibility to maintain order and see that his charges received what was due them in accordance with the provisions legislated by Congress and interpreted by the Office of Indian Affairs. The agent was also authorized to pay for certain services, such as for ice when the ice-making machine temporarily malfunctioned, and to hire and fire according to the operating procedures set forth by the Washington office. It was a bureaucratic position, subject to all of the frustration that an indifferent bureaucracy often imposes on those who seek to carry out its will.

Located some twenty miles east of Globe, Arizona, and bounded on the north by the Salt and Black Rivers, the sprawling San Carlos Reservation encompassed approximately 2,800 square miles. San Carlos was created from the original Apache reservation system that had been set aside in 1872. Although there had been an agency at San Carlos from the beginning, it did not become a separate reservation for two decades. Then, in 1896 the northern one-third of the original White Mountain Apache Reservation was renamed Fort Apache, with the remaining segment being officially classified as the San Carlos Reservation. Broadly, the mission of both the San Carlos and Fort Apache Reservations was to control all of the various Apache bands west of the Rio Grande River. Like other reservation systems it was

A view of San Carlos in September 1996. *Author photo.*

viewed as the gateway to Indian acculturation, and as elsewhere it proved a concept that delivered less than it promised.[7]

San Carlos may well have been the most ill-conceived of all Western reservation systems. To begin with, the location itself was regarded as simply awful. Historian Robert Utley describes it as a "hot, barren, malarial flat along Arizona's Gila River." The Apache war leader Victorio and some of his followers reportedly vowed that death was better than being incarcerated at San Carlos. Another, unidentified Chiricahua Apache thought most everything about San Carlos was dreadful. "The heat was terrible. The insects were terrible. The water was terrible." But there was more to it than that. Over and above the location itself, the deeper problem lay with the Indian Bureau's failure to recognize that not all Apache bands enjoyed friendly relations with one another. As a consequence, when these various bands were ordered to share the same reservation, it was an invitation to trouble.[8]

Until 1885, agency administrators were civilians appointed by the Office of Indian Affairs. However, feuding between agents and the military led to poor management practices, with the Indians usually paying the price for this squabbling. In 1885 control passed to the War Department, which assigned army officers to manage the reservations, a system that remained in place until 1900 when civilian agents were once again appointed.

Although one could find examples of fair and efficient agents who truly worked on behalf of their charges, by and large the reservation system, regardless of who was at the helm, did not receive high marks. Graft, incompetence, and the often abusive use of power drew harsh criticism, whether the agent was an army officer or a civilian. Given his own background in civil service reform, President Theodore Roosevelt may well have seen in his friend Luther Kelly a man who could be counted on to do right by the Indians, to be an example of Roosevelt's square deal philosophy.[9]

Notwithstanding the largely negative views of San Carlos, then as now, it is interesting to note that Luther Kelly genuinely liked the place. He and May were located in a nice roomy house that had formerly served as the residence of his predecessor, Mr. Taggart. And after the Philippines it seemed exactly the right spot. Contact with the world beyond San Carlos was through Globe to Phoenix. The agency headquarters, nerve center of the reservation, was situated on the line of the Gila Valley, Globe and Northern Railway, which connected with the Southern Pacific at Bowie, Arizona, and offered a second option for travel east or west.[10]

Early in his tenure at San Carlos, he sent his old comrade Gen. Oscar Long some Moro cloth from the Philippines and reported that he was pleasantly situated at San Carlos and enjoyed the climate and people.[11] Two months later, he wrote to Gen. Jesse Lee, saying "I am glad I left the Islands. This is a fine hot old country here, and I enjoy it very much." To another, he remarked that the dry heat was not unpleasant "if you have plenty of ice."[12]

Nor did his appreciation of San Carlos appear to diminish with the passing years. In November 1908, just weeks before he was replaced, Kelly wrote to William Howard Taft, extolling the virtues of San Carlos and inviting him to visit. By late 1908, Kelly probably suspected that his days at San Carlos might be numbered. Taft was now president-elect, and like any bureaucrat Kelly was simply looking to his own future.[13]

Kelly was enthusiastic about his new assignment and filled with ideas as to what might be done to improve the lot of his charges. He was, by spirit and personal code, a man who was not satisfied with anything less than his own best, a trait that had been made abundantly clear with any job he had ever undertaken.

When in Washington, President Roosevelt had asked Kelly to report on conditions at San Carlos as soon as he had had an opportunity to

Luther S. Kelly as the
Indian Agent at San Carlos
Apache Reservation,
Arizona, 1904–1908.
George Bille Collection.

size up the reservation. Accordingly, on 7 April Kelly provided the
president with an assessment of San Carlos, based on two months'
experience and observation. The population of the reservation, he
informed the president, consisted of 1,666 Apaches, 43 Mohaves, and
381 Tontos. But the picture was not a pleasant one. These Indians were
poor, Kelly pointed out, with most barely subsisting, thanks to a Bureau
of Indian Affairs' policy that sought to encourage self-sufficiency by
reducing the amount of rations, so that now only the aged and helpless
were actually issued food. In place of rations, some $18,000 had been
made available for Indian labor during fiscal year 1903–1904, but this
had provided only "scanty" relief for a few.[14]

"These Indians are intelligent, law abiding and fairly industrious,"
he informed the president, "but like most Indians are thriftless and lack
habits of economy." They were glad to have work, but there were few
jobs to be had on the reservation, so most sought employment with
railroads and mines outside the reservation. That Kelly was impressed

Apache students at San Carlos about 1905. *George Bille Collection.*

with the work ethic of these Apaches, however, is made clear in a letter
to George Bird Grinnell in which he states that they [the Apaches] were
"far ahead of the sioux [*sic*] as I knew them, and are willing to work."[15]

In August, Kelly was able to provide the Commissioner of Indian
Affairs with a more detailed picture of conditions. There was plenty
about which to be pleased and to feel encouraged. Much had already
been done at San Carlos in the way of establishing schools, law enforcement, and a judicial system. At Talkai, twelve miles north of San Carlos,
the Rice Bonded School, built of native white-ash stone, served the
educational needs of some 200 Apaches. Additionally, a boarding
school had the capacity to handle up to 100 pupils. Kelly advised the
commissioner that the students—all Apaches—made good progress
during the school year, at the conclusion of which they returned home,
there to revert to the traditional Apache lifestyle.[16]

In addition, the German Lutheran Society also operated a mission
school on the San Carlos River, but attendance was poor, with only
twenty students enrolled. Kelly attributed the low attendance to the
school's poor location. Despite its location, however, Kelly believed
that the mission school exerted a very positive influence on its students and he would welcome more schools of this type.

Although cattle raising was encouraged, the Apaches had few animals and were largely indifferent to the idea of becoming cattlemen. They were, Kelly observed, more inclined to kill the animals for beef so that herds remained small. As a consequence, permission was now required to kill a steer or an old cow and the animal's hide must be shown to the proper official.

Law and order was maintained through a police force consisting of a captain and fifteen privates, armed with Springfield carbines and .38 caliber revolvers. A police court, composed of three salaried Indian judges, had been established to deal with a variety of offenses ranging from drunkenness and disorderly conduct to horse-stealing and attempted murder.

Finally, Kelly reported that since his arrival in February, sixty shade trees, plus twenty-four English walnut, three crab, and three apricot trees had been planted. A decade later, Kelly would be planting his own fruit trees in Paradise, California, perhaps inspired by his experience here at San Carlos.[17]

When Kelly arrived at San Carlos in 1904, the use of Apache labor had increased significantly, enough so that local labor unions were beginning to oppose the practice. Apaches would work for less, usually far less, than what an employer would have to pay white laborers. As anthropologist Richard J. Perry points out, Apache labor was much exploited around the turn of the century. But faced with the Indian Bureau's policy of reducing rations and promoting self-sufficiency, the Apaches were left with little choice but to accept whatever work they could find.[18]

Probably the single most important source of employment for the Apaches during Kelly's administration was the Roosevelt Dam. Built on the Upper Salt River northwest of San Carlos by the U.S. Reclamation Service between 1902 and 1911, at a cost of ten million dollars, the dam eventually resulted in the creation of Lake Roosevelt. At ten miles long and two miles wide, it was then the world's largest artificial lake. During the construction of the dam, the famed army scout Al Sieber was killed by a falling boulder while supervising Apache workers in 1907. There is no record of Kelly and Sieber having ever met, but given that Kelly was the agent and Sieber was supervising Apache working parties, it seems hard to imagine that the two old scouts could have avoided seeing each other. And, assuming they did meet, one imagines that the exchange of experiences, which must surely have followed, would have been well worth recording.[19]

Whether or not Kelly made any effort to improve working conditions for his charges is left to our own surmise, though one is hard pressed to imagine exactly what he might have done to change the picture noticeably. He could hardly forbid the Apaches from accepting these jobs, nor were there any Federal laws governing minimum wage or working conditions. It is regrettable, too, that Kelly left no record of how exactly he felt about the reservation system, but he may well have viewed it as the only practical way of dealing with what had long been called the "Indian problem." He did believe, though, that the time had come to parcel out the reservation land to the Indians in severalty, viz., to individual Indians rather than simply to the tribe as a whole. And from the evidence we have of his tenure at San Carlos, it seems clear Kelly also believed that for these Indians, agriculture was the path that led to a successful recasting of their identity. In this he was not, of course, the first agent—nor the first white man, for that matter—who was convinced that the success of the acculturation program lay in agriculture. The prevailing winds of political wisdom carried this philosophy to all corners of the nation; it was the cornerstone of the reservation concept.[20]

Here at San Carlos, the problem was water. "Continued drought has affected this reservation heavily," Kelly advised the Commissioner of Indian Affairs in August 1904. "Springs are drying up, and ground on which hay was formerly gathered to fill government contracts is now bare of vegetation."[21] Interestingly enough, a year later Kelly was reporting that the extraordinary precipitation since January (1905) caused considerable flooding and washed away all irrigation ditches. Despite this, crops were planted and generally yielded a good harvest of wheat, barley, and corn.[22]

Owing to the scarcity of water, the San Carlos Apaches were crowded along the reservation's few water courses, a situation that compelled some to leave the reservation in search of better land. But Kelly believed there was potential here. There was more than enough land to provide each family with a small farm, if water could be obtained. Kelly's solution was to locate underground water and told President Roosevelt he had requested that the Indian Bureau provide a boring machine to drill for water, but thus far the department had not acted on his request. Whether or not mentioning his request to Roosevelt speeded up the process is unknown, but when Kelly wrote to George Bird Grinnell a month later, he had received the boring machine. Finally, Kelly told Roosevelt, he had recommended to the Indian Bureau that San Carlos be opened to mining exploration, with a tax levied on any earnings that might be realized from future mining operations.[23]

When he first arrived at San Carlos, Kelly told George Van Horn Moseley that the Indians regarded him as a tough taskmaster, saying that he "had a 'bad eye,'" and that "they would not have the free and easy times, they had formerly enjoyed." The attitude implies that Kelly's predecessor had perhaps managed the agency with a loose rein. Kelly apparently struck them as an agent who would run a tighter ship, and in this they were probably correct. There is no record of how the Apaches eventually came to regard Kelly, but he had never had a problem in developing a solid working rapport with native peoples, as any examination of his Western frontier experiences will attest to. He had long since developed a philosophy of dealing with native peoples and it seems unlikely that he would have altered this viewpoint when he arrived at San Carlos. With this in mind, it seems reasonable to assume that in time these Apaches came to see their new agent as a man who could be trusted and who would work on their behalf, but at the same time would brook no foolishness.[24]

Early on, Kelly discovered that being an employee of the Indian Bureau was quite unlike being in the military. "This Interior dept. is not like the department of war," he told George Van Horn Moseley. But regardless of which department of government one was involved with, snarls could and did occur. Red tape and delays were as much a part of life in the bureaucratic jungle in 1900 as they are today. And as time went on, he was to find out just how vexing it could be for a middle manager in the government bureaucracy.[25]

Since no personal records have survived, one cannot evaluate Kelly's financial situation, but it was probably never particularly strong. We do know that while at San Carlos Kelly maintained bank accounts at First National Bank of Glenwood Springs, Colorado, and National Metropolitan Bank of Washington, D.C., as well as at banks in Globe and Prescott, Arizona. May also had an account at Home Savings Bank, Detroit, Michigan.[26]

Kelly's government service work since 1891, including Alaska and the Philippines, would seem to have provided a decent enough living but not much beyond that. And the government was not always good about taking care of its own, as when Kelly attempted to recover the travel expense and back pay that was owed him. Kelly figured that he ought to get reimbursed for travel expense from the Philippines to San Carlos, reasoning, correctly, that he was being reassigned as a federal employee and that he ought not to have to bear the expense of moving.

The problem, however, was that two agencies were involved here—the Philippine government and the Bureau of Indian Affairs, Department of the Interior—and neither wanted to accept the burden of paying for his travel. About the same time, he also requested two months' extra back pay from the War Department, using General Order No. 13, dated 17 January 1899 as a basis. There is no record of his ever receiving either.[27]

From the time of his arrival at San Carlos, Kelly continually sought to better his and May's financial position by one means or another. He still owned some 150 acres of Colorado ranch land, which certainly qualified as an investment, and he had also purchased two town lots in Grand Junction, Colorado, during the 1880s, but lost them for failure to pay taxes. When this was brought to his attention, he immediately enlisted the Grand Junction firm of Rich and Hutchinson to redeem the property.[28]

During the spring and summer of 1904, Kelly corresponded with one Thomas Glover of Parachute, Colorado, about the possibility of selling or leasing the ranch land. Kelly was at first interested in having someone work the land on a five-year lease, but later leaned toward selling the land, although May wanted to hang onto the property, perhaps believing it would appreciate in value. But finally, in January 1907, the property was sold to Charles J. Johnson and E. E. Yoeman of Grand Valley for two thousand dollars, or about thirteen dollars an acre. Initially, the money was deposited in First National Bank, Glenwood Springs, then later transferred to May's bank in Detroit.[29]

The Kellys' lifestyle may have been modest, but their home always reflected a taste for culture. To the extent circumstances permitted, there always seemed to be a place in their home for music and books. Kelly was a regular customer of the Victor Talking Machine Company, from whom he ordered records of such popular tunes of the day as "Silver Threads Among the Gold," "The Old Oaken Bucket," and "My Old Kentucky Home." But his and May's tastes were fairly eclectic and included renditions of "Lorelei," "Titl's Serenade," and "Air des Larmes." Kelly also devised a way to improve the sound on the Victor machine by stretching a thin sheet of rubber over the end of the sound box and, as he explained to Sydney Prescott of the Patent Department, he was pleased with the results.[30]

Kelly was also interested in newly published accounts of frontier life and adventures, particularly those that dealt with his own sphere of experience. Joseph Henry Taylor, author of *Frontier and Indian Life and Kaleidoscopic Lives*, sent him a complimentary copy of the book, which had first appeared in 1889. The Taylor book, set in the Upper Missouri

River region during the 1860s and 1870s, reawakened old memories for Kelly, who had known that country about as well as anyone in those days. In writing to Taylor, Kelly thanked him for the book, remarking that "[i]t reminds me of old times on the Missouri," adding somewhat wistfully that "I suppose there are very few of the old timers now on the river. The buffalo do not often come now in sight of old fort Union, and one cannot sneak up the Yellowstone river and kill a deer when disposed." In addition to books, Kelly subscribed to publications such as *Forest & Stream*, of which his old friend George Bird Grinnell was editor-in-chief, and the *Indian School Journal*.[31]

Although he enjoyed reading and listening to music, Kelly needed outdoor physical activity, a trait that would remain a part of his life until eventually ruled out by failing health. Here at San Carlos, that need was satisfied by occasional hunting forays. He and May also found satisfaction in working the land, creating a garden that flourished with ripe corn and melons, among other things, illustrating that this land, despite its harshness was, indeed, capable of being productive. Although Kelly does not mention it specifically, they had almost certainly produced crops in Colorado, and would do so to a much greater extent when they settled in Paradise, California, a dozen years later.[32]

If the Kellys' gardening efforts were successful, it was not because of the particularly favorable climate. Sunshine was in abundance but moisture was not, and if a garden was to produce in these parts it required more than a little attention. In a July 1904 letter to a Mr. White, Kelly talked about the dry conditions, contrasting that with the effects of hard rains produced by summer monsoons. There had evidently been some talk of providing the Indians with clear water, rather than relying on flood waters, a project Kelly regarded as costly and impractical.

> Rains have been very backward, and river has been dry since you left until a couple of days ago. There is now about a foot of muddy water. I have had no reason [Kelly continued] to change my opinion that the demand will take all the flood water that can form here in this basin, and that there will never be any accumulation of any consequence. Of course if the government wants to pile up a million tons of mud, and give them clear water, and has the money to spend that way, there is nothing more to be said.[33]

Early in his tenure at San Carlos, Kelly and May were visited by Luther's thirteen-year-old nephew William D., the second of that name,

Luther W. Kelly (left) and William D. Kelly II (right) were sons of William D. Kelly I and nephews of Luther S. Kelly. William D. II spent time with Uncle Luther and Aunt May at San Carlos and again in Nevada. *George Bille Collection.*

who lived with his uncle and aunt for three months during 1904 and would join them again in Nevada a few years later. For a teenage boy this was a memorable experience. He was spending time with the famous Yellowstone Kelly, his uncle and the hero of his boyhood.[34]

The Indian agent's daily life was involved in arbitrating, or otherwise resolving, a variety of problems, ranging from those of a nagging sort, such as when the ice-plant machinery broke down, to more serious matters, of which the volatile mix of Indians and alcohol was far and away the worst. The Indian and the bottle had been bad news for four hundred years and the reservation system exacerbated the problem. Kelly had certainly seen plenty of instances of alcohol abuse during his frontier years and he saw it as a serious problem, one that wreaked havoc with the Indians. As agent at San Carlos, he was in a position to have some influence on the situation, at least in his small sphere of authority.

In May 1904, for example, Kelly wrote to the general superintendent of the Indian school in Phoenix describing the problem of halting the illicit liquor trade on the reservation. One individual in particular was apparently responsible for much of this illicit trade. Kelly wanted to apprehend the man, but had thus far been unsuccessful in his efforts. And the politics of local law enforcement frequently worked against the apprehension of these individuals, even when they could be had. When a culprit was nabbed by Globe policemen—whom Kelly thought "energetic men"—federal authorities refused to pay travel expenses to Tucson for these officers, sending instead a United States marshal or county sheriff to bring the prisoner back to Tucson, thereby depriving Globe policemen of earning some extra cash.[35]

The sale of liquor to Indians was by law prohibited on or off the reservation; that was clear enough. However, the legality of transporting liquor across the reservation by railroad was not quite as clear-cut. The Gila Valley, Globe & Northern Railroad, for instance, would haul a shipment to a designated point on the reservation and off-load it there for pickup by a saloon keeper, one W. C. Albriton, who then hauled the liquor to his establishment just across the reservation boundary. Writing to the commissioner of the practice, Kelly reported that he had forbidden Mr. Albriton to use the reservation roads to haul his liquor, which meant that Albriton could only reach his saloon by a round-about way and Kelly was glad to know it worked a hardship on the saloon keeper.[36]

But despite the best efforts of Kelly and local officials, Indians had no difficulty obtaining liquor. In June, Kelly wrote again to the super-intendent of the Indian boarding school in Phoenix, regarding a dozen or so Indian girls, ranging in age from fourteen to eighteen, "who are going to the bad because of their own ignorance and the cupidity and love of liquor of their parents." The situation prompted Kelly, a month later, to send one John Filleman to Globe under orders to pick up all Indian girls between the ages of fourteen and twenty who were without visible means of support. In addition, he asked the sheriff at Globe to appoint one William Grey a special deputy to make arrests of people selling liquor to Indians, including a black man who was living with an Apache woman. In Kelly's view, the fact that the two were living togeth-er, however, did not give him the right to provide her with liquor.[37]

Another troublesome problem had to do with loose horses on the reservation. The animals tended to damage Indian farms and also cre-ated a problem for legitimate stockmen who had grazing privileges. Although allowing stock to run loose on the reservation was illegal, Kelly got little support in his efforts to enforce the law here. The United States Marshal had failed to honor his requests and the United States Attorney informed him that there was no statute under which such animals could be legally seized. Kelly referred the matter upstairs, telling the commissioner that if this "decision is to stand, the result will be a crowding of the reservation of all kinds of stock by more or less irresponsible people to the injury of the Indian farms, and the interests of reputable stockmen who have grazing privileges." The ruling apparently stood and Kelly was compelled to deal with the problem as best he was able.[38]

A problem of a different sort occurred in October 1905, when the sheriff of Gila County notified Kelly that scarlet fever had broken out among Indians in Globe and requested that all Indians be removed to the reservation immediately. However, after investigating the matter, agency physician Doctor Carl Boyd advised Kelly that the report was without foundation.[39]

Although the Apache wars had ended with Geronimo's surrender in 1886, memories of those often fierce and unsettled times remained fresh in the minds of many Arizona residents, who never completely lost their fear of yet another outbreak. Accordingly, when in early 1905 there surfaced rumors of a possible outbreak among the White Mountain Apaches, who reportedly were buying arms, Kelly reported to the Indian Commissioner that, after talking to the Fort Apache agent, he was satisfied that the rumors were largely groundless. It was well known that Indians had been armed for years and used their weapons—primarily shotguns—for hunting.[40]

Typical of any bureaucracy, whether state or federal, is dealing with the legacy of a prior administration. During his tenure in office (1897–1904), Commissioner William Jones had created the position of "farmer" at San Carlos in order to provide a clerk in the Washington office with an opportunity to, in Kelly's words, "improve his lungs at this station." Kelly saw no need for such a position and did not want the man, but, he informed the General Supervisor of Reservations, "the late commissioner sent him here, saying that he was a protégé of a certain congressman who was kind on appropriations and to do the best he could with him."[41]

Getting along with people had never been a particular problem for Kelly, until he arrived at San Carlos. One suspects that the root cause of his people problems here stemmed from individuals who were employed on the reservation in one capacity or another and who sought to take advantage of the federal bureaucracy to further their own ends but in Luther Kelly found an agent who refused to cooperate as had his predecessors. In addition, according to Kelly anyway, there was a certain click in Globe that worked to undermine his authority; for what reason we don't know, but perhaps it was his refusal to look the other way with regard to the treatment or exploitation of Indians.

Problems began early and ran late. In 1905, for example, there was a conflict with one Ruth Gibbs, a former matron at the San Carlos boarding school, who wished to remain on the payroll during the period when the school was closed and while she was on furlough. Since this was an unusual request, Kelly requested authorization from headquarters and was turned down, prompting a protest from Gibbs who went over Kelly's head. She has joined the "little coterie of ex-employees and small politicians in Globe, Arizona, who are trying to make trouble for me in my position as agent," Kelly told the commissioner.[42]

In December 1905, Kelly was again forced to respond to charges leveled by Assistant District Attorney (for Graham County) E. J. Edwards, who wrote to the commissioner, criticizing Kelly on several counts, including the deportation of a man from San Carlos; his handling of Indians charged with stealing cattle; and permitting Indians to visit Globe in large numbers. In a letter to Frank Mead, Kelly acknowledged having read Edwards's letter, in which the Assistant D.A. tried to make him [Kelly] "out a monster of inhumanity and in other ways incapable of conducting properly the affairs of this agency." The charges, Kelly went on to say, "are a mass of misrepresentation, the facts perverted in the most devilish manner, and for reasons that are apparent to me but which I will not go into at this time."[43]

To the specifics, Kelly responded by saying that the man deported was sent off in an orderly way without harshness. As for the Indians alleged to have stolen cattle, he would have tried them before the Indian court, but lacked sufficient evidence. And Kelly denied allowing Indians to visit Globe in large numbers, saying he was very careful about the number of permits issued. "Indians with passes to work at the Salt River dam (Roosevelt), stop in Globe, on their way, and this cannot be helped. The whites set a very bad example there in the way of liquor."[44]

Another instance occurred in the fall of 1908 when Kelly suspended a wheelwright named John R. Kemp for using disrespectful language to him. Kelly explained the matter to the commissioner and speculated as to why it might have happened.

> I have always treated Mr. Kemp with the utmost considera-
> tion. Have made it a point to sympathize with him and ask
> his opinion in matters relating to his work, in which he
> showed considerable skill.

It was a great surprise his turning upon me the way he did, as our relations have always been cordial and friendly with mutual respect for each other.

The fact that I have issued a certain quantity of oil and fuel to the Agency Physician, Farmer and Assistant Farmer for their official use and none to the Wheelwright, except at the shop appears to have awakened his resentment.[45]

Kemp, of course, painted a far different picture of the situation in his letter to the commissioner. Kemp freely admitted having used disrespectful language, but pointed out that "there had been provocation sufficient to cause a free American citizen to say all he charges me with having said and more too." Kelly had treated him in an inconsiderate manner and acted "bossy." He also accused Kelly of having favorites among the employees. "Some of the favored are provided with wood and kerosene oil for use at their quarters, while others are not favored." In conclusion, Kemp argued that he had been misrepresented, that he was justified in saying what he had said to Kelly, and that "the gravity of my offense was not extreme enough to justify my suspension."[46]

Kelly was realistic enough to recognize that incidents of this nature could well lead to his removal as agent at San Carlos. If there was sufficient smoke and agitation, he would be an embarrassment to the department and the commissioner would be forced to replace him. He was discouraged by the back-biting and small-mindedness of so many with whom he was compelled to deal and laid his case out before the President himself as early as 1905, when he had only been at the agency for a year.

I have also to advise you that it may be possible that I will be deprived of my office of agent here owing to the misrepresentation and malice of small politicians, ex-employees and others, who are not pleased with my administration here. I court fullest investigation of course, which can only result in taking up my time and causing me some disquiet, but the pressure may be too much for the department.

I am not a young man now, having served in the last year of the Civil War, as well as the Spanish war.

I shall always be grateful for the interest you have taken in my career and in honoring me with office.[47]

The letter is interesting: honest, certainly, but perhaps more importantly, a model of political adroitness. On the face of it, anyway, Kelly would appear to be making an effort to protect himself and secure his position before the axe fell. In a sense, he wasn't entirely out of line in going over the commissioner's head. Roosevelt had, after all, asked him [Kelly] to report directly to the White House on conditions at San Carlos. There is no record as to whether Roosevelt acted on Kelly's letter in any special way. At the time, the Commissioner of Indian Affairs was Francis E. Leupp, who had replaced William Jones in 1905. Leupp was a man whose judgment Roosevelt trusted completely, and it would not be far fetched to imagine the President chatting with the commissioner, suggesting that he hoped Kelly, whom he had always admired and respected, could be retained. That is conjecture, of course, but what is fact is that Kelly did remain at San Carlos through the end of the Roosevelt administration.[48]

During his tenure at San Carlos, we know that Kelly visited the East several times, although exactly when is not known. The record shows that he applied for annual leave on at least four occasions, but it is not clear whether the requests were approved and if so whether he and May used that time to travel east. But we know that he visited Washington (and probably Philadelphia as well) because he was a member of President Roosevelt's "tennis cabinet."[49]

A feature of Theodore Roosevelt's second administration, the "tennis cabinet" consisted of a group of Roosevelt's cronies, friends, and political allies who often joined the President on vigorous outings whenever they chanced to find themselves in the Washington area. These outings were frequently, though not always, conducted in Rock Creek Park. The idea had grown out of the President's fondness for playing tennis and gradually evolved into a loosely knit group of men who enjoyed good, hearty outdoor activity and, of course, a close association with President Theodore Roosevelt. The cabinet included such luminaries as Maj. Gen. Leonard Wood, Chief of the Forest Service Gifford Pinchot, Secretary of the Interior James Garfield, and United States Civil Service Commissioner Alford W. Cooley, along with old Western comrades such as Ben Daniels, Seth Bullock, and Luther Kelly.[50]

In November, Kelly visited several caves located on the reservation, having promised George Bird Grinnell he would do so. When he first arrived at San Carlos, he had explored these caves and told Grinnell that they contained large quantities of bat guano, which he proposed to market on the Indians' behalf. On this occasion, he made a more detailed examination of the caves, finding evidence of ancient dwellers and their lifestyle, which he knew anthropologist Grinnell would be interested in.[51]

With the election of William Howard Taft in November 1908, President Theodore Roosevelt's second administration drew to a close. As the year wound steadily down and election day approached, Kelly may have wondered whether he would be retained at San Carlos once Roosevelt was out of office, but if so, he was not troubling himself about the election and figured one way or another all would work out.[52] And indeed they would if he had anything to do with it. Scarcely a week after the election, Kelly wrote to president-elect Taft, inviting him to San Carlos.

> On your way to the southwest cannot you come to this agency for a few days rest, 'far from the madding crowd?'
>
> It is a genial climate, quiet retired place, with fine quail and turkey hunting. Quail are found in walking distance, turkey two days ride in the mountains.
>
> You may remember me. I was a Captain in the 40th Vol. in command at Dapitan, Mindanao, when you appointed me Treasurer of the Province of Surigao. I have been Indian Agent for the Apaches for nearly five years.
>
> If you could bring Mrs. Taft with you, you would have a pleasant time.

The invitation was cordial and genuine enough, though clearly an effort on Kelly's part to secure his position at San Carlos. Taft, not surprisingly, declined the invitation.[53]

The beginning of the end of Kelly's time at San Carlos happened in December 1908, when he was demoted from agency superintendent to superintendent of the Indian School at a lesser salary; it was clearly a step down. The transfer may well have been with the idea in mind of encouraging Kelly to resign. However, his acceptance of the school post on 5 December made it clear that he had no intention of resigning. It was equally clear, though, that the commissioner wanted a new man on the station. What with the various complaints lodged against him, Kelly had proven to be something of an irritant at San Carlos, but his relationship with the President made it awkward to remove him while Roosevelt was still in office. However, now with T.R. preparing to leave the White House, Leupp no longer felt an obligation to retain Kelly at San Carlos. Accordingly, on 24 December 1908—Christmas Eve, no less—the commissioner advised Kelly that he was being transferred to the Keshena Indian School at Green Bay, Wisconsin, at an annual salary of $1,800. Formal notice of the new appointment reached Kelly on 30 December.

The commissioner was authorized to pay all expenses in obtaining corporate surety on a $50,000 bond for Kelly. Ironically, his replacement
was to be Lewis B. Weaver, who had recently arrived at San Carlos to fill
the newly created position of "Additional Farmer." Kelly was to learn of
his replacement under unfortunate circumstances.[54]

Kelly and Weaver had not gotten on well at all. Privately, Kelly dis-
approved of Weaver's being there at all, but he also perceived a certain
impertinence and underhandedness on Weaver's part. He explained to
the commissioner:

[O]n December 30, when I detailed the Additional Farmer,
Mr. Weaver, an employee of three months standing, at this
agency to do certain work, he flourished a letter from your
office of an official character, though marked personal, in
which it was stated that he had been appointed Superintendent
of this agency at a salary of $1200. This was in the presence
of other employees.[55]

Weaver defended himself.

On December 30, 1908 I was detailed to go the saw-mill, a distance of thirty-five miles to take charge of the mill while the
sawyer took a vacation of fifteen or thirty days.

I asked Capt. Kelly if he thought best that I should be
going away just at that time, thinking from remarks he had
been making for days previous that he knew of my appointment, until he asked me why I thought I should not go.

In answer to his question I took one page of the letter out
of my pocket and read to him that my appointment as
SUPERINTENDENT of the SAN CARLOS AGENCY had been
signed. Capt. Kelly said 'Let me see that' and reaching took it
from my hand, read some of it and returned it to me. I told
him that the letter was of a personal nature, and that as to the
matter of going to the saw-mill, I was perfectly willing to go,
and that I was entirely under his instructions and had no
idea of disobeying them.

I at once left for the saw-mill and remained there until
he sent for me a few days later.[56]

It seems clear that a decision to replace Kelly had been made
some time before the incident related here and that if Kelly knew or

suspected he was going to be replaced, as Weaver alleged, Kelly evidently did not know that it was Weaver who had been appointed as his replacement and he would understandably have been upset to learn about it from Weaver, rather than in a proper manner, from the commissioner.

In any event, he was not pleased with what he regarded as shabby treatment and said so in a 4 January letter to Roosevelt. Indeed, that he expected something like this three years earlier is clear from his 1905 letter to Roosevelt. He felt slighted. Was this the thanks one got for good and faithful service?

> Mr. Leupp recently wrote me that after consulting with you and the Secretary of the Interior, he had decided to place a younger and more active man at this agency.
>
> I have been offered the agency at Kishena [*sic*], Wis., but after consideration, I have decided that if I am too old for this place, I am not young enough for the other and so have declined it.
>
> As the office has made it impossible for me to remain here, having reduced the salary and appointed a young inexperienced employee at this agency to take my place, there is nothing left for me to do but leave the service.
>
> I wish to thank you for the five years that I have spent in Arizona. I do this with the more satisfaction that I have never asked you for anything, directly or indirectly, unless it was for your endorsement when I reentered the Volunteers, during the Insurrection in the Philippines.[57]

Considering his earlier 1905 letter to Roosevelt, which certainly seemed to invite the President's intercession on his behalf, albeit in a circumspect way, one is hard pressed to agree with the final paragraph of this letter. Not that there was anything in the world out of line with what Kelly had done. In the 1905 letter, he had simply laid the matter before the President, which indeed he had been asked to do when he was sent to San Carlos, and if in so doing it somehow reinforced his position, where was the harm in that? But it was clearly a request for a little assistance, even though he did not want to see it as such. Kelly was a proud man; a man who had been self-reliant since he was fifteen and in his own mind, anyway, would never have resorted to a tactic that might be construed as importuning.

On the other hand, the use of political influence was no stranger to Kelly's career. In addition to being appointed agent at San Carlos, influence had gotten him into the War Department, to Alaska twice, and helped him secure a position in the military. The thing was how one saw the use of such influence. Other than what he said to Theodore Roosevelt in his 1909 letter, we don't really know how Kelly felt, but it seems safe to conclude that he regarded himself as a man appointed to a post because of his ability, not purely as a result of political influence. He would be the last to deny that he had had help throughout his career, but he was not a man to take advantage of a relationship, unlike Nelson Miles who was perfectly shameless in advancing his own career. And this, it would appear, was a distinction that Kelly hoped Roosevelt would appreciate.

Upon receipt of Kelly's letter of 4 January, Roosevelt expressed his regrets and wished him well. There was little more Roosevelt could have done anyway. He was a lame duck president and not on particularly good terms with Congress. Still, he thought enough of Kelly to express his disappointment and regret.

> Your letter causes me sincere regret. Mr. Leupp had told me of the circumstances, and I had hoped that you would be willing to accept the agency offered you. It has been a matter of peculiar pride to me to have you serve under me, for I admire your past record, your character, your standards. May all good fortune go with you! I accept your resignation with genuine regret.
> Sincerely yours,
> Theodore Roosevelt.[58]

On the same day that he wrote to Roosevelt, Kelly also wrote to the commissioner, officially declining to accept the Keshena position. Then, in mid-January, amid the contretemps of his final unpleasant hours at San Carlos, more allegations against Kelly came to the fore, further adding to his personal anguish. Two employees, Rabinnovitz and Jones, charged that Kelly had issued wood and kerosene oil to employees, contrary to explicit department regulations. Hints of fraud and malfeasance were in the wind, the implications of which must have been unbearable to a man of Kelly's private instincts and personal code of standards.[59]

As a consequence of these allegations, Special Indian Agent Wilbut T. Elliott, was sent to San Carlos under orders to "look very carefully into this matter as a part of the general examination of Superintendent Kelly's accounts, both cash and property. If, in the course of this examination, other matters affecting Captain Kelly's management of his post come to your attention, notify the office at once of their character."[60]

One can only speculate as to what was going on. Both employees may have been disgruntled over some earlier issue with Kelly and sought the first opportunity to even the score. Perhaps they felt slighted at not also having been issued wood and kerosene. Kelly may have been out of line in issuing these items but, for whatever reason, judged it important enough to make a departure from the rules. It will never be possible to determine exactly what happened with any of these complaints, whether it be that of Ruth Gibbs, wheelwright John Kemp, or the matter of the wood and kerosene. But insofar as can be determined, Special Agent Elliott reported nothing of a questionable nature in Kelly's management of the agency. No charges were ever preferred.[61]

The San Carlos assignment had begun on a bright note. Kelly may well have seen his future with the Bureau of Indian Affairs. And why not? Given his background, few could offer stronger credentials, insofar as working with and understanding Indians was concerned. But rapport with the Indians was only part of what running a reservation was all about. The rest of it had to do with keeping one's nostrils in the wind, playing the shifting ebbs and tides of political maneuvering—and therein lay the crux of the problem. Luther Kelly was not a political critter... on any level, local or otherwise. He knew how the reservation ought to be run, but sometimes those ideas ran contrary to the notions of others and in the end it proved his undoing.

There was a little more to it than that, of course. There was the matter of how one dealt with the surrounding white community at large. Here would be a tight line to walk: how to deal fairly and squarely with the Indians without seeming to be overly prejudiced on their behalf. The bias against Indians was particularly strong in Arizona where memories of the Apache wars were still plenty fresh, and this undoubtedly played a role in how he was perceived by some in the Globe community. The surprising thing, though, is that none of these troubles seemed to generate a great deal of angst within Kelly's soul. None of this really soured him on San Carlos. Indeed, as we shall see, within a few years he would ask to return.

So five years drew to a close. It had been the longest time he and May had been together since leaving Colorado. And for the most part it had been a satisfying five years, even though the finish had

ended on a rather disappointing note. Now it was time to look elsewhere. On 19 January he tendered his official resignation to the
Commissioner of Indian Affairs. The following day he turned the
management of the agency over to Weaver, and he and May prepared to head east.

Chapter Fourteen

NEVADA,
1909–1915

**I have your good letter of March 18 but will not reply to
it at length until I return from Reno, Nev. where I expect to
go tomorrow to look at a mining property for some people.[1]**

Allowing some time to prepare for their move after relinquishing
command of the reservation on 20 January, the Kellys probably
arrived in the East sometime in February. In any case, it was certainly
before March because Luther was on hand for the final gathering of
outgoing President Theodore Roosevelt's tennis cabinet. On Monday,
1 March 1909, three days before President William Howard Taft was slat-
ed to assume the reins of the presidency, Roosevelt invited his tennis
cabinet—thirty-one members strong—to join him for a farewell White
House luncheon. On that morning, Roosevelt conferred with his personal aide, Archie Butt, about the arrangements.

> I have thirty-one at my Cabinet luncheon, and we want to
> seat it irrespective of rank and mix the tennis players with
> the wolf hunters and the 'two-gun' men so that the various

President Theodore Roosevelt's "Tennis Cabinet." Luther S. Kelly is standing ninth from the right, holding a cigar. *Theodore Roosevelt Collection, Harvard College Library.*

elements of what is known as my tennis cabinet will get acquainted. The papers have made a good deal of fun of my tennis cabinet, but they have never known how extensive or what a part it has played in my administrations. It will be gathered together to-day for the first time, and I regard this luncheon as my only official recognition of it.[2]

And a grand affair it was, too—food, spirits, and conviviality in abundance. As the luncheon drew to a close, Roosevelt's old Dakota companion and one time Black Hills lawman Seth Bullock "suddenly reached forward, swept aside a mass of flowers which made a center-piece on the table, and revealed a bronze cougar by Proctor, which was a parting gift to me." Afterward, the group, in company with Proctor's cougar, were photographed on the White House lawn.[3]

What words may have passed between Kelly and the outgoing president is not known. Given the circumstances, there was likely little if any opportunity to discuss what had happened at San Carlos, or what Kelly's future plans might involve. If T.R. had any suggestions, we have no record of them.

In any event, Kelly wasted little time exploring the job market. He wanted to return to Arizona and on 15 April wrote to President Taft requesting an appointment as Supervisor of the Census in Arizona. The request was duly processed and although the report on his past record was a good one, he was passed over for the appointment.

Then in June, he wrote to Assistant Commissioner of Indian Affairs Robert G. Valentine, saying he "would be pleased to consider a vacancy in the Sioux country." Again, the request was politely acknowledged with no resultant action. In view of his earlier rejection of the Wisconsin post, this request for a position in the land of the Sioux, where the winters are on par with those in Wisconsin, seems strange indeed. Perhaps it was a yen to return to the country of his old haunts. One suspects that the San Carlos episode had prejudiced the Indian Bureau's opinion of Kelly.[4]

While in the East, Kelly enjoyed something of a vacation, exploring central New York and the Adirondacks. Perhaps he also returned to the Finger Lakes country of his boyhood to renew old acquaintances. If May was along, there is no record of it, although it seems likely she would have accompanied him.[5]

In July, perhaps at the invitation of a friend, Luther was at Fort Myer, Virginia, where he was privileged to witness Orville Wright's successful completion of the army's first aviation acceptance trials, in a round-trip flight from Fort Myer to Alexandria, Virginia. During this same trial a year earlier, the plane had crashed, badly injuring Wright and killing his passenger, Lt. Thomas Selfridge, who thus became the first person to die in an airplane crash. Selfridge Field, Michigan, is named in his honor. Kelly did not record his feelings of that moment, as he witnessed a bit of history being made, but it would be surprising indeed if he did not feel a sense of having been passed by. Perhaps as he watched Wright's ungainly looking aircraft take to the skies, he contrasted that moment with images of the great buffalo herds and the still wild frontier he remembered from his young manhood and marveled at the changes wrought in his own lifetime.[6]

How long the Kellys remained in the East is not clear; it may have been until the end of 1909, perhaps until the affairs of his brother's estate were settled. William D. Kelly's death from a heart attack at age fifty-seven was, insofar as we know, completely unexpected and his passing surely left a void in the lives of Luther and his siblings. In the past it had been William who lobbied on Luther's behalf, writing to the President, Secretary of War, or whoever's assistance was needed. However, with William gone, brother Albert, himself an eminently successful coal entrepreneur, stepped forward and wrote to the Secretary of the Interior, Richard A. Ballinger, in an effort to secure his brother a position in the Indian service. Ballinger responded saying he was unable to say when or whether a position would open up for Kelly. The long and short of it, of course, was that the Bureau of Indian Affairs probably did not want Kelly back and no position was going to be offered; it was that simple.[7]

At any rate, 1910 found Kelly in Nevada, accompanied by his nephew William D. II, who remained with his uncle at least until spring and possibly through the summer.[8] Exactly what attracted Kelly to southwest Nevada to begin with is not entirely clear, but the area had been in the throes of gold fever for several years and was still going strong. Even if the peak of the boom had passed, there remained plenty of mining-related opportunities for an enterprising spirit and since there was nothing else on his plate at the moment, he may simply have decided to see what might be harvested out of this situation.

And as for nephew William, the lad was coming on nineteen and was no doubt feeling a sense of loss over his father's unexpected death. With this in mind, Luther may have decided that a taste of life in what one historian has called the Old West's last great gold rush,[8] would be just the thing to help nephew get his mind off his loss. May did not make the journey this time, but would join her husband later.[9]

The discovery of gold in Esmeralda County, Nevada, around the turn of the century stirred the fires of imagination and hope as gold strikes had been wont to do since Sutter's Mill, Colorado, Virginia City, Montana, the Black Hills, and the Klondike had set pulses to racing for nearly a century. And so it did in Nevada. The whole business had been triggered by the discovery of gold around Tonopah in 1900. From here, prospectors began fanning out into the surrounding hills, and in 1902 more gold was found around what came to be called Goldfield. The strike was good sized, too. In point of fact, the town was originally called Grandpa because those who named it figured the strike was so rich it was going to wind up the granddaddy of all strikes. Later, however, the name was changed to Goldfield.[10]

Goldfield in those days was synonymous with excitement, attracting a plethora of veteran prospectors and opportunists, as well as mining engineers and investors—a reflection of how the past half-century had affected the maturation of a gold camp. But if there was a difference to be noted between, say, Virginia City and Goldfield, there were plenty of similarities as well. Here, veterans of the Black Hills and the Klondike might stand at the bar next to a trained mining engineer, or gamble with the Earp brothers. Both Wyatt and Virgil were here in '05. Wyatt eventually moved on to Los Angeles, while Virgil succumbed to the effects of pneumonia later that year.[11]

This was Goldfield's peak; everything was done in a big way. During 1906, for example, with the mines producing a record $15 million in ore, the burgeoning sports promoter Tex Rickard sponsored a nationally recognized boxing match between Battling Nelson and the lightweight champion, a black man, Joe Gans. The match, held out of doors on Goldfield's main street, lasted a record forty-two rounds, with Gans eventually winning because of a foul by Nelson.

Rail service connected Goldfield to Tonopah, and by 1905 streets were lit by electricity produced in Bishop, California.[12] By 1906 Goldfield's population stood at fifteen thousand and there was no end in sight. Buildings sprouted up almost faster than they could be counted, and within a year it was the largest city in Nevada, with a population of twenty thousand, five banks, three newspapers, a stock exchange, and of course, a plethora of gambling establishments, saloons, and bordellos.

A national recession in 1907, coupled with a hard-fought miners' strike, hurt Goldfield's economic picture, but by 1910, when Kelly arrived, recovery was underway and indeed, mine production peaked that very year, so if the boom was slowly fading, plenty of excitement yet remained. From Goldfield's plush and exclusive Montezuma Club, Kelly wrote to President Taft, expressing his appreciation for being considered for the position with the census bureau in Arizona. "I have the honor to thank you for the interest displayed and to say that I realize the difficulties of your position, the demands made upon your time, the clamor of politicians and the just reservations of Bureau Chiefs in filling appointments."[13]

Although he spent time in Goldfield, Kelly apparently focused his efforts around the small mining camp of Lida, some twenty miles southwest of Goldfield. Lida (or Alida, named for the wife of one David Buel of Austin, Nevada), was located in a small canyon between Mount Jackson and the Silver Peak Range. What once was Lida is today high desert ranch land. Save for a small cemetery north of where the town proper once sat, and the remains of a post office, there is little to remind one of the throbbing boom times of a century ago. Gold had been discovered here in the late 1860s and a modest boom followed in

Remains of the post office, Lida, Nevada, 1992. *Author photo.*

the 1870s, but within a decade had faded. However, when Goldfield burst into full flower around 1905–1906, Lida experienced a rebirth that proved spirited if short-lived, with a hotel, schools, stores, and its own post office.[14]

Kelly is listed on the 1910 census as a miner, a label he was to carry for some years, even after moving to Paradise, California, in 1915. However, if mining/ prospecting was his primary means of support during the Nevada years it must have been in the employ of others, because he never filed a claim on any strike of his own and one is hard pressed to imagine how he and May might have survived for five and a half years without him having found enough color to support the two of them. We do know that on at least one occasion he was engaged to look over some potential mining property for someone and may have done this on a regular basis.[15]

In 1914 he was appointed justice of the peace for Lida to replace the deceased T. M. Jones. This would have provided some income at least, as well as renewing his acquaintance with the law, which he had found so much to his liking in Colorado thirty years earlier.[16]

But in any case, finances must have been tight for the Kellys. They were getting by but probably not much more than that. He had applied

Author on the site of
Lida, Nevada, 1992.
Author photo.

for a pension, which was approved in August 1912, adding thirteen dollars a month to their income. But Kelly still entertained hopes of landing another federal government position, if not an army billet. Early in 1912 he wrote to Secretary of War Henry L. Stimson, regarding a bill that had been introduced in Congress in April 1911. Senate Bill S.393, introduced by Senator George Nixon, called for Kelly to be placed on the retired list of the army with the rank of captain. Although he was sixty-two, Kelly obviously believed himself still capable of active duty. To the commissioner of pensions, Kelly wrote

> I have the honor to enclose copy of a bill now in the hands of the Senate Committee together with my military and civil history and ask favorable consideration should the bill in question be brought to your attention. I believe I am still able for active service should the measure be brought to a successful issue.[17]

By 1910, Kelly's military and civilian service records were impressive, as were his patriotic affiliations. He was a member of the GAR (Grand Army of the Republic); Sons of the American Revolution; Society of the War of 1812; and the Naval and Military Order of the Spanish-American War.[18]

Much effort had gone into the drafting of this bill and Kelly remained ever hopeful of its passage. To Theodore Roosevelt, he wrote:

> This is the culmination of two years effort in this direction, the bills introduced (by Senator Penrose) in 1909–1910, differing in that they included surviving Union and Confederate veterans who served as officers in the U.S. Volunteers, in the War with Spain and the Insurrection in the Philippines. But they failed to pass.
>
> I would like this bill to pass on its merits but I know enough of politics to perceive that a bill to pass must first have the favor of the President of the Senate and the Speaker of the House.
>
> Now I would have wished this bill to be introduced by the Senator from New York, my native state, but I am not acquainted with the gentleman, and chance came in my way through the Senator from Nevada, who granted my request. I am bound to get into the regular establishment if I can.
>
> I do not ask your assistance but I would like your good wishes.[19]

Although Kelly did not directly ask for Roosevelt's intercession, he was clearly hoping the former president would do just that. However, Roosevelt responded, saying he had made it a point not to interfere with legislation since leaving the White House and was sure Kelly would understand.[20]

The bill did not pass and a year later, in March 1913, a disappointed Kelly wrote to the Secretary of the Interior, reapplying for the post at San Carlos.

> I have the honor to file in your office my application for appointment as Superintendent of the San Carlos Indian Reservation, in Arizona. I was U.S. Agent for this reservation from 1904 to 1908 inclusive, and was getting along very well until H.G. [R.G.] Valentine, the private secretary to the Commissioner of Indian Affairs, and later Assistant

Commissioner, wishing to place a favorite, a young man, a very good taxidermist, but totally inexperienced in Indian affairs, caused me to be transferred to an Agency in Northern Wisconsin, when learning of the circumstances of the transfer, I resigned rather than go to a cold climate in the beginning of winter.

Whenever there occurs a vacancy of the post at San Carlos, I respectfully wish to be considered and herewith submit my record for your information.[21]

In view of what had happened at San Carlos, this request comes across as just a little startling, but it also shows that Kelly was much less troubled by the events that surrounded his first tour of duty than one might have suspected on the basis of the documentary evidence. Not that it made any difference, though, because the request was politely answered and filed accordingly.

During Kelly's Nevada years, he had occasion to meet several people, either miners or individuals looking to invest in promising mining property and who were to play a meaningful role in his and May's final years. Of these, none would prove more important than Dudley and Minnie Barnes. Whether these individuals had arrived in Nevada as a group, or whether a combination of circumstances and mutual interest brought them together, is not clear. At any rate, in 1915, the group, which by this time included Luther and May, elected to move to Paradise, California. Located about ninety miles north of Sacramento, the community of Paradise had gained attention because of its genial climate and fruit-growing potential. Possibly some of the group Kelly had gotten to know originally hailed from Paradise and painted an attractive enough picture of that community to draw Luther and May. But however it happened, the Kellys decided to see how Paradise looked to them. So it was that Luther, the ever restless spirit, and his wife May prepared for their final move.

Chapter Fifteen

PARADISE, CALIFORNIA:
The End of the Trail,
1915–1928

**I know that you will be pleased to know that I have built
a home in this beautiful section of California,
overlooking the valley of the Sacramento.[1]**

Luther and May arrived in Paradise sometime after the first of the year, 1915, but in any event it was well before 15 May, because by that time Luther had decided to purchase a sixty-acre tract of land on Clark Road from E. D. and Carrie Sharp for ten dollars in gold coin. Surprisingly, perhaps, May's name is omitted from the deed of sale. Financially, Luther and May were probably not particularly well off. Luther had received $2,500 from brother William's estate and that may have provided the wherewithal for any needed improvements on the property. For neighbors, the Kellys could look to the younger Dudley and Minnie Barnes, who provided a relationship that was to grow and flourish in the years ahead.[2]

Located in Butte County, some ninety miles north of Sacramento, Paradise had gradually evolved into an attractive and promising community. In 1890, the population of Paradise was only 500, but with arrival of the Butte County Railroad in 1903—soon to be acquired by the Southern Pacific—the community, situated along what was known as Paradise Ridge, or simply the Ridge, began to find its identity and grow.

Featuring a genial climate with abundant sunshine, mild winters, and cooler summers than those found in California's interior valleys, the rich volcanic soil of the Paradise area was particularly suited to growing fruit. Indeed, by 1916 the community was producing bumper crops of fruit and had earned the title of the apple-growing center of California.[3]

Among the very earliest white settlers who arrived in the region during the middle part of the nineteenth century were prospectors who had been unsuccessful in striking pay dirt elsewhere in the state and sought to try their luck hereabouts. As a community of sorts gradually developed, it was made up largely of saloons and brothels, one of the former of which was known as the "Pair-O-Dice," which was said to have been the origin of the town's present name. Yet another candidate for the naming was an early pioneer who, after traveling long and hard, declared that upon reaching the area he had arrived in Paradise. It is indeed a lovely area and however the name came to be, it is entirely appropriate.[4]

Luther Kelly took to fruit ranching as though he had been born to it. Eventually, he came to take pride in calling himself an orchardist. He named the ranch Cedar Lodge early on, because the pathway leading up to the house was flanked by a row of cedar trees on either side.[5] Despite all he had done during the course of his life, Kelly seems not to have lost his attraction for the soil, for growing things. Recall that on his marriage license he listed himself as a farmer. There was something in this way of life that reached out and touched him.

Although he would never have the entire piece of property producing crops, by 1922 he did have five acres under cultivation, with another five acres in timber and brush and the balance in lava soil. The cultivated section carried fourteen types of fruit-bearing trees, including apple, apricot, cherry, fig, pear, peach, prune, almond, walnut, nectarine, olive, and orange. Altogether, his property numbered 487 trees, of which 329 were fruit-bearing, most of these being almond and prune.[6]

He was proud of what his ranch produced, too, and among his circle of friends and acquaintances Kelly was gaining a reputation as a

A rock marker erected in 1990 remembers the Kellys as former residents of Paradise, California. Once the path to their home, Cedar Lodge, on Clark Road, was flanked by stately cedar trees. As of August 1992, only two cedars remained. The site is now owned by Paradise Marine. *Author photo.*

grower of tasty fruit. Friends were always pleased to receive a box from Cedar Lodge. George Bird Grinnell's reaction was typical.

> I fear that I never acknowledged to you the box of delicious
> English walnuts which you were kind enough to send me
> just about the time of the holidays. I say they were delicious,
> but really I had very little opportunity to get at them.
> Mrs. Grinnell pounced on them and, I think, devoured them
> all. She said that they were the best that she had ever tasted;
> so actually these thanks come from her rather than they
> do from me.[7]

Kelly was always eager to talk about the various secrets and processes that led to the production of fine and tasty fruit. The best way to treat prunes, he explained to Brininstool, was to dry them in the shade, a trick he had stumbled on by accident. Many growers, he pointed out, dipped prunes in lye to accelerate the drying process in the sun. However, the batch Brininstool received would, said Kelly, keep well if stored in a cool, dry location, but eventually they will dry and lose their bloom.[8]

Friends usually received these boxes of fruits and nuts as a gift, especially during the holiday season. On occasion, someone would order a box of prunes or walnuts, for instance, but otherwise, marketing his produce posed something of a problem. Glenwood Nursery in distant Rochester, New York, expressed serious interest in carrying some of his English walnuts and there were a few other outlets as well, but it was tough for one individual orchardist to effectively market his produce, no matter the quality. He and May raised one hundred pounds of walnuts using their own grafts, but were only able to sell forty pounds to customers in Sacramento. The balance was disposed as gifts to friends.[9]

During his years in Paradise, Kelly wrote frequently to a wide circle of friends and acquaintances, including former president Theodore Roosevelt; writer/historian Earl Alonzo Brininstool; old comrade from the Fifth Infantry days, now retired Brig. Gen. Oscar Fitzalan Long; and artists Edwin Deming and Charles M. Russell, among others. The contents of these letters ranged from reminiscences of the old days—not surprisingly—to descriptions of Cedar Lodge, and increasingly now to health-related issues.

To Charles Stobie, a western artist and former scout whom he had known in Colorado forty years earlier, Kelly wrote that he was quite able to work, and found "recreation in rooting out boulders and stumps where I want to set out almonds and vines. If I cannot break up a 300 pound rock with the 12 lb hammer (powder costs too much now) I hitch the horse to it and work it out, then move to a stone wall I am building just below the slope." Though seven months shy of seventy, he was obviously still able to perform hard physical labor, but then, save for the few years in Chicago and Governor's Island, his had always been a vigorous physical life, so continuing to derive satisfaction from such activity is not all that surprising. Indeed, if anything is surprising, it is how he managed to satisfy this need during those years in Chicago, New York, and Washington. With his and May's arrival in Paradise, Kelly's adventuring days may have come to an end, but there remained considerable vitality in that restless spirit, and the demands of Cedar Lodge provided a necessary outlet.[10]

That he was both pleased with and proud of Cedar Lodge, there can be no doubt. In February 1917, he painted a glowing word picture of his ranch for Theodore Roosevelt.

I know that you will be pleased to know that I have built a home in this beautiful section of California, overlooking the valley of the Sacramento.

The card picture will give you an idea of the near surroundings, but does not show the beautiful slope to Cherry run with its rushing streams, its pools, cascades and falls.

I have under way an orchard of olives, almonds, prunes, figs, walnuts, all of which do well here without irrigation.

The climate is mild and I have almonds and peach just coming into bloom.

Of timber I have oaks, white oak, black oak and live oak, with pines, bay, red bud and manzanita, so that if I choose to fall [sic] a tree, I have some latitude of choice, but in making a clearing (in which I take delight) I save the finest trees to make the ranch one great park.

I have in all sixty-five acres, too much for one man to care for, and I intend some day to dispose of 40 acres, so that I may improve the remaining 25 in a manner that I have in view.[11]

A week later, Roosevelt, in failing health, responded with as much gusto as he could muster, sending three bully cheers for Kelly and complimenting him on the looks of Cedar Lodge. While T.R. wished he could make the journey to California, he did not believe there was "any such good fortune in store for me." It proved a prophetic statement, for within two years Roosevelt would be dead.[12]

Of all his correspondents, he wrote most frequently to Earl Alonzo Brininstool, the self-styled poet and writer/historian who lived in Los Angeles. Twenty years younger than Kelly, Earl Brininstool was born in Warsaw, New York, but moved to California in 1895. A newspaperman by trade, he developed a fascination with the history of the American West, which eventually led him to write poetry, articles, and books about the West, with emphasis on the Indian Wars. Between 1905 and his death in 1957, his articles appeared frequently in such publications of the day as *Hunter-Trader-Trapper*, *Winners of the West*, and *Forest & Stream*. Book-length publications included *Fighting Red Cloud's Warriors* and *The Bozeman Trail* (with Grace Raymond Hebard), *The True Story of the Killing of Billy the Kid*, and *A Trooper with Custer*.

During the course of his life, Brininstool corresponded regularly with many of the old scouts, buffalo hunters, and personalities of the Old West. Brininstool and Kelly began their correspondence at least as early as 1918. In all likelihood the relationship was initiated by Brininstool, who had somehow learned that Kelly had settled in Paradise and recognized another opportunity to make contact with one of the real-life Western figures.[13]

As might be expected, much of what Kelly and Brininstool corresponded about concerned the story of the Western frontier. Brininstool would ask whether Kelly had known Custer's scout, Lonesome Charley Reynolds, or Jim Bridger, and Kelly would respond, often with an interesting anecdote or two. He remembered, for example, that even in poor hunting country, "Lonesome" Charley Reynolds could usually make a killing when no one else could.[14]

Many of Brininstool's early letters addressed Kelly as major, which of course, was a higher grade than he had ever attained in the army, but was rather an honorary title bestowed on Indian agents, a practice Kelly found ridiculous. Captain was good enough for him.[15]

Over the years, Kelly had become a member of several veterans and patriotic organizations, such as the Sons of the American Revolution and the GAR, among others, but now in his twilight years he told Brininstool that he was too far removed to be active in any of those organizations; had simply tired of paying his dues and so resigned from most of these groups. He did, however, wish to be a member of the Order of Indian Wars, because it meant a connection with events that he had been directly involved with. Friends such as Gen. Oscar Long, Gen. John Lincoln Clem, and Col. Homer Wheeler vouched for him.[16]

Next to the sense of accomplishment he derived from developing Cedar Lodge, visiting with old friends provided his greatest source of enjoyment. Sometimes friends, such as Eugene Grubb, who Kelly and May had known in Colorado and who had since made a name for himself as the "Potato King," would stop by for a visit, or Kelly might pay a call on his old comrade Oscar Long in Piedmont, California, and Earl Brininstool made at least one visit to Cedar Lodge. Mostly, however, such contact was by letter.[17]

Brininstool and Kelly would often send one another a photo or a book and Brininstool, of course, was always glad to have Kelly's comments. And given his natural bent for history anyway, it is not surprising that Kelly was interested in virtually anything about the Old West that his pen pal down in Los Angeles wanted to send along. He enjoyed Brininstool's *The True Story of the Killing of Billy the Kid* and was very much interested in the two-volume history of the Bozeman Trail that Brininstool and Grace Hebard had co-authored. He was fascinated by the account of the Wagon Box Fight. "That was a soldiers fight under

Luther S. Kelly
and Earl Alonzo
Brininstool at
Cedar Lodge, 1927.
*Amon Carter Museum,
Fort Worth, Texas.*

the stress of dire necessity and in the shadow of despair. Well fought."
Kelly appreciated a photo of Brininstool's den, saying it had a familiar
look and wished Brininstool could see his [Kelly's] Navajo blankets and
belts, as well as his souvenirs from the Philippines.[18]

As the twenties wore on, life at Cedar Lodge gradually became more
difficult for the Kellys due to health problems. In June 1923, May lost all
the vision in her right eye and had begun to lose sight in the left eye as
well. With Luther also suffering from deteriorating vision, the routine of
daily life grew ever more taxing. As an added responsibility, sometime in
the early twenties, May's brother George came to live with them. A former railroad conductor, George, who was a cripple, helped out around
the house to the extent that he was able, but, given Luther and May's
physical condition, he was also something of a burden as well. When
George died in 1925, Kelly told Brininstool that he had just buried his
brother-in-law, an aged cripple "who has been quite a care."[19]

The situation in the Kelly household, prior to George's death, provides another peek at Kelly's innate sense of humor. He billed himself

Luther and May Kelly at Cedar Lodge home. Photo probably taken in the 1920s. The caption on the print provides an example of Kelly's dry sense of humor. It reads: "The lady and the tiger, grim visaged war at the entrance, Manzanita Gate, Cedar Lodge." *George Bille Collection.*

as chief cook, while May's brother, whom Kelly called an old man, washed dishes, collected wood, and did the sweeping. The amusing aspect of this is that George was three years Kelly's junior.[20]

Luther and May tended to be a fairly private couple, though far from antisocial. As they had done in Colorado and elsewhere, they developed a circle of friends with whom they shared special moments and occasions, but probably to a lessening extent as their general health and eyesight began to fail. To celebrate Luther's seventy-third birthday, May, perhaps ably assisted by Dudley and Minnie Barnes, hosted a birthday picnic under the cedar trees. Some of the ladies "wanted to have a peep at my scrapbook," Kelly told Brininstool afterward.[21]

In addition to the Barnes's a friendship also developed between Luther and one, John Bille, another early Paradise resident. Bille was fond of relating an amusing anecdote about Kelly, which says much about the man and his impish sense of humor. On this particular occasion, Bille was out chopping firewood when he became conscious of someone's presence. Turning, he found Kelly standing there quietly watching. Addressing Kelly, Bille remarked that he didn't give a man much warning, to wit Kelly replied it was why he was still around.[22]

Another view of Luther and May at the front entrance of Cedar Lodge, about 1925–1927. *George Bille Collection.*

During the course of his life, Kelly had been blest with a strong constitution and robust health, notwithstanding the swollen veins in his left testicle, which was a source of some discomfort from time to time, though apparently not enough to interfere with a vigorous lifestyle. However, in 1908 he began to experience some additional health problems in the form of recurring double vision and was convinced that his long-standing testicle condition was related to the impairment of his vision.

I first began to have double vision in 1908 while holding the position of U.S. Indian Agent at San Carlos, Arizona. The disability manifested itself very lightly at that time and I paid little attention to it, but in the summer of 1909, it became a disagreeable incident so that two or three times in the day I was obliged to halt in whatever occupation I was engaged in until it passed away, which it frequently did in a few minutes. If walking I was obliged to pause for I could

Luther S. Kelly.
Probably taken about
the time of World War I,
or slightly later.
Photo furnished by the
Amon Carter Museum,
Fort Worth, Texas, and
used by permission of
Helen E. and Homer E.
Britzman Collection,
Taylor Museum for
Southwestern Studies,
Colorado Springs
Fine Arts Center.

not keep a straight course. This affects both eyes and the double vision is horizontal.

Since 1909, it is rare that a day passes that I am not held
by this embarrassing complaint at least three or four times in
a day. It follows mostly after manual exertion, but occurs
sometimes while in conversation or while reading. There is
no pain felt, it simply arrests movement in any occupation in
which I engage.[23]

It is interesting that Kelly believed the varicose veins in his testicle
led to a low state of vitality and eventually to his vision problem, which,
in turn, prevented him from obtaining employment. The remark about
low vitality is puzzling, especially in view of his 1919 letter to Charles
Stobie, in which he describes his vigorous work around the ranch. If
one chooses to believe his statement to Stobie, how then does one rec-
oncile his 1915 declaration of health for an invalid pension? The latter
seems a contradiction of the former and I am inclined to believe that

Kelly, in an effort to strengthen his case for a pension, exaggerated the effects of his condition.

If the double-vision problem persisted, Kelly left no record of it and it does not seem to have interfered with the way he went about his daily life, although in May 1915, he applied for a $17 increase in the monthly pension he had been receiving for three years, claiming that he had been unable to perform manual labor to support himself. Apparently, insofar as the Bureau of Pensions was concerned, his physical capability was limited, but two years later, with the advent of World War I, he had regained enough strength to offer his services in whatever way he might be most useful.

Again, it is difficult to see this claim as anything but an exaggeration, for clearly, by his own admission, he was able to engage in strenuous physical activity, although it does appear that he began to experience debilitating health problems a year or two after writing Stobie. In any case, the request was denied.[24]

Despite the contradictions implied above, his overall health seems to have been quite strong through the first few years in Paradise, at least judging from the tenor of his 1919 letter to Charles Stobie. However, the image conveyed by that letter—that is the picture of a man in robust health—is somewhat misleading. Quite apart from the double vision he experienced earlier, Kelly's general eyesight had begun to fail by 1920. And other health problems were close at hand. On 27 July 1920 he turned seventy-one. He had lived a strenuous life and so it is not surprising that the system began to fail.

At any rate, daily life at Cedar Lodge grew increasingly to be a question of how well or how poorly did we feel today. Aside from her own blindness, May seems to have been in reasonably good health. As for Luther, some days he felt strong, but others found him much less so, and on occasion either bedridden or forced to remain off his feet.[25]

But the breakdown began with his eyes. In June 1921, his old comrade Oscar Long helped arrange for Kelly's admission to Letterman General Hospital in San Francisco, where he underwent preliminary treatment for an eye operation that was scheduled for July. Upon returning to Paradise he told Brininstool that he felt better since his stay in San Francisco.[26] He was soon back in Letterman, however, where he underwent two further operations that seemed to do nothing more than cause acute discomfort. By early August he was home again and writing to Brininstool that he had endured discomfort and pain for more than a month and all to no avail. After two operations, his vision had not improved. Not only had he been miserable, but he had lost valuable time, which he could ill-afford to spare.[27]

In August he addressed the commissioner of pensions, in the hope of gaining an increase in his monthly pension, which by now had reached $50, and which was the sole source of his and May's support. He estimated it would be two years or longer before his orchard would be able to provide any real financial assistance. "I am now past 72 years of age," he wrote, "and until two years ago have been strong and healthy, delighting in out of door work of the most strenuous kind." He supported the claim with a letter from his physician, W. E. Mack, who reported that Kelly suffered the loss of all vision in his right eye and partial loss in his left eye. In addition, he suffered from Bright's Disease of the kidneys, "with dropsical effusion in both legs extending to the knees."

Despite Dr. Mack's letter, the Pension Bureau rejected the request on the grounds that "by reason of age and physical or mental disabilities you are helpless or blind or so nearly helpless or blind as to require the regular personal aid and attendance of another person." To this, Kelly penned a note to the commissioner, saying "I thank God that I am not as bad as all that and cheerfully forego any claim that places me in such category. Please God I have begun to mend since making application and am now on fair road to recovery—thanks to diet and sane exercise."[28]

In June 1922, Kelly wrote to the Secretary of the Interior, commenting on the secretary's recommendation to the Commissioner of Pensions that any increase of the $50 monthly pension, then in effect, be limited to those veterans age 80 and above. Limiting any increase to age 80, said Kelly, makes it "rather hard on the 'kids' of 73....I pray night and day that I may never reach the condition when I may have to apply for the increase on account of weakness and old age."[29]

By October, the picture had not improved much and Kelly was telling Brininstool that the eye remained bad and didn't seem to be healing. He was grateful, however, for his one good eye. But a month made a difference, because by mid-November he was able to report that the eye was healing and he was now able to do any kind of work.[30]

But if it wasn't one thing it was another. A week after writing Brininstool that he was able to do any kind of work, he was laid up with badly swollen legs, the result of poor circulation. The condition, presumably, kept him more or less incapacitated for several weeks, but in early February he told Brininstool that the eye had now healed and the legs were better.[31]

A month later, though, the circulatory problem was back and Kelly was *inflagrante de licto*, when the doctor caught him with rubber boots on after working in the fields, when he was supposed to be in bed. Again the legs were badly swollen from the knees down, which meant, he told Brininstool, that he must bid adieu to the hard physical labor of chopping down trees and blasting rocks, which he regarded as a source of great joy and relaxation.

The doctor, an Alaskan veteran, told Kelly to forget about the physical labor and instead work on his memoirs, threatening to get after him with a stuffed club if he did not comply; but the notion of him giving up all physical activity was totally out of character and in fact by June he was telling Brininstool that his legs were better, though weak after working the horse with a spring-toothed harrow.[32]

If Kelly did not always adhere to the doctor's orders to avoid physical exertion, he had concluded that diet was essential to good health. When Brininstool complained of having stomach problems, Kelly advised cutting back on heavy foods, pointing out that he himself now drank a quart of milk daily and used only whole wheat or bran bread, eggs, and fruit. His diet also included the juice of one lemon. The high-protein, almost exclusively meat diet of his young manhood was a thing of the past.[33]

Kelly had been working on his memoirs off and on since first settling in Paradise, and much as he was determined to finish the manuscript, it was impossible to spend all his time at the typewriter. Indeed, he was able to write only when his eyesight permitted. And beyond that, household responsibilities and tending to the needs of his trees demanded a certain amount of time. Brother-in-law George was of some help, but otherwise Kelly did most of the household chores and wrote when he could manage to stay awake.[34]

At least as early as 1919, Brininstool was urging him to get on with the project and offered to provide whatever assistance he could. Kelly plowed ahead as time and his and May's physical condition permitted, but it was slow going. He wished he could write his memoirs as quickly and easily as he wrote a letter, but where the former was concerned, he labored over the choice of just the right word and that took time.[35]

As the manuscript began to grow and take shape, Kelly was also in touch with another old friend, artist Edwin Willard Deming, who, like Brininstool, took a keen interest in the Kelly story. Deming, whose artistic depictions of Indian life had been well received, was enthusiastic about the project and encouraged Kelly to send his manuscript pages for retyping by a professional typist. When the half-finished script reached Deming in the spring of 1920, his enthusiasm was not at all dampened.

> The story is very interesting and you have told it in a simple direct way, just as you would tell it to a bunch of old timers around a campfire. The book will take a place with the "Winning of the West" by Teddy, "The Conquest of the Missouri,"... and many other narratives that tell the story of the romantic conquering of the Indian country.[36]

Deming believed he might be able to arrange for publication before the manuscript was finished. Kelly was skeptical, however, and his skepticism proved well founded. Nevertheless, Deming did eventually manage to interest Doubleday Page & Company in a partial script, but the publisher subsequently rejected it on the grounds that it would require too much editorial attention to put it in publishable form. "I was afraid that it was not a good plan to submit it in its unfinished state," Deming admitted. "The next time we submit it we will have it in complete shape." It was also Deming's suggestion that since Theodore Roosevelt was now dead, Kelly ought to contact Nelson Miles to write a foreword for the book.[37]

Meanwhile, Earl Brininstool had been lobbying on behalf of his publisher, Arthur H. Clark, who was about to publish a two-volume history of the Bozeman Trail by Brininstool and Wyoming State Historian Grace Raymond Hebard. Brininstool was very much pleased with Clark's work and urged Kelly to consider them as a publisher. Kelly ran the suggestion past Deming, who agreed that Clark would be a good choice. Kelly assured Brininstool not to be alarmed, that he would finish the narrative in good time. He had some good sources from which to draw: letters, a diary from Alaska and the Philippines, but white ants had, unfortunately, made something of a mess of parts of it all, making it difficult to read.[38]

Kelly had never met the artist Charles Marion Russell, but he had seen Russell's work and especially liked the artist's sketch of his duel with the two Sioux warriors that appeared in *Back-Trailing on the Old Frontiers*. Kelly wanted to use the sketch and Russell was pleased to know it would be included in the book. During the course of preparing his memoirs, Kelly wrote Russell expressing his regret that he had not known the artist in the early days.[39]

By the summer of 1924, the manuscript was nearly finished. Kelly believed the last four chapters, based mainly on his Philippines journal, were as good as anything he had written. George Bird Grinnell, who had been published by Yale, suggested that press would be a good home for the work and, after due deliberation, Kelly elected to accept Grinnell's advice. On 14 September, he wrote to R. V. Coleman of Yale, saying the manuscript was now finished and numbered 483 pages, including some twenty-five illustrations, together with a foreword by Nelson Miles. Also included, he told Coleman, was an

> old map which I made on tracing paper from a military map of the period about 1870, and used on the plains and mountains of Montana and Dakota, in the early days. It is chiefly valuable in showing the blank places in the region north and south of the Yellowstone River—a good many of which I filled in from my own travels and observation."[40]

What finally swayed Kelly to choose Yale over Arthur Clark is not clear. He did have a great deal of respect for Brininstool, after all, but in the end it may have been that Grinnell was from the eastern establishment and was a noted anthropologist and editor in his own right, and that perhaps carried a bit more weight. In any event, the manuscript was shipped off to New Haven under the title *Indian Man's Country: Alaska and the Philippines*. On 13 October, Coleman advised him that the manuscript had been turned over to the editorial board for consideration.[41]

Ordinarily manuscript decisions are lengthy processes, but in this instance, Kelly had a report within two weeks. Yale's reaction was very favorable. However, Coleman pointed out that a certain amount of editorial supervision would be required in order to put the manuscript into proper shape for publication. Coleman proposed turning the script over to an "eminent historical scholar for recommendations, which would then be passed on to the editorial board." If the board approved and Kelly agreed, a contract would be offered and publication would proceed. However, Coleman warned, this meant that Kelly would be putting himself "pretty thoroughly in our hands, and I want to be assured of your satisfaction with that" before proceeding. If accepted, Kelly was to receive a royalty of 7.5 percent of the retail price, until the editorial expense was recovered, after which he was to receive a straight 15 percent.[42]

The eminent historical scholar suggested by Coleman turned out to be Milo Milton Quaife, recently installed as editor of the Burton Historical Collection of the Detroit Public Library. A scholar of considerable repute who was then forty-four years old, Quaife was at the apex of a career that was to continue for another three decades. If a publisher of that day was to seek out a preeminent historian with editing experience, it would have been difficult to find one with stronger credentials than M. M. Quaife.

Prior to being named as editor of the Burton Collection, Quaife, who had earned degrees from Iowa College and the Universities of Missouri and Chicago, had served as editor of the Wisconsin State Historical Society's publications. He was active in the Mississippi Valley Historical Association and the author of a number of historical volumes, including his Ph.D. dissertation, *The Diary of James K. Polk During His Presidency.*[43]

With Kelly's approval of the overall plan, Coleman proceeded to contact Quaife, who subsequently read the manuscript and reported his findings on 15 December. Quaife was impressed with Kelly's first-person account of his life on the Plains, calling him a "reincarnation of Daniel Boone, as it were, and he puts into his journal a flavor of wild life and a fondness for it which should make his story attractive to all who entertain a like fondness." Quaife, however, did not like the idea of including that portion of Kelly's experiences in Alaska and the Philippines, which he felt carried the reader "into quite different fields and would, if published, constitute an anti-climax to the first."

Thus, Quaife recommended that the press consider publishing only that portion of Kelly's narrative which dealt with his Western experiences. Interestingly enough, at least one of the press's editors did not concur with Quaife. However, the editorial board, with or without Coleman's approval, accepted Quaife's assessment, which was then presented to Kelly, who agreed to both the arrangement and the contractual terms. The press had decided to title the published version *Yellowstone Kelly* and that, too, was fine. It remained only for the press to reach a satisfactory arrangement with either Milo Quaife or some other "eminent historian."[44]

Kelly does not seem to have been particularly upset that Yale wished to cut his manuscript in half. Indeed, after thinking about it he came to see a certain value in the notion of making Alaska and the Philippines a separate volume. And why not? Now the prospect of having two books to his credit held a certain appeal. He didn't know anything about Quaife, however, and asked Brininstool to do a little research on the man.[45]

By February, Quaife had agreed to undertake the editing of Kelly's manuscript, which he regarded as a gem, albeit one that required a fairly heavy editorial hand. While he clearly regarded the work as an important historical contribution, he obviously thought considerably less of Kelly's literary skill.

> [T]his narrative [said Quaife] provides an interesting and valuable first-hand picture of life on the western plains in the period to which it pertains. Suitably edited, it would seem well worth publishing. From the nature of the case Mr. Kelly, having lived a Daniel Boone career from his early years, could not be expected to be an expert or cultivated writer. Consequently, to prepare his manuscript for publication it should be thoroughly revised throughout. Such revision should aim to preserve the spirit and present simplicity of Mr. Kelly's narration and to exercise or refine, in so far as the circumstances of the case permit, present crudities of expression and of composition. I think the editorial work should be done as unobtrusively as possible, so that the finished narrative will appear to the reader as though it had come direct from Mr. Kelly. Of course it would be stated in the historical introduction (which should be provided) that the manuscript had been subjected to editorial revision.[46]

As noted, the press apparently agreed with Quaife's conclusions, here summarized and stated somewhat more succinctly than in his 15 December letter to Coleman. Once all were in agreement, Kelly's manuscript began its long route through the publication process. As with many authors, Kelly began to grow nervous as the months marched on and he heard nothing. "I suspect they may be waiting for the fall trade," he told Brininstool, "or working on the movie feature of the work, as they seem to lay a lot of stress on that part of the work." That fall, however, Coleman advised him that the book would not be out until the spring of 1926.[47]

Quaife described the manuscript's literary quality in harsher terms than it deserved. The original typescript differs little from the published book and is quite nicely written, as any reader will, I think, agree. The Alaska-Philippines typescript, on the other hand, is in rougher shape and would have required considerable editorial attention to put it into publishable condition, which may have influenced Quaife's view.

Despite failing eyesight and deteriorating health overall, Kelly continued to work, as he was able, on readying the Alaska-Philippines manuscript for submission to Yale. He was pleased with the foreword written by Nelson Miles for the volume about to be published and now asked William Howard Taft if he would consider preparing a similar statement for his Alaska-Philippines manuscript.

> Of all the general officers and commanders who served at home and abroad, who knew of my army service in the Islands, there is not one now living as far as I can learn. You are the only one left, Mr. Taft, and I would appreciate it very much if you could see your way to give me a short FORE-WORD for my forthcoming book."[48]

Taft was evidently a little surprised and embarrassed by the request, which was almost plaintive in nature and came from a man he scarcely recalled anymore. Still, he was gracious enough to respond, but declined the opportunity, saying he regretted that his knowledge of Kelly's previous history and work in the Philippines was "so dim, in view of the many things that have happened since that I could not write such a foreword as that you are doubtless entitled to." In view of how well they had got on when Taft visited him at Dapitan, Kelly was probably disappointed to receive that kind of turn-down.[49]

Yellowstone Kelly: The Memoirs of Luther S. Kelly was published in the spring of 1926, just as Coleman had promised. Reviews were good, suggesting strong sales ahead.

> His story reads like one of those vigorous fiction stories which so delighted boys of half a century ago. But to make the interest greater, this story is true. Here is history in a most entertaining form. — *Boston Transcript*

> What old "Yellowstone" has to say is extremely interesting, and he tells it in simple, straightforward fashion, with a wealth of absorbing detail. — *New York Times*

> Mr. Kelly writes, not as a novelist, but as a historian, and his work is rich in the best qualities of both. It is written in plain language, in most interesting fashion, and without undue boasting. — *The Outlook*

Kelly was pleased with the book and the way it had been placed before the public. Oscar Long, writing to thank Kelly for his copy, said he was "captivated by the narrative and read it attentively to the end. It brought back to me most vividly memories of the many campaigns of the past, when your soldier comrades and yourself suffered hardships, privations and dangers, which those who followed them were strangers to because the frontier had disappeared and civilization and settlements were made possible."[50]

In the spring of 1926, Kelly received an invitation from his old photographer friend L. A. Huffman, inviting him to attend the fiftieth anniversary of the Custer battle. Kelly wished he was in shape to go, but physical problems precluded him from doing so. Besides, he told Brininstool, he had to take care of May. Indeed, here was a case of the blind truly leading the blind. Kelly had installed a wire along the line of cedar trees leading out to the road so as to provide guidance for both of them.[51]

In September, Kelly wrote to Oscar Long, informing his old comrade that he could still use the typewriter, but was unable to read a newspaper. He was grateful to be able to go about his daily business, but was somewhat surprised "because according to my eye specialist I should have been under the knife more than a month ago." As for the book, he told Long that it was selling steadily, if not in great numbers. Yale seemed pleased with its performance thus far. He continued to work on his Alaska-Philippines manuscript, he told Long, and regarded it as a valuable piece of work, though one that required "some touching up and building of the opening chapter where it breaks from the original manuscript.[52]

By the spring of 1927, Kelly's correspondence had fallen off. He could no longer use the typewriter and was unable to read anything without the aid of a strong glass. In addition to his regular physician, he had been examined by two eye specialists, each of whom wrote to the Commissioner of Pensions, Winfield Scott, supporting Kelly's claim for an increase in his monthly pension. The act of 3 July 1926 did provide for a rate of $90 per month for an individual who was "totally helpless or blind." However, since Kelly did have some vision, he was not judged eligible.[53] He was expecting to have an eye operation soon and that, it was hoped, would restore at least some of his vision. Surgery was put on hold, however, when he came down with pneumonia during the late spring or early summer and was seriously ill for six weeks. Indeed, for two days, he hovered between life and death, he told Brininstool in an August letter so shaky the handwriting was barely decipherable. Thinking that the end was drawing near, he sent for a notary and dictated a codicil to his last will and testament, directing that his body be encased in "a suitable casket, plain but substantial and together with my Spanish war saber, a relic of the fight at La Lud, Luzon, February

The last known photograph of Luther S. "Yellowstone" Kelly, taken April 20, 1927. *Montana Historical Society, Helena*

1900, the whole to be tendered to the government of the State of Montana, through the Librarian, State Historical Society at Helena, Montana for such disposal as they may see fit." He had concluded that his body would rest easier in Montana, the scene of his earlier activities, than in "the vastness of Arlington," where he had originally planned to be buried.[54]

However, a fortnight later, he had rallied from the pneumonia and seemed to have recovered enough of his vision to return to work on his manuscript. He was still thinking of offering Alaska-Philippines to Houghton-Mifflin, once he got it ready for submission, although Yale was apparently still a candidate. Surprisingly, he also seemed to have in preparation what he called a short story, entitled "The Story of the

Mandan," which he described as an account of Mandan history from before the discovery of North America.[55]

On 18 May he was admitted to the U.S. Naval Hospital at Mare Island. His condition had again worsened and his eyesight had caused him to fall on several occasions. He was unable to make the journey alone and was taken to the hospital by a member of the Veterans Bureau. He remained hospitalized for six days, but there was little to be done for his condition. The doctors, probably due to his very poor overall physical condition, were reluctant to perform further eye surgery and advised him to wait until he had lost all vision. On the twenty-fourth he asked to return home and again was provided with an attendant to escort him.[56]

Probably during the fall of 1927 or the winter of 1928, he did manage to ship the Alaska-Philippines story off to Houghton-Mifflin, who subsequently rejected the manuscript. "They returned it," he told Edwin Deming, "saying they had one or two books and did not care to take up another at this time." He thought he might try the Century Company or another New York house thereafter and asked for Deming's recommendation. Insofar as his eyes were concerned, Deming had recommended a New York specialist, but Kelly knew there was no way he could manage a visit to New York. He had been trying to sell Cedar Lodge, he told Deming, but had thus far been unsuccessful and had given up until spring.[57]

In what was apparently his last letter to Earl Brininstool, Kelly reported that whatever vision remained would not last long. "I can still see to eat from my plate, but sight is going fast."[58] He still had not gotten the Alaska-Philippines manuscript off to another publisher and the way things played out, he never would.[59]

We know little of the last six months of Luther Kelly's life. If he corresponded with anyone during those weeks, the letters have not survived. In all likelihood, though, these were simply days of steadily declining health. On 9 December, he was stricken with influenza, but held on for another week. The end came finally, and we suspect probably mercifully, at 8:14 AM on 17 December 1928. Officially, the cause of death was listed as chronic nephritis, with influenza a contributory cause.[60]

Kelly had requested that his body be interred in Montana and that request had been directed to the State Historical Society's secretary, David Hilger. Although no written record of the Society's agreement to honor Kelly's request has survived, the state seems to have wasted no time in agreeing to accept the remains of one of its most illustrious pioneers.

The interment of Capt. Luther S. "Yellowstone" Kelly on the rim above Billings, Montana, June 26, 1929. *Montana State Historical Society, Helena.*

After Kelly's death, his body was consigned to the undertaking firm of Bicknell and Moore of Chico, California, where services were held on the morning of the nineteenth. Afterward, the body was prepared for rail transportation to Billings, Montana, accompanied by the Kellys' longtime friend and neighbor, Dudley Barnes. Upon arriving in Billings, Kelly's body was placed in the Billings mausoleum for burial at a later date.[61]

The exact site of Kelly's final resting place had not been decided upon at the time of his death. The Billings Commercial Club had responded to the idea with enthusiasm, proposing that the old scout be buried in Boot Hill on the rimrock (above the city of Billings. But apparently, as discussions progressed, a site other than Boot Hill was deemed more desirable and appropriate. According to one account, historian I. D. O'Donnell bought a piece of land some distance west of Boot Hill and donated it to May Kelly for Luther's final resting place, which was then named Kelly Mountain in honor of the famous scout.[62]

On 26 June 1929, Kelly's body lay in state in the Billings Commercial Club from 1:30 to 2:30, following which it was transported to Kelly

Mountain for burial. The impressive funeral procession was conducted with full military honors and included a number of state and city officials, Boy Scouts, and veterans groups. Following addresses by several notables, a volley from the firing squad, and the melancholy wail of taps, the body was lowered into its final resting place, a specially prepared, reinforced concrete crypt.

Over the crypt rests a small, plain granite slab, on the top of which is mounted a metal plate that reads:

LUTHER S. KELLY
NEW YORK
CAPTAIN 40 US VOL INF
JULY 27 1849 DEC 17 1928

Just below the gravesite stands a large interpretive sign summarizing Kelly's remarkable life.

YELLOWSTONE KELLY
    A LONG BREECH LOADING SPRINGFIELD RIFLE COV-
ERED FROM MUZZLE TO STOCK WITH THE SKIN OF A
HUGE BULL SNAKE, WAS CARRIED BY MAJOR LUTHER M.
(YELLOWSTONE) KELLY, SHAKESPEARE-QUOTING INDIAN
FIGHTER AND SCOUT. KELLY, NEW YORKER BORN APRIL
1849, AND CIVIL WAR VETERAN, GUIDED GOVERNMENT
EXPEDITIONS IN THE 1870'S-80'S INTO THE YELLOWSTONE
RIVER VALLEY. HE LATER SERVED WITH THE MILITARY IN
ALASKA AND THE PHILIPPINES AND THEN RETIRED TO
CALIFORNIA. BEFORE HIS DEATH, DEC. 17, 1928, HE ASKED
TO BE BURIED ON THIS POINT OVERLOOKING THE AREA
HE HAD SCOUTED.

The sign contains three errors. First, it incorrectly identifies Kelly as major, an official rank he never attained; his highest rank in the military was that of captain. Major was an honorary title bestowed on Indian agents of that day. Second, Kelly was born in July, not April. Finally, he did not specify this burial site, asking only to rest in Montana.

Initially, it was a spare and simple site, identified only by the granite marker. Later the marker was surrounded by a six-foot-high iron picket fence, which was removed sometime during the 1980s. Today the site appears much as it did in 1929.

Until recently, the area surrounding the gravesite received little attention. Then in 2001, largely through the efforts of Army Staff Sgt. Glenn Myers, the site has been spruced up so that it can once again stand as tall and straight as the memory it honors.

During his very nearly four score years, Luther Kelly had witnessed, and been a participant in, more history than most people experience even vicariously. Save for those few years in Chicago and the East, his had been a life of raw adventure, fraught with danger enough to demand an almost constant flow of adrenaline. He had known some of the most influential men of his day and become acquainted with parts of the world that were like the dark side of the moon to most Americans of his antiquity.

When the entire tapestry of his life is spread out before us, Luther Kelly emerges as a truly fascinating individual. To have done all that he did cannot help but strike us as remarkable. In the twilight of their years, few individuals of any age are able to reflect on the kind of life Kelly experienced. To have been, in a single lifetime, frontiersman, army scout, Alaskan explorer, soldier, and Indian agent, stands indeed as a remarkable record.

In the face of such a record, one is hard pressed to imagine him wishing his life had been different, but then who can really say what lingering regrets may beset any individual when they come to the end of the trail. Perhaps Kelly regretted leaving no descendants to follow.... Perhaps he regretted not having chosen a soldier's life earlier.... Perhaps he wished he had pursued a law career. And how nice it would have been to have witnessed publication of the Alaska-Philippines manuscript. But all possible regrets aside, one would have to acknowledge that the youth from Geneva had traveled far and done much. Goethe's dictum to "keep not firmly rooted, to briskly venture, briskly roam," could find no better example than Luther Sage Kelly.

Epilogue

In those years between Luther's death in 1928 and her own passing a
decade later, May Kelly arranged for a spray of flowers to be placed
on her husband's grave each year. Almost totally blind, Alice May Kelly
lived in a world of darkness, leaning heavily, we might imagine, on the
rich trove of memories that were her legacy from her forty-three years
of marriage to a remarkable man.[1]

With Luther gone, May came increasingly to rely on the care of
Dudley and Minnie Barnes, who undoubtedly tried to fill the void
left by Luther's passing as best they could. May's own end came on
22 August 1938 when she succumbed to the effects of pneumonia and
cardiac complications. She was laid to rest in the Paradise cemetery,
next to her brother George. How she felt about being separated from
Luther we shall never know, of course, but clearly they had come to a
meeting of minds about their respective final resting places. And in the
final analysis, was this really so very different from what their life
together had been, when she was often alone, while Luther was absent
on one adventure or another?

In the years since Kelly's interment, Billings and the Yellowstone
Valley have undergone noticeable and dramatic changes, and yet many
of the area's features remain intact and are clearly recognizable—for
example, the mighty "Rim" itself, rising a foreboding 400 feet above the
valley floor. Yellowstone Kelly's gravesite, situated along Black Otter
Trail, near the edge of the rim itself, embraces a truly grand view of the

majestic and historic Yellowstone Valley. If destiny ever decreed a fitting locale for one man's final resting place, surely this spot was meant for Yellowstone Kelly.

Notes

Chapter One

1. Luther S. Kelly, *Memoirs*, 3.
2. Ibid.
3. Durham, *Smithsonian Guide to Historic America*, 248–49.
4. Brumberg, *The Making of an Upstate Community*, 6.
5. Ibid., 9–13.
6. Ibid., 12–16.
7. Ibid., 15.
8. Ibid., 17, 19, 33–34.
9. Stelter, *History of the Ark Lodge*, 66; *American Ancestry*, 136; *The Kelly Family of Geneva*, 1; Musgrove, *History of the Town of Bristol*, 261–66.
10. Giles M. Kelly, *Genealogical Account of the Descendants of John Kelly*, 9. Although this branch of the Kellys seems to have been solidly English for some generations, Giles Kelly reports one story that has a Kelly of a much earlier generation leaving Ireland for England, and there, falling in love with and subsequently marrying a lady of high station.
11. *American Ancestry*, 136.
12. Ibid.; *The Kelly Family of Geneva*, 1; Stelter, *History of Ark Lodge*, 66.
13. Stelter, *History of the Ark Lodge*, 66.
14. *The Kelly Family of Geneva*, 2–3. There is some confusion as to the location of the Kelly house. According to the Geneva directory for 1857–1858, Jeannette was shown to be in residence on the north side of William St., east of Pulteney St. However, a story by reporter Arch Merrill, appearing in *The Geneva Gazette*, says that Luther S. Kelly was born in a house that stood on the corner of Pulteney St. and Elmwood Ave., where St. Stephen's Church now stands. One explanation is that the family moved sometime after Luther S. was born. See Letter to Dr. Richard E. Kelly, Buffalo, New York, November 4, 1971 (correspondent not identified; copy from Luther S. Kelly file, Geneva Historical Society, hereafter cited as Richard E. Kelly Letter, Nov. 4, 1971); and Merrill, "Boyhood Home Too

Dull for 'Yellowstone' Kelly." Both items found in the Luther S. Kelly file, Geneva Historical Society.

15. Ibid., 2.

16. The given name of Luther's second wife is variously spelled "Jenette," "Jeanette," "Jennette," and "Jeannette." I have used the last, which is the choice of Giles Kelly in his family history. See Giles M. Kelly, *A Genealogical Account of the Descendants of John Kelly*, 150. See also *American Ancestry*, 136.

17. *The Kelly Family of Geneva*, 2.

18. Richard E. Kelly Letter, 4 Nov. 1971. See also Brumberg, *The Making of an Upstate Community*; Lamar, *The Reader's Encyclopedia of the American West Community*, 52–53, 94; and Lamar, 160. See also the *Geneva Gazette*, 1854, no. 36.

19. Stelter, *History of the Ark Lodge*, 66; *The Kelly Family of Geneva*, 3–4.

20. Stelter, *History of the Ark Lodge*, 16–17. See also Stelter, "Who Was William Morgan?"

21. Ibid.

22. Ibid.

23. *The Geneva Gazette*, 1854, no. 32. See also issue no. 36 for that year. Unfortunately, no documentation presenting Kelly's side of the matter has survived.

24. Richard E. Kelly Letter, 4 Nov. 1971.

25. *American Ancestry*, 136; Richard E. Kelly Letter, 4 Nov. 1971; Musgrove, *History of the Town of Bristol*.

26. Luther S. Kelly file, Geneva Historical Society. Two-page typescript copy of Kelly family history and typescript copy of Jeannette E. Kelly's obituary, both from Luther S. Kelly file, Geneva Historical Society.

27. Brumberg, *The Making of an Upstate Community*, 51–57, 93.

28. Kelly, *Memoirs*, 1.

29. Brumberg, *The Making of an Upstate Community*, 108.

30. Luther S. Kelly file, Geneva Historical Society.

31. Kelly, *Memoirs*, 2.

32. Ibid.

33. Ibid.

34. Luther Kelly's name appears on the rolls only for the academic year ending November 15, 1865. Based on this, it appears he may only have attended the school for a few months before entering the army. Letter from Syracuse University Archives to author, 27 Jan. 1972.

35. Kelly, *Memoirs*, 2.

36. Ibid., 2–3. Kelly relates the story—probably apocryphal—of the young man who purchased a pair of size nine shoes so that he could tell the recruiting officer he was "over" eighteen. In any case, he seems to have lied about his age.

37. Ibid.

38. Ibid., 2–3.

39. McFeely, *Grant*, 175.

40. Kelly, *Memoirs*, 3.

41. Ibid., 3–4.

42. Luther S. Kelly, copy of sworn statement made to Bureau of Pensions, 20 July 1915. The condition with which Kelly was afflicted is known as *varicocele* or dilated testicular veins. The condition may have been caused by a blood clot and is associated with a 25–65 percent rate of sterility.

Personal communication to author from Roger P. Blair, M.D., 25 Nov. 1997.
See also Wyngaarden and Smith, *Cecil Textbook of Medicine*, Vol. 2, 1372.

43.   Ibid., 4; Long, *The Civil War Day by Day*, 693.

44.   Kelly, *Memoirs*, 4–5. Shinplasters were government-issue currency that resembled postage stamps. Because they were similar to small pieces of paper that people often moistened in vinegar or some other substance and then applied to an afflicted part of their anatomy such as the shin, they were called shinplasters. See Flexner, *Listening to America*, 191.

45.   Kelly, *Memoirs*, 5–6; Boatner, *Civil War Dictionary*, 191. Whoever it was that Kelly saw, it was not Custer, who had taken part in the Grand Review on May 23. See Utley, *Cavalier in Buckskin*, 35.

46.   Kelly, *Memoirs*, 6.

47.   Ibid., 5–6.

48.   Ibid., 6.

49.   Ibid., 6–7; Post Returns, Fort Ripley, Minnesota, April 1849–December 1865, Roll 1026, January 1866–July 1877. Roll 1027; Prucha, *Broadax and Bayonet*, 28; Baker, *The Muster Roll*, 1–23; Prucha, *American Indian Treaties*, 196.

50.   Kelly, *Memoirs*, 7.

51.   Ibid., 8–9; Kelly to Earl A. Brininstool, 15 Nov. 1922 (hereafter cited as Kelly to EAB, with appropriate dates); the E. A. Brininstool Collection, University of Texas. The Kelly-Brininstool letters may be found in two repositories: as part of the Earl A. Brininstool Collection in the Center for American History at the University of Texas, Austin, cited as the E. A. Brininstool Collection, University of Texas, and the Earl A. Brininstool Collection, Brigham Young University, Provo, UT, cited as the E. A. Brininstool Collection, BYU. [See ch2n3.]

52.   Karie, *Fort Sisseton*, 5; Utley, *Frontier Regulars*, 125; Kane, *Military Life in Dakota*, 44–46.

53.   Kelly, *Memoirs*, 9; Karie, *Fort Sisseton*, 1, 11.

54.   Kelly, *Memoirs*, 10–11. Galvanized Yankees were Confederate prisoners who had volunteered to serve against Indians on the frontier, rather than languish in prison. See Utley, *Frontiersmen in Blue*, 308.

55.   Kelly, *Memoirs*, 10–12.

56.   Ibid.; Keenan, *The Great Sioux Uprising*, 17–22.

57.   Kelly, *Memoirs*, 10–12.

58.   Rickey, *Forty Miles a Day*, 126.

59.   Ibid., 115; Kelly, *Memoirs*, 13.

60.   Kelly, *Memoirs*, 12; Kane, *Military Life in Dakota*, 44.

61.   Kelly, *Memoirs*, 12.

62.   Ibid., 13; Kane, *Military Life in Dakota*, 44n.

63.   Kelly, *Memoirs*, 13.

64.   Ibid.; Greene, *Yellowstone Command*, 54–63, 74. Kelly, *Memoirs*, 14.

Chapter Two

1.   Kelly, *Memoirs*, 15.

2.   Giles M. Kelly, *A Genealogical Account of the Descendants of John Kelly; American Ancestry*, 136.

3.   Kelly, *Memoirs*, 24; Kelly to EAB, 15 May 1920, the E. A. Brininstool Collection, University of Texas.

4.   Interestingly, one observer did in fact regard Kelly as "reckless," probably because of his famous encounter with two Sioux warriors while carrying

the mail between Forts Buford and Stevenson. See Taylor, *Frontier and Indian Life*, 80.

5. Kelly, *Memoirs*, 15.
6. Ibid.
7. Utley, *The Lance and the Shield*, 102–3; Thomas et al., *The Native Americans*, 165.
8. Gilman et al., *The Red River Trails*, 16–17; Kelly, *Memoirs*, 20.
9. Kelly, *Memoirs*, 16–18.
10. Ibid., 17–18.
11. Ibid.
12. Kelly, *Memoirs*, 19–20.
13 Ibid.
14. Ibid., 20–21.
15. Ibid., 21; Utley, *The Lance and the Shield*, 39–40.
16. Kelly, *Memoirs*, 22.
17. Ibid.
18. Ibid.
19. Ibid.
20. Ibid., 23–24.
21. Ibid., 24–25.
22. Kane, *Military Life in Dakota*, 22, 44, 79. Both sites are now under the waters of Lake Sakakawea, created by Garrison Dam.
23. Kelly, *Memoirs*, 25. Kelly did not recall the name of the agent, but it was probably Samuel Latta. See Utley, *The Lance and the Shield*, 48–49.
24. Kelly, *Memoirs*, 30.
25. Ibid., 27–30.
26. Ibid., 30.
27. Kelly, *Memoirs*, 26; Hanson, *The Conquest of the Missouri*, 159; Kelly to EAB, 13 January 1920 and 13 November 1921, the E. A. Brininstool Collection, University of Texas. Innis, *Briefly Buford*, 14.
28. Kelly spelled it Girard, as do several others. See Evans, *Custer's Last Fight*; Nichols, *In Custer's Shadow*; and Fox, *Archaeology, History, and Custer's Last Battle*. Most historians, however, seem to favor Gerard and I have chosen to follow that spelling. For examples of the Gerard usage, see Utley, *Cavalier in Buckskin*; Sklenar, *To Hell with Honor*; Gray, *Custer's Last Campaign*; Kuhlman, *Legend into History*, and Michno, *Lakota Noon*.
29. Kelly, *Memoirs*, 27; Kelly to EAB, 1 July 1925, E. A. Brininstool Collection, University of Texas.
30. Kelly, *Memoirs*, 31. Sun-of-the-Star may have been an Arikara or Ree known as Star Man. See also Kane, *Military Life in Dakota*, 100.
31. Kelly, *Memoirs*, 32–33.
32. Ibid., 33–34.
33. Taylor, *Frontier and Indian Life*, 88.
34. Kane, *Military Life in Dakota*, 154–55, 172–73. It is not clear exactly when Kelly arrived at Fort Buford. In his memoirs, he says he left Fort Berthold in November, so it seems likely he would have arrived at Buford just before or soon after Captain Clarke assumed command. See Kelly, *Memoirs*, 31.
35. Athearn, *Forts of the Upper Missouri*, 227; Kane, *Military Life in Dakota*, 22n, 46.
36. Kelly, *Memoirs*, 40. See also Kelly to EAB, 27 September 1922, the E. A. Brininstool Collection, University of Texas. Many years later, Kelly

received a letter from a man who had been a sergeant at Fort Buford when Kelly arrived at the post. "I remember you very well when you first came to Buford," the sergeant told Kelly. "You were tall and young with brown hair and I thought you were a girl." The source for this is found in a footnote on page 53 of the typescript used as the source for his published memoirs. For some reason, this footnote—along with a second, here cited in n39—were omitted from the published version of Kelly's memoirs. The typescript was made available through the courtesy of the Thomas Minckler Collection, Billings, Montana.

37. Kelly, *Memoirs*, 41–42.

38. Ibid., 43–44; Kelly to EAB, 27 Sept. 1922, E. A. Brininstool Collection, University of Texas; Kane, *Military Life in Dakota*, 355.

39. The story of Kelly's famous duel with the two Sioux warriors appears in several accounts, the most reliable of which are Kelly's personal memoirs, 44–49, and Kane, *Military Life in Dakota*, 356–57. These two versions vary somewhat in the details of the fight. I have chosen to rely mostly on the one found in Kane's work because it is Kelly's own account related soon after the incident, while that found in Kelly's *Memoirs* is based on recollections half a century later. For other versions, see Russell, *Back-Trailing on the Old Frontiers* and the *Anaconda* (MT) *Standard*, 17 Sept. 1922. For an exaggerated version of this affair, see Curry, "Personal Recollections of the Famous 'Yellowstone' Kelly." An interesting anecdote about Kelly's duel with the Sioux was later related by H. H. Larned, then a trader at Fort Berthold, who obtained the buffalo robes Kelly took from the Sioux. The robes apparently had bullet holes in them. Larned judged one of the robes to be especially nice and, in red pencil, wrote an account of the fight on the inside of the robe. Eventually, the robe, along with others, wound up in England and Larned received a letter from someone from the *London Times*, inquiring about the story, which, by that time, was no longer completely legible. Larned supplied details and eventually the *Times* published an account of Kelly's fight. See Kelly, typescript of published memoirs, footnote on p. 53.

40. "Yellowstone Kelly...Dies on Coast," *Billings Gazette*, 28 December 1928; Kelly, *Memoirs*, 50. Why the Indians should have called Kelly "little" seems curious. At five feet, eleven and a half inches, he was above average height for that time. Perhaps they were referring to his youth?

41. Kelly, *Memoirs*, 47.

42. Ibid., 48–49; Kelly to EAB, 1 February 1925, the E. A. Brininstool Collection, University of Texas.

43. Kelly to EAB, 26 November 1922. E. A. Brininstool Collection, University of Texas.

44. Ibid., 50–51.

45. Ibid., 70–71. Kelly to EAB, 30 August 1924, the E. A. Brininstool Collection, University of Texas. As has been noted, Sitting Bull tolerated traders because they served a useful purpose. See Utley, *The Lance and the Shield*, 39–40.

46. Kelly, *Memoirs*, 53.

47. Kelly to EAB, 15 May 1920, the E. A. Brininstool Collection, University of Texas.

48. Taylor, *Frontier and Indian Life*, 80; Kelly, *Memoirs*, 53–54.

49. Ibid., 57–58. Fort Peck is actually northwest of Fort Buford, but mostly west.

50. Ibid.

51. The lines are from Goethe's *The Apprenticeship of Wilhelm Meister* (1795–96).
52. Ibid., 57.
53. Wright, "Letters from Man on Kelly Mountain." This fight may well have been the one Kelly referred to when he talked about using a Springfield while his Henry was out of commission. See Kelly to EAB, 13 November 1921, the E. A. Brininstool Collection, University of Texas. See Figure 9, the photo of Kelly seated, the Springfield in front of him, clearly showing part of his little finger missing. It does seem odd that Kelly made no mention of this incident in his memoirs; obviously he recalled the amputation with great clarity.
54. Wright, "Letters from Man on Kelly Mountain."
55. Kelly, *Memoirs*, 51–52.
56. Ibid.
57. Ibid., 78–83. The "Ed" mentioned here may well have been Ed Lambert, though Kelly does not mention his last name. Young George Towne may also have been part of the group, since he and Kelly were together during this period. See Wright, "Letters from Man on Kelly Mountain."

Chapter Three

1. Kelly, *Memoirs*, 68.
2. Brown, *Plainsmen of the Yellowstone*, 13–18; James W. Forsyth, "Report of an Expedition Up the Yellowstone...1875"; George A. Forsyth, "Report of an Expedition Up the Yellowstone...1873."
3. A newspaper story claims that a man named Ball created the name. See "Local Resident's Father Spent Year with Yellowstone Kelly"; and *Winners of the West*, 30 January 1929.
4. Kelly, *Memoirs*, 67.
5. Ibid., 68.
6. Ibid.
7. Ibid., 69–70.
8. Ibid., 71.
9. DeVoto, *Across the Wide Missouri*, 116; Mails, *Mystic Warriors*, 564–66.
10. Kelly, *Memoirs*, 75–76.
11. Ibid., 72–73.
12. Ibid., 73–75.
13. Ibid.
14. Ibid., 75–77.
15. Ibid., 74, 84–85.
16. Marmaduke Van Sweringen, a young white man who was captured by the Shawnees and eventually rose to become the prominent and feared war chief Blue Jacket, is probably the most striking example of a white man turned Indian. Blue Jacket's story may be found in Eckert, *The Frontiersman*, and Faragher, *Daniel Boone*, 259–60.
17. Kelly, *Memoirs*, 87.
18. Ibid., 84.
19. Ibid., 85–86.
20. Ibid., 87.
21. Ibid., 87; DeBarthe, *Life and Adventures of Frank Grouard*, 36–37.
22. Kelly, *Memoirs*, 88.
23. Ibid., 89; Overholser, *Fort Benton*, 69.
24. Kelly, *Memoirs*, 90.

25. Ibid. Kelly is in error about the date here, which had to have been 1870, because by 1871 Reed was no longer agent. See Koury, *Guarding the Carroll Trail*, 14. Also, Kelly's description of Reed is at odds with that found in Koury's study, which describes both Reed and Bowles as a pair of unsavory characters. It should be pointed out that in later years, at any rate, Kelly seldom if ever spoke critically of a man. Indeed, he seems to have found superlatives for almost anyone he wrote about. For example, "Custer was a splendid cavalry leader," Kelly to EAB, 2 May 1926, the E. A. Brininstool Collection, University of Texas; and "[Kit] Carson was a noble character," Kelly to CMR, 12 April 1925, KFC.

26. Kelly, *Memoirs*, 94–97; Taylor, *Frontier and Indian Life*, 97.

27. Ibid., 98. In his memoirs, Kelly mistakenly refers to the vessel as the *Far West*, but in fact it was the *Key West*; Hanson, *The Conquest of the Missouri*, 149–51; George A. Forsyth, "Report of an Expedition Up the Yellowstone ...1873," 1–2; Dixon, *Hero of Beecher Island*, 103–5.

28. Hanson, *The Conquest of the Missouri*, 8; Way, *Way's Packet Directory*, 271; Dixon, *Hero of Beecher Island*, 104.

29. Hanson, *The Conquest of the Missouri*, 152–53; Kelly, *Memoirs*, 98.

30. George A. Forsyth, "Report of an Expedition Up the Yellowstone ...1873," 2; Dixon, *Hero of Beecher Island*, 104; Kelly, *Memoirs*, 98.

31. Kelly, *Memoirs*, 99.

32. Ibid., 99–100.

33. Ibid., 101; George A. Forsyth, "Report of an Expedition Up the Yellowstone ...1873," 3; Hanson, *The Conquest of the Missouri*, 161.

34. George A. Forsyth, "Report of an Expedition Up the Yellowstone ...1873," 5–6; Hanson, *The Conquest of the Missouri*, 164–66.

35. Dixon, *Hero of Beecher Island*, 105; Kelly, *Memoirs*, 101.

36. Kelly, *Memoirs*, 101.

37. Kelly, *Memoirs*, 101–2. In his biography of Forsyth, David Dixon says that the high point Forsyth climbed was at the Powder River rather than at Glendive as stated by Kelly in his memoirs. Forsyth does not specifically mention such an ascent in his report, though the document does suggest he did so while at or near the Powder River. In recalling the experience many years later, Kelly may well have been confused as to whether the ascent was at Glendive or the Powder. Dixon also makes no reference to a party that Forsyth was expecting to locate, nor does Forsyth himself refer to it in his official report.

38. George A. Forsyth, "Report of an Expedition Up the Yellowstone ...1873," 9–10; Dixon, *Hero of Beecher Island*, 105.

39. Dixon, *Hero of Beecher Island*, 105; Hanson, *The Conquest of the Missouri*, 168.

40. Kelly, *Memoirs*, 102.

41. Ibid., 103; Overholser, *Fort Benton*, 131.

42. Kelly, *Memoirs*, 103. Here again, Kelly makes a point of saying that under the right circumstances, the Henry was indeed capable of bringing down a buffalo.

43. Kelly, *Memoirs*, 104.

44. There is some disagreement on whether the spelling should be Bear's Paw, Bears Paw, Bear Paws, or Bear Paw. Jerome A. Greene's recent and excellent study of the Nez Perce War uses Bear's Paw and since his work seems likely to become the definitive account of that war, I have elected to accept his spelling. See Greene, *Nez Perce Summer*, 461. For sources

that use Bear Paw, see Hampton, *Children of Grace*, Haines, *An Elusive Victory*, and Lavender, *Let Me Be Free*. Luther Kelly also used Bear Paw. The National Park Service has also elected to adopt the singular version as the name of the Nez Perce National Historic Park.

45. Kelly's chronology here would seem to be off by a year. If indeed he did join Broadwater's bull train late in 1873, he could not have gone directly to Carroll as his memoirs state, since Carroll did not come into existence until the spring of 1874. However, a man named Peter Koch did establish a trading post late in 1873 near what was later Camp Lewis, and it is possible that Kelly confused Koch's trading post with that of Carroll. See Koury, *Guarding the Carroll Trail*, 7; Overholser, *Fort Benton*, 83.

46. Overholser, *Fort Benton*, 178–80; Koury, *Guarding the Carroll Trail*, 9–14.

47. Kelly, *Memoirs*, 104–5; Overholser, *Fort Benton*, 68, 83–84. Kelly says that Carroll was on the right bank of the Missouri, but that would only be true if one was traveling downriver.

48. The site would be near the present bridge that spans the Missouri River on Highway 191 at the James Kipp Recreation Area. Little remains of Carroll today.

49. Koury, *Guarding the Carroll Trail*, 9–16; Overholser, *Fort Benton*, 82–83, 178–80; Bonney, *Battle Drums and Geysers*, 44; Kelly, *Memoirs*, 90, 117.

50. Kelly, *Memoirs*, 117; G. Bird Grinnell to L. Kelly, 26 April 1921 and 21 June 1921.

51. Kelly, *Memoirs*, 117.

52. Koury, *Guarding the Carroll Trail*, 19–25; Kelly, *Memoirs*, 90–91, 117, 135.

53. Grinnell, "Stories of an Heroic Age." See also Kelly, *Memoirs*, 135–36; Kelly to EAB, 22 October 1922. The E. A. Brininstool Collection, University of Texas. The details of this incident, as described in his memoirs and in the letter to Earl Brininstool, differ slightly from this version, which I adopted because the account would have been fresher in Kelly's mind when he related it to Grinnell.

54. Kelly, *Memoirs*, 105–8.

55. Ibid., 106.

56. Ibid., 107–8. Kelly had first known Cornelius Cusick as a lieutenant at Fort Buford. When Kelly sold him the mare, Cusick was a captain in the Twenty-second Infantry, serving under Col. Nelson Miles, as was Kelly himself by that time.

57. Kelly, *Memoirs*, 91–92.

58. Ibid., 109, 136.

59. Ibid., 126–27.

60. Ibid., 74, 121. Flat Willow Creek heads in the Little Snowy Mountains and flows east into today's Petrolia Reservoir.

61. Ibid., 74.

62. Ibid., 110.

63. Ibid., 111.

64. Ibid., 110–11.

65. Ibid., 112.

66. Ibid., 113. The "Stoneys" were a Canadian tribe of the Assiniboine family.

67. Ibid., 113–14.

68. Ibid., 114.

69. Ibid., 115–16.

70. Ibid., 116.

71. Ibid., 118; Kelly to C. M. Russell, 12 April 1925. In his memoirs, Kelly refers to the one brother as Jean, but in his letter to C.M.R. it is spelled Gene.

72. Kelly, *Memoirs*, 118.

73. Ibid., 119.

74. Ibid., 123.

75. Ibid., p 121–22.

76. Ibid., 126.

77. Ibid., 128–29.

78. Ibid., 130–31.

79. Ibid., 131.

80. Ibid., 131–36; Thane, "When 'Yellowstone' Kelly Hunted in Judith Basin."

81. Ibid., 136–37.

82. Ibid., 137.

Chapter Four

1. Kelly, *Memoirs*, 146.

2. Prucha, *American Indian Treaties*, 282–83; Gray, *Centennial Campaign*, 9–15; Utley, *Cavalier in Buckskin*, 112–13.

3. Ibid.

4. Utley, *Cavalier in Buckskin*, 117–22; Adjutant General's Office, *Chronological List of Actions*, 51, 55.

5. Utley, *Cavalier in Buckskin*, 133–35.

6. Ibid., 145–47, 156; Gray, *Centennial Campaign*, 21–26.

7. Utley, *Cavalier in Buckskin*, 156–57.

8. Gray, *Centennial Campaign*, 47–58.

9. Ibid., 110–24.

10. Ibid., 151–97; Utley, *Cavalier in Buckskin*, 3–12.

11. Hedren, *Fort Laramie in 1876*, 133–34; Greene, *Battles and Skirmishes of the Great Sioux War*, 79–91.

12. Greene, *Yellowstone Command*, 1–3; Utley, "War Houses in the Sioux Country," *Montana Magazine* 35, no. 4, 18–25.

13. Greene, *Slim Buttes*, 9–11.

14. Ibid., 33–58.

15. Greene, *Yellowstone Command*, 55–57.

16. Ibid., 16; Hedren, *Fort Laramie*, 142.

17. Ibid., 58–60.

18. Ibid.

19. Ibid., 56–57.

20. Ibid. The post actually had several names until the permanent post was designated Fort Keogh in July 1878. See also Frink and Barthelmess, *Photographer on an Army Mule*, 78; Greene, Yellowstone Command, 185–86, 220.

21. Kelly, *Memoirs*, 135, 141. Kelly to EAB, 17 September 1920, E. A. Brininstool Collection, University of Texas. Although Kelly had seen much of the Yellowstone Valley by this time, he apparently had not gotten as far as the confluence of the Big Horn and Yellowstone Rivers, because in a 1926 letter to Charles Kessler he told the latter that Fort Pease, located just below the mouth of the Big Horn, had been burned by the time he visited that point on the river. See Kelly to Charles Kessler, 19 September 1926, Thomas Minckler Collection.

22. Kelly, *Memoirs*, 69, 146; Kelly to C. M. Russell, 2 October 1922; Kelly to EAB, 17 September 1920, E. A. Brininstool Collection, University of Texas.

23. Kelly, *Memoirs*, 140–45.
24. Greene, *Yellowstone Command*, 47–53.
25. Kelly, *Memoirs*, 146.
26. Ibid., 148–49; Prodgers, *Champion Buffalo Hunter*, 1. Kelly's arrival had to have been between 17 and 23 August. See Greene, *Yellowstone Command*, 47–53. See also, Kelly to Walter Camp, 15 April 1911, KFC.
27. Kelly, *Memoirs*, 146.
28. Ibid., 147–49. This is a wonderful story—so Kellyesque in nature, and even better because it is really true. Miles also talks about the incident in his memoirs. See Miles, *Personal Recollections and Observations*, Vol. 1, 217. According to his memoirs, Kelly arrived at the site of the cantonment with one companion, but the memoirs go on to state that after his talk with Miles, he returned to the camp of his "hunter friends," which may or may not have been the miners with whom he'd started back upriver.
29. The meeting between Kelly and Miles had to have been after 10 September, the date on which Miles arrived at the site of the new cantonment. Miles had also recently received authorization to hire a complement of twenty-five scouts. See Greene, *Yellowstone Command*, 60, 69. See also roster of Miles's scouts.
30. Greene, *Yellowstone Command*, 69–70.
31. Ibid., 74, 76.
32. Ibid., 69–70. Custer's command numbered 31 officers and 566 enlisted men, a total of 597. See Gray, *Custer's Last Campaign*, 204. At the beginning of the summer campaign, Crook had a force of some 900 officers and men. Terry's Dakota Column (including Custer) was slightly larger, and later, of course, the reinforced Terry-Crook combine numbered 4,000. Mangum, *Battle of the Rosebud*, 28; Utley, *Cavalier in Buckskin*, 167, Greene, *Yellowstone Command*, 43. The above figures do not reflect civilian packers and Indian auxiliaries.
33. Greene, *Yellowstone Command*, 70.
34. Ibid., 73, 81.
35. Ibid., 73.
36. Ibid., 74. Despite the fact that appropriations for civilian scouts seem to have been reduced, at one point to as few as four, Miles apparently found the means to keep at least a dozen on hand. During the next three years, the number of scouts and guides attached to the command would vary from month to month, ranging from a low of five to a high of twenty-four. See roster of Scouts, Cantonment Tongue River and Fort Keogh. For a more complete discussion of scouts and the military, see Dunlay, *Wolves for the Blue Soldiers*, 69–90.
37. Miles, *Personal Recollections and Observations*, Vol. 1, 221; Greene, *Yellowstone Command*, 78.
38. Kelly, *Memoirs*, 149–50.
39. Although Kelly apparently had high regard for Smith's skills, they evidently had a misunderstanding during the course of this particular mission. Kelly says nothing about it in his memoirs, nor does Smith make any mention of such an incident. However, many years later, Kelly told Earl Brininstool that Smith "did not fall in with the discipline necessary in the field, and we had a disagreement of no consequence." Whether this affected Smith's status as a scout is not known, but he seems to have been discharged on 9 November and his name thereafter does not appear on the roster of scouts. See Kelly to EAB, 23 June 1922, the E. A.

Brininstool Collection, University of Texas, and Prodgers, *The Champion Buffalo Hunter*. See also Roster of Scouts.

40. According to Greene, *Yellowstone Command* (80–81), this mission took place in October, but the authorizations from Miles and Baldwin are dated 18 and 19 September, respectively. See Letters Sent for Cantonment Tongue River, National Archives, Reg. 393, Part V, entry no. 2. The Baldwin order to Vic Smith presents something of a puzzle. According to Baldwin's biographer, the captain left Tongue River on 31 August to return to Fort Leavenworth and bring back the Fifth Infantry's regimental band, which he did, arriving back at the cantonment in mid-October. This being the case, one wonders how he could have issued an order to Smith dated 19 September. One possible explanation is that Baldwin's deputy issued the order in his name. See Steinbach, *A Long March*, 99, 104–5.

41. Kelly, *Memoirs*, 150.

42. Ibid.

43. Ibid., 151.

44. Ibid., 151–52.

45. Ibid., 149–50.

46. Ibid., 153.

47. Ibid., 152; Greene, *Yellowstone Command*, 111; DeMontravel, *A Hero to His Fighting Men*, 91.

48. Kelly, *Memoirs*, 152–53.

49. Greene, *Yellowstone Command*, 78–80; Miles, *Personal Recollections and Observations*, Vol. 1, 221.

50. Greene, *Yellowstone Command*, 80–83; Gray, "Sitting Bull Strikes the Glendive Supply Trains," 25–32.

51. In his memoirs, Kelly states that a courier brought word of the attack on the supply train. See Kelly, *Memoirs*, 153. Miles makes no mention of a courier, and in fact apparently penned a note to Sherman on the sixteenth, in which he expressed his concern for the safety of the train and planned to start out the next day to see what might have happened to it. See DeMontravel, *A Hero to His Fighting Men*, 85. However, in his Annual Report for 1876, Gen. William T. Sherman alludes to Miles having received "intelligence" of the attack. See Pohanka, *Nelson A. Miles*, 97. An enlisted man in the Fifth Infantry also stated that Miles was alerted to the attack on the supply train by a scout. See Brown, *Terror of the Badlands*, 5. John Gray suggests that the four scouts were Albert Gaeheder, Liver-Eating Johnson, Vic Smith, and Bill Sellew. See Gray, "Sitting Bull Strikes the Glendive Supply Trains."

52. John Gray speculates that this was Albert Gaeheder. See Gray, "Sitting Bull Strikes The Glendive Supply Trains."

53. Ibid.; Greene, *Yellowstone Command*, 86.

54. Greene, *Yellowstone Command*, 90–91.

55. Ibid., 88–89.

56. Brown, *Terror of the Badlands*, 5. Greene, *Yellowstone Command*, 88–91. The words were Bruguier's, but as Robert Utley has suggested, he probably captured the essence of Sitting Bull's feelings. See Utley, *The Lance and the Shield*, 170.

57. Greene, *Yellowstone Command*, 92.

58. Ibid. In his memoirs, Kelly claims to have been accompanied by four other scouts. Kelly also says the assignment was made near Sunday

Creek, but that would have to be wrong. The assignment was made *after* Miles and Otis met near Custer Creek, which is quite some distance east of Sunday Creek. See Kelly, *Memoirs*, 154. See also Prodgers, *The Champion Buffalo Hunter*, 68–69.

59.   Vic Smith's memoirs identify the place as Chokecherry Creek. Prodgers, *The Champion Buffalo Hunter*, 68.

60.   Kelly, *Memoirs*, 154; Prodgers, *The Champion Buffalo Hunter*, 68–69. The Cheyenne reference is puzzling, since none were with Sitting Bull, whose trail it is clear the scouts were following. Most of the Northern Cheyennes had, by this time, moved south into Wyoming. See Greene, *Yellowstone Command*, 66–67. The identity of the two white women is unknown. The only source for this is Smith's memoirs.

61.   Greene, *Yellowstone Command*, 92–94.

62.   Kelly, *Memoirs*, 155–56; Greene, *Yellowstone Command*, 102–4.

63.   Smith, "Where the Buffalo Went," 44.

64.   Kelly, *Memoirs*, 156–57; Prodgers, *The Champion Buffalo Hunter*, 189–90.

65.   Prodgers, *The Champion Buffalo Hunter*, 157; Greene, *Yellowstone Command*, 104–6.

66.   Greene, *Yellowstone Command*, 105–6.

67.   Ibid., 106; Kelly, *Memoirs*, 157–58.

68.   Greene, *Yellowstone Command*, 93, 106–7.

69.   Kelly, *Memoirs*, 158.

70.   Ibid.; Greene, *Yellowstone Command*, 107–8.

71.   Greene, *Yellowstone Command*, 107.

72.   Ibid., 107–8. Ibid., 111–13.

Chapter Five

1.   Kelly, *Memoirs*, 161.

2.   Greene, *Yellowstone Command*, 114–15.

3.   Ibid., 119–20.

4.   Kelly, *Memoirs*, 160–61.

5.   Kelly, *Memoirs*, 158; Greene, *Yellowstone Command*, 123.

6.   Ibid.; Utley, *The Lance and the Shield*, 177; Greene, *Yellowstone Command*, 123–24.

7.   Kelly, *Memoirs*, 161; Greene, *Yellowstone Command*, 127.

8.   Kelly, *Memoirs*, 161.

9.   Ibid., 162. A slightly different version was told by scout Jack Jackson, who claimed that they all spent the night at the trader's home and that they were entertained by the trader's wife who played the guitar for them. According to Jackson, a Hunkpapa named Long Fox entered the trading post while the scouts were eating. When asked where Sitting Bull's camp was located, he told them on the Red Water. He reportedly asked the trader not to let Sitting Bull persuade his chief to join them. See Logan, "An Episode in the Life of Yellowstone Kelly."

10.   Kelly, *Memoirs*, 162. Kelly's comment about the Indian boy is interesting and says a great deal about the attitude toward Indians held by many white men of that era, even those such as Kelly who had great respect for their culture and way of life.

11.   Ibid., 162–63.

12.   Ibid., 163–64.

13.   Ibid., 164. Jack Johnson later claimed that Kelly purposely walked out into full view of the Indians, hoping to draw fire, thereby enabling his

companions to spot their positions. See Logan, "An Episode in the Life of Yellowstone Kelly."

14. Snyder Diary, 24 November 1876.
15. Ibid., 4 December, 1876; Kelly, *Memoirs*, 165.
16. Greene, *Yellowstone Command*, 131; Snyder Diary, 8 December, 1876.
17. Greene, *Yellowstone Command*, 124–34.
18. Ibid.
19. Greene, *Yellowstone Command*, 135–46; Utley, *The Lance and the Shield*, 177–79.
20. Greene, *Yellowstone Command*, 155–56.
21. Ibid., 157.
22. Ibid., 153–54.
23. Ibid., 147–54.
24. Greene, *Yellowstone Command*, 151–52; Kelly, *Memoirs*, 166.
25. Greene, *Yellowstone Command*, 157; Kelly, *Memoirs*, 166.
26. Greene, *Yellowstone Command*, 158; Rickey, "The Battle of Wolf Mountain," 48. In a letter to Kelly, Oscar Long later claimed the temperature stood at forty below. See Long to Kelly, 14 July, 1920. However, since the 30-degree temperature was recorded in the official Journal of the Marches at the time, it would seem more reliable than a recollection made nearly half a century later.
27. It is not entirely clear exactly who was in the scouting contingent. Kelly says he had three Johnsons with him and Greene also says that James Parker was a member of the group. See Kelly, *Memoirs*, 167, and Greene, *Yellowstone Command*, 157–58, 164.
28. Greene, *Yellowstone Command*, 161–62; Kelly, *Memoirs*, 167.
29. Greene, *Yellowstone Command*, 162; Kelly, *Memoirs*, 167–68. Kelly remembered that two soldiers were killed and told W. R. Felton that it was a rule in 1876 and later along the Yellowstone to conceal where soldiers were buried so as to prevent Indians from digging them up. Kelly to W. R. Felton, 28 January 1912, KFC.
30. Kelly, *Memoirs*, 168–69.
31. Kelly, "Memoranda on the Wolf Mountain Campaign," in Brady, *Northwestern Fights and Fighters.* In his memoirs, Kelly says the Crows "touched each gently with a coup stick," but he makes no mention of this in his Wolf Mountain Memoranda. See Kelly, *Memoirs*, 169–70. See also Greene, *Yellowstone Command*, 164.
32. Kelly, *Memoirs*, 170; Kelly, "Memoranda on Wolf Mountain"; Greene, *Yellowstone Command*, 164–65.
33. Kelly to EAB, 31 March 1923, E. A. Brininstool Collection, University of Texas.
34. Kelly, *Memoirs*, 170; Kelly, "Memoranda on Wolf Mountain."
35. Ibid.
36. Kelly, *Memoirs*, 171; Kelly, "Memoranda on Wolf Mountain." In his memoirs, Kelly says the Indian scouts approached to within 200 yards, but in his "Memoranda" he says 300 yards. I have accepted the higher figure simply because it was an estimate made a dozen years earlier.
37. Ibid. In his Wolf Mountain Memoranda, Kelly says they drove off five Indians.
38. Kelly, Wolf Mountain Memoranda; Greene, *Yellowstone Command*, 165. In his memoirs, Thomas Leforge implies that Kelly acted scared. He says that Kelly immediately turned and headed back to the troops when the

scouts charged the Indians and then took credit for informing the troops. According to Leforge, Kelly was "twitted" about his act, which he (Leforge) somewhat excuses by saying that Kelly was employed as a guide, not a fighter (see Marquis, *Memoirs of a White Crow Indian*, 272–73). Leforge's left-handed allegation is difficult to sustain. First of all, such behavior would have been completely out of character for Kelly, who, if anything, was occasionally accused of being a bit reckless. One has only to consider his fight with the two Lakotas while carrying dispatches to Fort Stevenson, among other examples. Moreover, his (Kelly's) description of the action here is simply too detailed to dismiss out of hand. Second, the distinction between "guide" and "scout" was often blurred, particularly where the white scouts were concerned, and there is ample evidence to support Kelly's participation in other combat situations, so why would this instance have been any different? Jerome Greene says Miles learned that the scouts were in action because the troops could hear the sound of gunfire. (Greene, *Yellowstone Command*, 164). If, for some reason, relations between Kelly and Leforge were strained, there is no evidence of it in either Kelly's memoirs or his later correspondence. Years later, Kelly told Earl Brininstool that if Leforge was still alive, "he could give you some good stuff on that campaign." See Kelly to EAB, 31 March 1923, E. A. Brininstool Collection, University of Texas. Possibly, Leforge was irritated that Kelly had called for the scouts to charge the Indians, an act that Kelly himself admitted was rash and resulted in Leforge losing his horse.

39. Greene, *Yellowstone Command*, 165; Kelly, *Memoirs*, 171–72.
40. Kelly, *Memoirs*, 172.
41. The site of Battle Butte is near present Birney, Montana, about 115 miles from Cantonment Tongue River. Greene, *Yellowstone Command*, 165–66.
42. Greene, *Yellowstone Command*, 166.
43. Ibid. By the time his Personal Recollections & Observations was published in 1896, the number had grown to 1,000. See *Personal Recollections & Observations of General Nelson A. Miles*, Vol. 1, 237.
44. Greene, *Yellowstone Command*, 166; Rickey, "The Battle of Wolf Mountain," 49.
45. Kelly, *Memoirs*, 173; Thane, "When Yellowstone Kelly Was Scout"; Rickey, "The Battle of Wolf Mountain," 49; Greene, *Yellowstone Command*, 166. The most recent study of the Miles campaigns of 1876–1877, including the Battle of Wolf Mountain, will be found in Jerome Greene's excellent *Yellowstone Command*.
46. Kelly, *Memoirs*, 173–74; Greene, *Yellowstone Command*, 168–69; Rickey, "The Battle of Wolf Mountain," 49–50.
47. Kelly, *Memoirs*, 174; Greene, *Yellowstone Command*, 169–71, 175; Rickey, "The Battle of Wolf Mountain," 49–50.
48. Greene, *Yellowstone Command*, 171.
49. Ibid., 172–73; Rickey, "The Battle of Wolf Mountain," 52.
50. Greene, *Yellowstone Command*, 178; Rickey, "The Battle of Wolf Mountain," 53.
51. Greene, *Yellowstone Command*, 178–80; Rickey, "The Battle of Wolf Mountain," 53–54.
52. Greene, *Yellowstone Command*, 182–87.
53. Ibid., 181–82. Miles actually retained three scouts: Kelly, Billy Cross, and John Bruguier, along with James Parker as an expressman and Tom

Leforge, interpreter. Additionally, J. Johnson signed on as a guide in April. See Roster of Miles's Scouts, 1877, Cantonment Tongue River, MT.

54.   *New Northwest*, 8 March 1878.

Chapter Six

1.   Kelly, *Memoirs*, 176.

2.   Ibid., 180. In his memoirs, Kelly simply says the scout took place in early spring, but since he composed his official report from Wolf Point, Montana, on 9 April, he would necessarily have had to depart from the cantonment before that date. I have arbitrarily selected mid-March. See "Kelly's Report from Wolf Point, Montana, April 9, 1877," found in his Military Service File.

3.   Kelly, *Memoirs*, 180. Kelly claims that Red Mike was now a scout, though he is not listed on the roster of scouts at the cantonment. John Haddo (or Haddoo), was a corporal in Company B, Fifth Infantry. Haddo/Haddoo was awarded a Medal of Honor for his conduct in the Battle of Wolf Mountains. My source for the Haddo information was furnished by Richard Lea of Fort Collins, Colorado, who has done extensive research into medal-of-honor winners in the Indian wars.

4.   Kelly, *Memoirs*, 181.

5.   Ibid., 181–84.

6.   Ibid.; Kelly's "Report from Wolf Point"; Utley, *The Lance and the Shield*, 181. I have assumed this report was prepared for Miles, though it is not so specified.

7.   This turned out to be the campaign that resulted in Miles's attack on the village of the Minniconjou Sioux, Lame Deer, marking the end of the Great Sioux War. See Greene, *Yellowstone Command*, 201–8.

8.   Kelly, *Memoirs*, 176. Another possible explanation for the letters is that Kelly had a notion of remaining in the East and the letters were intended to open some doors for him. However, there is not a hint of this in his memoirs or personal correspondence, so the likelihood seems remote.

9.   Ibid., 176; Kelly, "Report from Wolf Point"; Roster of Scouts.

10.   Kelly, *Memoirs*, 176–77.

11.   Brust, "Oh What a River," 31.

12.   Kelly, *Memoirs*, 177.

13.   O. P. Stearns to Luther Kelly, 23 September 1922.

14.   Kelly, *Memoirs*, 177.

15.   Kelly, *Memoirs*, 177–78; Kelly to L. A. Huffman, 27 March 1921, KFC; Brown and Felton, *The Frontier Years*, 32, 239. Tobacco Gardens was so named because of the wild mullein, a member of the figwort family that apparently resembles the tobacco plant. Kelly's memoirs are the only source I have seen mention the Indian meeting with General Sheridan.

16.   Kelly, *Memoirs*, 178–79.

17.   Greene, *Yellowstone Command*, 183–85.

18.   Ibid., 187–200; Johnson, *The Unregimented General*, 153–70.

19.   Greene, *Yellowstone Command*, 201–15.

20.   Ibid., 184–85; Johnson, *The Unregimented General*, 181.

21.   Kelly, *Memoirs*, 185.

22.   Ibid., 184.

23.   The body of literature on the Nez Perce War is substantial. I have relied primarily on the following: Jerome Greene's *Nez Perce Summer*, as well as *Children of Grace*, by Bruce Hampton; *Following the Nez Perce Trail*, by

Cheryl Wilfong; *Frontier Regulars*, by Robert Utley; Jerome Greene's
Yellowstone Command; and *Flight of the Nez Perce*, by Mark Brown.

24. Greene, *Nez Perce Summer*, 20–21; Hampton, *Children of Grace*, 55; Utley,
     Frontier Regulars, 307–8.
25. Greene, *Nez Perce Summer*, 30, 36–42; Hampton, *Children of Grace*, 1–18;
     Utley, *Frontier Regulars*, 309–10.
26. Greene, *Nez Perce Summer*, 44, 103; Utley, *Frontier Regulars*, 311–12.
27. Greene, *Nez Perce Summer*, 60–72, 80–96, 117–40, 170–201.
28. Ibid., 204–7.
29. Miles to Sturgis, 27 August 1877. Nelson Miles Papers, Indian Wars, 1869–1886.
     U.S. Army Military History Institute, Carlisle Barracks, Pennsylvania.
30. Greene, *Nez Perce Summer*, 208–30; Utley, *Frontier Regulars*, 319–20;
     Hampton, *Children of Grace*, 221, 264–70. Many years later, Kelly told Earl
     Brininstool that he had once thought to write an article on the Nez Perce
     Campaign, and in connection with such had occasion to contact Colonel
     Sturgis, who subsequently sent him a lengthy manuscript telling of those
     events from his (Sturgis's) viewpoint. The manuscript, which remained
     among Kelly's personal papers, regrettably was lost, along with other
     valuable papers. Sturgis's views would doubtless have proved an inter-
     esting addition to the body of literature on the Nez Perce epic. See Kelly
     to EAB, 7 June 1926, E. A. Brininstool Collection, University of Texas.
31. Kelly, *Memoirs*, 186; Greene, *Nez Perce Summer*, 247.
32. Kelly, *Memoirs*, 91, 186.
33. Ibid., 186.
34. Ibid.; *Annual Report of the Secretary of War, 1877–1878*, Vol. 2, No. 1, Part
     Two, Vol. 1, 515; Greene, *Nez Perce Summer*, 248–50.
35. Kelly identifies the steamer as being the *Far West* (Kelly, "Engagement with
     the Nez Perces in Bearpaw Mountains, 1877," 4), while Virginia Johnson
     says it was the *Benton* (*The Unregimented General*, 194–195), and Robert
     Steinbach calls it the *Fontenelle* (*A Long March*, 129), as does Bruce
     Hampton (*Children of Grace*, 286). Jerome Greene (*Nez Perce Summer*, 255)
     also refers to the *Fontenelle*. Apparently both the *Benton* and *Fontenelle*
     were in the vicinity, which probably accounts for the confusion.
36. Kelly, *Memoirs*, 186; Kelly, "Engagement with the Nez Perces," 3–4.
     Mention of the "tussle" between Miles and Baldwin appears only in
     Kelly's memoirs, but he says nothing about it in his account of the cam-
     paign written for George Bird Grinnell in 1909.
37. Wilfong, *Following the Nez Perce Trail*, 294; Hampton, *Children of Grace*,
     286; Utley, *Frontier Regulars*, 321; Kelly, "Engagement with the Nez
     Perces," 3–4.
38. Kelly, *Memoirs*, 188.
39. Ibid., 189; Kelly, "Engagement with the Nez Perces," 5; Greene, *Nez Perce
     Summer*, 259.
40. Kelly, *Memoirs*, 189.
41. In his memoirs, Kelly says they had not progressed very far when they
     were "overhauled by Lieutenant Maus"; however, in his account of the
     campaign written for George Bird Grinnell, Kelly implies that they joined
     Maus. See Kelly, *Memoirs*, 189; Kelly, "Engagement with the Nez Perces," 5.
42. Kelly, *Memoirs*, 190.
43. Ibid., 189–91; Kelly, "Engagement with the Nez Perces," 5.
44. Kelly, *Memoirs*, 191; Kelly, "Engagement with the Nez Perces," 6–7.
45. Ibid.

46. Kelly, *Memoirs*, 191–92.

47. Ibid., 192; Kelly, "Engagement with the Nez Perces," 7–8.

48. Kelly, *Memoirs*, 192.

49. *Annual Report of the Secretary of War, 1877–1878*, 515; Kelly, "Engagement with the Nez Perces," 10. Kelly, *Memoirs*, 192. The chronology in Kelly's memoirs is confusing. It could not have been later than the twenty-eighth when Maus's detachment rode out to locate Miles after discovering the two Nez Perce herders and, indeed, it may well have been late on the twenty-seventh. In any case, if the troops were, as Kelly claimed, no more than a mile ahead when the scouts picked up the trail, they surely would have caught up with them before the thirtieth. He does, however, make it clear that they missed seeing the troops because of poor visibility, which suggests that Maus and his scouts must obviously have spent a day or more searching the countryside before finally locating Miles on 30 September.

50. *Annual Report of the Secretary of War, 1877–1878*, 515–16; Utley, *Frontier Regulars*, 322; Hampton, *Children of Grace*, 289–95; Greene, *Nez Perce Summer*, 260–66.

51. Kelly, *Memoirs*, 193; Greene, *Nez Perce Summer*, 271–91; Hampton, *Children of Grace*, 292–97.

52. Kelly, *Memoirs*, 193–94; Kelly, "Engagement with the Nez Perces," 10.

53. Kelly, *Memoirs*, 195.

54. Kelly, "Engagement with the Nez Perces," 10; Wilfong, *Following the Nez Perce Trail*, 314–15; Hampton, Children of Grace, 298, 310. Kelly claimed that the Sioux and Cheyenne auxiliaries precipitated the attack before Miles was ready and had they not done so, Kelly thought the Nez Perce might have surrendered sooner than they did.

55. Kelly, *Memoirs*, 197. This apparently was a white horse belonging to Mary Miles. See Johnson, *The Unregimented General*, 207.

56. Ibid.

Chapter Seven

1. Kelly, *Memoirs*, 199–200.

2. Utley, *The Lance and Shield*, 191; Manzione, *I Am Looking to the North*, 67–68, 81–82.

3. Manzione, *I Am Looking to the North*, 76–78.

4. Ibid., 81–82, 100–101.

5. Kelly, *Memoirs*, 199.

6. Ibid., 200.

7. According to a story appearing in the *Geneva* (New York) *Gazette* on 15 February 1878, Kelly suffered frostbite during the course of this mission. See also Johnson, *The Unregimented General*, 206.

8. Kelly, *Memoirs*, 200–201.

9. Kelly to EAB, 26 November 1922, E. A. Brininstool Collection, University of Texas.

10. Ibid.; Kelly, *Memoirs*, 202.

11. Kelly, *Memoirs*, 203; Zimmerman, *Frontier Soldier*, 115–17.

12. Kelly, *Memoirs*, 203–4.

13. Ibid., 204.

14. Ibid., 205.

15. Ibid., 205–6.

16. Ibid.; Hampton, *Children of Grace*, 312–13; Lavender, *Let Me Be Free*, 323;

DeMontravel, *A Hero to His Fighting Men*, 125.

17.   Greene, *Nez Perce Summer*, 328–31; Hampton, *Children of Grace*, 314–16; DeMontravel, *A Hero to His Fighting Men*, 130–36.

18.   Hampton, *Children of Grace*, 317–18; Kelly to EAB, 10 January 1921, E. A. Brininstool Collection, University of Texas.

19.   Hampton, *Children of Grace*, 317–18; Lewis Crawford to Kelly, 18 June 1923, KFC.

20.   Baird, Memoranda of Events, Yellowstone Command; Snyder Diary, 25 October 1877; Greene, *Yellowstone Command*, 220.

21.   Kelly, *Memoirs*, 206–7; Kelly to EAB, 12 March 1919, E. A. Brininstool Collection, University of Texas.

22.   Kelly, *Memoirs*, 206–7. Kelly refers to Sergeant Gilbert and Privates Leavitt and Fox, though without their first names. However, since Sergeant Gilbert seems to have been on at least one other assignment with Kelly, I have chosen to retain his last name in the narrative.

23.   Ibid., 208–9.

24.   Ibid., 209.

25.   Ibid., 210.

26.   Ibid.

27.   Ibid.; Kelly to EAB, 12 March 1919, E. A. Brininstool Collection, University of Texas.

28.   Hedren, *Fort Laramie in 1876*, 171–72.

29.   Kelly, *Memoirs*, 211. In his memoirs, Kelly does refer to Pollock as the commanding officer, but in a letter to Earl Brininstool he says it was Major Powell. Pollock, however, was the commanding officer, not Capt. James Powell, Twenty-seventh Infantry, who had retired from the army in January 1868. See Kelly to EAB, 12 March 1919, EAB Collection, University of Texas, and *Portraits of Fort Phil Kearny*, 208. Exactly what military post this might have been is unclear, and Alberts makes no mention of this in his biography of Wesley Merritt. See Alberts, *Brandy Station to Manila Bay*, 248–49.

30.   Kelly, *Memoirs*, 211; Kelly to EAB, 12 March 1919, E. A. Brininstool Collection, University of Texas.

31.   Kelly, *Memoirs*, 211.

32.   Ibid., 213; Haines, *Yellowstone Place Names*, 7–8.

33.   Kelly, *Memoirs*, 213; Haines, *The Yellowstone Story*, Vol. 1, 10.

34.   Kelly, *Memoirs*, 213–14.

35.   Ibid., 214. Forts Keogh and Custer were both built in the year following the Custer disaster. Originally named Big Horn Post, it was officially named Fort Custer in November 1877. Prucha, *Guide to Military Posts*, 69.

36.   Kelly, *Memoirs*, 215. The Black Canyon Kelly refers to is probably Shell Canyon.

37.   Kelly, *Memoirs*, 217. Kelly says only that he was accompanied by one of the other men, whom I have assume was Gilbert. It is interesting that Kelly evidently made an assumption that there were no other prospecting parties in the park. Since this was the primary object of their mission, after all, it seems odd that Kelly would not have investigated the northern reaches of the park, closer to the reservation boundary.

38.   Kelly, *Memoirs*, 217–18.

39.   Kelly, *Memoirs*, 219.

40.   *The Rubáiyát of Omar Khayyám*, Edward Fitzgerald Translation, verse xii.

41.   Kelly *Memoirs*, 219.

42. Ibid., 219–20.

43. Ibid., 221.

44. Ibid., 222; Haines, *Yellowstone Place Names*, 107–9. Philetus W. Norris was appointed the first superintendent of Yellowstone National Park in August 1877. See Haines, *The Yellowstone Story*, Vol. 1, 216.

45. Ibid., 222.

46. Ibid.

47. Haines, *The Yellowstone Story*, Vol. 1, 201–3.

48. Many years later, Kelly received a letter from a retired army officer who then lived in Bozeman and recalled having the famous scout pointed out to him. The writer, F. L. Graham, said, "that name meant so much to me, as it did to anyone native of Montana." F. L. Graham to Kelly, 8 February 1920, KFC.

49. Kelly, *Memoirs*, 167, 223; DeMontravel, *A Hero to His Fighting Men*, 139–40; Johnson, *The Unregimented General*, 212–13; Miles, *Personal Recollections*, Vol. 1, 294–99; Utley, *Frontier Regulars*, 333.

50. Kelly, *Memoirs*, 223; DeMontravel, *A Hero to His Fighting Men*, 140.

51. Kelly, *Memoirs*, 223. Kelly does not elaborate on exactly what they did after leaving Miles's party, but he had to have been back at Fort Keogh by November because he was discharged as a scout on 30 November. He was not carried on the roster of scouts for July and August, but was back on the roster for the period September–November. Quite possibly, he was detached for the Yellowstone assignment, then reinstated in September.

52. The source for Kelly going east to get married is the *Bismarck Tribune* for 2 December 1878 and the *Bozeman Avant-Courier*, 2 January 1879. In none of his correspondence or writings does Kelly himself make any mention of a planned wedding, but the idea is intriguing, nonetheless. It does seem odd that he would have made a second trip east in consecutive years, without some compelling reason. Quite possibly, he met a young woman during his visit the previous year and fell in love; perhaps they even set a tentative date, but she changed her mind during the course of the year. While it would have been perfectly in character for Kelly to have said nothing of the matter, it does seem that some hint of his purpose would have reached the papers. It is also possible that when asked by a *Bismarck Tribune* reporter why he was going east, Kelly simply replied facetiously that he planned to get married. In any case, a number of explanations are possible, but all that is known for certain is that he did visit his old New York home in 1879.

53. Again, as with the marriage question, the *Bismarck Tribune* seems to be the only source for Kelly's plan to go into the cattle business. And once again, this may have been nothing more than a casual remark on Kelly's part, which some reporter took more seriously than Kelly intended. See the *Bismarck Tribune*, 12 April 1879. Miles had spent the winter of 1878–1879 in Washington, serving on the army's Equipment Board. See Johnson, *The Unregimented General*, 215–17.

54. Kelly, *Memoirs*, 224; Utley, *The Lance and the Shield*, 206; DeMontravel, *A Hero to His Fighting Men*, 142–43.

55. Kelly, *Memoirs*, 223–24. Since the work of the Reeve Boundary Survey was begun in the summer of 1879 and completed before the onset of winter, Kelly's service as guide for the cavalry escort must have been in the summer or late fall of 1879. See Superintendent P. W. Norris, "Report upon

Yellowstone National Park for the Year 1879," in "Report to the Secretary of the Interior for the Year 1879" (Washington, D.C.: U.S. Government Printing Office, 12–13).

56. I have assumed here that Kelly is referring to the Stinking Water River, an early name for the present Shoshone River. See Haines, *Yellowstone Place Names*, 11.

57. Kelly, *Memoirs*, 224.

58. Ibid., 224.

59. Ibid., 227–28.

60. Ibid., 227.

61. Ibid., 226.

62. Ibid., 227.

63. Ibid., 228.

64. Ibid., 228; Haines, *Yellowstone Place Names*, 433–34.

65. Kelly's memoirs jump abruptly from Yellowstone Park to the winter of 1879–1880. He says nothing about when he left or where he was going. See Kelly, *Memoirs*, 229.

66. Ibid., 229.

67. Ibid.; Kelly to W. R. Felton, 28 January 1912, KFC.

68. Kelly, *Memoirs*, 230.

69. Ibid., 231–32; Pohanka, *Nelson A. Miles*, 127.

70. Kelly, *Memoirs*, 236–37.

71. Ibid., 240. To say that the Indians who had surrendered were content in their camps is not quite a fair statement, as any student of the Indian wars will agree, though it evidently seemed that way to Kelly and probably to others.

Chapter Eight

1. Kelly, *Memoirs*, 245.

2. Ibid., 240.

3. Ibid., 240–41.

4. Ibid., 241.

5. Ibid., 241; Thrapp, *Frontier Biography*, Vol. 1, 302.

6. Simmons, *The Utes of Colorado*, 179; Utley, *Frontier Regulars*, 342.

7. Utley, *Frontier Regulars*, 341–43; Simmons, *The Utes of Colorado*, 19, 180–81; Thrapp, *Frontier Biography*, Vol. 2, 968; Miller, *Hollow Victory*, 4–5.

8. Simmons, *The Utes of Colorado*, 180–81; Miller, *Hollow Victory*, 4–5.

9. Ibid.

10. There are several good accounts of the Milk River fight. I have mostly relied on Mark Miller's *Hollow Victory* and Utley's *Frontier Regulars*, 342–48. Simmons' *The Utes of Colorado* was also helpful.

11. Utley, *Frontier Regulars*, 347–48; Simmons, *The Utes of Colorado*, 186–94.

12. Utley, *Frontier Regulars*, 349–50. In his biography of Merritt, Don Alberts says that Merritt left a mixed force of cavalry and infantry at the cantonment. See Alberts, *Brandy Station to Manila Bay*, 256 '

13. This spot was probably in the vicinity of present Plateau City. See Kelly, *Memoirs*, 244–45, and *Memoirs of Experiences in Alaska and the Philippines*. Luther Kelly's *Memoirs*, published by Yale University Press in 1926, consisted only of his Western experiences. The press declined to publish the Alaska-Philippines portion.

14. Kelly, *Memoirs of Experiences in Alaska and the Philippines*.

15. Kelly's memoirs are a bit confusing on this point. He had to have been at

the White River cantonment at least as early as the summer of 1881, because there is reference to letters written by Kelly from White River to one James Gilson, a scout at Cantonment Uncompahgre, regarding Indian affairs. See Letters from Col. Ranald Mackenzie to General John Pope, commanding the Department of Missouri, dated 12 and 18 June 1881, found in Luther S. Kelly Military Service file. See also Kelly, *Memoirs*, 244–45, and Heitman, *Historical Register*, Vol. 1, 384.

16. Kelly, *Memoirs*, 244–45; Kelly to EAB, 12 March 1919, E. A. Brininstool Collection, University of Texas. Kelly recalled that Bridger was then living "on or near Snake river [*sic*], Colo. with his two unmarried daughters. I had in mind to go there and visit him, but did not." For the best account of the Forest Service and the wilderness concept, see Baldwin, *The Quiet Revolution*.

17. Kelly to Adjutant White River, 4 December 1882, Kelly, Military Service File.

18. Ibid., 248–49. Kelly to Adjutant White River, 4 December 1882, Kelly, Military Service File; Kelly *Memoirs of Experiences in Alaska and the Philippines*, 2.

19. Kelly to Adjutant, White River Cantonment, 27 December 1882, Kelly, Military Service File.

20. Kelly to Adjutant, White River Cantonment, 23 February 1883, Kelly, Military Service File.

21. Kelly to Adjutant, White River Cantonment, 29 March 1883, Kelly, Military Service File. The Hog Back Canyon Kelly refers to is probably today's Grand Hogback which runs generally north-south between Meeker and Rifle. The route Kelly recommended was later built by Capt. Stephen Baker with two companies of the Sixth Infantry. Kelly, *Memoirs*, 255.

22. Letter Lt. Oberlin M. Carter to Adj. Gen., Department of Missouri, 10 August 1883, Kelly, Military Service File.

23. Kelly to Miles, 24 July 1884, Nelson Miles Family Papers, Library of Congress. Evacuation Creek flows southeast out of White River at the approximate junction of that river with Utah State Highway 45. Once inside the Colorado state line, Evacuation Creek branches into Texas and Missouri Creeks.

24. "Lute" was apparently the nickname Kelly acquired as a boy, for this is how Murray addressed him in correspondence. See Murray to Kelly, 6 October 1926, KFC. Catlin, George B., "The Wild West of a Real Man" (unidentified newspaper article from Kelly file, Geneva Historical Society).

25. Certified copy of marriage record, Michigan Department of Public Health, 9 October 1974. *Detroit Free Press*, 25 September 1885, 5; *Dictionary of American Biography*, 309. My assumption that Kelly went to Detroit to get married is based on a talk given to the Women's Improvement Club of Paradise, California, by May Kelly in 1932, during which she described how Kelly had arranged for a caretaker to look after his home while he went to Detroit to get married. See article from Paradise, California, newspaper, 19 November 1932, in E. A. Brininstool Collection, BYU University, Provo, Utah.

26. Article from Paradise, California, newspaper, 19 November 1932, in E. A. Brininstool Collection, BYU University, Provo, Utah.

27. Ibid. Kelly's grandniece told the author that her mother had said May was sometimes afraid to stay by herself, but was also afraid to go.

28. Copy of document describing transfer of assets found in BLM Records,

Serial #COCOAA 006326, State of Colorado.

29. Kelly's possible role as a hunting guide is pure conjecture on my part, but it is logical. Roosevelt was well acquainted with Kelly by the time of the Spanish-American War, though exactly where and when they first met is not known. The guide business, I think, offers a plausible theory. See *Theodore Roosevelt: An Autobiography*, 46–47.

30. Charles P. Hiller to Rev. Norman L. Jensen, 10 March 1942, in *Grand Valley United Methodist Church, Parachute, Colorado, 1888–1998*. Copy of letter furnished by Parachute Public Library.

31. Obituary notice of Jeannette Kelly found in the L. S. Kelly file, Geneva Historical Society, and "The Kelly Family of Geneva," typescript, also in the L. S. Kelly file of the Geneva (New York) Historical Society.

32. Ferdinand Vandeveer Hayden reportedly named the area Parachute in 1879 because the pattern of the three streams flowing into the Grand River at this point resembled a parachute. See Murray, *Lest We Forget*, 1; Gulliford, *Garfield County, Colorado*, 28.

33. Luther Kelly to Frank D. Baldwin, 12 July 1891, Kelly, Military Service File.

34. Ibid.; Kelly to Miles, 25 July 1884, Kelly, Military Service File.

35. Pohanka, *Nelson A. Miles*, 189; DeMontravel, *A Hero to His Fighting Men*, 196–98.

36. Utley, *The Indian Frontier*, 253–54.

37. Ibid., 255; Utley, *Frontier Regulars*, 414–15.

38. Utley, *The Indian Frontier*, 255–56; Utley, *Frontier Regulars*, 415–16.

39. Utley, *Frontier Regulars*, 418–19.

40. Kelly to Frank Baldwin, 12 July 1891, Kelly, Military Service File.

41. Ibid.; Skogen, *Indian Depredation Claims*, 96, 102.

42. Kelly, Civilian Personnel Record File, National Archives.

43. Kelly, Military Service Record. In his memoirs, Kelly says only that army friends found a place for him in the War Department. See Kelly, *Memoirs*, 255. May Kelly says that Miles sent for her husband. See Article from Paradise, California, newspaper, 19 November 1932, in E. A. Brininstool Collection, BYU University, Provo, Utah.

Chapter Nine

1. Kelly, *Memoirs*, 255.

2. Kelly, Military Service File; Hutton, *Phil Sheridan and His Army*, 153.

3. Roster of Geo. H. Thomas Post, No. 5, Grand Army of the Republic, Revised 27 August 1892, 25; *The History of the George H. Thomas Post No. 5.* Photocopy from Chicago Historical Society.

4. Schulman, Bruce R., "Interactive Guide to the World's Columbian Exposition," found online at http://users.vnet/schulman/Columbian/columbian.html; Kelly, *Memoirs of Experiences in Alaska and the Philippines*, 4; *Webster's Biographical Dictionary*, 444.

5. Kelly, *Memoirs of Experiences in Alaska and the Philippines*, 5.

6. Ibid., 5–6; Greene, *Yellowstone Command*, 42.

7. Kelly, *Memoirs of Experiences in Alaska and the Philippines*, 6–7.

8. Kelly, *Memoirs of Experiences in Alaska and the Philippines*, 4.

9. Ibid.

10. DeMontravel, *A Hero to His Fighting Men*, 214–24.

11. Adjutant General's Office and Civilian Employment Record, in Kelly, Military Service File.

12. DeMontravel, *A Hero to His Fighting Men*, 226.

13.   Kelly, *Memoirs of Experiences in Alaska and the Philippines*, 8.
14.   Memo, War Dept., Adjutant General's Office and Civilian Employment Record found in Kelly, Military Service File. Kelly to L. A. Huffman, 27 March 1921, KFC.
15.   Kelly, *Memoirs of Experiences in Alaska and the Philippines*, 8.
16.   Kelly, *Memoirs of Experiences in Alaska and the Philippines*, 9. See also Chapter 8, n29.
17.   Brown and Felton, *The Frontier Years*, 105; Kelly, *Memoirs of Experiences in Alaska and the Philippines*, 157.
18.   For contrasting views on Miles's education, see Johnson, *The Unregimented General*, 5, and DeMontravel, *A Hero to His Fighting Men*, 4.
19.   Johnson, *The Unregimented General*, 5.
20.   Brown and Felton, *The Frontier Years*, 105.
21.   Miles's biographer, Virginia Johnson, claimed that Kelly was one of the few people with whom Miles could relax. See Johnson, *The Unregimented General*, 5, 112, 135. See also Kelly's memoirs; Luther Kelly, Military Service File; Kelly to Miles, 24 July 1884, Nelson Miles Papers, Library of Congress.
22.   Miles's biographer, Virginia Johnson, claimed that Kelly was one of the few people with whom Miles could relax. See Johnson, *The Unregimented General*, 5, 112, 135. See also Kelly's memoirs; Luther Kelly, Military Service File; Kelly to Miles, 24 July 1884, Nelson Miles Papers, Library of Congress.
23.   Memo, War Dept., Adjutant General's Office and Civilian Employment Record found in Kelly, Military Service File. See also, Kelly to EAB, 28 January 1923, E. A. Brininstool Collection, University of Texas, and New York Senator T. C. Platt from W. L. Swert, 30 May 1898. Kelly, Military Service File.

Chapter Ten

1.   Kelly, *Memoirs of Experiences in Alaska and the Philippines*, 15.
2.   Webb, *The Last Frontier*, 119–41; Sherwood, *Exploration of Alaska*, 145–68.
3.   Sherwood, *Exploration of Alaska*, 98–18; Webb, *The Last Frontier*, 104.
4.   Ray, *Compilation of Narratives of Exploration in Alaska*, 497–501. Hereafter cited as *Compilation of Narratives*; Sherwood, *Exploration of Alaska*, 155; Nielson, *Armed Forces on a Northern Frontier*, 65.
5.   Ray, *Compilation of Narratives*, 497–501; Nielson, *Armed Forces on a Northern Frontier*, 74; Sherwood, *Exploration of Alaska*, 155–57; Webb, *The Last Frontier*, 145–46.
6.   Ray, *Compilation of Narratives*, 498. Lapland may be defined as the northern sections of Norway, Sweden, Finland, and a part of Russia.
7.   Sherwood, *Exploration of Alaska*, 155; Ray, *Compilation of Narratives*, 497–501.
8.   U.S. War Dept., *Reports of Explorations in the Territory of Alaska (Cooks Inlet, Sushitna, Copper, and Tanana Rivers), 1898*, 5–6. Hereafter cited as *Reports of Explorations*. Official accounts of the Glenn and Abercrombie expeditions may be found in two places: the *Compilation of Narratives of Explorations in Alaska*, prepared for the U.S. Senate, and No. XXV, *Reports of Explorations in the Territory of Alaska*, which was prepared as the more official version of the two expeditions for submission to the secretary of war. Although both may be legitimately regarded as

"official," the *Reports of Explorations* is longer and contains details omitted from the *Compilation of Narratives*.

9.   Kelly, *Memoirs of Experiences in Alaska and the Philippines*, 12; Kelly to EAB, 1 July 1925, E. A. Brininstool Collection, University of Texas.

10.   Ibid. Kelly remembered the name as Devoe. *Compilation of Narratives*, 499; Heitman, *Historical Dictionary*, 370.

11.   Ibid.; Kelly, Military Service Record; U.S. Government Civilian Employment Record.

12.   Kelly, *Memoirs of Experiences in Alaska and the Philippines*, 15; Ray, *Compilation of Narratives*, 499–500.

13.   Castner, J. C., "A Historical Topic—Exploration in Alaska," 7. Hereafter cited as Castner "Explorations" 7.

14.   Kelly, *Memoirs of Experiences in Alaska and the Philippines*, 15–16.

15.   Ray, *Compilation of Narratives*, 499–501; Glenn, *Reports of Explorations*, 11. Kelly, *Memoirs of Experiences in Alaska and the Philippines*, 19–20. In his memoirs, Kelly says the reindeer were shipped aboard the *George W. Elder*, but he may have been thinking of the Harriman Expedition which did sail on the *Elder* the following year. See Kelly, *Memoirs of Experiences in Alaska and the Philippines*, 19.

16.   Grinnell to Kelly, 9 April 1898, KFC. According to Grinnell's letter, Kelly had written to him on 27 March, though the letter seems not to have survived.

17.   Grinnell to Kelly, 27 April 1898, KFC. Grinnell was off considerably in his prediction that an invasion of Cuba would not take place before autumn, when in fact it happened in June.

18.   Ibid., 21.

19.   Kelly, *Memoirs of Experiences in Alaska and the Philippines*, 21–22. Kelly incorrectly refers to the newspaper as the "Times-Intelligence." He does not elaborate further on the identity of young Robe.

20.   Ibid., 22.

21.   Castner "Explorations," 7. Reindeer Moss is not a true moss, but a lichen, composed of both algae and fungi. Because it has no roots, it is able to grow on rocks, taking nourishment from the air. It is able to withstand extreme cold and dryness. Davis, "Reindeer Moss."

22.   Glenn, *Reports of Explorations*, 11; *Compilation of Narratives*, 498, 501. It is estimated that in terms of real dollars (in the year 2001), the $76,000 would have been the equivalent of approximately $1.5 million. See Sahr, "Consumer Price Index Conversion Factors."

23.   Glenn, *Reports of Explorations*, 12–14; Sherwood, *Exploration of Alaska*, 167.

24.   Glenn, *Reports of Explorations*, 14–15. Kelly says little about the trip across the Gulf of Alaska, but implies that they were aboard the *Aliance*, not the *Valencia*. See Kelly, *Memoirs of Experiences in Alaska and the Philippines*, 24–25.

25.   Glenn, *Reports of Explorations*, 15–17; Mendenhall, "A Reconnaissance from Resurrection Bay to the Tanana River, Alaska, in 1898," *Twentieth Annual Report of the United States Geological Survey, Part VII, Explorations in Alaska, 1898*, 272. Hereafter cited as Mendenhall, "From Resurrection Bay to the Tanana."

26.   Glenn, *Reports of Explorations*, 6.

27.   Ibid., 17; Musicant, *Empire by Default*, 188–90.

28.   Sherwood, *Exploration of Alaska*, 156.

29.   Kelly, Military Service Record. On 27 May 1898, Miles recommended that Kelly be appointed a lieutenant in one of the new immune regiments. See Chapter Eleven for an explanation of the "immunes."

30.   Kelly, *Memoirs of Experiences in Alaska and the Philippines*, 14. For a detailed explanation of the army's role in the war with Spain, see Graham A. Cosmas, *An Army for Empire*.

31.   Kelly, Military Service Record.

32.   Glenn, *Reports of Explorations*, 17–18; Mendenhall, "From Resurrection Bay to the Tanana," 272; Kelly, *Memoirs of Experiences in Alaska and the Philippines*, 27.

33.   Kelly, *Reports of Explorations*, 6; Castner, "Explorations in Alaska," 8.

34.   From Glenn's description of the area, it may be that the bay he refers to is present Granite Bay on the eastern shore of Esther Island. See Glenn, *Reports of Explorations*, 19.

35.   Glenn, *Reports of Explorations*, 19–20.

36.   Ibid., 21; *Compilation of Narratives*, 632.

37.   Mendenhall, *Reconnaissances from Resurrection Bay to the Tanana River, Notebook No. 1*, 6, hereafter cited as Mendenhall, *Notebook No. 1*. Mendenhall's official reports of the expedition were based on his daily journals, which he titled notebooks. His observations and experiences of the Glenn expedition were recorded in three such field notebooks, which often contain details not included in the official reports, as for example, this outing of 26 April. George Howe was a Hospital Corps private attached to the expedition. The name of the sixth man, as mentioned in Mendenhall's notebook, is unreadable, but it was probably one of the privates not identified on the roster of the expedition.

38.   Kelly, *Memoirs of Experiences in Alaska and the Philippines*, 43.

39.   *Compilation of Narratives*, 632; Mendenhall, "From Resurrection Bay to the Tanana," 273.

40.   Ibid., 21.

41.   The official reports spell this officer's name as "Learnard"; however, Heitman's Historical Register identifies him as "Learned." See Glenn, *Reports of Explorations*, 22; *Compilation of Narratives*, 630; Mendenhall, "From Resurrection Bay to the Tanana," 273; Heitman, 621.

42.   Glenn, *Reports of Explorations*, 22–23; *Compilation of Narratives*, 632.

43.   Castner, *Lieutenant Castner's Alaskan Exploration*, 7–8; Mendenhall, *Notebook Number 1*, 9.

44.   Kelly, *Memoirs of Experiences in Alaska and the Philippines*, 31.

45.   Glenn, *Reports of Explorations*, 30.

46.   Ibid., 30–31.

47.   Kelly to EAB, 25 April 1923, E. A. Brininstool Collection, University of Texas.

48.   Kelly, *Reports of Explorations*, 289–90; Glenn, *Reports of Explorations*, 33. See also Kelly's sub-report, "From Cabin Creek to the Valley of the Yukla, Alaska," in *Compilation of Narratives*, 684.

49.   Mendenhall says it was the twenty-first. Mendenhall, *Notebook Number 1*, 10.

50.   Glenn, *Reports of Explorations*, 32–34.

51.   Kelly, *Reports of Explorations*, 292–93; *Compilation of Narratives*, 685–86.

52.   Glenn, *Reports of Explorations*, 34; Mendenhall, *Notebook Number 1*, 11.

53.   Glenn, *Reports of Explorations*, 35–36; Mendenhall, *Notebook Number 1*, 12. Mendenhall's route from Resurrection Bay to Sunrise may well have followed the present Iditarod Trail for at least part of the way.

54. Ibid., 37.
55. Kelly, *Reports of Explorations*, 290–91; Kelly, "From Cabin Creek to the Valley of the Yukla," 684.
56. Kelly, *Reports of Explorations*, 291; Kelly, *Compilation of Narratives*, 685. The glacial or "blue" bear is a rare species found only on the coast of Alaska between Prince William Sound and Ketchikan. See Schooler, *The Blue Bear*.
57. Kelly, *Memoirs of Experiences in Alaska and the Philippines*, 37.
58. Ibid.
59. Castner, *Lieutenant Castner's Alaskan Exploration*, 15–16.
60. Kelly, *Reports of Explorations*, 292; *Compilation of Narratives*, 685.
61. Castner, *Lieutenant Castner's Alaskan Exploration*, 14.
62. Glenn, *Reports of Explorations*, 47–51; *Compilation of Narratives*, 633.
63. Castner, *Lieutenant Castner's Alaskan Exploration*, 22–23.
64. Ibid., 23. By the time Kelly arrived, Castner's party had run out of rations and was forced to subsist on a diet of mutton and dried apples until one of the packers arrived with a small supply of rations on the eleventh.
65. Kelly, *Memoirs of Experiences in Alaska and the Philippines*, 53.
66. Ibid., 23–24.
67. Ibid., 26.
68. Mendenhall, "From Resurrection Bay to the Tanana," 281; Castner, *Lieutenant Castner's Alaskan Exploration*, 26; Glenn, *Reports of Explorations*, 56, 72–73; Kelly to Theodore Roosevelt, 29 January 1915, Theodore Roosevelt Collection, Library of Congress.
69. Kelly to Theodore Roosevelt, 29 January 1915, Theodore Roosevelt Collection, Library of Congress.
70. Glenn, *Reports of Explorations*, 76; Kelly, *Memoirs of Experiences in Alaska and the Philippines*, 77. Castner reported that he was supposed to be issued rations for twenty days but actually only received a ten-day supply, and a fifty-pound sack of flour was mostly moldy. Castner, *Lieutenant Castner's Alaskan Exploration*, 42.
71. Glenn, *Reports of Explorations*, 79. Mendenhall called this "Camp Disconsolate." See Mendenhall, "From Resurrection Bay to the Tanana," 287.
72. Glenn, *Reports of Explorations*, 86; Mendenhall, *Notebook Number 1*, 73.
73. Glenn, *Reports of Explorations*, 80–81; Kelly, *Memoirs of Experiences in Alaska and the Philippines*, 83.
74. Glenn, *Reports of Explorations*, 88–89; Mendenhall, "From Resurrection Bay to the Tanana," 290.
75. Glenn, *Reports of Explorations*, 92; Kelly, *Memoirs of Experiences in Alaska and the Philippines*, 87. The order directing Kelly to report for duty was received at Vancouver Barracks on 25 July 1898 and forwarded immediately. Kelly acknowledged receipt of same on 25 October. Kelly, Military Service Record. See also Mendenhall, "From Resurrection Bay to the Tanana," 290. The Union League was a Republican organization, dominated by wealthy businessmen, of which William D. Kelly was one. As a strong financial supporter of the Republican party, W. D. Kelly's recommendation to the President would have carried significant weight. See also Morris, *Theodore Rex*, 34.
76. The ordeal of Lieutenant Castner's party is described in *Lieutenant Castner's Alaskan Exploration*, 47–68, and Castner, "Exploration in Alaska."

77.   Kelly to Alfred H. Brooks, 2 April 1907, KFC; Webb, *The Last Frontier*, 147, 250.

78.   Glenn, *Reports of Explorations*, 122; Sherwood, *Exploration of Alaska*, 160; Webb, *The Last Frontier*, 147–48.

Chapter Eleven

1.   Kelly to Theodore Roosevelt, 29 January 1915, Theodore Roosevelt Collection, Library of Congress.

2.   Kelly, *Memoirs of Experiences in Alaska and the Philippines*, 88.

3.   Ibid., 89.

4.   Ibid., 91.

5.   Wm. D. Kelly II to author, 3 May 1972.

6.   Kelly, *Memoirs of Experiences in Alaska and the Philippines*, 94. Kelly, Military Service Record. According to his military service record, Kelly evidently believed his original commission was as a lieutenant because that is how he reported in from Vancouver Barracks. His memoirs, however, suggest he thought he had been appointed a captain. See Kelly, Military Service Record.

7.   Kelly, *Memoirs of Experiences in Alaska and the Philippines*, 94–95.

8.   Ibid., 94–95.

9.   Cosmas, *An Army for Empire*, 127–30.

10.   *Correspondence Relating to the War with Spain*, 627.

11.   Kelly, *Memoirs of Experiences in Alaska and the Philippines*, 95–96.

12.   Ibid., 96.

13.   Ibid., 97.

14.   Ibid.

15.   Ibid., 102.

16.   Kelly, Military Service Record.

17.   Kelly, *Memoirs of Experiences in Alaska and the Philippines*, 99.

18.   Linn, *The Philippine War*, 32–34.

19.   Ibid., 42, 89–90; Musicant, *Empire By Default*, 626–29.

20.   Linn, *The Philippine War*, 90, 125.

21.   Kelly, Military Service Record; Kelly, *Memoirs of Experiences in Alaska and the Philippines*, 100.

22.   Kelly, *Memoirs of Experiences in Alaska and the Philippines*, 100.

23.   Ibid., 101. At this time, Nelson Miles was something of a *persona non grata* with the McKinley administration because of the political turmoil created over his accusations in what came to be known as the "Beef Scandal," in the aftermath of the Spanish-American War. For a discussion of this affair, see Cosmas, *An Army for Empire*. Theodore Roosevelt, although a hero of the Spanish-American War and then governor of New York, was also not a favorite of the McKinley administration. See Morris, *The Rise of Theodore Roosevelt*, and Brands, *The Last Romantic*.

24.   Kelly, *Memoirs of Experiences in Alaska and the Philippines*, 102.

25.   Ibid., 102–3.

26.   The two principal secondary sources for the Harriman expedition are Goetzmann and Sloan, *Looking Far North*, and Klein, *The Life & Legend of E. H. Harriman*. I have used both in the preparation of this chapter.

27.   Klein, *E. H. Harriman*, 183.

28.   Goetzmann and Sloan, *Looking Far North*, 207–8.

29.   Ibid., 208; Kelly to EAB, 12 March 1919, E. A. Brininstool Collection, University of Texas. Goetzmann and Sloan identify Kelly as having been

a scout for Custer, which of course he was not. In point of fact, it does not seem likely the two men ever met. In his biography of Harriman, Maury Klein repeats the misidentification.

30. Kelly, *Memoirs of Experiences in Alaska and the Philippines*, 104.

31. Ibid., 105–6; *American Ancestry*, Vol. 11. Kelly was then a member of the Society of the War of 1812. It seems odd that Harriman wondered whether Kelly had been in that war, because Kelly would have to have been more than 100 years old. The foregoing is taken from a genealogy of the Kelly family, given to author by the late William D. Kelly II.   .

32. Kelly, *Memoirs of Experiences in Alaska and the Philippines*, 106–7; Goetzman and Sloan, *Looking Far North*, 24.

33. Kelly, *Memoirs of Experiences in Alaska and the Philippines*, 107.

34. Ibid.

35. Kelly, *Memoirs of Experiences in Alaska and the Philippines*, 109; Burroughs, *My Boyhood*, 575; Goetzmann and Sloan, *Looking Far North*, 29–32; Klein, *E. H. Harriman*, 187–88; Kearny, "Reminiscences of the Harriman Expedition."

36. Burroughs, *My Boyhood*, 220–21.

37. Goetzmann and Sloan, *Looking Far North*, 55–67.

38. Ibid., 68–69.

39. Goetzmann and Sloan, *Looking Far North*, 69–71; Klein, *E. H. Harriman*, 189.

40. Merriam, *Journals of Harriman Alaska Expedition*, Vol. 1, 53–55; Goetzmann and Sloan, *Looking Far North*, 69; Klein, *E. H. Harriman*, 189.

41. Goetzmann and Sloan, *Looking Far North*, 89–91; Merriam, *Journals of Harriman Alaska Expedition*, Vol. 1, 71.

42. Goetzmann and Sloan, *Looking Far North*, 95–105; Merriam, *Harriman Alaska Expedition*, 78.

43. Kelly, *Memoirs of Experiences in Alaska and the Philippines*, 116; Goetzman and Sloan, *Looking Far North*, 8–10, 12, 97–98.

44. Kelly, *Memoirs of Experiences in Alaska and the Philippines*, 117–21.

45. Burroughs, "Summer Holidays In Alaskan Waters," 576; Burroughs, *Harriman Alaska Expedition*, 79. The accepted spelling at that time seems to have been Kadiak, rather than Kodiak, and seems to have been Burroughs's preference as well.

46. Burroughs, *Harriman Alaska Expedition*, 80–81.

47. Goetzmann and Sloan, *Looking Far North*, 121–22; Klein, *E. H. Harriman*, 195; Kelly, *Memoirs of Experiences in Alaska and the Philippines*, 120–24

48. Burroughs, "Summer Holidays in Alaskan Waters," 582; Goetzmann and Sloan, *Looking Far North*, 122–23; Klein, E. H. Harriman, 195–96.

49. Goetzmann and Sloan, *Looking Far North*, 129; Klein, *E. H. Harriman*, 196.

50. Klein, *E. H. Harriman*, 198.

51. Merriam, *Journals of Harriman Alaska Expedition*, Vol. 1, 222.

52. Kearny, "Reminiscences of the Harriman Expedition"; Klein, *E. H. Harriman*, 199; Goetzmann and Sloan, *Looking Far North*, 152.

53. Dall, *Journal of the Harriman Expedition.*

54. Kelly, *Memoirs of Experiences in Alaska and the Philippines*, 124–25; Goetzman and Sloan, *Looking Far North*, 163–68.

55. Kelly, *Memoirs of Experiences in Alaska and the Philippines*, 126; Kelly, Military Service Record.

56. Kelly, *Memoirs of Experiences in Alaska and the Philippines*, 127.

57. Kelly to Theodore Roosevelt, 29 January 1915, Theodore Roosevelt Collection, Library of Congress (referring to Robert Louis Stevenson's 1879 work, *Travels with a Donkey in the Cévennes*).

Chapter Twelve

1. Kelly, *Memoirs of Experiences in Alaska and the Philippines*, 190.
2. Kelly, Military Service Record.
3. Ibid.; Linn, *The Philippine War*, 126–27.
4. Kelly, Military Service Record.
5. Ibid.; Kelly, *Memoirs of Experiences in Alaska and the Philippines*, 128.
6. Kelly, *Memoirs of Experiences in Alaska and the Philippines*, 130.
7. "Major Movements and Events, 40th U.S. Volunteer Infantry, 1899–1901," found in Jesse Proctor Folder, 1898-W-995, Spanish-American War Survey Collection, Archives, U.S. Army Military History Institute, Carlisle Barracks, PA. Hereafter cited as "Major Movements and Events, 40th USV."
8. Kelly, *Memoirs of Experiences in Alaska and the Philippines*, 131, 133.
9. Linn, *The Philippine War*, 160–61.
10. Ibid.
11. Linn, *The Philippine War*, 174. The Bicol Peninsula was so-named because Bicol was the language of the region.
12. Ibid.
13. Tagalog is the most prominent of the various languages used throughout the Philippine Archipelago. Bicol, on the other hand, is spoken on the Bicol Peninsula.
14. Linn, *The Philippine War*, 174–75. For a discussion of the overall prosecution of the Philippine-American War and the various issues involved therewith, I have drawn heavily on Brian Linn's two excellent studies, *The Philippine War, 1899–1902* and *The U.S. Army and Counterinsurgency in the Philippine War, 1899–1902*. Another outstanding study of the Philippine conflict is John Morgan Gates, *Schoolbooks and Krags.*
15. Linn, *The Philippine War*, 175–76.
16. Ibid.
17. Ibid.
18. Ibid., 176–78. Interestingly, United States forces also landed at Legaspi during the liberation of the Philippines in World War II.
19. Linn, *The Philippine War*, 178; Heitman, *Historical Register*, 207; Greene, *Nez Perce Summer*, 206.
20. "Major Movements and Events of the 40th USV: Report of Brigadier General James M. Bell," found in *Report of the Lieutenant-General Commanding the Army, Annual Reports of the War Department*, Vol. 4075, 668, hereafter cited as Bell's Report.
21. Report of Major General J. C. Bates, found in *Report of the Lieutenant-General Commanding the Army, Annual Reports of the War Department*, Part IV, Serial 4075, 661–62, hereafter cited as Bates' Report.
22. Olson, *Historical Dictionary of the Spanish Empire*, 134.
23. Kelly, *Memoirs of Experiences in Alaska and the Philippines*, 135.
24. Bates' Report, 662–63.
25. Ibid., 672.
26. Kelly, *Memoirs of Experiences in Alaska and the Philippines*, 137; Report of E. A. Godwin, Colonel, Fortieth Volunteer Infantry, found in *Report of*

*the Lieutenant-General Commanding the Army, Annual Reports of
the War Department*, Part IV, Serial 4075, 671–72, hereafter cited as
Godwin's Report. See also, Linn, *The Philippine War*, 175–76.

27.   Kelly, *Memoirs of Experiences in Alaska and the Philippines*, 138.
28.   Ibid., 139; Bates' Report, 664; Godwin's Report, 671–72; Report of
      M. M. McNamee, Major, Fortieth Volunteer Infantry, found in
      *Report of the Lieutenant-General Commanding the Army, Annual
      Reports of the War Department*, Part IV, Serial 4075, 671–72, hereafter
      cited as McNamee's Report.
29.   McNamee's Report, 677–79.
30.   Ibid.
31.   Ibid., 679.
32.   Ibid.
33.   Ibid.
34.   McNamee's Report, 679; Kelly, *Memoirs of Experiences in Alaska and the
      Philippines*, 148.
35.   Kelly, *Memoirs of Experiences in Alaska and the Philippines*, 144.
36.   Kelly to EAB, 22 August 1927, E.A. Brininstool Collection, University of
      Texas; Kelly, *Memoirs of Experiences in Alaska and the Philippines*, 147;
      McNamee's Report, 679; *Army-Navy Journal*, 10 December 1910.
37.   Bates' Report, 666–67.
38.   Kelly, *Memoirs of Experiences in Alaska and the Philippines*, 153, 156.
      In his memoirs, Kelly says Rizal was executed in 1899, but in fact it
      was 1896. See Keenan, *Encyclopedia of the Spanish-American and
      Philippine-American Wars*, 329–30.
39.   Kelly, *Memoirs of Experiences in Alaska and the Philippines*, 156–57.
40.   Ibid., 158.
41.   Bates' Report, 667.
42.   Kelly to EAB, 30 August 1924, E. A. Brininstool Collection, University of
      Texas. Kelly apparently kept a daily journal while in the Philippines, but
      it seems not to have survived. See also Kelly to EAB, 9 July 1924, E. A.
      Brininstool Collection, University of Texas.
43.   Bates' Report, 695, 698–99; Bell's Report, 2–3.
44.   Post Returns, Dapitan, Mindanao, April 1900; *Kelly's Report*, October 12,
      1900, found in *Annual Reports of the War Department for the Fiscal
      Year Ended June 30, 1901, Report of the Lieutenant-General
      Commanding The Army*, Part IV, Serial 4274, hereafter cited as Kelly's
      Report. Bell's Report gives 3 April as the date of arrival. See also Bates'
      Report, 694–97.
45.   Linn, *The Philippine War*, 180.
46.   Ibid., 123, 178; Beede, *The War of 1898*, 42.
47.   Bates' Report, 697.
48.   Bell's Report, 2–3; Godwin's Report, 266–71.
49.   Kelly, *Memoirs of Experiences in Alaska and the Philippines*, 163.
50.   Ibid., 165.
51.   Ibid., 165–66.
52.   Kelly's Report, 272.
53.   Kelly to T.R., 5 September 1900. Theodore Roosevelt Collection, Library of
      Congress.
54.   T.R. to Kelly, 27 November 1900, in Theodore Roosevelt Collection,
      Library of Congress.
55.   Kelly, *Memoirs of Experiences in Alaska and the Philippines*, 185–86.

56. Godwin's Report, 271; Bates' Report, 702. Kelly, *Memoirs of Experiences in Alaska and the Philippines*, 188.

57. Ibid., 183, 185–86.

58. Ibid., 179, 185–86.

59. Kelly, *Memoirs of Experiences in Alaska and the Philippines*, 180–81.

60. Kelly to EAB, 13 December 1922, E. A. Brininstool Collection, University of Texas. Kelly evidently brought the cannon back to the States, but at some point it disappeared from his collection of souvenirs.

61. Bell's Report, 2–3; "Army Service Experiences Questionnaire, James C. Keeler," 40th Regiment, U.S. Volunteer Infantry, Spanish-American War Survey Collection, Archives, U.S. Army Military History Institute, Carlisle Barracks, PA.

62. "Efficiency Report of Captain Luther S. Kelly, 40th Infantry," found in Kelly, Military Service Record. The lesser marks for discipline and command capacity suggest that Colonel Godwin thought Kelly a good but not outstanding officer. This may serve to explain the colonel's refusal to recommend Kelly for a Medal of Honor. If anything was, in fact, said about the burials, it may have cost Kelly points with his commanding officer.

63. Beede, *The War of 1898*, 531–33; Karnow, *In Our Image*, 168–74.

64. Ibid.; Linn, *The Philippine War*, 216.

65. Ibid.

66. Kelly, *Memoirs of Experiences in Alaska and the Philippines*, 190.

67. Ibid. The description of this moment is so characteristic of Kelly, who excused himself from the gathering, saying in his *Memoirs* that "[a]t this point I thot [sic] the conversation was getting rather personal."

68. Beede, *The War of 1898*, 533; Karnow, *In Our Image*, 168–74; Linn, *The Philippine War*, 216–17.

69. Kelly to T.R., 29 January 1915, found in Theodore Roosevelt Collection, Library of Congress. See also Kelly to Nelson Miles, July 24, 1884. See Chapter 16, note 23, of this book.

70. Linn, *The Philippine War*, 223.

71. Kelly, *Memoirs of Experiences in Alaska and the Philippines*, 192, 194; Kelly, Military Service Record; Beede, *The War of 1898*, 78–79. He remained a volunteer officer until mustered out at Surigao on 30 June 1901.

72. Kelly, *Memoirs of Experiences in Alaska and the Philippines*, 194.

73. Ibid., 195.

74. Ibid.

75. Ibid., 195–96.

76. War Dept., Division of Insular Affairs, 2d Indorsement [sic], 26 February 1902; 4th Indorsement [sic], 29 March 1902; 6th Indorsement [sic], 15 April 1902; M. E. Olmstead to Secretary of War, 24 March 1902; Division of Insular Affairs to Mrs. Luther S. Kelly, 7 April 1902; Division of Insular Affairs to William D. Kelly, 16 April 1902. All of the above found in Luther S. Kelly, Civilian Personnel File, National Archives, Record Group 350, #4665–6.

77. Clipping from Paradise, California, newspaper, November 1932.

78. "Report of the Provincial Governor of the Province of Surigao," found in *Report of the Philippine Commission*, 921.

79. Kelly, *Memoirs of Experiences in Alaska and the Philippines*, 200–201.

80. Kelly, Military Service Record; *Report of the Philippine Commission*, 30;

War Department, Annual Reports, 1903, Part IV, Serial 4630, 242–43; *Army and Navy Journal,* 28 March 1903; Nichols, *In Custer's Shadow,* 271. Kelly later told Earl Brininstool that he was acting governor when General Lee arrived. See Kelly to EAB, 30 June 1921, E. A. Brininstool Collection, University of Texas.

81. Lee to Davis, *War Department Annual Reports, June 30, 1903,* Vol. 3, House Document, 58th Congress, Serial 4630, 251.

82. Theodore Roosevelt to Kelly, 25 March 1903. Kelly, Military Service File.

83. Theodore Roosevelt to Secretary of War, 18 March 1901, in Kelly, Military Service Record.

84. AAG to M. E. Olmstead, 1 April 1903; AAG to Boies Penrose, 27 April 1903, found in Kelly, Military Service Record.

85. George Bird Grinnell to Theodore Roosevelt, 24 March 1903, found in Luther S. Kelly, Civilian Personnel File, National Archives, Record Group 350, #4665–5.

86. William D. Kelly to E. A. Hitchcock, 11 May 1903, found in Luther S. Kelly, Civilian Personnel File, National Archives, Record Group 350, #4665–6.

87. E. A. Hitchcock to Elihu Root, 4 June 1903; Translation of cablegram sent to Governor William Howard Taft, 5 June 1903. Luther S. Kelly, Civilian Personnel File, National Archives, Record Group 350, #4665–6.

88. Acting Secretary of War to E. A. Hitchcock, 10 and 22 June 1903; Government of the Philippine Islands, Executive Bureau, Manila, to Chief, Bureau of Insular Affairs, Washington, 21 July 1903; Philippine Civil Service Board to the U.S. Civil Service Commission, Washington, 11 November 1903. Luther S. Kelly, Civilian Personnel File.

Chapter Thirteen

1. Kelly to William H. Taft, 8 November 1908. William Howard Taft Papers, Library of Congress.

2. Kelly to George Van Horn Moseley, 8 April 1904; National Archives, Record Group 75, Letters Received, 1881–1907, 1904-#4832. Moseley, whom Kelly had known in the Philippines, was a lieutenant in the 9th Cavalry. See also Chapter 12, note 87. In his letter to Moseley, Kelly says, "[W]e stopped at the Palmer House for a couple of nights." It is not clear whether the "we" refers to May, or perhaps to a fellow officer who was also bound for the East. As far as we know, May and Anna had returned from their visit to the Philippines in 1903, so it seems unlikely that May would have been in Chicago with him.

3. Mount Airy did not become an official community until after World War I, but it apparently was used unofficially by residents prior to that time. Germantown (PA) Historical Society, Phone conversation with Marion Rosenbaum.

4. Prucha, *The Great Father,* Vol. 2, 763.

5. Linn, *The Philippine War,* 317–20; Morris, *Theodore Rex,* 97–99.

6. Kelly to George Van Horn Moseley, 8 April 1904. National Archives, Record Group 75, Letters Received, 1881–1907, 1904-#4832, Treasury Department to Commissioner of Indian Affairs. For the Miles–Roosevelt controversy, see Morris, *Theodore Rex,* 78–80, 97–103, and DeMontravel, *A Hero to His Fighting Men,* 346–48.

7. San Carlos Agency, MS707, Arizona Historical Society, hereafter cited as San Carlos File, Arizona Historical Society; Worcester, *The Apaches,* 168–69; Hoxie, *Encyclopedia of North American Indians,* 29.

8. For descriptions of San Carlos, see Utley, *The Indian Frontier*, 193–94; Thrapp, *Victorio*, 213; Perry, *Apache Reservation*, 119.

9. San Carlos File, Arizona Historical Society. The Arizona Historical Society file says that civilian agents were again appointed beginning in 1900. For a discussion of the reservation system and the government's management thereof, see Prucha, *The Great Father*, especially Vol. II, 716–35, 763. See also Brands, *The Last Romantic*, 541–66.

10. Kelly, Luther S., Report of Agent for San Carlos Agency, 1904, 152. In *Annual Report of the Commissioner of Indian Affairs, June 30, 1904*, Serial 4798. Hereafter cited as Kelly, San Carlos Annual Report.

11. Kelly to Long, 10 April 1904, San Carlos File, Arizona Historical Society; Kelly to George Van Horn Moseley, 8 April 1904. During the 1930s, the Kelly house, agency headquarters, and other sites that existed during Kelly's tenure as agent were covered by the waters of Coolidge Dam. Any Indian whose land was covered by those waters was given a new tract near the town of Rice, which had been the site of the Indian boarding school. San Carlos Agency, MS707, Arizona Historical Society, 6–7. See also Nancy Felton to L. A. Huffman, 27 January 1930, and W. E. Tiffany to L. S. Kelly, October 10, 1926, KFC.

12. Kelly to Lee, 9 July 1904. See also Kelly to Thomas Glover, 11 July 1904, KFC.

13. Kelly to Taft, 8 November 1908; Taft-Secretary to Kelly, 14 November 1908, William Howard Taft Papers, Library of Congress.

14. Kelly to Theodore Roosevelt, 7 April 1904, San Carlos File, Arizona Historical Society.

15. Ibid.; Kelly to George Bird Grinnell, 24 May 1904, San Carlos File, Arizona Historical Society.

16. Kelly, San Carlos Annual Report, 151.

17. Ibid., 151–53.

18. Perry, *Apache Reservation*, 142–43.

19. Rogge et al., *Raising Arizona's Dams*, 7; Thrapp, *Frontier Biography*, Vol. 3, 1306–7. Dan Thrapp suggests the possibility that Sieber's death was not an accident.

20. Kelly to Frank Mead, 29 November 1905, San Carlos File, Arizona Historical Society.

21. Kelly, San Carlos Annual Report, 1904, 153.

22. Ibid., 176.

23. Kelly to Frank Mead, 29 November 1905, San Carlos File, Arizona Historical Society; Kelly to George Bird Grinnell, 24 May 1904, San Carlos File, Arizona Historical Society.

24. Kelly to George Van Horn Moseley, 8 April 1904, San Carlos File, Arizona Historical Society.

25. Ibid.

26. See Kelly to First National Bank, Glenwood Springs, 3 January 1907; Kelly to Home Savings Bank, Detroit, 8 March 1907; Kelly to National Metropolitan Bank, 7 April 1908, San Carlos File, Arizona Historical Society. Since Kelly and May did occasionally travel to Washington and Detroit, they may have had these accounts simply as a matter of convenience.

27. Kelly to Executive Secretary, Philippine Commission, 26 April 1904; Kelly to War Department, 13 May 1904; See also Kelly to Secretary of War, 31 August 1904; San Carlos File, Arizona Historical Society.

28. Kelly to Rich and Hutchinson, 10 February and 26 March 1908, San Carlos File, Arizona Historical Society.

29. Kelly to Thomas A. Glover, 14 May 1904, and 11 July 1904; Kelly to First National Bank, Glenwood Springs, 3 January 1907; Kelly to Home Savings Bank, Detroit, 8 March 1907, San Carlos File, Arizona Historical Society. See also Chapter 8, note 28.

30. Kelly to Victor Talking Machine Company, 7 May and 7 July 1907; Kelly to Sydney Prescott, Victor Talking Machine Company, 24 October 1908, San Carlos File, Arizona Historical Society.

31. Kelly to *Forest & Stream*, 16 November 1905; Kelly to Joseph H. Taylor, 26 November 1907, San Carlos File, Arizona Historical Society.

32. Kelly to Mr. White, 24 July 1904, San Carlos File, Arizona Historical Society. The letter gives no indication as to White's first name, but he apparently had been a former resident of the area, perhaps a government employee.

33. Ibid.

34. In one letter to the author, William D. Kelly II says he lived at San Carlos in 1903, but another letter says 1904. Since Kelly did not arrive at San Carlos until 1904, WDK was obviously in error as to the 1903 date. WDK also claimed he was with Kelly in Nevada in 1905 and again in 1907, which is also in error since Kelly did not actually leave San Carlos until 1909. See WDK to Author 3 May 1972 and 28 November 1972. Five male descendants of William D. Kelly I carry the same given name. Of these, three William D. Kellys are still alive.

35. Kelly to Frank Mead, General Superintendent, Indian School, Phoenix, 28 May 1904; Kelly to Commissioner of Indian Affairs, 23 July 1904, San Carlos File, Arizona Historical Society.

36. Kelly to Commissioner of Indians Affairs, 25 August 1904. National Archives, Record Group 75, Letters Received, 1881–1907, no. 59243. See also Kelly to Frederick Nave, U.S. Attorney, 26 June 1904, San Carlos File, Arizona Historical Society.

37. Kelly to Superintendent Mead, 29 June 1904; Kelly to Filleman, 10 July 1904; Kelly to E. P. Shanley, 6 January 1905; Kelly to William Grey, 28 January 1905; Gila County Sheriff to Kelly, 2 March 1905, San Carlos File, Arizona Historical Society.

38. U.S. Attorney Frederick Nave to Kelly, 20 September 1904; Kelly to Commissioner, 23 September 1904; Kelly to Frederick Nave, 23 October 1904, San Carlos File, Arizona Historical Society.

39. Kelly to Commissioner of Indian Affairs, 27 October 1905. National Archives, Record Group 75 Letters Received, 1881–1907.

40. Ibid., 13 February 1905.

41. Kelly to Frank Mead, General Supervisor of Reservations, 1 February 1905, San Carlos File, Arizona Historical Society. Kelly later claimed it was Robert G. Valentine, then secretary to the commissioner and later commissioner himself, who was responsible for the appointment. See Chapter Fourteen, note 21.

42. The picture is not as clear as one might have hoped for, but given Kelly's past history and the evidence on hand, it seems fairly safe to say that such was the story. Kelly to Commissioner of Indian Affairs, 21 October 1905; Ruth Gibbs to Commissioner, undated letter, National Archives, Record Group 75, Letters Received, 1881–1907.

43. Kelly to Frank Mead, 11 December 1905, San Carlos File, Arizona Historical Society.

44. Ibid.

45. Kelly to Commissioner of Indian Affairs, 3 September 1908, San Carlos File, Arizona Historical Society.

46. Kemp to Commissioner, 3 September 1908, San Carlos File, Arizona Historical Society.

47. Kelly to Theodore Roosevelt, 30 September 1905, San Carlos File, Arizona Historical Society.

48. Roosevelt, *Theodore Roosevelt: An Autobiography*, 377.

49. Kelly's requests for thirty days annual leave were made on 13 August 1904, 21 November 1904, 10 September 1905, and 2 March 1906. Kelly to Commissioner of Indian Affairs, National Archives, Record Group 75, Letters Received 1881–1907. These are the only requests that seem to have survived, but in all probability there were one or two others.

50. Roosevelt, *Theodore Roosevelt: An Autobiography*, 46–48; Miller, *Theodore Roosevelt: A Life*, 415; Morris, *Theodore Rex*, 512; Edmund Morris to author, 21 March 1981. See also *The Saturday Evening Post*, 19 May 1906.

51. Kelly to George Bird Grinnell, 24 May 1904 and 29 November 1908, San Carlos File, Arizona Historical Society.

52. Kelly to R. S. Connell, 3 August 1908, San Carlos File, Arizona Historical Society.

53. Kelly to William Howard Taft, 8 November 1908, Taft Papers, Library of Congress. *Far from the Madding Crowd* was a highly acclaimed 1874 novel by Thomas Hardy.

54. R. G. Valentine, Acting Commissioner to Secretary of the Interior, 16 December 1908. Commissioner Francis Leupp to Kelly, 24 December 1908; Assistant Secretary of the Interior Wilson to Commissioner Leupp, 30 December 1908, San Carlos File, Arizona Historical Society.

55. Kelly to Commissioner, 4 January 1909, San Carlos File, Arizona Historical Society.

56. Lewis B. Weaver to R. G. Valentine, Assistant Commissioner of Indian Affairs, 18 January 1909, San Carlos File, Arizona Historical Society.

57. Kelly to Roosevelt, 30 September 1905 and 4 January 1909. National Archives, Record Group 75, Letters Received, 1881–1907; San Carlos File, Arizona Historical Society. See Kelly to Secretary of the Interior, 16 March 1913, San Carlos File, Arizona Historical Society.

58. Theodore Roosevelt to Kelly, 9 January 1909, San Carlos File, Arizona Historical Society. See also Morris, *Theodore Rex*, 546.

59. Kelly to Commissioner, 4 January 1909; Kelly to Secretary of the Interior, 16 March 1913. Memo, Office of Indian Affairs, 21 January 1909, San Carlos File, Arizona Historical Society

60. Acting Commissioner R. G. Valentine to Wilbur T. Elliott, 13 January 1909, San Carlos File, Arizona Historical Society.

61. Nothing in the San Carlos records indicates that Kelly was ever implicated in or charged with any wrongdoing during his tenure at the agency. Certainly he never believed he left behind anything but an unblemished record, which is supported by his later efforts to secure another position in the Indian Bureau, hardly something he would have attempted had he known he was on the black list. And, it is most unlikely that he would have been offered the Keshena post in the face of any real malfeasance while in office. See letter from Gen. C. R. Edwards to Fred V. Carpenter, Secretary to the President, 24 April 1909, San Carlos File, Arizona Historical Society.

Chapter Fourteen

1. Kelly to L. A. Huffman, 1 April 1912, KFC.
2. Abbott, *The Letters of Archie Butt*, 365.
3. Miller, *Theodore Roosevelt: A Life*, 493–94; Roosevelt, *Theodore Roosevelt: An Autobiography*, 47–48.
4. William Howard Taft to Kelly, 26 April 1909, William Howard Taft Papers, Library of Congress; Kelly to R. G. Valentine, 21 June 1909, Kelly, Civilian Personnel File, National Archives.
5. Kelly to R. G. Valentine, 21 June 1909, Kelly, Civilian Personnel File, National Archives.
6. Kelly to L. A. Huffman, 27 March 1921, KFC. Prendergast, Curtis, *The First Aviators*, 58–59, 85.
7. Albert Kelly to R. A. Ballinger, 10 January 1910; Ballinger to Albert Kelly, 11 January 1910, Kelly, Civilian Personnel File.
8. It is possible that Kelly arrived in Nevada in late 1909 or early 1910, but in any event he was there at least as early as April because the 1910 census shows Luther and William living in Lida, Nevada. May's name does not appear, however. See Thirteenth Census of the U.S., 1910 for Lida, Esmeralda County, Enumeration District No. 23, Sheet 5.
9. Zanjani, *Goldfield*, 236. In a letter to the author, William D. Kelly II said he accompanied his uncle to Nevada in 1905 and again in 1907. This could certainly have happened. While at San Carlos, Kelly could have taken some annual leave and visited Nevada with his nephew. If so, it would mean that Kelly had an opportunity to see what the Nevada boom was all about before heading out to the area again in 1910. See also WDK to Author, 3 May and 28 November 1972.
10. May was in Lida by at least 1914, if not earlier, as I have a copy of an envelope addressed to her in Lida, with a 1914 date.
11. Paher, *Goldfield: Boom Town of Nevada*, 3; Zanjani, *Goldfield*, 16–17.
12. Thrapp, *Frontier Biography*, Vol. 1, 447–48.
13. Ibid., 15; Paher, *Nevada Ghost Towns & Mining Camps*, 386, 397, 404; Zanjani, *Goldfield*, 232; Kelly to President Taft, 22 May 1910, William Howard Taft Papers, Library of Congress.
14. Paher, *Nevada Ghost Towns & Mining Camps*, 383, 410–11.
15. Thirteenth Census of the U.S., 1910 for Lida, Esmeralda County, Enumeration District No. 23, Sheet 5; Carlson, *Nevada Place Names*, 155; Paher, *Nevada Ghost Towns*, 410. When the author visited the site of Lida in 1996, the only visible reminder of the town's mining era was the remains of the post office. The site is now on private ranchland. A capsule history of Lida is presented on an interpretive sign that may be reached via a public access road.
16. Kelly to L. A. Huffman, 11 April 1912, KFC; Listing of Justices of the Peace, Esmeralda County, Nevada, page 7. See also Chapter 8, note 32.
17. Kelly, Military Service Record; Kelly to Commissioner of Pensions, 4 May 1915, Kelly Pension File.
18. Ibid.
19. Kelly to T.R., 17 January 1911, Theodore Roosevelt Collection, Library of Congress.
20. T.R. to Kelly, 30 January 1911, Theodore Roosevelt Collection, Library of Congress.
21. Kelly to Secretary of the Interior, 16 March 1913, San Carlos File, Arizona Historical Society.

Chapter Fifteen

1. Kelly to T.R., 11 February 1917, Theodore Roosevelt Collection, Library of Congress.
2. Photocopy of deed of sale between Luther S. Kelly and E. D. and Carrie Sharp; Kelly, William D., "Last Will and Testament," KFC. It seems incredible that sixty acres could have been acquired for $10 gold.
3. *Paradise and Beyond*, 17–20.
4. Ibid., 18.
5. Cedar Lodge is (or was in 1996) owned by Paradise Marine, which evidently found it necessary to cut down the last of Kelly's cedar trees. The site is marked by a large boulder with a plaque.
6. Listing of trees on Kelly's property, found in Kelly family papers.
7. Grinnell to Kelly, 14 February 1921, KFC.
8. Kelly to EAB, 26 November 1922, E. A. Brininstool Collection, University of Texas.
9. Kelly to EAB, 30 November 1920 and 26 November 1922, E. A. Brininstool Collection, University of Texas.
10. Kelly to Charles Stobie, 4 January 1919, Western History Department, Denver Public Library. See also Thrapp, *Frontier Biography*, Vol. 3, 1371–72. See also note 19.
11. Kelly to T.R., 11 February 1917, Theodore Roosevelt Collection, Library of Congress.
12. T.R. to Kelly, 20 February 1917, Theodore Roosevelt Collection, Library of Congress. Roosevelt died on 6 January 1919.
13. Thrapp, *Frontier Biography*, Vol. 1, 169–70.
14. Kelly to EAB, 10 June 1919, E. A. Brininstool Collection, BYU; and Kelly to EAB, 12 March 1919, E. A. Brininstool Collection, University of Texas.
15. Kelly to EAB, 11 May 1921, E. A. Brininstool Collection, University of Texas.
16. Kelly to EAB, 1 July and 8 August 1925, E. A. Brininstool Collection, University of Texas.
17. Kelly to EAB, 6 February 1921, E. A. Brininstool Collection, University of Texas.
18. Kelly to EAB, 25 May 1923, E. A. Brininstool Collection, University of Texas. As noted elsewhere, Kelly collected a number of interesting artifacts and memorabilia from his various adventures, most of which, like his Philippines journal, have not, to my knowledge, survived.
19. Kelly to EAB, 17 June 1925, E. A. Brininstool Collection, University of Texas.
20. Kelly to EAB, 1 June 1923, 29 July 1924, and 17 June 1925, E. A. Brininstool Collection, University of Texas. See also U.S. Census for Detroit, Wayne County, Michigan, 1880, Sheet 127. George Morrison's handicap is unknown.
21. Kelly to EAB, 30 August 1922, E. A. Brininstool Collection, University of Texas.
22. Randolph, "Paradise Offers Peace to Many Backgrounds," *Oroville* (CA) *Mercury-Register*, 13 May 1982.
23. Declaration of Invalid Pension and Sworn Statement of Kelly, 26 July 1916, Kelly, Luther S., Pension File, (XC2, 733, 187), Department of Veterans Affairs, Seattle, Washington, hereafter cited as Kelly, Pension File.
24. Kelly to Commissioner of Pensions, 4 May 1915, Kelly Pension File; Kelly to Secretary of War, 8 April 1917, Kelly Military Service File. Commissioner of Pensions to Kelly, 17 May 1915, Kelly Pension File.

25. For a picture of the fluctuation in Kelly's health, see Kelly to EAB, 30 June, 11 August, 13 November, and 22 November 1921; also 6 February and 7 June 1922 and 29 July 1924. All may be found in E. A. Brininstool Collection, University of Texas.

26. Kelly to EAB, 30 June 1921, E. A. Brininstool Collection, University of Texas.

27. Kelly to EAB, 11 August 1921, E. A. Brininstool Collection, University of Texas.

28. Kelly to Commissioner of Pensions, 30 August 1921; W. E. Mack, M.D., to Commissioner of Pensions, 28 February 1922; Commissioner of Pensions to Kelly, 8 June 1922; Kelly to Commissioner, 14 June 1922, Kelly Pension File. Bright's Disease is the same as nephritis.

29. Kelly to Secretary of the Interior, 29 June 1922, Kelly Pension File.

30. Kelly to EAB, 11 October and 13 November 1921, E. A. Brininstool Collection, University of Texas.

31. Kelly to EAB, 22 November 1921 and 6 February 1922, E. A. Brininstool Collection, University of Texas.

32. Kelly to EAB, 8 March 1922, E. A. Brininstool Collection, University of Texas.

33. Kelly to EAB, 30 August 1922, E. A. Brininstool Collection, University of Texas.

34. Kelly to EAB, 7 June 1922 and 29 July 1924, E. A. Brininstool Collection, University of Texas. Exactly when Kelly began work on his memoirs is not clear, though it could certainly have been before he arrived in Paradise, perhaps while he was at San Carlos.

35. EAB to Kelly, 3 March 1919 and 3 August 1920; Kelly to EAB 12 March 1919, 30 July 1920, and 1 June 1923, E. A. Brininstool Collection, University of Texas.

36. Deming to Kelly, 14 May 1920, KFC. Exactly when Kelly and Deming first met is not known, but it was likely in 1897 in New York, when both men had an opportunity to visit with Chief Joseph of the Nez Perce, who was then in the Washington-New York area attempting to lobby for a permanent home for his people in the Wallowa Valley. See Hampton, *Children of Grace*, 333.

37. Deming to Kelly, 14 May 1920 and 26 July 1921, KFC.

38. EAB to Kelly 30 June 1921, The E. A. Brininstool Collection, BYU, and Kelly to EAB, 7 June 1922, E. A. Brininstool Collection, University of Texas.

39. Kelly to Charles M. Russell, 12 April 1925, Helen E. and Homer E. Britzman Collection, Taylor Museum for Southwestern Studies of the Colorado Springs Fine Arts Center, Colorado Springs, Colorado.

40. Kelly to EAB, 29 July and 30 August 1924, E. A. Brininstool Collection, University of Texas; Kelly to R. V. Coleman, 12 August and 14 September 1924; Kelly to EAB, 8 January 1924, E. A. Brininstool Collection, University of Texas; correspondence relating to the publication of *Yellowstone Kelly: The Memoirs of Luther S. Kelly*, Records of the Yale University Press, Manuscripts and Archives, Yale University Library, hereafter cited as Kelly Publication File. In his 12 August letter to Coleman, Kelly says the script numbered 480 pages with 20 illustrations, but a month later he had added 3 pages and five illustrations. The original of the map, which was reproduced in his memoirs, is today in the Parmly Billings (Montana) Public Library.

41. Kelly to EAB, 22 October 1924, E. A. Brininstool Collection, University of

Texas; Coleman to Kelly, 13 October 1924, Kelly Publication File.

42. Coleman to Kelly, 27 October 1924, Kelly Publication File.

43. Lamar, *The New Encyclopedia of the American West*, 932.

44. Quaife to Coleman, 15 December 1924; Undated memo to Coleman;
    Coleman to Quaife, 6 February 1925, and Coleman to Kelly, 6 February
    1925, both in Kelly Publication File; Kelly to EAB, 31 March 1925, E. A.
    Brininstool Collection, University of Texas.

45. Kelly to Coleman, 29 January 1925, Kelly Publication File; Kelly to EAB,
    15 February and 31 March 1925, E. A. Brininstool Collection, University
    of Texas.

46. Quaife to Coleman, 19 February 1925, Kelly Publication File.

47. Ibid.; Memo, Yale University Press, 7 December 1925, Kelly Publication
    File. Kelly to EAB, 8 August and 30 October 1925, E. A. Brininstool
    Collection, University of Texas.

48. Kelly to EAB, 21 March 1926, E. A. Brininstool Collection, University of
    Texas; Kelly to Taft, 24 September 1927, William Howard Taft Papers,
    Library of Congress.

49. Taft to Kelly, 1 October 1927, William Howard Taft Papers, Library
    of Congress.

50. Oscar Long to Kelly, 28 April 1926, KFC.

51. Kelly to EAB, 7 June 1926, E. A. Brininstool Collection, University of Texas.

52. Kelly to Oscar Long, 25 September 1926, KFC.

53. Kelly, Pension File.

54. Kelly, Luther, Codicil to Last Will and Testament. See also Kelly to EAB,
    18 March and 2 August 1927, and 13 August 1927, E. A. Brininstool
    Collection, University of Texas; "Yellowstone Kelly, Scout Wills His
    Body to Montana."

55. Kelly to EAB, 2 and 13 August 1927, E. A. Brininstool Collection, University
    of Texas. As far as I have been able to determine, this story never
    appeared in print. During the latter part of his life, Kelly evidently wrote
    a number of pieces, though it is not clear whether they were ever pub-
    lished. *The Reader's Guide* and other reference sources reveal nothing in
    this regard. Nevertheless, there are tantalizing references to publication.
    For example, in 1915, Theodore Roosevelt wrote regarding an article on
    "Peace and War" that Kelly had apparently written, about which
    Roosevelt says, "The closing sentence ought to be blazoned in letters of
    gold in every school house of this land; and all the professional pacifists
    should be obliged to learn it by heart." See Theodore Roosevelt to Kelly,
    13 February 1915, Theodore Roosevelt Collection, Library of Congress.

56. Kelly, Pension File; Kelly to EAB, 8 June 1928, E. A. Brininstool Collection,
    University of Texas. Kelly told Brininstool he had been hospitalized for a
    couple of weeks, but in fact, he was admitted on 18 May and discharged
    on the twenty-fourth or twenty-fifth.

57. Kelly to Deming. The letter is undated, but was probably written in the
    late fall of 1927 or winter of 1928, KFC.

58. Kelly to EAB, 8 June 1928, E. A. Brininstool Collection, University of Texas.

59. This manuscript, in keeping with the provisions of Kelly's last will and
    testament, was consigned to his nephew, Dr. Luther W. Kelly.

60. Kelly, Pension File.

61. "Yellowstone Kelly Is Laid to Rest," *Billings Gazette*, 19 December 1928,
    Chico (CA) *Enterprise*, 18 December 1928.

62. It is not clear whether it became Kelly Mountain before or after Kelly was

laid to rest there. See *Winners of the West*, 30 January 1929; Bragg, "Famed Frontiersman of Billings Area Now Helps Boost Savings Bond Sales," *Billings Gazette*, 29 January 1956; Bragg, "Sacrifice Cliff isn't where they say it is," *Billings Gazette*, 10 June 1979.

Epilogue

1.   "Wreath Sent By Mrs. Kelly," *Billings Gazette.*

Bibliography

Manuscript Materials

Baird, George W. "Memoranda of Movements of and Events in Yellowstone Command, from October 1876 to October 1878." In Baird Papers, Kansas State Historical Society.

Brown, Edwin M. *Terror of the Badlands: An Account of Col. Nelson A. Miles's Campaign Against the Sioux, 1876–1877.* Helena: Montana Historical Society Library.

Brown, William Carey, Collection, Archives, University of Colorado Libraries, Boulder, Colorado.

Curry, Thomas L. "Personal Recollections of the Famous 'Yellowstone' Kelly." Typescript in Library, Montana Historical Society, Helena.

Dall, William Healy. *Journal of the Harriman Expedition.* Dall Papers, Smithsonian Institution Archives.

Kearney, Thomas. "Reminiscences of the Harriman Expedition." Letter to Dr. Waldo L. Schmitt, in Waldo LaSalle Schmitt Papers, Smithsonian Institution Archives.

The Kelly Family of Geneva, Luther S. Kelly File. Geneva, NY, Historical Society.

Kelly, Luther S. "Engagement with the Nez Perces in Bearpaw Mountains, 1877." George Bird Grinnell Collection, Manuscript 441, Braun Research Library, Southwest Museum, Los Angeles.

———. Typescript from which *"Yellowstone Kelly": The Memoirs of Luther S. Kelly* was originally published by Yale University Press in 1926. Copy of typescript provided through the courtesy of Thomas Minckler Collection, Billings, Montana.

———. Memoirs of Experiences in Alaska and the Philippines. Unpublished manuscript in Yale Collection of Western Americana, Beinecke Rare Book and Manuscript Library, New Haven, CT.

Kelly, William Dunham. "Last Will and Testament." KFC.

Merriam, C. Hart. *Journals of the Harriman Alaska Expedition, 1899.* 3 vols. C. Hart Merriam Papers, Library of Congress.

Records of the Yale University Press. Manuscripts and Archives, Yale
    University Library.
Reed, John Scott. "Burden and Honor: The United States Volunteers in the
    Southern Philippines, 1899–1901." Ph.D. dissertation, University of
    Southern California, 1994.
Snyder, Captain Simon, Company F, 5th U.S. Infantry. Diary for the years
    1876–1877.
Spanish-American War Survey Collection. Folder: Jesse Proctor, 1898-W-995.
    Co. H. 40th U.S. Volunteer Infantry. Carlisle Barracks, PA: U.S. Army
    Military History Institute.
Theodore Roosevelt Papers, Library of Congress.
William Howard Taft Papers, Library of Congress.

Government Documents and Publications

Annual Reports of the Commissioner of Indian Affairs, 1904 (Serial 4798); 1905
    (Serial 4959).
Annual Reports of the Secretary of War, 1876–1882, 1901–1903.
*Correspondence Relating To The War With Spain And Conditions Growing Out
    Of The Same, Including The Insurrection In The Philippine Islands And
    The China Relief Expedition Between The Adjutant-General Of The Army
    And Military Commanders In The United States, Cuba, Porto Rico, China,
    And The Philippine Islands, From April 15, 1898, to July 30, 1902. With An
    Appendix Giving The Organization of Army Corps And A Brief History Of
    The Volunteer Organizations In The Service Of The United States During
    The War With Spain*, In Two Volumes. Washington: Government Printing
    Office, 1902.
Forsyth, Maj. George A. "Report of an Expedition Up the Yellowstone River
    Made in 1873." Box 45, Philip H. Sheridan Papers, Manuscript Division,
    Library of Congress.
Glenn, E. F., and Abercrombie, W. R. War Department, U.S., Adjutant-General's
    Office. Publication XXV, Military Information Division. *Reports of
    Explorations in the Territory of Alaska, Cook Inlet, Sushitna, Copper, and
    Tanana Rivers, 1898*. Washington, D.C.: U.S. Government Printing
    Office, 1900.
Kelly, Luther S. Military Service Record, National Archives.
———. Pension File, National Archives.
———. Civilian Personnel File, National Archives.
Mendenhall, Walter C. *Reconnaissances from Resurrection Bay to the Tanana
    River. Notebook Number 1*, U.S.G.S. Anchorage, AK, Field Office, 1898.
Miles, Nelson A. Papers of the Commanding General, 1898–1925. Box T-1, U.S.
    Army Military History Institute, Carlisle Barracks, PA.
Norris, Superintendent P. W. "Report upon Yellowstone National Park for the
    Year 1879." Washington, D.C.: U.S. Government Printing Office.
Ray, Patrick Henry, 8th Infantry. *Compilation of Narratives of Exploration in
    Alaska*, Senate Report 1023, 56th Congress, 1st Session. Washington, D.C.:
    U.S. Government Printing Office, 1900. Serial 3896.
*Report of the Commission Appointed By Direction Of The President Of The
    United States To Meet With The Sioux Chief Sitting Bull*. Washington,
    D.C.: Government Printing Office, 1877.
Report of the Lieutenant-General Commanding the Army. In Seven Parts, Part 4,
    found in *Annual Reports of the War Department for the Fiscal Year Ended
    June 30, 1900*. Washington, D.C.: U.S. Government Printing Office, 1900.

Returns from U.S. Military Posts, 1800–1916. National Archives and Records Services: Roll 158, Fort Buford, ND, June 1866–Dec. 1879; Roll 992, Fort Ransom, ND, June 1867–April 1872; Roll 1026 Fort Ripley, MN, April 1849–Dec. 1865; Roll 1027, Jan. 1866–July 1877, Roll, 1179 Fort Sisseton (Wadsworth), SD, June 1864–Dec. 1872; Roll 572 Fort Keogh, MT, Sept. 1876–Dec. 1886; Roll 288, Post at Dapitan, Mindanao, Philippine Islands, April 1900, July 1912.

Spanish-American War Survey Collection Archives. U.S. Army Military History Institute, Carlisle Barracks, PA.

Thirteenth Census of the United States for Esmeralda County, Nevada, 1910.

United States Geological Survey, *Twentieth Annual Report to the Secretary of the Interior, 1898–99*, in Seven Parts. Washington, D.C.: Government Printing Office.

U.S. Senate: *Affairs in the Philippines: Hearings Before the Committee on the Philippines*. Washington: U.S. Government Printing Office, 1902.

Correspondence

There are two major bodies of Luther Kelly correspondence: The E. A. Brininstool Collection, located in two repositories: the E. A. Brininstool Collection, Center for American History, the University of Texas at Austin, cited throughout as the E. A. Brininstool Collection, University of Texas; the E. A. Brininstool Collection, L. Tom Perry Special Collections, Harold B. Lee Library, Brigham Young University, Provo, UT, cited throughout as the E. A. Brininstool Collection, BYU; and the Kelly Family Collection, cited as KFC. Other bodies of correspondence include NARA, Record Group 75, Letters Sent and Received, 1881–1907, Commissioner and Assistant Commissioner of Indian Affairs; Library of Congress; Theodore Roosevelt and William Howard Taft Collections, respectively, Library of Congress, and Records of the Yale University Press, Manuscripts and Archives, Yale University Library. In addition, Luther Kelly corresponded with several individuals during the latter part of his life. Copies of these letters are cited in the appropriate endnotes.

Selected Newspapers & Periodicals

Anaconda (MT) *Standard; Army and Navy Journal; Billings* (MT) *Gazette; Bismarck* (ND) *Tribune; Chico* (CA) *Daily Enterprise; Chico* (CA) *Record; Fergus County* (MT) *Argus; Frontier Times; Geneva* (NY) *Courier; Glacier* (MT) *Courier; Globe* (AZ) *Silver Belt; Great Falls* (MT) *Tribune; Kansas City Times; Mississippi Valley Historical Review; New Northwest; Oroville* (CA) *Mercury-Register; Paradise* (CA) *Progress Review; Park County* (MT) *News; Real West; Recreation; Rocky Mountain Husbandman; Terry* (MT) *Tribune; The West; Winners of the West*.

Articles

The Yellowstone Kelly file in the Parmly Billings (Montana) Public Library contains more than thirty newspaper articles about Kelly. Most of these appeared in the years after his death and say essentially the same thing. I have listed here only those articles that are cited in the narrative.

Anderson, Harry H. "Indian Peace Talkers and the Conclusion of the Sioux War of 1876." *Nebraska History* 44, December 1963.

———. "Nelson A. Miles and the Sioux War of 1876–1877." *Chicago Westerners Brand Book*, 16, June 1959, 25–27, 32.

Baird, George W. "General Miles's Indian Campaigns." *Century Magazine*, no. 42, July 1891.

Barron, Marietta. "The Letters of a U.S. Soldier Reflect the Savagery of the Philippine Insurrection." *Military History* 17, no. 2, June 2000.

Bragg, Addison R. "Famed Frontiersman of Billings Area Now Helps Boost Savings Bond." *Billings Gazette*, January 29, 1956.

———. "Sacrifice Cliff isn't where they say it is." *Billings Gazette*, June 10, 1979.

Breihan, Carl. "Yellowstone Kelly." *Real West*, September 1980.

Brust, James, ed. "'Oh what a river': Adaline Forsee's Journal of a Trip from St. Louis to Cantonment Tongue River, 1877." *North Dakota History* 64, no. 2, Spring 1997.

Bundy Rex, "Yellowstone Kelly, The Little Man with a Strong Heart." *Real West*, August 1970.

"Burial of Yellowstone Kelly on Kelly Mountain, Near Billings, Montana, Wednesday, June 26, 1929." *Winners of the West*, June 30, 1929.

Burroughs, John, "Summer Holidays in Alaskan Waters." *Century Illustrated* 60, August 1900.

"Captain Luther Sage Kelly, Noted Indian Scout, Dies at Residence in Paradise." *Chico* (CA) *Daily Enterprise*, December 17, 1928.

Castner, Joseph C. "Exploration in Alaska." A speech published in *Press Bulletin no. 27*, Hawaiian Engineering Association (Honolulu), 1910.

Conway, Dan R. "The Plainsman on the Frontier with 'Yellowstone' Kelly on His Adventure in the Territory of the Hostile Sioux." *Fergus County* (MT) *Argus*, September 23, 1926.

"Crypt Put in Place on Kelly Mountain for Burial June 26." *Billings Gazette*, June 15, 1929.

Davis, T. Neal. "Reindeer Moss." Article no. 428, *Alaska Science Forum*, September 22, 1980.

Forsyth, Lt. Col. James W. "Report of an Expedition Up the Yellowstone River Made in 1875." Washington, D.C.: U.S. Government Printing Office, 1875.

"Gallant Service of a Volunteer." *Army and Navy Journal*, December 2, 1910.

Gannett, Henry. "The Harriman Alaska Expedition." Washington, D.C.: *The National Geographic Magazine* 10, no. 507, 1899.

Gray, Fred Morton. "Saga of Yellowstone Kelly." *Real West*, January 1960.

———. "Yellowstone Kelly, Indian Fighter." *The West*, April 1965.

Gray, John S. "Lame Deer Fight Ends Sioux War." *Chicago Westerners Brand Book*, no. 3, May 1974.

———. "Sitting Bull Strikes the Glendive Supply Trains," *Chicago Westerners Brand Book*, no. 4, June 1971.

Grinnell, George Bird. "Stories of an Heroic Age." *Forest and Stream*, January 30, 1897.

"High Tribute Paid Capt. Luther S. Kelly As Large Crowd Attends Burial Ceremony of Noted Indian Scout on Mountain Top." *Chico* (CA) *Daily Enterprise*, July 13, 1929.

Hough, Alfred Lacy. "A Winter Campaign Against the Sioux." Ed. by Robert G. Athearn. *Mississippi Valley Historical Review* 35, September 1948, 272–84.

"Impressive Ceremonies Will Mark Burial Here of 'Yellowstone' Kelly." *Billings Gazette*, June 1929.

Keenan, Jerry. "Yellowstone Kelly: From New York to Paradise," *Montana: The Magazine of Western History* 40, no. 3, Summer 1990.

Kelly, Alice May Morrison. Untitled article describing Alice May Kelly's arrival in Colorado following her marriage to Luther S. Kelly. Unidentified

newspaper article dated 19 November 1932, in the E. A. Brininstool
Collection, BYU.

"Kelly, Indian Scout, Soldier Dead at Home in Paradise After Life of Adventure."
Chico (CA) *Record*, December 18, 1928.

Kelly, Luther S. Sub-report "From Cabin Creek to the Valley of the Yukla," found
in Glenn, E. F. and Abercrombie, W. R. Reports of Explorations in the
Territory of Alaska, 1899 and reprinted in *Compilation of Narratives of
Exploration in Alaska*, 1900.

———. "The Last Man." *Chico* (CA) *Daily Enterprise*, Monday, May 30, 1927.

———. "Memorandum on the Wolf Mountain Campaign." Found in Brady,
C. T., *Northwestern Fights and Fighters*. Garden City, NY: Doubleday &
Page, 1913.

———. "Recollections of the Frontier." *Recreation*, June 1896.

"Kelly to Rest on Yellowstone." *Chico* (CA) *Daily Enterprise*, December 13, 1928.

"Kelly's Widow Sends Wreath." *Billings Gazette*, December 21, 1930.

Lass, William E. "Steamboats on the Yellowstone." *Montana: The Magazine of
Western History* 35, no. 4, Autumn 1985.

Lindsey, Alton, A. "The Harriman Alaska Expedition of 1899, Including the
Identities of Those in the Staff Picture." *BioScience* 28, no. 6, June 1978.

"Local Resident's Father Spent Year with Yellowstone Kelly." *Billings Gazette*,
September 19, 1960.

"Locate Site of Memorial." *Billings Gazette*, June 11, 1929.

Logan, Sidney M. "An Episode in the Life of Yellowstone Kelly, As Related by
His Fellow Comrade in Arms, Jack Johnson." *Park County* (MT) *News*.
No date.

"Luther P.[*sic*] Kelly: A Geneva Boy Among the Indians." *Geneva* (NY) *Gazette*,
February 15, 1878.

"Man Near Missoula Was Acquaintance of Famed Frontiersman." *Billings
Gazette*, June 1929.

Martin, Manning. "Yellowstone Kelly." *Frontier Times*, January 1974.

Mendenhall, W. C. "A Reconnaissance from Resurrection Bay to the Tanana
River, Alaska, 1898." In "Explorations in Alaska," Part VII, *20th Annual
Report, U.S. Geological Survey*. Washington, D.C.: U.S. Government
Printing Office, 1899.

Merrill, Arch. "Boyhood Home Too Dull for 'Yellowstone' Kelly. *Geneva* (NY)
Courier, undated.

"Old Picture Recalls Career of Picturesque Scout." *Winners of the West*,
December 1938.

Pearson, Jeffrey V. "Nelson A. Miles, Crazy Horse, and the Battle of Wolf
Mountains." *Montana: The Magazine of Western History* 51, no. 4,
Winter 2001.

Randolph, Charles. "Paradise Offers Peace to Many Vagabonds." *Oroville* (CA)
Mercury-Register, March 13, 1982.

Rickey, Don. "The Battle of Wolf Mountain." *Montana: The Magazine of Western
History*, Spring 1963, 44–54.

Sahr, Robert C. "Consumer Price Index (CPI) Conversion Factors to Convert to
Dollars of the Year 2000." Corvallis, OR: Sahr, Robert C., Political Science
Department, Oregon State University.

Seyburn, Lt. S. Y., U.S.A., Adj., Tenth Infantry. "Tenth Regiment of Infantry."
Journal of the Military Service Institution of the U.S., Vol. 13, 1892.

Smith, Vic. "Where the Buffalo Went." *Recreation*, vol. 7, July 1897, 44.

Stelter, Brother John H., M.D. "Question of the Month . . . Who Was William

Morgan who disappeared 150 Years Ago on September 19, 1826?" Luther S. Kelly File, Geneva Historical Society.

"The Tennis Board." *The Saturday Evening Post*, May 19, 1906.

Thane, Eric. "When 'Yellowstone' Kelly Hunted in Judith Basin." *Billings Gazette*, January 29, 1940.

———. "When Yellowstone Kelly Was Scout for General Nelson A. Miles." *Rocky Mountain Husbandman*, no date.

Utley, Robert M. "War Houses in the Sioux Country." *Montana: The Magazine of Western History* 35, no. 4, Autumn 1985.

"Vet Groups Meet Here This Week." *Billings Gazette*, June 23, 1929.

"Vets Request Kelly Marker." *Billings Gazette*, April 24, 1935.

"Wreath Sent By Mrs. Kelly." *Billings Gazette*, 1934?

Wright, Kathryn. "Letters from Man on Kelly Mountain." *Midland Empire Magazine, Billings Gazette*, March 5, 1964.

"'Yellowstone Kelly' The Famous Scout in Geneva." *Geneva* (NY) *Courier*, January 29, 1879.

"Yellowstone Kelly, Indian Fighter." *The West*, April 1965.

"Yellowstone Kelly Is Laid to Rest." *Billings Gazette*, December 19, 1928.

"'Yellowstone' Kelly, Indian Fighter, Scout and Guide, Was One of the Youngest Plainsman of the 60s and Hero of Many Adventures." *The Anaconda* (MT) *Standard*, September 17, 1922.

"Yellowstone Kelly: The Man-Who-Never-Lays-Down-His-Gun," *New Northwest*, March 8, 1878.

"'Yellowstone' Kelly, Scout, Trapper and Pioneer of Montana, Dies on Coast." *Billings Gazette*, December 28, 1928.

"'Yellowstone' Kelly Well Known Indian Scout Dies; Will Be Buried at Billings." *Winners of the West*, January 30, 1929.

"Yellowstone Kelly, Scout Wills His Body to Montana." Unidentified newspaper article, possibly the *Billings Gazette*, August 5, 1927.

Books

Abbott, Lawrence, ed. *The Letters of Archie Butt*. Garden City, NY: Doubleday, Page Co., 1924.

Adjutant General's Office. *Chronological List of Actions, &, With Indians from January 15, 1837 to January, 1891*. Fort Collins, CO: The Old Army Press, 1979.

Alberts, Don E. *Brandy Station to Manila Bay: A Biography of General Wesley Merritt*. Austin, TX: Presidial Press, 1980.

American Ancestry, Vol. 12. Albany, NY.

Athearn, Robert G. *Forts of the Upper Missouri*. Lincoln: University of Nebraska Press, 1972.

———. *William Tecumseh Sherman and the Settlement of the West*. Norman: The University of Oklahoma Press, 1995.

Bade, W. F. *The Life and Letters of John Muir*. 2 Vols. Boston: Houghton Mifflin, 1929.

Bain, David Haward. *Sitting in Darkness, Americans in the Philippines*. Boston, MA: Houghton Mifflin Co., 1984.

Baker, Robert Orr. *The Muster Roll: A Biography of Fort Ripley, Minnesota*. St. Paul, MN: H. M. Smyth Co., no date.

Baldwin, Donald N. *The Quiet Revolution: The Grass Roots of Today's Wilderness Preservation Movement*. Boulder, CO: Pruett Publishing Co., 1972.

Barry, Susan, and John Barry, eds. *This Is What I Remember: People of White*

River County. 2 vols. Meeker, CO: The Rio Blanco County Historical Society, 1978.

Beede, Benjamin R., ed. *The War of 1898 and U.S. Interventions 1898–1934: An Encyclopedia*. New York: Garland Publishing, Inc., 1994.

Boatner, Mark M., III. *The Civil War Dictionary*. New York: David McKay Company, 1959.

Bond, Fred G. *Flatboating on the Yellowstone, 1877*. With an introduction and epilogue by Diana Yares. Staten Island, NY: Ward Hill Press, 1998.

Bonney, Orrin H., and Lorraine Bonney. *Battle Drums and Geysers: The Life and Journals of Lieutenant Gustavus Cheyney Doane, Soldier and Explorer of the Yellowstone and Snake River Regions*. Chicago, IL: Swallow Press, Inc., 1970.

Brands, H. W., *TR: The Last Romantic*. New York: Basic Books, 1997.

Brown, Mark H. *The Plainsmen of the Yellowstone*. Lincoln: University of Nebraska Press, 1969.

Brown, Mark H., and W. R. Felton. *The Frontier Years: L. A. Huffman, Photographer of the Plains*. New York: Henry Holt and Company, 1955.

Brumberg, G. David. *The Making of An Upstate Community: Geneva, New York*. Geneva, NY: The Geneva Bicentennial Commission, 1976.

Burdick, Usher L. *Tales From Buffalo Land: The Story of Fort Buford*. Baltimore: Wirth Bros., 1940.

Burroughs, John. *My Boyhood*. With a conclusion by his son Julian Burroughs. Garden City, NY: Doubleday Page & Company, 1922.

Carlson, Helen. *Nevada Place Names*. Reno: University of Nevada Press, 1974.

Castner, Lt. Joseph C. *Lieutenant Castner's Alaskan Exploration, 1898: A Journey of Hardship and Suffering*. Anchorage, AK: Cook Inlet Historical Society, 1984.

Coe, W. R. and A. Robertson. *Nemerteans: Bryozoa, Harriman Alaska Expedition, 1899*. Kraus Reprint, 1904.

Cosmas, Graham A. *An Army for Empire: The United States Army in the Spanish-American War*. College Station: Texas A&M University Press, 1994.

De Barthe, Joe. *Life and Adventures of Frank Grouard*. Norman: University of Oklahoma Press, 1958.

DeMontravel, Peter R. *A Hero to His Fighting Men: Nelson A. Miles, 1839–1925*. Kent, OH: Kent State University Press, 1998.

DeVoto, Bernard. *Across the Wide Missouri*. Cambridge, MA: Houghton Mifflin Company, 1947.

Dictionary of American Biography. 20 volumes. New York: Charles Scribner's Sons, 1928.

Dixon, David. *Hero of Beecher Island: The Life and Military Career of George A. Forsyth*. Lincoln: University of Nebraska Press, 1994.

Dunlay, Thomas W. *Wolves for the Blue Soldiers: Indian Scouts and Auxiliaries with the United States Army, 1860–90*. Lincoln: University of Nebraska Press, 1982.

Durham, Michael S. *The Smithsonian Guide to Historic America: The Mid-Atlantic States*. New York: Stewart, Tabori Chang, 1989.

Eckert, Allan. *The Frontiersman: A Narrative*. Boston, MA: Little Brown, 1967.

Eggan, Fred. *The Philippines*. 4 vols. New Haven: Human Relations Area Files, Yale, 1955.

Elliott, Russell R. *Nevada's Twentieth-Century Mining Boom: Tonopah, Goldfield, Ely*. Reno: University of Nevada Press, 1966.

Evans, David C., *Custer's Last Fight: The Story of the Battle of the Little Big Horn.* El Segundo, CA: Upton & Sons, 1999.

Faragher, John Mack. *Daniel Boone: The Life and Legend of an American Pioneer.* New York: Henry Holt, 1992.

Faust, Karl Irving. *Campaigning in the Philippines.* Reprint. NY: Arno Press, 1970.

Flexner, Stuart Berg. *Listening to America: An Illustrated History of Words and Phrases from our Lively and Splendid Past.* New York: Simon and Schuster, 1982.

Fox, Richard Allen, Jr. *Archaeology, History, and Custer's Last Battle.* Norman: University of Oklahoma Press, 1993.

Frink, Maurice, with Casey Barthelmess. *Photographer on an Army Mule.* Norman: University of Oklahoma Press, 1965.

FPK/BTA. *Portraits of Fort Phil Kearny.* Banner, WY: The Fort Phil Kearny/Bozeman Trail Association, 1993.

Gates, John M. *Schoolbooks and Krags: The United States Army in the Philippines, 1898–1902,* Westport, CT, Greenwood Press, Inc., 1973.

George H. Thomas Post. *The History of the George H. Thomas Post No. 5, Department of Illinois, Grand Army of the Republic for Twenty-five Years.* Photocopy from Chicago, Illinois, Historical Society.

Gilman, Rhoda R., Carolyn Gilman, and Deborah M. Stultz. *The Red River Trails, Oxcart Routes Between St. Paul and the Selkirk Settlement, 1820–1870.* St. Paul: The Minnesota Historical Society, 1979.

Goetzmann, William H., and Kay Sloan. *Looking Far North: The Harriman Expedition to Alaska, 1899.* New York: The Viking Press, 1982.

Gray, John S. *Centennial Campaign: The Sioux War of 1876.* Fort Collins, CO: The Old Army Press, 1976.

———. *Custer's Last Campaign: Mitch Boyer and the Little Bighorn Reconstructed.* Lincoln: University of Nebraska Press, 1991.

Greene, Jerome A. *Yellowstone Command: Colonel Nelson A. Miles and the Great Sioux War, 1876–1877.* Lincoln: University of Nebraska Press, 1972.

———. *Slim Buttes, 1876: An Episode of the Great Sioux War.* Norman: University of Oklahoma Press, 1982.

———, ed. and ann. *Frontier Soldier: An Enlisted Man's Journal of the Sioux and Nez Perce Campaigns, 1877,* by William F. Zimmer. Helena: Montana Historical Society Press, 1998.

———. *Battles and Skirmishes of the Great Sioux War, 1876–1877: The Military View.* Norman: University of Oklahoma Press, 1993.

———. *Nez Perce Summer 1877: The U.S. Army and the Nee-Me-Poo Crisis.* Helena: Montana Historical Society Press, 2000.

Gulliford, Andrew. *Garfield County, Colorado: The First Hundred Years, 1883–1983.* Glenwood Springs, CO: The Grand River Museum Alliance, 1983.

Haines, Aubrey L. *An Elusive Victory: The Battle of the Big Hole.* West Glacier, MT: The Glacier Natural History Association, 1991.

———. *Yellowstone Place Names: Mirrors of History.* Niwot: University Press of Colorado, 1996.

———. *The Yellowstone Story: A History of Our First National Park.* Vol. 1. Niwot: University Press of Colorado, 1977.

Hampton, Bruce, *Children of Grace: The Nez Perce War of 1877.* New York: Henry Holt and Co., 1994.

Hanson, Joseph Mills. *The Conquest of the Missouri: Being the Story of the Life and Exploits of Captain Grant Marsh.* New York: Murray Hill Books, 1909.

Harper's History of the War in the Philippines. New York: Harper & Bros., 1900.

Hart, Herbert M. *Tour Guide to Old Western Forts: The Posts & Camps of the Army, Navy & Marines on the Western Frontier, 1804–1916.* Boulder and Ft. Collins, CO: Pruett Publishing Co. & Old Army Press, 1980.

Hedren, Paul L. *Fort Laramie in 1876: Chronicle of a Frontier Post at War.* Lincoln: University of Nebraska Press, 1988.

Heitman, Francis B. *Historical Register and Dictionary of the United States Army from Its Organization, September 29, 1789, to March 2, 1903.* Vol. 1. Urbana: University of Illinois Press, 1965.

Hoxie, Frederick E., ed. *Encyclopedia of North American Indians.* Boston, MA: Houghton Mifflin, 1996.

Hutton, Paul Andrew. *Phil Sheridan and His Army.* Lincoln: University of Nebraska Press, 1985.

Innis, Ben. *Briefly Buford.* Privately printed, 1963.

Johnson, Virginia W. *The Unregimented General: A Biography of Nelson A. Miles.* Boston, MA: Houghton Mifflin Company, 1962.

Jusserand, Jean Jules. *What Me Befell: The Reminiscences of Jean Jules Jusserand.* Boston, MA: Houghton Mifflin, 1933.

Kane, Lucile M., trans. and ed. *Military Life in Dakota: The Journal of Philippe Regis de Trobriand.* Lincoln: University of Nebraska Press, 1981.

Karie, Karen *Fort Sisseton: Our Living Heritage.* Sisseton: South Dakota Dept. of Game, Fish, and Parks. No date.

Karnow, Stanley. *In Our Image: America's Image in the Philippines.* New York: Random House, 1989.

Keenan, Jerry. *The Great Sioux Uprising: Rebellion on the Plains, August–September 1862.* Cambridge, MA: DaCapo Press, 2003.

———. *Encyclopedia of the Spanish-American and Philippine-American Wars.* Santa Barbara, CA: ABC-Clio, 2001.

Kelly, Giles M. *A Genealogical Account of the Descendants of John Kelly of Newbury, Massachusetts, U.S.A.* Albany, NY: Joel Munsell's Sons, 1886.

Kelly, Luther S., *"Yellowstone Kelly": The Memoirs of Luther S. Kelly.* Edited by M. M. Quaife. New Haven, CT: Yale University Press, 1926.

Kennan, George. *E. H. Harriman: A Biography.* 2 vols. Boston: Houghton Mifflin Co., 1922.

Klein, Maury. *The Life & Legend of E. H. Harriman.* Chapel Hill: The University of North Carolina Press, 2000.

Koury, Michael J. *Guarding the Carroll Trail: Camp Lewis 1874–1875.* Edited by Glen C. Morton. Lewistown: The Central Montana Historical Association, 1994.

Kuhlman, Charles. *Legend into History.* Ft. Collins, CO: The Old Army Press, 1977.

Lamar, Howard R., ed. *The Reader's Encyclopedia of the American West.* New York: Thomas Y. Crowell, 1977.

———. *The New Encyclopedia of the American West.* New Haven, CT: Yale University Press, 1998.

Lavender, David. *Let Me Be Free: The Nez Perce Tragedy.* New York: Harper Collins, 1992.

Lincoln, Francis Church. *Mining Districts & Mineral Resources of Nevada.* Las Vegas: Nevada Newsletter Publishing Company, 1923.

Linn, Brian McAllister. *The Philippine War 1899–1902.* Lawrence: University Press of Kansas, 2000.

———. *Guardians of Empire: The U.S. Army and the Pacific, 1902–1940.* Chapel

Hill: University of North Carolina Press, 1997.

———. *The U.S. Army and Counterinsurgency in the Philippine War, 1899–1902.* Chapel Hill: University of North Carolina Press, 1989.

Long, E. B., with Barbara Long. *The Civil War Day By Day: An Almanac, 1861–1865.* New York: Doubleday & Co., Inc., 1971.

Lounsberry, Col. Clement A. *Early History of North Dakota: Essential Outlines of American History.* New York: Liberty Press, 1919.

Mails, Thomas E. *Mystic Warriors of the Plains: The Culture, Arts, Crafts, and Religion of the Plains Indians.* New York: Mallard Press, 1991.

Mangum, Neil C. *Battle of the Rosebud: Prelude to the Little Bighorn.* El Segundo, CA: Upton & Sons, 1987.

Manzione, Joseph. *"I Am Looking to the North for My Life": Sitting Bull 1876–1881.* Salt Lake City: University of Utah Press, 1991.

Marquis, Thomas B. *Memoirs of a White Crow Indian (Thomas H. Leforge).* Lincoln: University of Nebraska Press, 1974.

McFarling, Lloyd, ed. *Exploring the Northern Plains 1804–1876.* Caldwell, ID: The Caxton Printers, Ltd., 1955.

McFeely, William S. *Grant: A Biography.* New York: W. W. Norton & Company, 1982.

McGinnis, Anthony. *Counting Coup and Cutting Horses: Indian Tribal Warfare on the Northern Plains 1738–1889.* Evergreen, CO: Cordillera Press, Inc, 1990.

Melody, Michael Edward. *The Apaches: A Critical Bibliography.* Bloomington: Indiana University Press, 1977.

———. *The Apache.* New York: Chelsea House, 1989.

Merriam, C. Hart, ed. *Journals of Harriman Alaska Expedition.* 13 vols. Garden City, NY: Doubleday, Page & Co., 1901–1914.

Michno, Gregory F. *Lakota Noon: The Indian Narrative of Custer's Defeat.* Missoula, MT: Mountain Press Publishing Company, 1997.

Miles, Nelson A. *Personal Recollections and Observations of General Nelson A. Miles.* 2 vols. Lincoln: University of Nebraska Press, 1992.

Miller, Mark E. *Hollow Victory: The White River Expedition of 1879 and the Battle of Milk Creek.* Boulder: University Press of Colorado, 1997.

Miller, Nathan. *Theodore Roosevelt: A Life.* New York: William Morrow, 1992.

Millet, Francis Davis. *The Expedition to the Philippines.* New York: Harper and Brothers, 1898.

Morris, Edmund. *The Rise of Theodore Roosevelt.* New York: Coward, McCann & Geohegan, Inc., 1979.

———. *Theodore Rex.* New York: Random House, 2001.

Muir, John. *Travels in Alaska.* Boston: Houghton Mifflin Co., 1915.

———. *John of the Mountains: Unpublished Journals of John Muir.* Boston: Houghton Mifflin, 1938.

Murray, Erlene Durrant. *Lest We Forget: A Short History of Early Grand Valley, Colorado, Originally Called Parachute, Colorado.* No Publisher. Copy in Parachute, Colorado Public Library.

Musgrove, Richard W. *History of the Town of Bristol, Grafton County, New Hampshire,* vol. 2. Bristol, NH: Richard W. Musgrove, 1904.

Musicant, Ivan. *Empire by Default: The Spanish-American War and the Dawn of the American Century.* New York: Henry Holt, 1998.

National Park Service. *Nez Perce Country Official National Park Handbook.* Washington, D.C.: National Park Service, 1983.

Nichols, Ronald H. *In Custer's Shadow: Major Marcus Reno.* Ft. Collins, CO: The Old Army Press, 1999.

Nielson, Jonathan M. *Armed Forces on a Northern Frontier: The Military in Alaska's History, 1867–1887,* Contributions in Military Studies, no. 74. Westport, CT: Greenwood Press, 1988.

Olson, James S., Editor-in-Chief. *Historical Dictionary of the Spanish Empire, 1402–1975.* Westport, CT: Greenwood Press, 1992.

Overholser, Joel. *Fort Benton: World's Innermost Port.* Fort Benton, MT: Joel Overholser, 1987.

Paher, Stanley W. *Nevada Ghost Towns & Mining Camps.* Las Vegas: Nevada Publications, 1970.

———. *Goldfield: Boom Town of Nevada.* Las Vegas: Nevada Publications, 1977.

Paradise and Beyond. Paradise, CA: Paradise Fact and Folklore, Inc., 1981.

Perry, Richard J. *Apache Reservation: Indigenous Peoples and the American State.* Austin: University of Texas Press, 1993.

Pohanka, Brian C. *Nelson A. Miles: A Documentary Biography of His U.S. Military Career 1861–1903.* Glendale, CA: The Arthur H. Clark Company, 1985.

Prendergast, Curtis. *The First Aviators.* Alexandria, VA: Time-Life Books, 1980.

Prodgers, Jeannette, ed. *The Champion Buffalo Hunter: The Frontier Memoirs of Yellowstone Vic Smith.* Helena, MT: Falcon Publishing Co., 1997.

Prucha, Francis Paul. *Guide to the Military Posts of the U.S.* Madison: State Historical Society of Wisconsin, 1964.

———. *Broadax and Bayonet: The Role of the United States Army in the Development of the Northwest, 1815–1860.* Lincoln: University of Nebraska Press, 1967.

———. *American Indian Treaties: The History of a Political Anomaly.* Berkeley: University of California Press, 1994.

———. *The Great Father.* 2 vols. Lincoln: The University of Nebraska Press, 1984.

Remele, Larry, ed. *Fort Totten Military Post and Indian School, 1867–1959.* Bismarck: State Historical Society of North Dakota, 1986.

Rickey, Don Jr. *Forty Miles a Day on Beans and Hay.* Norman: University of Oklahoma Press, 1963.

Rogge, A. E., D. Lorne McWatters, Melissa Keane, and Richard P. Emanuel. *Raising Arizona's Dams: Daily Life, Danger, and Discrimination in the Dam Construction Camps of Central Arizona, 1890s-1940s.* Tucson: The University of Arizona Press, 1995.

Roosevelt, Theodore. *Theodore Roosevelt: An Autobiography,* New York: The Macmillan Co., 1916.

Roth, Russell. *Muddy Glory: America's Indian Wars in the Philippines, 1899–1935.* West Haven, MA: Christopher Publishing House, 1981.

Russell, Charles M. *Back-Trailing on the Old Frontiers.* Great Falls, MT: Cheely-Raban Syndicate, 1922. Second printing, 1986.

Schooler, Lynn. *The Blue Bear: A True Story of Friendship, Tragedy, and Survival in the Alaskan Wilderness.* New York: Harper Collins, 2002.

Sexton, William T. *Soldiers in the Sun.* Harrisburg, PA: Military Service Publishing Co., 1939.

Sherman, William C. *Prairie Mosaic: An Ethnic Atlas of Rural, North Dakota.* Fargo: North Dakota Institute for Regional Studies, 1983.

Sherwood, Morgan B. *Exploration of Alaska 1865–1900.* Fairbanks: University of Alaska Press, 1992.

Simmons, Virginia McConnell. *The Ute Indians of Colorado and New Mexico.* Boulder: University Press of Colorado, 2000.

Skinner, Woodward B. *The Apache Rock Crumbles.* Self-published, 1985.

Sklenar, Larry, *To Hell with Honor: Custer and the Little Bighorn*. Norman: University of Oklahoma Press, 2000.

Skogen, Larry C. *Indian Depredation Claims, 1796–1920*. Norman: University of Oklahoma Press, 1996.

South Dakota Department of Game, Fish, and Parks. *Fort Sisseton (Fort Wadsworth) 1864–1889*. Sisseton, SD: No date.

Steinbach, Robert H. *A Long March: The Lives of Frank and Alice Baldwin*. Austin: University of Texas Press, 1989.

Stelter, John H. *History of the Ark Lodge #33, Fraternal Order of Masons, 1807–1957*. Geneva, NY: 1957.

Storey, Moorfield, and Marcial P. Lichauco. *The Conquest of the Philippines by the U.S., 1898–1925*. Ayer Co. reprint of 1926 edition.

Taylor, John R. M. *The Philippine Insurrection Against the United States: A Compilation of Documents with Notes and Introduction*. 5 vols. Parsay City, Philippines: Eugenio Lopez Foundation, 1971.

Taylor, Joseph Henry. *Frontier and Indian Life and Kaleidoscopic Lives*. Washburn, ND: Washburn's Fiftieth Anniversary Committee, 1932.

Thomas, David Hurst, Jay Miller, Richard White, Peter Nabokov, and Philip J. Deloria. *The Native Americans: An Illustrated History*. Atlanta, GA: Turner Publishing Company, 1993.

Thrapp, Dan L. *Encyclopedia of Frontier Biography:* 3 vols. Glendale, CA: The Arthur H. Clark Company, 1988.

———. *Victorio and the Mimbres Apaches*. Norman: University of Oklahoma Press, 1980.

Topping, E. S. *The Chronicles of the Yellowstone*. Minneapolis, MN: Ross & Haines, Inc., 1968.

Utley, Robert M. *Cavalier in Buckskin: George Armstrong Custer and the Western Military Frontier*. Norman: University of Oklahoma Press, 1988.

———. *Frontiersmen in Blue: The United States Army and the Indian, 1848–1865*. New York: Macmillan Publishing Co., Inc., 1967.

———. *Frontier Regulars: The United States Army and the Indian, 1866–1890*. New York: Macmillan Publishing Co., Inc., 1973.

———. *The Lance and the Shield: The Life and Times of Sitting Bull*. New York: Henry Holt, 1993.

———. *The Indian Frontier of the American West, 1846–1890*. Albuquerque: University of New Mexico Press, 1984.

Way, Frederick, Jr., comp. *Way's Packet Directory, 1848–1983*. Athens: Ohio University Press, 1983.

Webb, Melody. *The Last Frontier: A History of the Yukon Basin of Canada and Alaska*. Albuquerque: University of New Mexico Press, 1985.

Webster's Biographical Dictionary. Springfield, MA: G&C Merriam Co., Publishers, 1956.

Werstein, Irving. *Ninety-eight: The Story of the Spanish-American War and the Philippine Insurrection*. New York: Cooper Square, 1966.

Wilfong, Cheryl, *Following the Nez Perce Trail: A Guide to the Nee-Me-Poo National Historical Trail with Eyewitness Accounts*. Corvallis: Oregon State University Press, 1990.

Wolff, Leon. *Little Brown Brother*. New York: Longmans Green & Co., Ltd., 1961.

Wooster, Robert. *Nelson A. Miles & the Twilight of the Frontier Army*. Lincoln: University of Nebraska Press, 1993.

Worcester, Donald E. *The Apaches: Eagles of the Southwest*. Norman: University of Oklahoma Press, 1984.

Wyngaarden, James B., and Lloyd H. Smith Jr., eds. *Cecil Textbook of Medicine*, vol. 2. Philadelphia, PA: W. B. Saunders Company, 1985.

Young, Hall. *Alaska Days with John Muir*. New York: Fleming Revell, 1915.

Zanjani, Sally. *Goldfield: The Last Gold Rush on the Western Frontier*. Athens, OH: Swallow Press, 1992.

Zarbin, Earl A. *Roosevelt Dam: A History to 1911*. Phoenix, AZ: Salt River Project, 1984.

Zimmer, William F. *Frontier Soldier: An Enlisted Man's Journal of the Sioux and Nez Perce Campaigns, 1877*. Helena: Montana Historical Society Press, 1998.

Index

Page numbers in italics indicate illustrations. The abbreviation "Dak." stands for the Dakota Territory, and "Phil." indicates the Philippines.